Nature's Cruel Stepdames

Medieval & Renaissance Literary Studies

Nature's Cruel Stepdames

Murderous Women
in the
Street Literature
of Seventeenth
Century England

Susan C. Staub

Duquesne University Press
Pittsburgh, Pa.

Published in the United States of America by:
DUQUESNE UNIVERSITY PRESS
600 Forbes Avenue
Pittsburgh, Pennsylvania 15282

Library of Congress Cataloging-in-Publication Data
Staub, Susan C.
    Nature's cruel stepdames : murderous women in the street literature of
seventeenth century England / Susan C. Staub.
        p. cm. — (Medieval & Renaissance literary studies)
    Summary: "A selection of seventeenth century pamphlets revealing
the popular press's obsessive concern with female violence — usually
domestic — and a discussion of the texts' historical and cultural
contexts" — Provided by publisher.
    Includes bibliographical references and index.
    ISBN 0–8207–0356–7 (cloth : alk. paper)
    1. Street literature — England — History and criticism. 2. English
literature — Early modern, 1500–1700 — History and criticism. 3. Women
and literature — England — History — 17th century. 4. English literature —
Early modern, 1500–1700. 5. Female offenders — Literary collections.
6. Women murderers — Literary collections. 7. Infanticide — Literary
collections. 8. Murder — Literary collections. 9. Female offenders in
literature. 10. Women murderers in literature. 11. Street literature —
England. 12. Infanticide in literature. 13. Murder in literature. I. Title.
II. Medieval and Renaissance literary studies
    PR972.S73 2004
    820.9'3522'09032—dc22
                                                         2004021250

∞ Printed on acid-free paper.

Contents

List of Illustrations

Acknowledgments

My interest in sixteenth and seventeenth century crime literature is long held and derives from my fascination with early modern drama. That fascination was heightened by my participation in the 1992 National Endowment for the Humanities summer institute at the Folger, "The Theatre in History: The Social Function of Renaissance Dramatic Genres." I am grateful to Jean Howard, the director of the institute, and my fellow seminar members for helping me think about both the drama and the pamphlets in new ways. I would also like to acknowledge the generous financial support of the Appalachian Foundation in awarding me a Board of Trustees Travel Studies Grant for research in England, and the Appalachian State University Research Council for providing grants to allow me to do research at the Folger Shakespeare Library in Washington, D.C., and at Houghton Library at Harvard. This work would not have been possible without the support of my chairs, first Dan Hurley and currently Dave Haney, who have given me course reductions to complete this project.

I am also grateful to my colleagues at Appalachian who have listened to me talk endlessly about what came to be known as my "Renaissance women behaving badly" book. Several colleagues read and commented on various portions of this volume, in particular Chip Arnold and Grace McEntee, who read the entire Part 1; Lynn Sanders and Tina Groover, who read early versions of the Anne Greene material; and the two Toms, McGowan and McLaughlin, who were always ready and willing to help me grapple with the knotty bits — Tom McGowan with linguistic issues in the pamphlets and Tom McLaughlin with interpretative issues. I would also like to thank several students who assisted me with this project: Amy Walter-Welch, who in the very early stages helped me decide what needed footnoting from a student's point of view and whose input was invaluable; and Katie James, Lucas Pasley, and Mary Clai Waters, who checked my documentation. And finally, I am grateful to the copyeditor at Duquesne University Press, whose careful proofreading and suggestions for regularizing the pamphlets helped make this a better book.

Very early versions of the material on murdering wives and Anne Greene were published in *Renaissance Papers* (1995 and 1997) and are republished here by permission of the Southeastern Renaissance Conference. Other material from Part 1 has appeared as "Early Modern Medea: Representations of Child Murder in the Street Literature of Seventeenth Century England" in *Maternal Measures: Figuring Caregiving in the Early Modern Period*, edited by Naomi Miller and Naomi Yavneh (Ashgate Press, 2000); "Bloody Relations: Murderous Wives in the Street Literature of Early Modern England" in *Domestic Arrangements in Early Modern England*, edited by Kari McBride (Duquesne University Press, 2002); and "'News from the Dead': The Strange Story of a Woman Who Gave Birth, Was Executed and Was Resurrected as a Virgin" in *The Single Woman in Medieval and Early Modern England: Her Life and Representation*, edited by Laurel Amtower and Dorothea Kehler (Arizona Center for Medieval and Renaissance Studies, 2003).

Part 1: The Contexts

1

Women's Crimes in the Popular Press

Those women that in blood delight,
Are ruled by the Devill,
Else how can th' wife her husband kill,
Or th' Mother her owne childs blood spill.
— Martin Parker, "A Warning for Wives"

This book seeks to make accessible some of the crime pamphlets published in the popular English press from 1604 to 1692. The years covered by this volume, basically the entire seventeenth century, witnessed great religious, cultural, and political changes. Although "pamphlet literature" suggests something both ephemeral and trivial and examining it might seem an indirect way to consider some of these changes, it is at least partially because these writings are ephemeral that they are valuable. Because they were produced quickly and for a general audience, they may more clearly reflect the period's contradictory attitudes, particularly toward women, than more thoughtfully and self-consciously written literature might. And because they were printed cheaply and in great quantities, we can assume that they either reflected popular culture or helped to shape it. Although I label these texts "popular" because they were cheap and widely distributed, I do not mean to place them in opposition to elite literature; these works are important precisely because their readership crosses class categories.

Historically, the pamphlet has endured its share of scorn. Thomas Bodley, for example, dubbed pamphlets "baggage books" and banned them as "not worth the custody" of the library he established at Oxford in 1603.[1] Even the kind of literature represented by the pamphlet is problematic. According to the *Oxford English Dictionary*, a "pamphlet" is "a small treatise occupying fewer pages or sheets than would make a book." But beyond the defining characteristic of size, the term could be used to classify many genres, "including issues of single plays, romances, poems, novelettes, newspapers, news-letters, and other periodicals." Shakespeare even uses the word to describe *The Rape of Lucrece* in his dedication to the Earl of Southampton: "this pamphlet without beginning is but a superfluous moiety," he modestly writes. Both the words "pamphlet" and "moiety" seem meant to serve as a disclaimer, setting the work up as something diminutive and of little worth.

Fortunately, recent scholars have recognized the value of these works, if only as an alternative way of studying more canonical texts. Increasingly, many have called for a "different kind of textual intercourse . . . a promiscuous conversation of many texts" beyond the purely literary.[2] Feminist scholars, in particular, have sought to "write history from below," in the words of Jean Howard, that is, to revise literary and cultural history to take into account those in "subordinated gender and class positions."[3] One way to write history from below is by juxtaposing literary writings with popular writings that have, until recently, been given only marginalized status in literary history. In fact, George Orwell's mid-twentieth century statement that "the great function of the pamphlet is to act as a sort of foot-note or marginal comment on official history" best encapsulates what I see as the pamphlet's significance.[4] The footnote can often take the reader in surprising directions. And yet, despite increasing interest in alternative texts, many of these popular or nonliterary texts are not readily available to the twenty-first century reader.

In the decade since Howard stressed the need to look at alternative texts, much work has been done in the recovery of domestic texts and writings by women from the period. Popular, nonliterary texts are now recognized as an important area of study. Crime pamphlets, in particular, are receiving long overdue attention; for instance, recent book-length analyses such as those by Frances Dolan and Joy Wiltenburg consider the role these writings play in revealing attitudes about women and domestic life in the period. Others have examined these texts for the light they shed on the rise of print culture and literacy and on the spread of Protestant ideology and other religious ideas. More broadly, crime pamphlets have been studied for the way they reflect the changing attitudes and perceptions of the English people between the mid-sixteenth and the mid-eighteenth centuries.[5] Nonetheless, few have been reproduced.[6] This study of women and crime in the popular press seeks to remedy that situation by providing both an analysis of early modern crime pamphlets and an edition of some of the texts discussed.

In general, popular pamphlets, sometimes also called newsbooks, were occasional, brief publications, ranging from 2 to 60 pages in length. They were usually published in response to a sensational or phenomenal event, something as simple as an earthquake, the appearance of a "blazing star" (a comet), or other natural act of God; or something as strange as the birth of a two-headed baby or the miraculous return to life of an executed criminal. Many pamphlets also treated religious and political controversies. But in the pamphlets devoted to crime, one of the most popular subjects was murder, particularly murder by women. This study will focus on crime pamphlets dealing with murderous women.

The history of the popular pamphlet is shadowy. Because, as Adam Fox points out, "we have the texts but not the contexts," much of what we might suggest about the readership and purpose of these texts is purely conjectural.[7] We do know that many of these writings were posted or sold in public places, and since they cost only a penny or twopence, a wider range of consumers could afford them than could afford more elaborate literary texts. As Tessa Watt points out, however, it is difficult to ascertain the exact audience for these kinds of publications: the "idea that the broadsides and chapbooks were aimed at and consumed by a definable social group may be a myth. The audience presupposed within the cheap print itself appears to be inclusive rather than exclusive."[8] Literacy during this period is equally difficult to assess, and these texts further muddy the waters. While scholars conjecture literacy rates as high as 78 percent for London men (with literacy defined as the ability to sign one's name), most agree that the literacy rate for women was much lower.[9] Yet several of the pamphlets that I include in this volume specifically address a female readership. Still others offer evidence of women's writing ability. In *A True Discourse Of the practises of Elizabeth Caldwell*, for instance, Caldwell purportedly writes a long letter to her husband before her execution; another pamphlet, *Fair Warning to Murderers of Infants*, depicts the woman dictating a letter to her children because she cannot write. This text does offer evidence that she can read, however, referring to specific religious writings that she read while in prison to help her repent her actions. Because pamphlet literature circulated so widely, we can speculate that it had influence even over those who could not read. As Fox posits, "Perhaps a majority of people may not yet have been able to read it for themselves, but it was also the case that the vernacular repertoire was being structured and determined by this print, and a multitude of other written materials, in fundamental ways."[10]

Although a few crime pamphlets have been attributed to literary figures such as Thomas Kyd (1558–94), John Taylor (1580–1653), and Anthony Munday (1553–1633), most of the authors' names are lost to history as many pamphlets were published anonymously. Most crime pamphlets seem to be written by preachers or other clergymen seeking to warn and edify their readers. Yet there can be no denying that even religious figures wrote because these stories were so titillating and sensational. The stories they related were, in the words of Peter Lake, "the literary equivalent of a John Carpenter film."[11] And money must have played at least some motivating role in the author's decision to put the account on paper. For example, Henry Goodcole, one of the most prolific crime writers from the period and author of two pamphlets included in this volume, apparently wrote to supplement his salary as ordinary of Newgate Prison. The publication of one or two crime accounts could likely more than double his meager annual stipend.[12] That these pamphlets proved so lucrative suggests a public fascination with crime, and the authors' exploitation of this fascination as well as of their subjects highlights the "morally ambiguous nature" of these writings. Lake goes so far as to label them "pornographic," explaining, "Examples of extreme violence, sexual licence [*sic*], outlandish and disgusting acts were presented to the reader, ostensibly for his or her moral instruction but, in fact, in order not merely to edify but also to shock, titillate and engender the *frisson* of horror laced with disapproval which allows both pleasure and excitement at the enormities described to be combined with a reconfirmed sense of the reader's own moral superiority."[13] As this study shows, such ambivalence is characteristic of the genre.

Clearly, the public was fascinated with criminal women. A cursory survey of ballad entries in the Stationers' Register for the years 1569–1640 reveals no fewer than 25 titles depicting female murderers.[14] These ballads, coupled with the many pamphlets and plays based on true-life crimes committed by women, suggest a high level of popular anxiety about female criminality during the period. Judging from the number of these narratives, one might believe that there was a sudden surge in female violence at this time, but such was not the case. Surviving historical records offer no evidence of an increase in husband murder during the late sixteenth and seventeenth centuries. Yet ballads, pamphlets, and plays present a disproportionate number of female murderers as opposed to male murderers. The popular press shows an almost obsessive concern with female violence, and this violence is almost always domestic. The public's appetite for these writings suggests more than a taste for blood and gore; it evinces a cultural pre-occupation with women's behavior and, because the violence depicted is predominantly domestic, points toward growing instability within the institution of marriage. But more importantly for my analysis, this literature suggests that the conflict within the marital realm brought with it a concomitant change in the status of women, however dubious. That women were shown committing and being executed for their crimes marks a new consciousness of them as individuals.

While women committed far fewer violent crimes than did men, the number of pamphlets devoted to the subject of crimes by women, at least until the mid–seventeenth century, suggests otherwise.[15] In the popular imagination, male authority was under siege. Central to an analysis of this literature is how its portrayal of female criminals betrays anxiety about female power and sexuality at a time when increased female power was possible, if not likely.[16]

Although pamphlet writers often embellish the stories they tell and, despite their frequent protests to the contrary, are not overly concerned with factual details and evidence, their stories (and the fact that they tell them) offer a rich store from which to examine the social conditions, legal rights, and attitudes toward women in the early modern period. It is easy to dismiss these writings as tabloid hack-work or simply as additional examples of the misogynistic railings so prevalent at the time, but they offer a much more complex view of women than such simplistic assessments allow. As I will show, the crime literature of early modern England articulates an ambivalent attitude towards women, picturing them as both powerful and weak, sympathetic and sinister.

These popular texts illustrate the precarious and often contra-dictory legal position that early modern women found themselves in. Examinations of women and crime in the early modern period are especially rewarding because they afford an opportunity to explore the legal fiction of the wife as *feme covert*. Legally, wives were "covered" by their husbands; they had no identities apart from them. But their legal situation proved much more complicated than the term *feme covert* implies, and legal status was equally complicated for unmarried women and widows. Although theoretically women had no legal identity apart from their husbands and fathers, prosecutions of women for serious crimes (specifically, husband murder, infanticide, and witchcraft) increased dramatically during the period.

The first widespread prosecutions of women during the age occurred as laws were instituted or reinterpreted to regulate female sexual and social behavior. As Christina Larner explains in her study of witch trials of the period: "Previously kept out of the courts on the grounds that their fathers or husbands were legally responsible for their actions and that crimes committed by them must have been through coercion by their men folk, women suddenly appeared in the courts in large numbers, the old women as witches, the young as infanticides."[17] Despite this "criminalization of women,"[18] there was no real growth in the number of violent crimes committed by them. Nonetheless, new laws increasingly targeted women, making it easier to prosecute them as bastard bearers, adulterers, and infanticides. Even the law that defined husband murder as petty treason safeguarded the hierarchical relations within marriage. Issues previously regarded as the domain of the church shifted to the state, and private domestic matters became matters of public concern. Although the common definition of the household as a miniature commonwealth with the husband as its ruler suggests that domestic relations were in some sense already linked to the public good, this analogy seems to take on greater importance in the late sixteenth and the seventeenth centuries as women emerge from the domestic to the public sphere.[19]

Oddly enough, one might argue (as several scholars have) that the increased prosecution of women actually marks a progression toward female agency and subjectivity; women as felons were granted a legal status heretofore denied them. Further, prosecuted women were recognized as individuals separate from men and were granted the opportunity to speak, if only from the scaffold. Even though these scaffold speeches were a kind of highly structured and coerced discourse, they afforded women at least a limited voice. Many of the pamphlets included in this volume purport to include the true confessions of women, albeit filtered through the perspective of a male writer. And in at least two of them, as noted earlier, the authors include letters either written or dictated by the accused woman, offering even more complex examples of female voice.

Although the authors maintain that their narratives are based on actual cases, it is not always possible to verify that these women even existed. Most accounts do seem to be skeletally based on historical events, problematically positioning the fictive voice with that of the historical woman. The authors repeatedly insist on their truth telling, often explaining that they are compelled to write only to counter the many falsehoods and rumors that are spreading both orally and in the press about the event in question. With the inclusion of specific details such as full names, places, and ages, they take great pains to establish the authenticity of their narratives. Many of these cases are also presented as firsthand accounts by witnesses, confessors, or ministers; nonetheless, all are embellished by their authors and most seem designed to support the dominant patriarchal discourse. Whether the women in these accounts existed or not, these pamphlets were written to advance the male author's particular message, a message that may be as basic as the need for women to obey their husbands, as *Murther, Murther. Or, A bloody Relation how Anne Hamton . . . murthered her deare Husband* seeks to emphasize, or the dangers of misguided religious fervor, as illustrated in *Bloody Newes from Dover.* To modern audiences both these narratives seem too generic and sensational to be true. Strangely, because these writings are often so polemical, even verifiable cases, such as the story of Anne Greene told in Richard Watkins's *Newes from the Dead,* sometimes take on the aura of myth.

Since these narratives blur the distinction between so-called history and fiction, we must look instead for the truth that they do convey, a truth that may have nothing to do with literal fact. "The artifice of fiction," as Natalie Zemon Davis suggests in her study of sixteenth century French letters of pardon, "did not necessarily lend falsity to an account; it might well bring verisimilitude or a moral truth."[20] And such is the case here. When we look at these narratives as shaped and constructed in much the same way a fictional work of literature might be, it becomes easier to understand how a story such as that told by Richard Watkins can echo so many other narrative forms (the saints' lives, the miracles of the virgin, the French canard or *occasionnel*) and yet still be based on an actual and verifiable case. In spite of the authors' frequent protests to the contrary, these texts are historical fiction; they are "feigned history," to borrow Francis Bacon's term for poetry.[21] Thus we must attend to the way these stories are told as much as to the fact that they are told.

These texts offer representations of female voices, not necessarily the actual voices. While all of the authors of these texts speak in the first person, the women's speech they recount is invariably in the third person, with only two exceptions (the letters of Caldwell and Goodenough), and both of those are problematic. Even if we accept these two as recorded female speech, they are shaped by the culturally defined structure of the confession, a structure that allows female speech as a way of silencing it. It seems obvious that the female voice is being packaged within a masculine structure. Still, I do not mean to argue that we hear nothing of the woman's voice in these texts; neither would I argue the complete absence of female subjectivity in them. As E. Jane Burns persuasively posits in her study of female characters in Old French literature, the female speaker, even one invented by a male author, "moves toward subjectivity in a way that necessarily destabilizes and redefines the notion of subjectivity itself."[22] Further, in their attempts to manage the female voice, there is often a curious slippage or instability in these narratives; an unintended side effect of these stories is that in their policing of the unruly woman, they often critique the very patriarchy they mean to support. While we are not necessarily recovering authentic female voices even when women speak in these accounts, we do get a glimpse of female experience in seventeenth century England. Despite these ambiguities (or perhaps because of them), these crime pamphlets provide an important source for "reflecting on the conditions under which the socially marginalized (for example, poor, unmarried women) could be constructed as subjects."[23]

Ostensibly, these writers seek to edify their readers — to inculcate proper behavior and warn of the dreadful consequences of wickedness. As a ballad writer from the period admonishes:

> Let all good wives a warning take,
>   in Country and in City,
> And thinke how they shall at a stake
>   be burned without pitty.
> If they can have such barbarous hearts,
> What man or woman will take their parts,
>   Oh women, Murderous women,
>   whereon are your minds?
>
> — "A Warning for Wives"[24]

In actuality, they do much more. In addition to providing source material for many Renaissance plays, these pamphlets offer clues about cultural ideologies and anxieties, especially those related to gender. The crimes that garnered the most attention are gender specific and fly in the face of woman's role as wife and mother: infanticide, child murder, and husband murder.[25] And often, as I will show, these crimes are conflated with other offenses (and other anxieties — religious and national, for example). This emphasis suggests a social order threatened by women asserting identities separate from that of subordinate wife. Yet in their focus on female criminality, these writings seek not so much to warn readers of the dangers of insubordinate women (although that is certainly a side effect), as to ensure that women remain in their properly ordained places as wives and mothers. These narratives function to regain control over the transgressive woman. Almost invariably, they do so by depicting women as victims, thereby robbing them of the autonomy the writers find so threatening.

Although these writings often view women criminals as aberrations, as deformities of nature, one suspects that they are meant to exemplify womankind in general since in the period all women were defined as aberrant. The assessment of women murderers in these pamphlets as "matchlesse monsters," "savages," "unnatural cruel beasts in woman's shapes," and "shee wolves" simply continues the traditional misogynistic rhetoric that defined women as imperfect, deformed men — "monsters" in Aristotle's term. Women fitting these descriptions, then, are not exceptional but represent womankind in general.

More often than not, the woman's actions in these pamphlets are explained as the result of sexual transgressions: sex out of wedlock, adultery, or promiscuity. Later in the century, when accounts dealing with married women who murder their children increase, the accounts still support stereotypical views of women. Although child murder by married women is not often explained as a result of female lustfulness, these narratives, too, depict the criminal as vain, misguided, and frail. Like Eve, all these women are easily seduced by the devil, who figures prominently in these accounts. Their characteristic gullibility is sometimes even considered a mitigating factor in women's guilt. And it is precisely this weakness that requires women's complete acquiescence to the superior and wiser male sex.

In choosing the texts for this volume, I had two goals. First, I sought to include both representative and unusual pamphlets. So, I include works such as *Deeds Against Nature and Monsters by kinde*, a fairly typical account of an unmarried mother who kills her illegitimate newborn by throwing it in a privy, and *Murther, Murther. Or, A bloody Relation how Anne Hamton . . . murthered her deare Husband*, the story of a wife who murders her husband simply because she wants more social and economic freedom. But I also offer more unusual narratives, narratives often as interesting for the way they relate their stories as for the stories they tell.

Richard Watkins's *Newes from the Dead*, for example, presents the bizarre tale of a woman who survives her execution, but with a narrative strategy that differs from a typical murder pamphlet in its analytical and scientific tone. Further, Watkins appends 24 pages of poetry written by Oxford students to his account, giving the text multiple and seemingly contradictory purposes. It is at once a scientific explanation of an extraordinary event (and concomitantly, a rather prurient examination of female bodily functions) and a literary interpretation of it. *A Hellish Murther Committed by a French Midwife*, in contrast, is organized as a kind of legal deposition of the witnesses in a petty treason (husband murder) trial and provides a fascinating example of the silencing of the female voice in a text that purports to focus on that voice. In its flurry of testimony, the confession of an unusually strong female murderer (one who murders her husband by strangling him and chopping his body into pieces) is reduced to a whisper. Another account, *Fair Warning to Murderers of Infants*, seems to belong as much to the genre of the mother's advice book as to the crime pamphlet since the bulk of the text is devoted to the murderous mother's legacy to her children, a letter entitled, "Advice of your Dying Mother." The irony of a mother who has murdered one of her children serving as an exemplar of maternal solicitude is typical of the many contradictions apparent in this literature. Gilbert Dugdale's *A True Discourse Of the practises of Elizabeth Caldwell* also presents a woman speaking publicly about appropriate conduct, in this case in a letter she writes while awaiting execution, in which she advises her husband of his moral and spiritual duties. Taking on the stance of a repentant sinner, the speaker in the letter is also remarkably harsh toward the husband, offering one of the earliest published critiques of spousal abuse. Although it is impossible to know if this letter was written by Caldwell or by Dugdale, its style is strikingly different from the narrative portion of the pamphlet. Accepting the letter as authentically that of a woman and including it in their survey of the earliest published works by Renaissance women, Elizabeth Tebeaux and Mary M.

Lay argue that Caldwell's letter is "typical of writing by women at this time" and "reflects the impassioned, disorganized expostulation of many pietistic writings by Renaissance women."[26] Ventriloquized or not, the wife's public voice overtakes that of the author in this text and makes explicit the contradictions inherent in the very definition of the wife as *feme covert*. Thus the pamphlet disciplines the woman at the same time that it publicizes and empowers her, critiquing its own and the period's oversimplified view of wifely subservience.

My second goal was to choose texts that correspond to the commonplace stages of the early modern woman's life: maid, wife, and widow. I added the role of mother to the familiar trio of stages because married mothers are profoundly important in the murder pamphlets of the period. In fact, although unmarried infanticidal mothers were apparently more prevalent in early modern England, the popular literature focuses more on married mothers who murder their children. This focus suggests that child murder by a wife was more shocking basically because it was less common, but it also indicates an anxiety about maternal power.

Stories of husband murderers, women who most blatantly overturn the definition of the wife as *feme covert*, comprise the first section of this volume. I begin with the married woman because she represents the norm of early modern society; in the words of T. E., a woman is "understood either married or to bee married."[27] Although husband murderers are clearly the most socially threatening of the violent women treated here, as indicated by the association of their crime with treason, several of these accounts present oddly sympathetic pictures of the criminals. In fact, one murderer, Elizabeth Caldwell in Dugdale's *A True Discourse Of the practises of Elizabeth Caldwell*, becomes a kind of martyr dying for the salvation of her husband. Strangely, most of these accounts emphasize the motivation for the wife's actions. In detailing why these women committed their crimes, the authors seek to explain — and hence contain — the crime. But the attention to motivation also gives the criminal limited psychological reality.

Women thus depicted are shown to be not entirely subsumed in their husbands but to have desires and wills of their own. By subtly challenging the legal definition of the wife, this literature seems to indict the entire marital framework; both the wives *and* husbands ignore the strictures on appropriate household behavior. Husbands are shown beating and raping their wives, speaking harshly, or neglecting them altogether, or squandering their family estates and leaving their dependents destitute. Wives respond with anger, adultery, and ultimately, violence.

The second section in this volume is devoted to married mothers, the figure in many ways most problematic in this literature. As mothers, these women possess very real and socially sanctioned authority; as wives, they must cede that authority to their husbands. These pamphlets seem to recognize this conflict by depicting these women as good mothers, *good mothers who murder their children.* Often their violence is perpetrated not to break free from patriarchal constraints but rather to conform to them. Although the texts are frequently ambivalent in their analysis of motivation, for the most part these women commit their crimes out of a concern for their children's physical, spiritual, and mental well-being. Margret Vincent in *A pittilesse Mother*, for example, kills her child out of a misplaced sense of religious piety. Mary Cook in *Blood for Blood* kills to save her child from the oppressive life that she herself suffers. And Mary Goodenough, the widowed mother of *Fair Warning to Murderers of Infants*, shows her undying sense of maternal duty in the letter of instruction she leaves as a legacy to her surviving children. And yet, despite sympathetic portrayals of these criminals, almost all these texts present maternal power as conflicted, with the mothers' actions representing a contest for power within the household.

In some ways the placement of widows in this volume replicates their position in early modern society. Just as their place was unclear then, I had difficulty deciding where to locate them in this text. It may seem inconsistent to place *Fair Warning to Murderers of Infants*, the story of the widow Mary Goodenough, with the married women, since I put the case of the widow Elizabeth Barnes with the unmarried women. But I include Goodenough here because she fits the definition of the good mother that this section considers. Although her desperate poverty parallels that of the unmarried infanticidal mothers, the pamphlet focuses on the letter she composes for her surviving children and thus on her voice. Therefore, she possesses a kind of agency and power that the unmarried women never exhibit.

The next selection of texts concerns unmarried women who murder their illegitimate babies. Although several laws were passed in the late sixteenth and early seventeenth centuries that specifically targeted unmarried women, for the most part the popular press ignores the crime of infanticide, a crime legally confined to unmarried women in 1624, when a statute was passed defining as murder the concealing of an illegitimate infant's death. Typically, the popular press treats only the most sensational of these cases. Though unmarried mothers who commit infanticide are constructed as monsters in this literature, closer examination reveals that they are actually the most powerless of any of the violent women included in this volume. Mostly poor servants struggling to survive in a society that holds little place for them, these women commit their crimes out of a desperate attempt to maintain their jobs and reputations. Their actions represent not a subversion of the social order but an endorsement of it. Although the last pamphlet I include in this section, *Natures Cruell Step-Dames*, reports on Elizabeth Barnes, a widow rather than a spinster, her case illustrates many characteristics of the unmarried infanticide. Poverty, marginalization, and a culture of shame all contribute to her crime.

The final section concerns one of the more unusual cases treated in the murder pamphlets, the miraculous story of Anne Greene, a woman who is executed for infanticide but is revived during a public autopsy. The story of the hanged woman revived exists in several versions both in English and French and offers a vivid example of the ways popular culture reshaped narratives to invest them with meanings appropriate to the culture and time. The two accounts that I consider most fully in my discussion of this case, Burdet's *A Wonder of Wonders* and Watkins's *Newes from the Dead*, utilize very different narrative strategies to relate the event. Burdet offers a more typical murder pamphlet, complete with crime, confession, and repentance. Nonetheless, his interest seems more in the injustice of the law than in the transgression of the woman. Watkins's interest, on the other hand, purportedly derives from the case's scientific significance, and his account is related in precise, analytical language. Yet both writers are compelled to explain why the law and providence do not seem to coincide in this instance. Confronted with a criminal whose punishment apparently offers no lesson about proper behavior because the execution fails, these pamphleteers attempt to reconstruct her into a socially acceptable version of proper womanhood.

The works examined in this volume were not written to be great literature, but to respond to, report on, or even to exploit events that early modern society found significant. Because these texts so richly reflect their culture, they offer an invaluable source for interrogating the domestic, economic, and legal conditions of seventeenth century women. It is crucial, then, to pay attention to what stories pamphlet writers found important enough to tell and to note how they told them.

2

The *Feme Covert* Uncovered
REPRESENTATIONS OF MURDEROUS WIVES

For thus doth St. Peter preach to them: "Ye wives, be ye in subjection to obey your own husband." To obey is another thing then to control or command, which yet they may do to their children and to their family, but as for their husbands, them must they obey and cease from commanding and perform subjection.
— *Homily on the State of Matrimony*

Marriage seems to have entailed many dangers to husbands of this period.
— Hyder E. Rollins, *A Pepysian Garland*

Husband murder — far more than infanticide or child murder — posed the greatest threat to the social order and received the most attention in the popular press. So severe a breach of the marital hierarchy was this offense that it was given its own legal category, that of petty treason. Petty treason "was an aggravated form of murder, as consisting in one of the following three acts: Homicide of a master by his servant; of a husband by his wife; and of an ecclesiastical superior by his inferior." Husband murder was analogous to high treason in that, like treason against the state, it abused "the obligations of duty, subjection, and allegiance" that an inferior owed a superior. Just as the treasonous subordinate violated the "confidence which the king presuppose[d] in his subject," so the insubordinate wife disrupted the "natural, civil, and even spiritual relations" she held with her husband.[1] Unlike infanticide and child murder, which stem largely from the perpetrator's desire to adhere to social formulations of appropriate behavior (the virtuous maid or good mother), husband murder overturns the domestic hierarchy.

Because this crime is such a blatant and brutal disruption of the ordered household, the popular press exhibits an almost obsessive concern with it. At least until the middle of the seventeenth century, accounts of husband murder greatly outnumber accounts of wife murder. Yet as several recent scholars have shown, women were not excessively violent during this period; in one survey of assize records from 1559 to 1625, wives, not husbands, were the victims in three quarters of the cases of spousal homicide.[2] We can assume that these numbers remained constant throughout the seventeenth century. Perhaps this literature focuses on murderous wives precisely because their crime was more unusual and hence more horrendous, but it seems equally likely that husband murder receives attention because it represented a fundamental subversion of the domestic hierarchy. There was, after all, some acceptance of male violence as a kind of household discipline; the wife's assault on her husband, on the other hand, was virtually never justified. The crisis depicted in these writings, however, represented not simply one of wifely insubordination; the husband's authority, and thereby that of the state, is called into question as well. Holinshed seemed to have an understanding of the enormous significance of these crimes when he decided to include an account of the 1551 murder of Thomas Arden by his wife in his *Chronicles of England, Scotland, and Ireland*. Noting that it is "but a private matter, and therefore as it were impertinent to this historie," he nonetheless decides that the case is important enough "to set it foorth somewhat at large." Holinshed seems to recognize that these cases had public significance and therefore belong to the realm of history.[3] Since both the political and the social structure hinged on the analogy between family and state, a challenge to the domestic hierarchy was a challenge to the civic order as well. These texts, then, interrogate the institution of marriage and the concomitant melding of private into public.

It has become a commonplace that early modern women had no legal existence apart from marriage. Maid, wife, or widow, they were governed by their relationship and subordination to husbands or future husbands. When T. E., the first commentator on laws relating specifically to women, defined women's legal status, his definition was clear and uncontested: "Women have no voyse in Parliament, They make no Lawes, they consent to none, they abrogate none. All of them are understood either married or to bee married and their desires are subject to their husband." The author continued with only measured sympathy, "I know no remedy, though some women can shift it well enough."[4] Thus, in theory, marriage represented a kind of civil death for women, granting them no recourse under the law for crimes they suffered nor accountability for those they committed.

But women's legal position in early modern England was less clear-cut than T. E.'s general assessment indicates. Actually, the very existence of T. E.'s text calls into question the idea that women had no legal existence in the period. With the heading "The Women's Lawier" running throughout the five books, the work appears to be a guide for lawyers preparing legal defenses of women. Why would there be a need for such a manual if women had no voice, no consent, no desire — no legal existence? As Frances Dolan has explained, even T. E.'s phrase "shift it well enough" "constitutes wives as subjects of desire" maneuvering "*within* a repressive situation, by bending, if not breaking the rules."[5] According to the *OED*, "to shift" is "to manage matters; to deal, to bargain, make arrangements," but also "to manage to effect one's purposes, or make a living, by one's own devices; to succeed" and "to act or live through with difficulty." And if we consider Dolan's gloss of "covert" as "sly" and "stealthy" maneuvering, by her very definition the *feme covert* undermines the system meant to contain her.[6] The definition of wives as *femes coverts*, as women legally covered or subsumed by their husbands, then, seems a kind of legal fiction that is everywhere confounded in the period. In fact, recent scholarship suggests that exceptions to coverture existed everywhere, particularly in the equity and church courts. And as Laura Gowing has shown, women were the chief litigants in defamation suits. Further, some women managed to maintain control over their property after marriage; other records show wives actually suing their own husbands.[7] Nonetheless, legal authorities often go to great extremes to maintain this definition of the wife, even to the point of creating the category of the "married spinster." The fiction of the married spinster allowed judges to separate the wife from her husband and hold her accountable for her actions, while at the same time maintaining her status as subordinate to her husband.[8] These ambiguities run throughout the period. As several recent scholars have shown, this was a time of unusual marital ferment in which women's place in the social and legal scheme was ambiguous at best.[9] Marriage was in crisis in the late sixteenth and early seventeenth centuries, "the site of a paradoxical struggle to create a private realm and to take control of it in the interests of the public good," as Catherine Belsey explains it.[10]

Conduct books and marriage manuals offer absolute statements on the need for wifely submission, arguing, "If she be not subject to her husband, things will goe backward, the house will come to ruine."[11] Yet even the *Homily on the State of Matrimony*, with which I began this section, opens a potential gap in the definition of the wife as subsumed in her husband. The *Homily* instructs wives to obey their husbands, pointing out that "to obey is another thing then to control or command, *which yet they may do to their children and to their families*" (emphasis mine). To "command" is to possess identity and agency. Ostensibly, this agency is limited to the household, and even there is restricted to children, servants, and other domestic matters. The husband remains the ultimate authority. Although the woman's position of wifely subjection is clearly delineated in text after text, the period displays considerable anxiety about that position.

The popular press also participated in this cultural exploration of female agency, and given the ambiguities evident in domestic and legal texts, it is no wonder that the pamphlet literature focuses on the household as the potential site of female power. But in its depiction of wifely power, the popular press almost always constructs female agency as violent.[12]

Murdering wives must certainly be among those who attempt "to shift it well enough" in the seventeenth century. Representations of wives who murder their husbands occupy an important place in the writings of early modern England — in legal tracts, dramas, ballads, and pamphlets. And at first glance, popular accounts of women who murder their husbands seem to be one place where women are represented as possessing unequivocal autonomy and subjectivity. As I have shown, in theory the married woman was subject to her husband; as T. E. styles it, a husband and wife "are but one person, and by this a married Woman perhaps may either doubt whether shee bee either none or no more then halfe a person."[13] Legally, the husband was held accountable for his wife's actions, her identity was contained within his. It has been argued, however, that in instances of serious crime, women gained a separate legal existence. T. E. explains, "In matters criminall and capitall causes, a feme covert shall answere without her husband."[14] Or, in the words of Margaret Doody, "Women as felons were legal beings."[15] In instances of capital offense women could be tried and executed just as men might be.[16] Further, in the pamphlets and ballads retelling these crimes, women are often given a voice as they confess and explain the motivations for their actions. Catherine Belsey points out the double effect of the required confession in this literature: "The supreme opportunity to speak was the moment of execution. The requirement for confessions from the scaffold, so that the people could see how church and state combined to protect them from the enemies of God and society, paradoxically also offered women a place from which to speak in public with a hitherto unimagined authority which was not diminished by the fact that it was demonic."[17] The popular crime literature of early modern England, then, further uncovers ambiguities inherent in the definition of wife as *feme covert*. As a wife, the woman has no identity apart from her husband, yet she is the center of the family, itself a microcosm of society at large. She is granted authority in matters of the household and over her children and servants. Likewise, she has no legal autonomy, yet in some instances she can be held accountable for her crimes. By exposing such contradictions these works provide a locus for female agency and voice, at least tacitly. While many of England's laws were constructed to contain women and to prevent them from transgressing the accepted social and sexual order, this literature shows them doing just that.

Clearly, these accounts mean to provide examples of the household gone awry, and by negation they offer a definition of the properly ordered family. Yet some of these narratives seem to be merely sensational and exaggerated accounts of wifely villainy and offer little explanation for the wife's actions. Because they offer no real motivation, they skirt the issue of wifely agency. The case of Anne Hamton, whose story is told in *Murther, Murther. Or, A bloody Relation how Anne Hamton, dwelling in Westminster nigh London, by poyson murthered her deare husband* (1641), offers a good example of popular depictions of marital breakdown. In this case, the husband is the picture of appropriate husbandly behavior. A "very laborious man," he delights "in nothing more but to see his wife pleasant."[18] The wife, on the other hand, gossips and spends all the money the husband earns. In the early modern period, the wife's duties in the household were rigidly defined and were meant to complement the duties of the husband. The husband's responsibility was to "get goods"; the wife's was to "gather them together and save them." The husband should "get money and provisions"; the wife was ordained not to spend vainly. The husband was instructed to be "skillful in talk"; the wife should "boast of silence."[19] Before the crime is committed, the husband in this narrative offers a textbook example of good husbandry. He exerts authority over his wife but does not abuse that authority:

"hee always spoke in a very loving manner unto her except she overmuch provoked him" (4). In contrast, the wife is a "light housewife," with all its connotations of moral laxity, who, while her husband is working, spends her time gossiping with one young fellow or another and wastes all the family's resources. The wife, then, disrupts the proper household that the husband attempts to uphold. This disruption is characterized as a contest for speech and money, two of the more common signifiers of power within the domestic sphere as presented in this literature.[20]

Once the murder's inception is recounted, the crime seems almost laughable because it is so excessive given the text's description of the wife's circumstances. Complaining that her husband "was an enemy to good fellowship," Anne is swiftly moved to murder when her landlady cajoles, "hang him, cut his throat, or poison him, for he is not fit to live upon the earth amongst good fellows" (4). Anne then proceeds to poison him with double the necessary dosage. Poison is the method most frequently used by wives to murder their husbands in popular accounts and represents a perversion of the prescribed wifely duty of providing nourishment for their families. This crime, then, constructs the wife as a kind of "anti-housewife."[21] The murder here occurs abruptly and quickly; the pamphleteer provides no real motivation for the wife's actions, thus denying Anne any real agency. She is goaded into action by her female companion. The text expresses incredible anxiety about female companionship and its potential intrusion into the ideally secure space of the household.

The pamphleteer insists that this story should serve as a warning to women of the dangers of insubordination. Speaking directly to his potential female readership, he admonishes, "Hearken to me you that be wives, and give attendance you which as yet are unmarried, regard the words of St. Paul which commands that every wife should love her own husband as Christ the church" (1). The title page offers the same admonition. Nonetheless, one suspects that the sensationalism of the case prompted its telling, more than morality. The author revels in the details of the death, describing the corrupted body in graphic terms: the corpse literally bursts with poison, the fingernails peel, the hands swell into great boils, the belly "seemed as if hot irons had been thrust into it" (5). In its depiction of the explosion of the husband's body, the narrative literalizes the explosion of the household that the prescriptive literature sought to prevent.

Although most crime pamphlets include a confession as a way to reincorporate the criminal into the social order, the confession here is deferred. Perhaps recognizing that his readers would expect to hear the criminal's repentance, the author calls the reader's attention to the omission and promises a more perfect relation later, one that he never gives. Whether intentional or not, however, this omission of the customary confession serves to silence the vocal, gossipy woman of the narration. The goal of containing the unruly woman is achieved in this text even more than if a confession had been delivered.

Yet in many ways, as frightening and horrific as their crimes are, many of these women do not really seem dangerous. Their actions are so extreme and so unmotivated that they seem caricatures. In the story of Anne Hamton, in fact, the author seems to recognize the ludicrousness of his narrative and opens the pamphlet with a disclaimer: "Gentle Reader, It is not my purpose to make thee now laugh" (1). Far more compelling are the accounts that try to explain the reasons for murder, thereby at least recognizing the potential for wifely agency. Interestingly, although they do not dwell on the fact, most of these accounts illustrate the wholesale breakdown of the marriage; both husband *and* wife are shown violating the household order.

Henry Goodcole's (1586–1641) *The Adultresses Funerall Day* (1635) vividly illustrates this more complex examination of marital disorder. Goodcole, chaplain at Newgate Prison and a master of the crime/confession genre,[22] depicts husband murder as a fundamental breakdown not just of domestic order, but of the natural order as well. He links it with other unnatural activities — "Catamatisme, Sodometry, Paracity, many headed murders and the like."

All are symptomatic of a world out of joint: "Now what the reason may be conjectured in these our latest, but worst dayes: that so many nefarious acts, equalling, if not farre surpassing those perpretated [*sic*] in former ages, should be new committed . . . I can give no other reason then this, the contempt of the feare of God, and the neglect of his Sabbath."[23] Although his explanation for the instability within the household is simplistic — heedless disregard of God's commandments, most specifically of the Sabbath — his narrative presents a much more detailed picture of marital discord. In *The Adultresses Funerall Day* he focuses on the most dangerous of the "grand Malefactors" plaguing the social order, the "poor wretched creature" Alice Clarke. Although this pamphlet relates the story of the murder of Alice's husband (a man ironically named Fortune), the word "adulteresses" in the title suggests that Goodcole's interest is as much in Alice's sexual transgression as in the murder. The title foregrounds the initial transgression that almost inevitably leads to the greater crime of murder in the narratives on husband murder. Almost all female misconduct derives from a sexual lapse. As the popular literature presents it, the consequences of female unchastity are devastating.

As Goodcole's narrative illustrates, while crime writers view murderous wives as fearful, commonly they also seek to explain their crimes away by offering sometimes elaborate motivations for them. Alice's story is a study in victimhood, from her early seduction and impregnation by her employer to a forced, loveless marriage, and finally to the abuse she suffers at the hands of her husband. Goodcole's stance seems strangely sympathetic, making allowances for the woman's actions in light of the circumstances she finds herself in. Comparing Alice to another notorious murderess of the day, Mistress Page of Plymouth, he admits, "Her injuries, and harsh and unmanly usage spurred by the instigations of the divell, *almost* compeld her to what she did . . . so they were *almost* beyond the strength of Nature for her to suffer" (sig. Bv; emphasis mine). The pamphlet offers most of the typical motivations for murder: spousal abuse and neglect, forced marriage, and seduction by another man. The difference is that it includes multiple motivations all in one case.

Believing in the power of confession to purge the sinner of guilt — "If a sinner be at any time silent, he is but the Devils Secretary"[24] — Goodcole devotes the greater part of his story to Alice's confession rather than to the actual crime. This confession serves two purposes: first, it provides a public display of the unruly woman surrendering to God, the ultimate patriarch. And second, perhaps unintentionally, it grants that woman at least limited authority and subjectivity: "to speak is to possess meaning, to have access to the language which defines, delimits and locates power. To speak is to become a subject."[25] Occupying center stage for the moment, the woman tells her life story, ordering it and offering justifications for it as she speaks.

The first explanation the wife offers for her crime is that she is in a forced, loveless marriage. Enforced marriage frequently provides motivation for husband murder. In Thomas Deloney's (1543?–1600) ballad on the murder of Page of Plymouth, for example, the wife laments,

> In blooming yeares my Father's greedy mind,
> Against my will, a match for me did find;
> Great wealth there was, yea, gold and mony store,
> But yet my heart had chosen long before.
>
>   . . . .
>
> My chosen eies could not his sight abide;
> My tender youth did scorne his aged side:
> Scant could I taste the meate whereon he fed;
> My legges did loath to lodge within his bed.[26]

While most murder accounts serve as a warning about what happens when women overstep their place as submissive wives, frequently they admonish husbands and fathers as well. In the *Murder of M. Page of Plymouth* (1591),[27] for example, the father is held at least partially responsible for Page's murder. He abuses parental authority by forcing his daughter to marry against her will. At a time when companionate marriages were becoming more common, a forced marriage was often considered no marriage at all.[28]

Alice Clarke also complains of physical abuse by her husband. The legitimacy of a husband beating his wife was heatedly debated in the prescriptive literature of the period. Although violence within the household was sometimes considered justifiable as necessary discipline, most theorists prohibited excessive physical correction. In his *Apologie for Women* (1609), William Heale, for instance, rejects this form of discipline outright, arguing that wife beating is "not only unlawful, but an odious, unmanly, and unseemelie thing."[29] In fact, Heale's discussion of wife beating uncovers another disjunction in the theory that the husband and wife are one flesh: "No man did ever willingly hurt himselfe; or if any man hath, certainely he maie iustly of all men bee helde a madde man: and therefore what mutual blowes can lawfully passe between man and wife; who are one and the selfesame?"[30] Since most marriage theorists decry excessive beating as a means of wife control, the wife's attack on her husband in this situation, if not justifiable, is at least understandable. Goodcole supports the wife in this claim, noting the marks on her body that prove the abuse she suffered. Husbands in this tract seem particularly unsympathetic and malicious. In another case that Goodcole briefly recounts as a parallel to Alice's, he depicts a husband refusing the antidote his wife offers repentantly once he has been poisoned: "Nay thou Strumpet and murderesse, I will receive no helpe at all but I am resolvd to die and leave the world be it for no other cause but to have thee burnt at a stake for my death" (sig. Bv–B2). In a strange way, the husband here snatches back sovereignty by not allowing the wife to save him and effectively killing himself by refusing the antidote, if we believe the confession here, and Goodcole intimates that we should not.

Rather than meeting blow with blow, Alice chooses the more passive but more effective action of poisoning her husband. Yet she claims at one point that she did not poison her husband at all, but that he grabbed the poison out of her pocket before she could stop him. She implies that the husband was actually suicidal, pointing out that he had earlier attempted to drown himself but was prevented from doing so at her urging. Despite other places where he expresses sympathy for Alice, here Goodcole views her insistence that her husband actually killed himself as little more than a rationalization. Nonetheless, he includes her rationalizations in his narrative, seemingly to undermine her credibility and negate the pity the reader may feel for her because she was abused. To pity her is to acknowledge her as a complete human being with her own needs and desires.

Finally, the wife argues that the murder was instigated by her lover, Henry White. White, she claims, convinced her to kill her husband and gave her the money to buy poison. "That it were better for one to be hanged, then to endure so discontented a life," he glozes, and promises to marry her upon her husband's death (sig. B2v). The instigation to murder by a lover is a fairly common element in these stories and serves to caution women to beware flattery and smooth words, whether of the devil or of their lovers. Furthermore, this explanation for the crime affords the woman little agency and thus, it would seem, little culpability — but such is not the case. Once the murder has been committed, White rejects Clarke, ostensibly in fear that having betrayed her husband she might betray him as well.[31] At this point Goodcole intercedes to censure men who seduce women: "A great clog unto such a mans conscience, if it be true, to seduce a woman unto his will, and so leave her" (sig. B3). Nonetheless, his sympathy is qualified by the phrase "if it be true."

Goodcole's attitude toward his subject is equivocal throughout. Sometimes he casts doubt on the confession by questioning Alice's veracity and by labeling her defense "a lame excuse, or strange delusion" (sig. B3). In other places he seems to verify the truth of her claims as he does when he notes the marks of abuse present on her body. He seems to exonerate her of total blame by placing at least partial responsibility on the men in her life — her father, her employer, her husband, and her lover. He even berates her neighbors for their failure to provide "good counsell" (sig. Bv), suggesting a kind of social control and responsibility beyond that of church and court. Crime writers frequently advocate neighborly responsibility. Goodcole implicates the neighbors in *Natures Cruell Step-Dames* as well, likening the mother's temptation to kill her child to a house on fire: if her house had been set on fire she would have raised such an outcry that her neighbors would immediately have helped her, but "her heart was here set on fire by hell," and they ignored her need.[32] Rarely, however, does Goodcole allow Alice's confession to stand completely on its own. Although he concedes some voice to the woman, this voice is never left unchecked by the male voice of the pamphleteer.

Thomas Kyd's *The Trueth of the most wicked and secret murthering of John Brewen* (1592) provides another example of an adulterous affair that leads to husband murder. Here Anne Welles's lover, John Parker, convinces her to poison Brewen, her husband, and marry him. Two years and two children later, Parker still refuses to marry Welles: "The varlet, hearing the great mone shee made unto him, was nothing moved therewith, but chorlishly answered, shee should not appoint him when to marrie: but if I were so minded (quoth he), I would be twise advised how I did wed with such a strumpet as thy selfe; and then reviled her most shamefully."[33] Like Clarke's lover, he argues that if she would poison her husband she might poison him as well. In this tale, too, the treatment of the woman is ambivalent. We learn that Brewen forced Anne to marry him under threat of imprisonment and that she is mistreated and abused by Parker. Although the sympathy toward Welles is measured, early in the narrative she is called a "proper young woman" and a "nice maiden." Parker, on the other hand, is "accursed," "chorlish," and a "varlet." Nonetheless, Anne suffers the greater punishment when the murder is discovered — she is burned at the stake, Parker is hanged.

Sympathetic treatment alongside vile invective is fairly common in these accounts. More unusual is the almost entirely benevolent depiction of the female criminal in Gilbert Dugdale's *A True*

Discourse Of the practises of Elizabeth Caldwell (1604), the story of a botched husband murder. The pamphlet is oddly reminiscent of *A Christall Glasse for Christian Women* (1603), in which Philip Stubbes eulogizes his dead wife Katherine as the perfect mirror of womanhood. In Dugdale's account, Elizabeth's complicity in the crime is minimal — she stands by while another woman puts ratsbane in her husband's oatcakes. Though she immediately regrets her compliance, before she can stop them, the husband and several neighbor children eat the cakes. As luck would have it, the poison only sickens her husband, who "by way of vomit [was] saved."[34] However, a neighbor's child, two dogs, and a cat do eventually die.

Like other accounts, the bulk of this narrative is devoted to Caldwell's confession, but there is little of Goodcole's characteristic ambivalence here. From the moment of her imprisonment, Caldwell is depicted as a godly woman more concerned with the conversion of her fellow prisoners than with her own fate: "from her first entrance into prison, till the time of her death, there was never heard by any, so much as an idle word to proceed out of her mouth, neither did she omit any time, during her imprisonment, in serving of God, and seeking pardon for her sinnes, with great zeale and industrie, continually meditating on the Bible, excluding herselfe from all companie, saving such as might yeeld her spirituall comforts, as learned Divines, and such, the faithfull servaunts of God" (sig. B2). Ironically, though an adulteress and an attempted murderer, Caldwell becomes the epitome of piety and rectitude. She takes an active part in the reformation of her fellow prisoners and in the 300 or so people who visit her daily. Although unusual for this kind of literature, the transformation of the criminal here is similar to that which occurs in yet another pamphlet, Richard Watkins's *Newes from the Dead* (1651). This account relates the strange case of Anne Greene, who was hanged for infanticide in 1650 but miraculously came back to life after her execution. In order to explain her survival and God's apparent beneficence toward her, Watkins remakes Anne into the archetype of proper womanhood. This pamphlet also includes a series of poems written by Oxford students, some of whom even compare Anne's resurrection to Christ's (see below). In both these cases the criminal becomes perversely sanctified through her crime.

As I have suggested, women in these criminal accounts are typically given some authority in their confessions. Here, however, not only is the woman allowed to speak but to write as well. Dugdale includes a letter purportedly in Caldwell's own hand (as indicated by a change in typeface for this portion of the pamphlet). In the letter, Caldwell reconstructs herself as a kind of Christian martyr, sacrificing herself for the salvation of her wayward husband: "if the losse of my blood, or life, or to endure any torments that the world can inflict upon me might procure your true conversion, I should esteeme it purchased at an easie rate" (sig. B4v). As often happens in these accounts, the recasting of the criminal as saint reconciles the criminal with the state in a final act of atonement. Yet the situation seems even more complex in this instance because Caldwell posits herself as the wronged party. She places the blame for her actions at least partially on her husband, who in his neglect of his wife left her at the mercy of seductive and sinful personages. "[Remember] howe poore you have many times left me, how long you have beene absent from mee, all which advantage the devill took to subvert me . . . wrought upon my weaknes, my povertie, and your absence, untill they made me yeeld to conspire with them the destruction of your bodie," Caldwell chides him (sig. Cv). While the text is overtly concerned with wifely submission, it seems equally aware of husbandly duty. In a twisted reversal of criminal culpability, Caldwell piously intimates that her husband is actually the one in need of heavenly forgiveness. Piety — not poison — inverts "the hierarchy of marital authority" in this pamphlet.[35] Through his actions the husband invalidates the social strictures that define female roles.

The autonomy granted the woman seems especially unusual here. Caldwell even dictates the terms upon which she dies, exhorting her companions to pray, calling for her Bible, reading and praying to God, and finally requesting that a hymn be sung as she meets her death. There is power here and Caldwell is given the privilege of speech, but except for her mild criticism of her husband, she speaks only in religious platitudes. Whereas her crime implies resistance, her confession defers to patriarchy. Further, the narrative does not end with Caldwell's death. As a counterpoint to the saintly and devout Caldwell, Dugdale returns to one of her conspirators in the crime, "that uncharitable creature, Isabel Hall, widdow," before ending his narrative. Like other female criminals, Hall is defined by her marital status and, as a widow, ultimately seems more dangerous than the married Caldwell because she exists outside of direct male control. As the narrative concludes, Dugdale shifts total blame onto Hall, calling her "the onely instrument of this timeless action" (sig. D3). Apparently, class plays as big a part as gender here. Caldwell is obviously a gentlewoman; Hall comes from the lower classes. Unlike Caldwell, who is contrite and repentant, Hall denies everything. Paradoxically, by rejecting speech, Hall retains her subjectivity and power. She is the unruly woman who refuses to be tamed by confession. When seen as a foil to Elizabeth Caldwell, Isabel Hall offers the real threat to the dominant social order. Although Dugdale seems, then, to express total sympathy for his subject, the shift in focus to Hall at the end of the narrative suggests a refusal to admit any goodness in a more average woman and allows him to complete the saint/sinner dichotomy. Caldwell, with all her contrition and devotion, is an anomaly.

Even in more notorious cases, the authors usually provide at least minimal explanations for the wives' actions, though such details are often not developed. In the story of Thomas Arden's murder, for example, Arden's land grabbing and greed at least partly mitigate his wife Alice's guilt and suggest that she was not the only one who wished him dead. Holinshed's account even intimates that Arden facilitates Alice's affair with the servant Mosby because of this greed: he "was yet so greatly gyven to seek his advauntage, and caryd so little how he came by it that in hope of atteynynge some benefits of the lord northe by meanes of this mosby who could do muche with hym, he winked at hir filthie disorder, and both permitted, and also invited Mosbie verie often to lodge in his house."[36] Arden's actions represent an abuse of male authority as he becomes the most reviled of early modern stereotypes — the wittol, or willing cuckold. This is hardly a sympathetic endorsement of Alice's behavior but does at least suggest the complexity of her actions.

Perhaps the most extreme depiction of the collapse of the household, and surely one of the most sensational accounts, is the story of Mary Hobry (or Aubrey), the French midwife who murdered her husband and disposed of his body by chopping it into parts and leaving the pieces in various places along the Strand. There are at least four versions of Hobry's crime: two pamphlets (one with an attached ballad, sung to the tune of "The Pious Chieftans's Exhortation") and two broadside ballads.[37] It is not hard to imagine why the story of Mary Hobry would have caught the early modern public's fancy. She is transgressive in every way: she is French, she is a midwife, and she is Catholic. And she is preternaturally strong, acting alone and accomplishing a feat of incredible physical strength. She does not choose poison, the typical female murder weapon, but brutally and physically kills her husband by strangling him with his own cravat. Although two of the accounts express doubt that she could have carried out the crime of strangling and disposing of her husband's body by herself, the court decides otherwise.

The most developed of these narratives is told in *A Hellish Murder Committed by a French Midwife* (1688). This pamphlet differs from the others included in this volume because it purports to be the actual legal deposition of the witnesses and of Mary Hobry herself. Its tone is legalistic and precise, and because it records the examinations of 18 witnesses, including Hobry's son, it renders the full horror of the crime in graphic detail. But it also provides a more vivid picture of the trouble within the household than other accounts do. In some ways the emphasis on Hobry's nationality —

she is almost always referred to as "the *French* midwife" — serves to construct her as cultural "other" and thus makes her less threatening. The pamphlet's record of her speech, frequently in French with an English translation provided by the author, further creates her as foreign — alien, incomprehensible, perhaps even base. (Interestingly, the French phrases are only presented in the witnesses' depositions; Hobry's testimony is recounted almost entirely in English, except for her signature at the end verifying its accuracy.) By emphasizing her foreignness, the text can offer consolation to the Englishman (or woman) reading it. No Englishwoman would perpetrate such a crime. The hints at Hobry's Catholicism may serve a similar purpose, at once demonizing her and the hated papist religion that she practices.[38]

Most of the witnesses are neighbors who recount the constant battles within the Hobry household. Given the amount of neighborly surveillance here, it seems particularly curious that no one did anything before the anger erupted into violence. As the neighbors relate it, the emphasis is almost completely on Hobry's angry speeches against her husband, what one deponent describes as "dangerous words." Although everyone agrees that Denis Hobry, the husband, is a drunk, a "Libertine and Debauchee to the Highest Degree" (39), they focus instead on Mary Hobry's abusive language. One witness testifies that he heard her curse her husband more than 40 times, calling him "Dog, Drunken Villain, and other the Foulest Words of Reproach" and "C'est un Chien; C'est un Yvrogne" (2). Repeatedly, the witnesses tell of Hobry's threats to murder her husband. The emphasis on female speech here is consistent with the early modern construct of gender, which places speech at the center of patriarchal authority. To have speech is to have agency, as I argued earlier. The woman who speaks neither in acquiescence nor in answer to her husband reveals an independence that endangers the patriarchal order. Since she ignores the social tenet requiring female silence, she may very well ignore other rules of marriage. Verbal assertiveness in women is associated with sexual assertiveness:

Love thy wife
As thy life,
Let her not go thou know'st not whither;
For you will alwayes live in strife
If she keep not her lips together,

as one seventeenth century balladeer phrased it.[39] In this account, adultery is never an issue; nonetheless, the authority of the patriarch, the husband, is undermined by Hobry's independence. And yet, strangely enough, in a text that so foregrounds unchecked female speech, Hobry's voice is obscured. Amid the voices of the many witnesses, hers is drowned out, as it must have been before she committed the crime. Though many of the witnesses chastise her for her transgressive speech, the text also shows the husband's abuse of Hobry. Nonetheless, her complaints fall on deaf ears. As the text presents it, a woman who speaks against her husband, even justifiably so, so transgresses appropriate female behavior that she deserves punishment. The text records Hobry's speech only to squelch it.

As a midwife, Hobry is self-sufficient. With her own profession, she earns money and respect and has an identity outside the household. In fact, as the narrative depicts it, she is the bread-winner, not the husband. The wife is described as "industrious," the husband as profligate. At least part of the conflict derives from the husband squandering all her hard-earned money on drink. By allowing the wife to earn the family's income, he abandons one of the important responsibilities that his authority is hinged upon. In particular, as a midwife, Hobry seems the very embodiment of female power. In her role as midwife, she presides over childbirth, itself a site of female empowerment. Further, the position of midwife, according to Adrian Wilson, overturned normal distinctions of class and rank, giving her authority over both men and women of a higher social class. And the midwife possessed a unique authority in early modern courts, offering expert testimony in cases of infanticide, child murder, and rape. As someone who often provided the crucial evidence verifying virginity, pregnancy, or the viability of a fetus, the midwife played a significant role in policing sexuality. This power, however, also brought with it an enormous amount of anxiety. As Percival Willughby depicts them, "midwives will follow their own ways, and will have their own wills."[40]

Nonetheless, despite the narrative's focus on her autonomy, we learn from her testimony that she, too, is a victim. The most telling detail, and the one that the text glosses quickly over, is the fact that she had endured years of sexual abuse, and on the night of the murder, her husband had raped her. The wife's description of the abuse she endured that night is graphic and brutal: first, the husband begins beating her in the stomach and breasts; then he grabs and squeezes her so hard that blood starts coming out of her mouth. Then, forcing upon her "the most Unnatural of Villainies," he "acted such a Violence upon her Body in despite of all Opposition that she could make, as forc'd from her a great deal of Blood, this Examinate crying out to her Landlady, who was (as she believes) out of distance of hearing her. This Examinate told him, *I will immediately Rise and Complain to the Neighbors*: Whereupon he took her Forcibly by the Arm, and threw her down on the Bed, being before sitting up to rise; and after this, Bit her like a Dog &c" (33–34). Despite the author's discreet "&c," the magnitude of the crime is clear. As Dolan points out, Hobry raises the "hue and cry" that the law says she must to prove that she did not consent. According to Bracton, the medieval legal writer, the raped woman "must go at once and while the deed is newly done, with the hue and cry, to the neighboring townships and there show the injury done her to men of good repute, the blood and her clothing stained with blood, and her torn garments."[41] But the situation for Hobry seems even more appalling than that of other victimized women because the rapist is her husband; the symbol of law enforcement within the household is here the lawbreaker. Further, since rape had been constructed as a property crime at least since the Middle Ages, consent was not legally at issue here at all. The wife is her husband's property, so any assault against her is a crime against the husband. But what happens when the perpetrator is the husband himself? If T. E.'s discussion of rape is any indication, no crime has occurred: "if any virgin, widdow, or single woman be ravished, shee her selfe may sue an Appeale of rape, prosecute the felon to death, and the kings pardon (as it seemeth) cannot helpe him. If a feme covert be ravished, shee cannot have an Appeale without her husband."[42] And yet the text, seemingly aware of the wife's dilemma, shows a remarkable amount of self-consciousness on the part of the wife. Her self-questioning — "What will become of me? What am I to do! Here am I Threatened to be Murder'd, and I have no way in the World to Deliver myself, but by Beginning with him" (34) — depicts her despair so sympathetically that her separateness as a human being is unequivocal. Such a strategy almost demands that the reader examine the boundaries of a husband's control over his wife's body.[43] It seems that the wife in this narrative has no choice: to save herself, she must kill her husband. The contradictory position of the wife that we have noticed throughout this literature is most acute here. Hobry is her husband's possession, legally without autonomy, yet she is accountable for her reaction to his brutalizing of her. The broadsheet version of this event, "A Warning-Piece to All Married Men and Women, Being the Full Confession of Mary Hobry, the French Midwife" (1688), shows even more sympathy for the wife, characterizing the husband's abuse

> at such an inhumane rate,
> That she a thousand times wish'd him ill Fate,
> And thought within herself to end the Strife,
> If she were forc'd, to take away his Life:
> The cause that mov'd him to those Tyrannies,
> Was her aversion to his Villainies.

It later depicts Hobry weeping and wishing for her own death. Nonetheless, in both narratives, the law only recognizes the death of the husband; Hobry's suffering seems of little consequence.

On the surface, the crime literature of early modern England presents women felons (and by extension all women) as threatening and monstrous — "matchlesse monsters of the female sex," as

Goodcole would have it. But if these women are monsters they seem distinctly impotent — monsters with talons blunted and claws clipped. Their actions are almost always explained with reference to men (or the devil), and we soon realize that it is not the woman's story that is being told here but the man's. If these women are subversive, they are so only momentarily and are quickly incorporated back into patriarchy as victims. As reprehensible as these women's actions may be, the narratives invariably show that men are ultimately in power. Containment is effected by glossing over blame. Although men are revealed to be culpable, that culpability is minimal. Similarly, women are held accountable for their actions, but they are rarely shown acting on their own. Although their crimes suggest that these women act in defiance of male control, the narratives persistently depict them acquiescing to men, whether in confession or murder. The pamphlets dealing with husband murder, then, give power to the women only to deny it. This contradiction is central to the genre and to the period.

3

Bloody Mothers

REPRESENTATIONS OF CHILD MURDER

> Children run to their mother, ask her advice about everything, ask
> her all sorts of questions, and whatever she answers they believe,
> admire, and consider as the gospel truth. Mothers, how many
> opportunities you have to make your children good or bad!
> — Juan Luis Vives, *The Education of a Christian Woman*

The figure of the murdering mother appears repeatedly in early
modern news pamphlets, broadsheets, and dramas and became
popular at the same time that domestic literature was busily re-
defining the mother's role. Conduct books, domestic manuals, and
sermons increasingly emphasized the intellectual and spiritual
duties of the mother in addition to her physical obligations. In
the words of one writer, mothers were to "nourish [their children's]
bodies as the pelican" and "suckle [their] minds with the milk of
good manners, training [them] up . . . in religion and learning."[1]
These responsibilities conferred an authority on the early modern
mother heretofore unmatched within the household.[2] Recent
research suggests further that some mothers possessed very real
economic power, playing significant roles in arranging their sons'
marriages and making decisions about wills and property.[3] It is
not surprising, then, that early modern writings on motherhood
attempted to contain maternal power by insisting on the mother's

41

intellectual and moral weakness at the same time that they affirmed her special place within the household.

The mother's role was ambiguous at best. Her authoritative position as mother conflicted with her subordinated position as wife. Although she seemed to have a unique power within the domestic sphere, she was pictured as subject to her husband. She might be the steward of the household in the husband's absence, but in his presence she remained his subordinate. Even more than the murdering wife, then, the murdering mother reveals the instability inherent in the family-state analogy. As we might expect, the increasing importance given to the mother in the late sixteenth and early seventeenth centuries opens up a potential site of conflict between motherly authority and wifely submission. Clearly, as Mary Beth Rose points out, "motherhood presents a test case for female power, making visible the destabilizing contradictions that that power comprises in English Renaissance society."[4] In fact, any woman involved in the nurturing and upbringing of the child, from pregnancy through breaching, could be suspect.

Anxiety about maternal nurture was everywhere present in England at this time, and the mother's role from conception through childhood was a contested site of female empowerment. Midwives, for example, came under increased scrutiny and regulation. Although some scholars argue that the regulation of midwifery stemmed from scientific developments such as the invention of the forceps, there is evidence of cultural anxiety about midwives. Recent scholars have largely discredited the association of midwifery with witchcraft; nonetheless, as we have seen, the midwife inhabited a position of power and authority not available to other women that was bound to make her threatening.[5] The popular literature reflects these concerns, depicting midwives as purveyors of immorality who help unmarried women (and occasionally married women) get rid of their unwanted pregnancies. One such pamphlet, *The Murderous Midwife, with her Roasted Punishment* (1673), describes a midwife "in great Credit and Repute, being made use of by most of the Great Ladies there, as indeed she was Mistress of her Trade, and skilful (though not honest) in her Art."[6] As the pamphlet progresses, neighbors grow increasingly suspicious because they see many pregnant women enter and leave the house, but never any babies. Finally, the neighbors obtain a warrant, search the house, and discover 62 infant bodies thrown in the privy. The midwife is tried and punished by being lifted over a fire in a cage filled with 16 wild cats. There she is mauled and roasted to death. Like other pamphlets from the period, this one revels in the details of a powerful woman getting her comeuppance.

The practice of wet-nursing was also heatedly critiqued; conduct books and mothers' manuals urged mothers to breast-feed their children rather than send them out to wet nurses. In this literature, mother's milk was granted an almost mystical significance — the power not only to convey and prevent disease but to pass on the character traits of the woman nursing the child. For this reason, mothers were encouraged to breast-feed their own children lest inappropriate lower-class traits be passed on to them. As Valerie Fildes explains, "Before 1800, the wet nurse (or the breastfeeding mother) did not just provide nourishment for the baby; she was believed to transmit to the child, along with her ideas, beliefs, intelligence, intellect, diet, and speech, all her physical, mental and emotional qualities. Effectively, she was seen to be reproducing herself; the child *was* the nurse; an extero-gestate foetus."[7] The insistence that the mother breast-feed her baby seems also to have had another more insidious purpose: to keep the mother within the properly ordained sphere of the household. As Elizabeth Clinton, Countess of Lincoln, chides, the mother who fails to nurse her children is guilty of "unmotherly affection, idlenesse, desire to have liberty to gadd from home, pride, foolish fineness, lust, wantonesse & the like evills."[8] Occasionally, the crime literature of the period also encouraged women to breast-feed their children, largely through scare tactics. By providing examples of malevolent wet nurses, this literature becomes part of the general social trend condemning the practice of sending children out. For example, in

A True Relation of the Most Horrid and Barbarous Murthers Committed by Abigail Hill of St. Olaves Southwark, on the persons of foure Infants (1658), Abigail Hill, the wet nurse or "foster mother" of several children, brutally murders four infants. Hill also "borrows" poor neighborhood children and, passing them off as her charges, brings them periodically to the parish overseers to receive quarters pay for them.[9] As Marina Warner has explained, the female breast, the ultimate sign of motherhood, takes on a kind of polyvalent symbolism — of wildness, autonomy, and strength, and of nurturance, provision, comfort — shared by Amazonian warriors, virgin goddesses, and the Christian figure of charity. The figure of the maternal body, as in the nursing and nurturing breast, "gave legitimacy to a body that is otherwise a source of peril."[10]

The mother's womb carried an equally important function: the womb was "the place wherein the seede of man is conceaved, fortified, conserved, nourished, and augmented." Although the focus in most of the discussions on the development of the fetus is on the nurturing of the child in the father's and God's image, there was some concern that even the mother's thoughts and fears could be detrimental to the healthy development of the unborn child in the womb. A wayward imagination could result in the birth of a monstrous baby. *The True Discripcion of a Childe with Ruffes* (1566), for example, describes a baby born with a ruff-like neck because his mother liked to dress in ruffs.[11]

Strangely, alongside theories of the mother's influence over her unborn children were concomitant theories that denied maternal power. One explanation of pregnancy, for example, held that the mother served only as an incubator to the fetus and played little or no role in the infant's development: "Mothers afford very little to the generation of the child, but onely are at the trouble to carry it, . . . as if the womb were hired by men, as Merchant Ships are to be straited by them; and to discharge their burden, . . . women grow luke-warm, and lose all humane affections toward their children."[12] Although this theory calls the widely accepted view of the mother as natural nurturer into question, motherly affection was widely considered desirable and even inevitable. Still, several writers warn mothers of the dangers of nurturing their children too much, especially boys. There was considerable concern that the mother might spoil her children with obsessive coddling and pampering: "For cheryssyng marreth the sonnes and hit utterly distroyeth the daughters."[13]

Recent scholarship has even interpreted the witch hunts as a "projection of hatred and aggression toward the mother, which is worked out through the persecution if not of the mother herself, of old, poor, or otherwise powerless women."[14] The search for the witch's teat — itself a perversion of the mother's nourishing breast — suggests a parallel construction of motherhood as malevolent and dangerous.[15] In fact, in response to the question of why the victims of witch hunts were overwhelmingly female, Deborah Willis conjectures that "witches were women" precisely "because women were mothers."[16]

Like the domestic tracts, the street literature participates in the ambivalent construction of motherhood during the period. And like domestic literature, the popular pamphlets are concerned with maternal duty. For the most part, however, these writings concentrate on instances when motherhood goes awry, on those cases when maternal nurture transmutes into maternal violence. Since women's power in early modern England is almost wholly within the household, the violence depicted is largely domestic, and at least in the case of married mothers, most often occurs at the point where motherly authority and wifely submission collide. At the same time that domestic texts and conduct books valorized motherhood, dubbing it "the salvation of [the female] sex," the popular press criminalized mothers. Not only is motherhood a source of redemption, but it is also the woman's punishment as a daughter of Eve. John Knox's discussion of motherhood in *The First Blast of the Trumpet Against the Monstrous Regiment of Women* vividly betrays the duality evident in the woman's role as wife and mother: "Two punishmentes are laid upon her [women], to witte, a dolor, anguishe and payn, as oft as ever she shal be mother:

and a subiection of her selfe, her appetites and will, to her husband, and to his will. Frome the former parte of this malediction can nether arte, nobilitie, policie, nor lawe made by man, deliver womankinde, but who soever atteineth to that honour to be mother, proveth in experience the effect and strength of godde's word."[17] Although the method might be different, the end result of both types of texts was the same: to limit maternal authority.

Despite the prevalence of "spinsters" in the court cases involving infant and child murder, the popular press rarely treated unmarried infanticides, choosing instead to focus on married women (and sometimes widows) who murdered their children, apparently because their crimes suggested a potential disruption of the marital structure and were thus more threatening. Child murder by married women only infrequently occurred, making it more notorious. As Malcolmson notes, "Documented instances of infanticide within marriage are exceptional. . . . women from genteel or middle-class families were seldom accused of infanticide; almost all of the women involved appear to have been from labouring, mechanic or farming backgrounds."[18] Infanticide committed by unmarried mothers, while not condoned, was at least understandable; the murder of infants and children by married mothers was not. The very fact that it occurred evoked the horrible power of the mother that conduct books, prescriptive literature, and even medical manuals tried to suppress. Because middle-class married women were generally not committing infanticide to maintain their socio-economic status, their actions more clearly indicted the patriarchal definition of domesticity and necessitated an examination of the motivation behind their crimes. In recounting these crimes, these texts explore the definition of the good mother and expose contradictions and anxieties about maternal authority.

Where it does treat unmarried infanticides, street literature represents these women as decidedly unnatural, monstrous, and sexually promiscuous (see the discussion of unmarried mothers in "To Avoid Their Shame," below). In contrast, the majority of the pamphlets dealing with married mothers do not sexualize the mothers and are at least partially sympathetic in their depictions of them. Because they are socially and religiously sanctified wives, these women are granted a measure of respect not typically given to the unmarried women. Their crimes are not an attempt to avoid the shame of motherhood; in fact, most of these women commit their crimes out of their sense of duty as mothers. For the most part, they do not define themselves against the social order but completely within it. This literature focuses precisely on those sites where the mother is deemed to have the most power — over the physical, spiritual and mental well-being of her children. In a perversion of the responsible mother of the conduct manuals, these mothers kill their children in order to save them from religious falsehood, from starvation, and occasionally, from the mother's own desperate psychological state. While mother's manuals and conduct books limit maternal power by emphasizing paternal governance, these pamphlets seek to undermine maternal authority by constructing it as dangerous and violent.

As noted earlier, one of the mother's chief responsibilities was to instill proper faith in her children, a responsibility that grants the mother an enormous amount of power not just over the child's earthly life but over its eternal soul. Although in many ways the Reformation replaced the parish priest with the godly father, who had ultimate responsibility for the spiritual instruction of the family, the mother's influence was also widely recognized. William Gouge, in *Of Domesticall Duties*, for instance, lists religious instruction as one of the special duties of mothers, a duty that most women seem to have taken quite seriously. In *The Mothers Legacie to her Unborne Childe*, one of the few places where we actually hear a mother's voice, Elizabeth Jocelin fears that her death in childbirth will prevent her "from executing that care I so exceedingly desired, I mean in religious training our Childe."[19]

Always looking for a sensational angle, several popular pamphlets treat the disastrous repercussions of misdirected and obsessive religious piety, thus playing on cultural anxieties about Catholicism and other religious sects. *A pittilesse Mother* (1616), for one, tells the story of Margret Vincent, a mother who murders her children out of an obsessive concern for the salvation of their souls when her husband refuses to allow them to be baptized in the Catholic Church. Her crime is not one of anger or hatred but rather stems from her concept of what it means to be a good mother. By defining good mothering as raising and educating her children in her true faith, Vincent sees no recourse but to kill them in order to deliver them from eternal damnation. This pamphlet is more openly propagandistic than other texts of this kind (though one could argue that virtually all of this literature has a propagandizing intent), and the story is told in large measure to warn of the dangers of Roman Catholicism. Addressed specifically to the "good Gentlewomen" whom the pamphlet depicts as particularly vulnerable to the machinations of the Catholic Church, the text is "both anti-Papist and misogynist," according to Betty Travitsky.[20] Just as women fall easily victim to Satan's wiles, so too are they easily swayed by false religion; they are, in the pamphlet writer's words, "the weak sex they [Roman Catholics] continually make prize of."[21] Margret Vincent is transgressive and dangerous not just as mother but in her recusancy as well, "both of which provided her with some grounds for resisting domestic patriarchy."[22] Although the pamphlet basically constructs Vincent as religiously misguided, it also defines her actions as a resistance to husbandly authority by defining her in opposition to her less gullible husband, a "good Gentleman" who accounted her persuasions "vaine and frivolous and she undutifull to make so fond an attempt" (sig. A3).

As the pamphlet begins, the author takes great pains to establish Vincent as a model of wifely and motherly gentleness, describing her as "discreete, civill, and of modest conversation" and "much esteemed of all that knewe her, for her modest and seemely carriage." Married for 12 or 14 years in comfort and concord, this "good soul," this "unfortunate gentlewoman," falls into the clutches of "Roman Wolves" who entangle the "sweet Lamb" with their subtle persuasions. For the most part, Vincent is portrayed as an innocent victim without agency, bewitched by the deceptive allure of the Catholic Church. The Catholic Church is presented as a seductive lover, offering such charming inducements that "hardly the female kinde can escape their inticements" (sig. A2v). The depiction of the woman as easily swayed by false doctrine builds on a long held tradition of women as intellectually and morally weaker than men and lends support to the argument that men should retain dominance over the household. The text illustrates the woman's limited power over her husband as she tries futilely to persuade him to convert, feeling that "she was appointed by the holy Church to shew him the light of true understanding" (sig. A3). Interestingly, though, the husband seems at least partially culpable and is described as snubbing Vincent with unkind speeches. Further, one place in the text suggests that the issue is not only religion but also the struggle for power within the household. "Oh Margret, Margret, how often have I perswaded thee from this damned Opinion, this damned Opinion, that hath undone us all," the husband moans. Flouting her role as submissive wife, Vincent, sounding oddly like Chaucer's Wife of Bath, admonishes her husband for not giving her sovereignty in the marriage: "Oh, Jarvis, this had never beene done if thou hast been ruld and by me converted" (sig. A4v). Although it is only suggested in this text, the conflict can be read as centering in parental power and authority; the father contends with the mother for control of the children. The woodcut on the title page, however, glosses over this bit of wifely intransigence, showing the mother less in control of her actions, being goaded by the devil to strangle her babies. Despite the mother's formidable power over her children, then, she is still the weaker sex, subject to all of the errors of the flesh and spirit, and in need of the close supervision of her husband.

A similar pamphlet from the mid-seventeenth century, *Bloody Newes from Dover* (1647), also exploits a contemporary religious dispute, in this case, the controversy over infant baptism. What in the narrative seems merely an illustration of female willfulness and susceptibility to fits of passion is revealed on the title page to be an example of the frightening results of misplaced faith. Much less developed and sympathetic than *A pittilesse Mother*, *Bloody Newes from Dover* relates the crime in less than half a page: John Champion, an honest tradesman, seeks to have his newborn baby christened. His wife (unnamed in the text, but named Mary and labeled an "Anabaptist" on the title page) refuses, greatly perplexing her husband (and the reader because the text itself says nothing about her religious beliefs and presents her actions as totally lacking in motivation). Six or seven weeks pass, until one day while the husband is away, "this wicked minded woman" takes "a great knife and cuts off the child's head." When the husband returns home, the wife calls him into the parlor, points to the bloody infant, and utters, "Behold husband, thy sweet Babe without a head, now go and baptize it; if you will, you must christen the head without a body: for here they lye separated."[23] Lacking the ambivalence of other texts, this pamphlet preys on cultural anxieties about various nonconforming religious sects that denied infant baptism, a fundamental tenet of the Church of England.[24] The entire story is told on the sensational title page, where the mother gruesomely offers the severed head to her shocked husband. Nonetheless, despite its stereotyping of the mother as a fiendish "Anabaptist" (a term used indiscriminately during the period for any radical sect),[25] the woodcut's emphasis on the literal head of the child at least points toward the metaphoric battle for the position of household head. Indeed, the author offers the following moral to his story: "Thus may we see, that where division and controversie doth arise, sad effects will suddenly follow: for no sooner can there a breach appear, but presently Sathan is ready to stop it up, by infusing his deluding spirit into their hearts, for the increasing of variance, discord, and contention."

Religion is the locus of maternal anxiety in these narratives because it offers women the potential for power, even if this power was not often realized. Many sects recognized the necessity of educating women so that they might read and understand scripture and pass this knowledge on to their children. Further, although

Bloody Newes from Dover.   20

BEING
A Tru:
RELATION
OF

The great and bloudy Murder, committed by *Mary Champion* (an Anabaptist) who cut off her Childs head, being 7.
weekes old, and held it to her husband to baptize. Also a-
nother great murder committed in the North, by a Scot-
tish Commander, for which Fact he was executed.

Printed in the Yeare of Discovery, *Feb,* 13. 1647: 1646

Bloody Newes from Dover, title page, shelfmark E.375 (20). By permission
of the British Library.

Protestantism may have actually increased paternal authority, virtually all churches sanctioned wifely disobedience in the name of true faith.[26] Some sects ostensibly allowed women equal participation in religious matters, occasionally even legitimizing political action.

Beyond spiritual sustenance, the mother was also responsible for the physical nurturance of her children, and other pamphlets relate the sad stories of mothers who kill their children because they cannot afford to feed them. In a single-page broadsheet entitled "The Distressed Mother, or a Sorrowful Wife in Tears" (1690?), the mother murders her two young children because they are starving. As the title suggests, the writer is completely sympathetic to the mother and places total blame for the tragedy on the profligate husband who has squandered the family's estate through riotous living, extravagance, and drink. In an especially pitiful passage, the author describes the murder after the child begs his mother for food: "Mother saith one, a little food, or I die." The mother sighs, "Where shall I get it? Your father hath lost his Patience, and his Wealth, and we all our Hopes, with his Mishaps. Alas! Alas! what shall become of me, or who shall succour you, my children? Better it is to Die with one Stroke, than so languish in a continual Famine." And with that explanation, the mother slits the children's throats from ear to ear and prepares to kill herself as well. Before she can commit suicide, however, the husband returns, "laden with wine," and she resolves to kill him instead: "Thou shalt Die, thou negligent Man, since thy ill Government hath been the Ruine of me and my Children." In a masterstroke of understatement, the pamphlet writer offers this moral: "Wives should beware of too much Fury, and Husbands [should] be more circumspect in their Families."[27] Instead of confirming female agency and will, this narrative serves to reinforce patriarchal power. The father is held completely responsible for the death of his family; his presence and careful supervision could easily have averted the tragedy. Without his good government over the household, the family is completely destroyed.

Still other accounts represent the mother's mental weakness and susceptibility to melancholy. Although their intent is to challenge motherly authority, they seem instead to indict the institution of marriage as oppressive and detrimental to the mother. The various narratives of Mary Cook, a suicidal mother who kills her favorite child, a two-year-old daughter, offer a good example of a mother driven to murder because she places no value on her own life. There are three versions of this story: *Blood for Blood*, *The Cruel Mother*, and *Inquest After Blood* (all 1670). That this story attracted so much attention suggests the extent to which seventeenth century England was grappling with its construction of motherhood.

Blood for Blood opens like *A pittilesse Mother* with a description of the mother's good character. A 37-year-old wife and mother of eight children,[28] Mary Cook "was of a very civil and sober life and conversation, living in the neighbourhood very inoffensively," but the writer also cautions that she was "of a very melancholy temper, which is the Anvil that the Devil delights to forge upon."[29] As discussions of hysteria, significantly called "the mother" in the Renaissance, explain, women were considered prone to various fits of temperament and melancholia. The womb, the source of women's salvation and power but also of her shame and frailty, was thought to wander, either from lack of sex or from retention of menstrual fluid. This wandering womb could cause all sorts of strange behaviors, from sorrow and depression to convulsions and disorientation.[30] The "remedy — a husband and regular sexual intercourse — declares the necessity for male control of this volatile female element," as Coppélia Kahn notes.[31] *The Cruel Mother* offers an additional reason for Cook's crime — an equally female one — when it reports that Cook miscarried while she was in prison. Since pregnancy was often viewed in the early modern period as a disease that could bring about irrational longings and fits of temperament, the murder can be explained as the result of periodic, natural female processes. In defining pregnancy negatively as a disease that subjects the woman to frightful bodily changes over which she has no control, medical literature from the period pathologized and diminished reproductive power. Like other writings from the period, these narratives seem deeply suspicious of female reproductive ability.[32]

Like other pamphlets discussed here, *Blood for Blood* holds the husband partially responsible for the tragedy that follows. As the narrative represents her, Mary Cook is frustrated because her husband is frequently absent and neglects his business at home. In a desperate cry of self-assertion, she tries to commit suicide numerous times over the course of a year and a half. Paradoxically, she endeavors to assert herself by erasing herself. Although her husband finally realizes that she is suicidal and knocks down all the hooks and nails in the cellar to prevent her from hanging herself, he never really hears her cries for help. After several aborted attempts at suicide, Cook finally kills her youngest child, not out of malice, but at least in this account, because she fears what will happen to the child after she is dead: "what should become of that child, which she so dearly loved, after she was dead: upon this she concludes, she had better rid that of life first, and then all her fears and cares for it would be at an end" (15). Later, when asked why she had perpetrated so atrocious an act, she replies because "she was weary of her life" (18).

The killing of the child because she is "weary of her life" suggests that in a strange way she associates the child's life with her own. In fact, *The Cruel Mother* makes the connection between the mother's life and the child's explicit, explaining that she killed the child so that "she by that means [should] come to her own end."[33] The murder in this instance derives largely from the mother's own lack of self-worth, and she projects that worthlessness onto her only daughter. In fact, she verbalizes her disgust with herself in terms of womanhood: "God had convinced her that her own righteousness was but unrighteousness, even as a filthy menstruous clothe, and therefore desired out of the sense of her own nothingness, and utter emptiness, to go out of herself" (*Blood for Blood*, 38). That Cook defines her self-disgust in terms of menstruation, the signal of potential motherhood, suggests a complex intermingling of selfhood and motherhood. As Marilyn Francus contends, "The roles of wife and mother frequently — perhaps usually — required the erasure of the self; and one suspects that her frustrations were profoundly typical (and perhaps all the more horrifying for that reason), as Mary Cook the person was eclipsed by Mary Cook the wife and mother."[34] Further, perhaps she surmises that her only female child will suffer the same sense of worthlessness that she herself does and seeks to save the child from the pain the mother suffers.[35] Apparently, this obsessive identification with the child was not unusual. Michael MacDonald notes in his study of suicide in the period that some seventeenth century mothers "were so strongly attached to their children that when they became depressed and suicidal they thought of their youngsters as extensions of the identity they wished to exterminate."[36] Indeed, Cook seems so completely defined by her role as mother that she fails to distinguish herself from her child. She views the child as merely an extension of herself, so much so that after she confesses to murder she worries that the child may suffer damnation because of the state of *her* soul. As such, the narrative posits the need to circumscribe domestic nurturance; as Frances Dolan explains, "maternal subjectivity is threatening when its boundaries expand to include — even consume — the offspring."[37]

In Mary Cook's case, the pamphlet writers are forced to confront an example of female agency and subjectivity in a way that those who write about unmarried infanticidal mothers are not. And taken together, these three accounts of Mary Cook's crime are remarkable for the various motivations they attribute to the mother, almost all of which seek to rob her of that agency. Both *Blood for Blood* and *The Cruel Mother* depict the mother's depression as a kind of satanic possession, and *Blood for Blood* even reports a rumor that Satan actually appeared to her. The narrators clearly want the reader to view her as a victim, describing her as "more like a Lamb going to the slaughter than a Murderer going to the Gallows" (46). In one account religion is blamed ("she was under trouble of mind about Religion," *Blood for Blood*, 33), as it is in *A pittilesse Mother* and *Bloody Newes from Dover*, but Cook denies this assertion: "her answer was, That there was nothing of any Religious Concernment in it" (34). *Inquest After Blood* constructs her as insane and reports that her husband brought forth several witnesses to attest to her madness. This defense fails because Cook provides lucid responses in her deposition.[38] In particular, she proves her competency by answering questions about the maintenance of the household. Ironically, as Francus points out, "Cook succeeded at the technical aspects of homemaking even as she subverted the ideological criteria."[39] Nonetheless, the various strategies to deflect maternal agency only serve to make it more ambivalent.

Although the account of Cook's fragile psychological state suggests that she was not really in control of her actions, the text is somewhat ambivalent on this point. Cook's actions express at least a limited challenge to patriarchal prerogative. In one tragic assertion of selfhood, she threatens to kill her youngest child if her husband goes out, but his compliance prevents this. Further, the murder occurs completely within the context of maternal and wifely duty, the husband in the background demanding his Sunday clothes and the baby in the cradle crying for its breakfast. Suddenly, in one shocking moment, the picture of domestic bliss goes haywire: "but she laying aside all Motherly Bowels, took the Babe out of the cradle, set her on her lap, took the knife out of her skirt, laid her left hand upon its face and chin, and with the other hand cut her throat at one stroke" (*Blood for Blood*, 15). Then, curiously, she stomps her foot to call for her husband! (Interestingly, the forwardness represented by the stamping of the foot is transformed into acquiescence on the scaffold, where she stomps her foot to indicate that she is willing and ready to die.) Before she is conveyed to Newgate, she takes off her rings, cuts the silver chaps from her scarf and gives her husband all the keys of the trunks, chests, and boxes in a symbolic ceding of her domestic place. And in one final jab at her husband's neglect, she chides, "O, if you had been more careful to look after me, you might have hinderd me from doing this" (20–21). Although these actions hint that the murder is a contest for power in the household, the greater weight given to the husband's neglect and to the wife's mental state actually serves to reinforce paternal authority by denying maternal competence.

And yet maternal power remains conflicted in these texts. In one final attempt at recognition, the pamphlet portrays Mary Cook asking that her story be recorded and published. If we agree with Mary Beth Rose that "the ideal society is based upon the sacrifice of the mother's desire,"[40] Cook remains dangerous despite the pamphlet writers' attempts to explain away her agency because she continues to assert herself even after death by seeking to have her story heard. Given the various retellings of her story, she is at least partially successful. The woman whose voice seemed to be ignored in life will finally be heard, if only because of her notoriety.

The depiction of the mother's desire to have her voice heard is the most striking feature of the last pamphlet that I will discuss in this section, *Fair Warning to Murderers of Infants: Being an Account of the Tryal, Codemnation and Execution of Mary Goodenough* (1692). Although Goodenough is not a married woman but a widow, her story belongs here because the text examines her authority, first as a criminal and then as a mother. Unlike the other women we have examined, however, her "good mothering" comes after the death of her baby. The text is not clear whether or not she murdered it intentionally or simply neglected it, noting that the child "perished for want of suitable Help and due Attendance."[41] What is important is that she concealed the death; as a result, her actions fall under the 1624 statute that defined the concealment of the death of an illegitimate baby as murder (see below, "To Avoid Their Shame").

The narrative begins with the death of Goodenough's child, but the bulk of the pamphlet is devoted to a lengthy letter the mother ostensibly dictates for her surviving children. As in other criminal accounts, the ideology of chastity that "made silence an equivalent of bodily purity" is shown to operate in crisis in this text.[42] But here the author represents the sanctioned female voice as the woman speaks not from her momentarily authorized position as criminal but from her socially approved position of mother. Goodenough speaks not in confession but in a long treatise of advice to her children that will be read to them only after her death. Mary Beth Rose convincingly argues that within literary and domestic texts of the period "maternal desire and agency . . . can be represented visibly (corporeally) only as dangerous, subordinate, or peripheral in relation to public, adult life" unless the mother is absent or dead. Thus "the best mother is . . . a dead mother."[43] Although Rose is explaining the phenomenon of the mother's advice book, a genre that at once transgresses and replicates patriarchal dictates, her argument seems equally valid for this text. Goodenough's letter, entitled "Advice of your Dying Mother," exhibits some of the same characteristics of the mother's advice books, and whether actually dictated by the mother or not, suggests that Dorothy Leigh and other writing mothers were influential enough for the pamphleteer to use them as models for his repentant mother.

Like Leigh's *Mothers Blessing*, Goodenough's letter of advice enjoys a liminal status poised between life and death and is offered as the mother's legacy to her children. And exactly like Elizabeth Jocelin's *Mothers Legacie to her Unborne Childe*, Goodenough seeks to provide the spiritual and moral guidance she will be unable to supply her children because she is dead. She speaks with a voice of maternal love and authority, thus becoming an exemplar of maternal solicitude, an irony apparently lost on the pamphleteer.

Goodenough's letter to her children extends the compulsory public confession of the typical crime pamphlet and transforms it into a pseudo mother's manual. The mother's manual is a genre that is itself contradictory — both public and private.[44] Likewise, the female criminal on the scaffold, and in the pamphlets, disrupts the normative opposition of public/male space and private/female space. The letter in *Fair Warning* further problematizes the two categories.[45] In addition, the fact that the advice in this instance comes from a mother who killed one of her children makes the form doubly fractured. What at first seems the grand irony of a murdering mother writing in support of family values is not so strange after all when we consider the ambivalent position of both the female criminal and the mother in the early modern period. She has already been made public through her crime and is no longer bound by the dictates of silence and modesty. Oddly enough, because she is already transgressive, her writing reincorporates her into society and refocuses the reader's attention on her role as good mother, which is perhaps the writer's intent.

Yet one of the strange things about this case is that Goodenough fails to provide the requisite confession. Her boldness in leaving a written legacy to her children is partially negated by her inability to speak publicly in confession. The refusal here is not depicted as a conscious act of will and self-assertion, but rather as a sign of her physical and mental impairment. The author apologizes for this breach of custom, explaining, "it could not be expected she should say much more; for she must needs be in great Confusion and Surprize, who in less than Two month's time, was Committed, Try'd, Condemn'd and Executed for her Crime. Besides, she seem'd never to have had any great Faculty or Freedom of Speech" (3). Still, the author assures the reader, she dies with a "great Abhorrence of Sin" and a "sincere desire to propagate" holiness in others. Her letter to her children serves to replace the missing confession, and while this omission emphasizes her weakness, the letter foregrounds her power as mother.[46]

The street literature of seventeenth century England preys on cultural anxiety about motherhood by carrying the mother's legitimate power to its most extreme manifestation and intermingling maternal power with other anxieties. The writers depict criminal mothers as "good mothers," but they pervert the ideal of the good mother by exaggerating and distorting maternal nurturance. By depicting violence as deriving from maternal duty, the popular press makes all mothers suspect. Although these texts are often sympathetic to their subjects, their sympathy brands these women as weak and provides further justification of the need to circumscribe maternal authority.

As these pamphlets suggest, the woman's role as wife *and* mother in early modern English society was highly conflicted. Although the crime pamphlets describe events that were extreme and extraordinary, they provide vivid examples of the period's interrogation of the proper scope of maternal authority. The texts discussed here illustrate how the murdering mother embodies both her society's expectations and its anxieties about motherhood by showing motherhood to be at once empowering and destructive. That the popular press's obsession with murdering mothers occurs at the same time that women were gaining greater power and authority within the domestic sphere is crucial. Paradoxically enough, while these accounts criminalize female subjectivity, they often also attempt to qualify maternal authority by casting the mother's actions as reactions to her weakness or to patriarchal neglect and irresponsibility. Maternal power is thus partially undermined and made less threatening.

4

"To Avoid Their Shame"

REPRESENTATIONS OF INFANTICIDE

The monsters of the Sea draw out their Breasts, and give Suck to their Young Ones. The barbarous Cruelties of some Midwives, Nurses and *even* Parents to young Children, may assure us, That there are greater Monsters upon the Land than are to be found in the Bottom of the Deep.

> — "The Cruel Midwife"

In his discussion of the duties of parents, William Gouge chastizes the many "lewd" and "unnaturall" mothers who "leave their new-borne children under stalls, at mens doores, in Church porches, yea many times in open field." Comparing them to ostriches that abandon their eggs in the dust and eagles that thrust their young from the nest, he finds these women even more unnatural than beasts.[1] Gouge writes in the midst of the "infanticide craze," a time of increased prosecution of unmarried women for the murder of their illegitimate children that some scholars liken to the more notorious witch-hunts occurring at the same time throughout early modern Europe.[2]

The pamphlet literature treating infanticide echoes Gouge's rhetoric, a rhetoric that is typical of the writing about unmarried mothers in general during the period, not just those who neglected or murdered their children. Since in early modern thought, as I have shown, a woman was "understood either married or to be married,"[3] single women, whether spinsters or widows, were often treated with suspicion and hostility. The situation for a single *mother* was even more dismal. Unwed mothers overstepped the marital order by having children out of wedlock, and they received some of the most scathing attacks in legal and religious treatises. Concerns about primogeniture, paternity, and purity of bloodlines as well as fears about the social drain illegitimacy placed on the parish stigmatized these women. Pregnancy and childbirth outside of marriage imposed a heavy burden not just on the young woman left with the child but on society as well, because the county in which the child was born was often considered responsible for its support should the mother be unable to care for it. Further, producing illegitimate children betrayed a sexuality, a life outside of marriage and beyond patriarchal control, that needed to be contained. As the authors of *Half Humankind* point out, "The Renaissance viewed woman as possessed of a powerful, potentially disruptive sexuality requiring control through rigid social institutions and carefully nurtured inhibitions within the woman herself."[4] In the opinion of Joseph Swetnam, in fact, any sign of sexuality outside of marriage deprived women of a legitimate place in society. Spurning such women as "wanton harlots," Swetnam argues,

> you have thus unluckily made your selves neither maidens, widows, nor wives, but more vile than filthy channel dirt fit to be swept out of the heart and suburbs of your Country. Oh, then suffer not this world's pleasure to take from you the good thoughts of an honest life! But down, down upon your knees, you earthly Serpents, and wash away your black sin with the crystal tears of true sorrow and repentance, so that when you wander from this enticing world, you may be washed and cleansed from this foul leprosy of nature.[5]

Admittedly, Swetnam was notorious even in his own time for the extremity of his views; nonetheless, his language is remarkably similar to that of legal and criminal writers from the period. The rhetoric of monstrosity and shame becomes even more vehement in descriptions of unmarried women who commit infanticide.

Women accused of causing their children's deaths, whether through abandonment, carelessness, or outright murder, are described as "matchlesse monsters of the female sex," "vipers," "savages," and "bloody dogs." As is the case with other unmarried mothers, their sexuality makes them particularly suspect. The word "lewd" occurs in virtually all the commentary on the subject: the tags "harlot," "strumpet," and "whore" are equally prevalent. One of the more famous examples, cited repeatedly in legal definitions of infanticide from the period, provides a good instance of this phrasing: "A *Harlot* delivered of a childe, hidde it in an Orchard (it being alive) and covered it with leaves, and a Kite stroke at it, and the childe dyed therof, and the mother was arraigned and executed for Murder."[6] In the late sixteenth and early seventeenth centuries, both legally and in popular culture, infanticide came to be associated almost exclusively with unmarried, sexually active women — the "looser sort," in Percival Willughby's words.[7] This focus on sexuality is limited to unmarried infanticidal mothers. In fact, despite the popular press's obsession with them, married women largely escaped prosecution. In a study of the Essex assize records from 1620 to 1680, J. A. Sharpe found that of the 84 women indicted for infanticide, only 7 were listed as married.[8]

Before 1560, cases of infanticide rarely appear in the assize records.[9] Infanticide was newly criminalized during this period; in the Middle Ages such cases were commonly considered the province of the church courts and were usually punishable by penance rather than death. Under Elizabeth's reign, however, as the regulation of personal conduct shifted from the church to the secular courts, infanticide came under heightened scrutiny. By some scholars' accounts there was as much as a 225 percent increase in the number of women indicted for this crime between 1576 and 1650.[10] This is not to say that infanticide was commonplace during the seventeenth century. Despite the pressures placed on unwed mothers, the records indicate that deliberately neglecting or killing children was rare.[11] Nonetheless, infanticide seems to have been sufficiently widespread (or at least feared) to warrant special legislation. In 1624 "An Acte to Prevent the Destroying and Murthering of Bastard Children" was passed, specifically targeting unmarried women who attempted to conceal the deaths of their illegitimate infants:

> Whereas many *lewd* Women that have been delivered of *Bastard* children, to avoid their shame and to escape punishment, do secretly bury or conceal the death of their children, and after, if the child be found dead, the said women do alledge, that the said child was born dead; whereas it falleth out sometimes (although hardly is it to be proved) that the said child or children were murthered by the said women, their *lewd* mothers, or by their assent or procurement: For the preventing therefore of this great mischief, be it enacted by the authority of the present parliament, . . . That if any woman be delivered of any issue of her body, male or female, which being born alive, should by the laws of this realm be a *bastard*, and that she endeavour privately, either by drowning or secret burying thereof, or any other way, either by her self or the procuring of others, so to conceal the death thereof, as that it may not come to light, whether it were born alive or not, but be concealed: in every such case the said mother so offending shall suffer death as in the case of murther, except such mother can make proof by one witness at the least, that the child (whose death was by her so intended to be concealed) was born dead.[12]

Reversing the normal rules of evidence, the statute presumed the mother's guilt in the death of an infant unless she could prove otherwise. Although the law made concealment of the death of a bastard child the indictable crime, hiding the pregnancy itself was viewed as substantiating evidence that the mother intended to do away with her infant. The case of Ann Price illustrates the law at work: a servant in the house of a gentlewoman, Price was impregnated by one of her fellow servants. She managed to hide her pregnancy so that "no Person in the house did in the least suspect her till after she was delivered." After the baby was born, she wrapped it in her apron and locked it in a box. When the child was inevitably discovered, Price claimed that, "finding her pains come fast upon her," she knocked on the floor with her shoe to call for help. Since she was three flights of stairs away, no one heard her. She was found guilty of murder, "the concealing of the Child being a material Point of Evidence against her."[13] Prior to the passage of "An Acte to Prevent the Destroying and Murthering of Bastard Children," the courts had to prove the infant had been born alive before convicting the mother of murder. After 1624, however, the law made concealment the crime and referred specifically to unmarried women because it covered only illegitimate children. Thus infanticide was legally a gendered crime and, like witchcraft, it was one of the few crimes where the accused was presumed guilty unless she could prove her innocence.

Given the often precarious situation of the mother, evidence of innocence was frequently difficult to find. In the absence of witnesses to a live birth, any indication that the mother had prepared for the birth — the hiring of a midwife or the purchase of linens, for instance — served as proof that she had not "intended to conceal" and was grounds for acquittal.[14] A married woman accused in the death of her infant was not bound by the same rules of evidence; in her case, a conviction could be obtained only if there was unequivocal proof that the child had been born alive and that she had deliberately killed it.

It is unclear whether the infanticide law actually saved children or had the reverse effect because of the way that it affirmed negative attitudes about unmarried mothers. While court records suggest that at least until the mid-seventeenth century an increased number of women were prosecuted for the murder of their newborns, the law did not seem primarily intended to protect the lives of bastard children. The repetition of such words as "lewd" and "bastard" indicates that this statute was more concerned with the initial crime of fornication and with illegitimacy rather than the actual death of the child. And given the spate of legislation passed in the decades prior to 1624, we can conjecture that economic concerns played at least as large a role as morality. For example, a 1576 statute allowed the courts to sentence parents to the county jail who failed to maintain their illegitimate children. Further legislation enacted in 1610 granted authorities the right to commit to the House of Correction "every Lewd Woman" who bore a chargeable bastard.[15] While begetting an illegitimate child was not a crime under English law, bearing a child that was chargeable to the parish was. Since this particular statute provided for the punishment of women only, it too served to intensify the social prejudices already pressuring unmarried mothers, stigmatizing them both for their lack of chastity and for their poverty.[16] Because of the shame associated with poverty, some scholars conjecture that while infanticide was never condoned, it was sometimes seen as preferable to charging the child to the parish. Thus, the study of infanticide "uncovers a perplexing relativity in popular attitudes towards the value of infant life which contrasts markedly with the clear prescriptions of contemporary official morality."[17] As Mark Jackson explains, "Contemporary preoccupations with unmarried women and with the fate of their illegitimate children stemmed from a variety of factors, notably from anxieties about the appropriate behaviour of single women and about the role of women in the family, from concerns about the concealment of illicit sex, and, perhaps most importantly, from fears about the financial burden of increasing numbers of illegitimate children."[18]

Given the apparent legal and social obsession with these crimes, it is surprising to discover that they are not accorded the attention in the popular literature that we would expect. Most often, accounts of infanticide receive summary treatment in the sessions papers that record the crimes tried during a particular assize. Even the few pamphlets that treat infanticide as defined by statute link it with other crimes, as if infanticide is not important enough — or shocking enough — to warrant a more extended and separate discussion. In many of the popular accounts, infanticide is just another one of many serious social ills that plagued the nation. As Frances E. Dolan points out, the popular literature tends to ignore infanticide as defined by law, preferring to focus instead on the more sensational murders, those "for which the statutes cannot account."[19] For this reason, pamphlets tended to cover anomalous crimes rather than commonplace ones: the story of a servant woman who murders several babies; the mother who plies her child with candies and cake and then slits its throat; an infanticide committed by an unlikely culprit, such as a woman from a higher social class; or even the case of a woman who survives her execution.[20]

Even in these anomalous accounts, however, the sometimes elaborate motivations attributed to other female criminals are mostly omitted, as if the motivation for murder is already understood: "to avoid their shame," in the words of the 1624 statute. Because of this conventional motivation, these women actually seem the least transgressive of the criminal women treated in the street literature. In a peculiar way, their crimes confirm the power of the state over their lives. They have so completely absorbed the dictates of their society and are so invested in maintaining the face of respectability, that they are compelled to commit the most atrocious of acts in order to protect their social identity. Just as infanticides have no place in society, these prosecuted women are accorded little space in the pamphlet literature. Powerless and marginalized in life, they remain shadowed even in the accounts of their crimes.

When stories of infanticides are told, ostensibly they are told to serve as a warning to other unmarried women. The author of *News from Tyburn* (1675), for instance, tells the story of Elizabeth Simmonds who threw her bastard child into a pond, claiming that the baby had died in childbirth and that the weather was too cold to bury it. Although Simmonds's crime is described as "heinous" and "unnatural," her subsequent penitence in prison is equally important. In "continual Tears and Lamentations" and in "very Pathetick Language," Simmonds begs "all young Maidens to take warning by her shameful death: To resist or rather fly all immodest motions and lascivious addresses; not believing the flatteries of men, nor giving up their Honour."[21] As this case illustrates, these writings seek first to contain the sexuality of the fallen woman by recuperating her back into the social order through confession and death, and second, to control the sexuality of other women by presenting the criminal as an exemplum of unchaste behavior. In effect, however, these stories perpetuate the culture of shame that leads to infanticide in the first place.[22]

The street literature detailing infanticide echoes the judgmental and moralistic tone of the polemical literature, and though it invariably describes the perpetrators as "whores," the women it deals with are rarely prostitutes. The term "whore" functions as a "free-floating signifier"[23] attached to any woman who fails to fit the model of chaste wife.[24] *Deeds Against Nature, and Monsters by kinde* (1614), for example, tells the story of Martha Scambler ("a lascivious, lewd and close strumpet"), an unmarried mother who kills her baby by throwing it in the privy and is only discovered when a yelping dog leads her neighbors to "the sweet Babe lying all besmeared with the filth of that loathsome place."[25] Although Scambler's story was written before the "Acte to Prevent the Destroying and Murthering of Bastard Children," it provides a representative example of the way popular literature treated unmarried women suspected of killing their illegitimate infants.

Like legal accounts of infanticide, *Deeds Against Nature* depicts the crime as unnatural and monstrous. That monstrousness is almost exclusively the result of Scambler's unrestrained sexuality, a sexuality that, according to the pamphlet writer, deprives her of her identity not just as a mother but also as a woman. The author explains that her delivery was all the easier because of "her lusty body, strong nature, and feare of shame" (sig. A4). (The word "shame" is used nine times in the course of the narrative about Scambler, another six times in the ballad attached to the narrative.) He depicts her as a "Caterpillar of nature, a creature more savage then a shee woolfe, more unnaturall then either bird or beast, for every creature hath a tender feeling of love to their young, except some few murtherous-minded strumpets, *woemen* I cannot call them." Since she is not a married woman, a *feme covert*, Scambler has "no husband to cover her act of shame." Thus the pamphlet places her in counterdistinction to the good, married mother, who "esteemes the fruit of her owne womb, the pretious and dearest

Jewell of the world, and for the cherishing of the same will (as it were) spend her lives purest blood, where, contrariwise the harlot (delighting in shame and sinne) makes no conscience to be the butcher of her owne seed" (sig. A3v). Such women must be punished, as much for their uncontrolled sexuality as for the murder of their babies.

Even the drawing that serves as the frontispiece to the pamphlet suggests the impact of her crime, a crime not just against nature but against the social order. As is typical, Scambler's crime is linked with that of another criminal: in this instance, John Arthur, a London beggar who murdered his mistress. Nonetheless, the greater social import of Scambler's crime as compared to Arthur's is indicated by both the words and by the woodcut on the title page: Arthur, "a London cripple," is shown hanging with only the executioner as his companion; Scambler, "a *lascivious* young Damsel," is depicted with five heavily armed guards in addition to the hangman. Although the phrase "young Damsel" suggests some ambivalence, the title page symbolically indicates that the sexually active, unmarried woman poses the greater threat to society.

By linking Scambler with the beggar John Arthur, the pamphlet writer also makes explicit the connection between her crime and poverty. In its representation of his crime, the narrative makes much of the way that Arthur uses his deformity to solicit the "charitie and devotions of almes-giving people" (sig. A2). Equating his poverty with moral depravity, the writer presents Arthur as thankless and base, spending the money given to him in "blasphemie, swearing, drunkennes, and such like, all damnable sinnes and such as be the nurses and breeders of others" (sig. A2v). Arthur is one of the undeserving poor — "rogues, vagabonds, and sturdy beggars and other lewd and idle persons"[26] — that the period distinguished from the truly needy. The criminalization of the poor was a characteristic response to crime in the period, and occurs repeatedly in the pamphlets. In another example, depicted in *A Warning to Sinners, Being a True Relation of a Poor Woman* (1660), the woman's poverty is regarded as "Gods Justice upon Notorious Sinners," as is her literally putrefying body.[27] As J. A. Sharpe notes, in this era of increased numbers of poor, these people shifted in popular imagination "from being God's poor to being the Devil's."[28] From Arthur's story to Scambler's (and to that of other poor, young women whose economic survival may have depended upon concealing pregnancies and illegitimate births) seems not much of a leap.[29] Their shared space in a single pamphlet suggests an economic as well as a moral connection between them. Infanticide is thus criminalized not just in terms of gender and marital status but also in terms of class. The irony, of course, is that the criminalization of poverty may have motivated infanticide by encouraging mothers to kill their babies to avoid slipping into poverty and being judged as in league with the devil.

As we might expect given the class prejudice of the law, servants are the primary target of infanticide indictments.[30] Female servants probably accounted for the majority of cases of infanticide brought before the courts. Keith Wrightson found that between 14 and 23 percent of all women bearing bastards in Lancashire and Essex named their masters as the father.[31] The percentage of masters involved in infanticide cases may have been even higher. In the Surrey assizes from 1660 to the end of the eighteenth century, for example, as many as two-thirds of the women accused were servants.[32] According to Cockburn, victims of neonatal infanticide were "typically, conceived on the fringes of the biological family — as the result of relationships with masters — or within the household — during affairs with fellow servants."[33] Since the birth of a child could mean the loss of a job and a home, it is no wonder that these women might choose desperate measures to avoid detection. Two mothers who were exploited by masters were Anne Greene, discussed below, and Jane Hattersley, whose story is told in a pamphlet attributed to Thomas Brewer (fl. 1624) entitled *The Bloudy Mother* (1609). For the most part, the pamphlets only chronicle stories of infanticides when there is something unusual about them. Anne Greene's story is told because she survives her execution and the pamphlet writers must somehow account for this phenomenon; Jane Hattersley's story is told because it is so sensational.

Hattersley, "the bloudy mother" of the pamphlet's title, conceives at least four babies by her master and murders three of them in the span of the twelve years covered by the text. (The pamphleteer hints there may be more: "Many great bellies had she, besides these here spoken of, but the unhappie loads of them could never be seene.")[34] The narrative opens with an account of the master, Adam Adamson, a man in "good account and recconing amongst his neighbours." Although married, the "vigor and strength of lust, carried his love from her [his wife] to a servaunt he kept." The text largely ignores the possibility of exploitation by the master, and instead constructs Hattersley as a prostitute, saying that she was as easy yielding to Adamson's demands "as if she had spent an apprenticeship in a house of such trading, as traines such as she to such damnable service and imployment" (sigs. A3v–A4). Hattersley is sexually suspect even beyond her relationship with Adamson, who refuses to care for her after she becomes pregnant the first time because he conveniently doubts the child is his. Hattersley is forced to rely on the charity of her neighbors who take her in and give her room and board. But, as the text conveys it, she abuses their charity by concealing her pregnancy with tucking and loose lacing. Running throughout the narrative is a kind of defensiveness about providing relief to the poor. Clearly, Hattersley, too, is one of the undeserving poor targeted by the various poor laws. Strangely enough, after the baby, "her load of woe and shame," is born and Hattersley strangles it, she is not brought up on murder charges. (Since the murder happened sometime before 1609 and as early as a few decades before the 1624 statute, Hattersley would have been charged with murder. Had the crime occurred after the passage of the 1624 law, she would almost certainly have been charged and found guilty of infanticide since her actions fit exactly those covered by the statute.) Before the mistress can fetch the constable, Hattersley cleans the baby of any signs of violence, and the constable assumes that it died by overlaying. Two more infant murders follow; a fourth baby is spared when it is taken to a wet nurse. As the narrative recounts it, the mother murders the babies and the father buries them.

Adamson's relationship with his servant inverts the natural order of the household, and, at least as the author presents it, Hattersley is granted power, at least temporarily, that should normally be accorded the wife: "So much he doted upon this Strumpet, that all the love and kindnes that was fully due to his ligitimate bed-mate, she was mistriss and commaundresse of: what she commaunded must be performed; what she requested, must be provided; and what she was displeasd with, to please her must be removed" (sig. A4). The confusion of roles that this pamphlet portrays seems endemic to the conditions of servitude in the seventeenth century. Although sexual relations between masters and servants upset the household order, they also seem an almost inevitable result of the correspondence often made between the duties of the servant and the duties of the wife toward the master/husband. As Laura Gowing puts it, "This very commensurability, which explained and justified the ordered household, implicitly suggested that sexual and economic power would be entwined in relations between masters and servants as it was between husbands and wives."[35] Both servants and wives owe the master of the household obedience and subservience, and both are frequently considered the husband's or master's property. For example, William Gouge, in arguing that a master has the right to deny his servant the freedom to marry, explains that masters have this power because servants are "part of his masters goods, and possessions." Nonetheless, he is careful to clarify the prohibition against masters having sexual relations with servants:

> They who in this kinde so farre debase themselves, as to give their servaunts power over their owne bodie, doe make both themselves, and their true lawfull bedfellow to be despised: themselves, in that such servants are so made one flesh, will thinke to keepe in awe such a master or mistresse, as they have knowne, through feare of

revealing their sinne: their bedfellow, in that such servants will thinke to be maintained, and boulstered up by the master or mistresse, whom they have so knowne. On this ground was Sarah despised in the eyes of Hagar her maid.[36]

Despite conduct writers' warnings, sexual relations between masters and servants seems a fairly common occurrence during the period. Paul Griffiths has found hundreds of cases in which masters abused their positions as household patriarchs. The story of Robert Parker, a London cook charged at Bridewell with fathering the illegitimate child of his maid Alice Ashemore, provides an example of typical attitudes. Although Parker admitted that he "had th' use and carnall knowledge of hir body for the space of a twelvemonth and somewhat more at his pleasure . . . [whenever] he could find her alone," he also insisted that this was his right as her master: "thowe art my servant / and I may doe with thee what I please."[37] The repercussions of this kind of household subversion are startlingly conveyed in this pamphlet, but in such a way as to indict the servant more than the master. At one point, the text portrays Hattersley's attempt to poison Adamson's wife to bring about the marriage that Adamson had promised her, and thus literally take the mistress's place. Not only is the gender hierarchy being overturned, but the social hierarchy as well. The narrative seems anxious not just about unruly women, but about servants who can invert the household status with their feminine wiles.

Other traditional formulations suggest just how unnatural Adamson's relationship with Hattersley is; according to Dod and Cleaver in *A Godlie Forme of Householde Government: For the Ordering of Private Families, according to the direction of Gods word* (1612), "The householder is called *Pater familias*, that is father of the family, because he should have a fatherly care over his servants as if they were his children."[38] Thus in early modern thought Adamson's relationship with his servant might be read as a kind of incest, but the text makes nothing of this point. Everything about Hattersley, on the other hand, is depicted as utterly monstrous and unnatural.

Yet what is most interesting about this pamphlet is the way that it seeks to ignore, but inadvertently conveys, the desperate situation of the mother. Clearly her place as a servant is threatened and her reputation as a woman is at risk. The writer talks about the power that Hattersley lords over her master, but never deals with the very real power Adamson wields over his servant. The true isolation and powerlessness of Hattersley becomes explicit at several points: when she is thrown out of the house and deprived of one of her gowns and in the descriptions of her third birth and her execution.

The description of the third birth is particularly telling. Here, the popular ritual associated with childbirth, itself an inversion of ordinary gender power relations, is inverted. As Adrian Wilson depicts it, "childbirth in seventeenth-century England was a social occasion," a ceremony characterized by its focus on the "female social space to which the mother now belonged." The mother-to-be would invite her female friends, neighbors, and relatives to join her for the birth and lying-in period. The birthing room became an exclusively female space set off from the everyday world of male power and authority. This time of female hegemony lasted from the beginning of labor to the churching ceremony about four weeks later.[39] Yet *The Bloudy Mother* conveys something entirely different in its perversion of the childbirth ritual. Instead of a world of communal female power and companionship, the narrative portrays a world of isolation and shame as it depicts Hattersley locked in the birthing chamber with her female neighbor spying at the keyhole. Even the open keyhole, the stereotypical means of invading private, enclosed spaces, suggests how disempowered Hattersley is, and at the same time insinuates her promiscuity. According to Wilson, in most birthing ceremonies the windows were covered and the keyholes plugged to demarcate the female social space and to exclude men. Hattersley is denied that privacy and enclosed space; just as her body has been open sexually so now her private space has been invaded.[40] The women here are not joined in a celebration of female power, but pitted against one another as the neighbor seeks proof of the illegitimate birth. The birthing chamber becomes a place of concealment, shame, and humiliation.[41]

The role played by the women in this pamphlet suggests much about the way mechanisms of sexual and social control operated during the period. At infanticide trials, women searched the accused's body for signs of childbirth; during the witch trials, they searched for signs of the devil's mark. One of the chief strategies for maintaining patriarchal order required that a distinction be made between individual women, giving authority to some (midwives, for one, as I have already shown, but also some married women) and ostracizing others.[42] Furthermore, although mistresses had a duty to protect their female servants, in instances in which the husband fathers the servant's baby, the situation is doubly loaded because the wife also feels an obligation to her household, her husband, and both their reputations. As Gowing so clearly summarizes the situation, "the plot of adultery was reduced to a conflict between two women, and men's sexual responsibility was projected onto their wives. In effect, the antagonistic relationships of women eased the dilemmas of men; with women's complicity, both the blame and the responsibility for sexual disorder was shifted away from masters and husbands."[43] The pamphlet reflects just such a shift, at least until the end of the narrative when it momentarily turns its attention to the fate of the master.

More pathetically, at her execution, Hattersley refuses to confess because Adamson has duped her into believing that a pardon is imminent. Seeking to ensure his own acquittal, he convinces her not to implicate him in the murders, and assures her of a reprieve after her sentence. Even as the execution time draws near, Hattersley remains steadfast and fearless as if she were a "stage player" acting the "part in ieast" (sig. B4v). And indeed, she is. She remains, in death as in life, the unwitting puppet of her master and society. By requiring her silence, Adamson controls Hattersley's speech much as he controlled her livelihood and her sexuality in the 12 years of her employment. As Foucault and others have argued, the scaffold confession served to manifest state power and to affirm the justice of the law.[44] According to J. A. Sharpe, "When felons stood on the gallows and confessed their guilt not only for the offence for which they suffered death, but for a whole catalogue of wrongdoing, and expressed their true repentance for the same, they were helping to assert the legitimacy of power which had brought them to their sad end."[45] Pamphlet writers emphasized the importance of confessions as a sign of providential power: confessions help purge the sin and prepare the sinner for death. Furthermore, the gallows speech serves to edify and admonish the spectators at the execution, for "dying men's wordes are ever remarkable, & their last deeds memorable for succeeding posterities, by them to be instructed, what vertues or vices they followed and imbraced, and by them to learne to imitate that which was good, and to eschew evill."[46] The confession, then, can empower the criminal on the scaffold, affording her a measure of authority that she lacks in everyday life. Power is located in speech.[47] But in Hattersley's case even that moment of power is thwarted. She dies pitifully and deluded, awaiting a reprieve that never arrives.

Yet for those who might fear that the aborted confession prevents the necessary restoration of social order, the pamphlet writer assures us that crime begets punishment. The author takes his readers beyond the time of the execution to the fate of Adamson. In a kind of addendum to his narrative that is unusual in its focus on the fortunes of the father, the writer describes the horrid death of Adamson, who fell into a "miserable consumption" and was literally devoured alive by worms and lice. Thus justice has been served and the workings of providence affirmed.

The assurance that divine providence will punish the wrongdoer, that "murder will out," in the words of one pamphleteer, is crucial to this literature.[48] For instance, in one of the few infanticide narratives dealing with a woman of a different social class, *Strange and Wonderful News from Durham, or the Virgins Caveat Against Infant Murther* (1679), the crime goes undetected for several months until the ghost of the infant begins appearing to various neighbors. When asked, "Who was its Mother, the Occasion of its Death and Walking, and who were privy to that hainous Offence," the "All-powerful God" lends the ghostly babe an "Articulate Voice" and allows it to respond, "beauteous Elizabeth."[49]

The subject of this literature is almost invariably the poor and socially displaced, mostly servants, but occasionally widows as well. Women comprised the majority of those who received poor relief in seventeenth century England, and most of those receiving relief were widows with small children.[50] Although there was some sympathy for widows, their representation in the street literature does not vary markedly from that of other unmarried women. For the most part, they, too, are monstrous and sexually promiscuous. As several recent scholars have shown, widows overturned the paradigm of woman as "chaste, silent, and obedient." They were sexually experienced, and were so often depicted as insatiable that they became comic stock characters in the drama of the period.[51] The accounts of widows who murder their children often seek to affirm this view of widowhood by focusing on the initial sexual transgression that results in violence. *A True Narrative of the Proceedings at the Sessions-house in the Old-Bayly* (1677), for example, describes a 40-year-old widow with six children, "of still too Youthful a temper," who barbarously murders her bastard infant by crushing its head and gouging its eyes with a pair of scissors. After she kills the infant, she places it on a platter and sets it on a shelf. The details here are so horrible they are almost laughable. Once discovered, the widow acts distracted and insists that she miscarried; but the courts decide that since "she had sense enough to endeavour to conceal it, she [should be] Convicted and Condemned."[52] Once again, it is concealment, the fear of something unknown and hence uncontrollable, that indicts the woman.

Other accounts suggest the ever present danger of the crime by recounting several cases within the same pamphlet. *Natures Cruell Step-Dames* (1637), Henry Goodcole's strange assortment of "matchlesse female monsters," discusses three infanticides and links them with the sexual crimes of pedophilia and prostitution.

The "step-dame" of the title (according to the *OED*, "a stepmother" and therefore not a true mother) suggests the unnatural relationship of these mothers to their children; the relationship is strained, outside of nature, marginalized, and monstrous. Acting counter to all that is maternal, these not-true mothers are "unnatural cruel Beasts in women's shapes": "The Swallow flieth high, and in the towring Trees, Churches, and Houses build their Nestes, to preserve their yong ones out of danger; the Sparrow watcheth alone on the House top, as carefull what it had hatched and brought foorth. Beasts, such as Lyons, Woolves, Tigers and Foxes, have secret caves and woods where they hide there young, to preserve and foster them alive: But these bloody dogs degenerate from them."[53] All of the crimes Goodcole relates are sexual in nature, positing a correspondence between social disorder and unregulated female sexuality. Perhaps the strangest thing about this pamphlet is its inclusion among the "cruel step-dames" of a father who rapes his nine-year-old daughter. Since his crime is one that is sexually perverse, Goodcole defines him as something "other," bestial, and monstrous — that is, as something female.

The longest of Goodcole's examples of these unnatural monsters concerns Elizabeth Barnes, a widowed mother who lures her child into the woods under the pretext of visiting a relative, plies the child with pies and fruit, and once she falls asleep "barbarously did cut [her] throat" (3). Barnes is different from the other murdering mothers treated in this chapter because she has been married and because the child she kills is the product of that marriage. She murders her eight-year-old daughter, and her crime does not fall under the 1624 statute; yet her story, like the other narratives discussed here, depicts sexual transgression as paramount. Readers eventually discover that though she is unmarried, Barnes is pregnant. Her narrative, then, conflates two anxieties — the independent, sexually experienced woman who is outside of male control and the malevolent mother with the power to give and take the life of the child. That Goodcole introduces Barnes first as a widow illustrates his attempt to contain her within a marital structure, but also suggests her marginalized status. In theory, as a widow she possesses more social freedom than the wife or maid; she might also enjoy some measure of economic independence, being free to run both her household and perhaps her own business.[54] But as scholar Barbara Todd and Goodcole's narrative illustrate, reality was probably much bleaker. Widowed women were often left with small children and with little to sustain them. Like the never-married mother, they must have felt tremendous pressure to maintain their children and avoid the shame of "charging them to the parish." Their dire circumstances made them eager to remarry and thus prey to unscrupulous suitors.[55] But the poor widows of early modern England had little to offer a husband; in a society that placed such a high premium on chastity, they might be looked upon as used goods, as "left over," in the words of Charles Carlton.[56]

In his recounting of the crime itself, Goodcole, like many of those who write about murderous wives, presents Barnes as a kind of "anti-housewife" who disrupts the appropriate order of the household.[57] The action takes place in the woods, a setting outside of the enclosed, confined space of the home, suggesting at once that Barnes is not subject to household control but also that she is homeless and unprotected. In some ways, the crime seems less threatening because it takes place outside. It does not pollute the inside domestic space. Paradoxically, the crime itself is contained because Barnes is not contained by husband and home. Still, the setting, Wormewall Wood, and other details of the story evoke a fairy tale and suggest a primitive anxiety about motherhood.[58] As a wife and mother, Barnes's primary responsibilities are to sustain her children and to maintain the household economy. As a widow, Barnes fails at both. Like the witch who destroys her victims by contaminating their food supply, the mother here uses food to coax her child to sleep so that she can murder her. The ideal mother nourishes her child, first in her womb and later at her breast and table. The association with the witch — "the anti-mother" — seems deliberate since killing babies was one of the primary accusations lodged against witches.[59] In addition to her failure at nurturance, Barnes is equally unsuccessful at managing the household economy; we learn through her confession that she has squandered her estate on her lover.

Goodcole dispenses with the crime itself rather quickly. With only a few details to suggest the atrocity of the murder, he spends the bulk of his narrative trying to entice a confession out of Barnes. Once he does so, he launches into a long diatribe about the importance of prayer. In both instances, the voiceless woman is commanded to speak, first in confession and then in prayer. Of course, the male writer really speaks here, acting as ventriloquist to his female subject and only giving her speech that affirms patriarchy.

From what Goodcole does say about Barnes's circumstances, we learn that she has been tricked out of her estate by Richard Evans, a tailor who promised to marry her, and "being by that meanes become poore and indebted, knew not what would become of her" (5). Such economic realities suggest an embedded narrative that the pamphlet neglects. As a widow and mother, Elizabeth Barnes may very well have been dependent upon the marriage market for survival. Once she is tricked out of her estate by the smooth words of her lover, she finds that she has no value in that market. The presence of a child simply adds to her dilemma. She decides that the solution is to kill her child and commit suicide. Examples of suicide or attempted suicide are not uncommon in the pamphlet accounts of infanticide, and the shame associated with unwed motherhood was commonly accepted as a motive. In 1614, Robert Negus testified that Elizabeth Goare, desperately poor and unmarried, "a little before her death, being unmarried, was delivered of a bastard girl and thereupon as this defendant verily believeth, drowned herself."[60] Although Goodcole is not overly concerned with the social implications of the crime, he does at least recognize that society is partially to blame and chastises the neighbors who ignored Barnes's obvious need for help. Interestingly, Richard Evans, the most direct cause of Elizabeth's downfall, is admonished only with the wish that he confess his transgressions in public. This portion of the pamphlet ends, "And so much for

Elizabeth Barnes," a dismissal that parallels the treatment of unmarried mothers in general in early modern society.

In figuring these women as monsters, the literature of infanticide perpetuates the culture of shame associated with being an unmarried mother and contributes to the very crime it claims to abhor. These women are shamed by their situations and shamed once again in the literature. Fortunately, as the century wore on, courts grew more lenient, especially if the woman were repentant and fit the stereotype of women as weak and misguided. Earlier in the century conviction rates in some counties were as high as 53 percent; by the end of the century, most women were acquitted.[61] By the eighteenth century government officials began speaking out against the 1624 statute, arguing that "nothing . . . could be more unjust or inconsistent with the principles of all law than first to force a woman through modesty to concealment, and then to hang her for that concealment."[62] As Keith Wrightson sums it up, "The history of infanticide provides examples not only of the processes by which crime is defined and redefined, but also of the complex interrelationships between law and social, moral and communal values."[63] These complex relationships and values are clearly evident in the popular literature detailing the crime of infanticide.

5

The Popular Press and Providence

EXPLAINING THE MIRACULOUS RECOVERY OF ANNE GREENE

On December 14, 1650, Anne Greene, unmarried servant to Thomas Read in Oxfordshire, was hanged for the murder of her newborn son. As she dangled from the scaffold, her friends, eager to lessen her pain, thumped her breasts and pulled on her legs with all their weight in an effort to hasten her death. At length, when everyone presumed she was dead, she was taken down, placed in a coffin, and carried to the private house of the town apothecary, where several local physicians were gathered to perform a dissection. Much to their amazement, however, when they opened the coffin they observed that she seemed to be breathing:

> They perceiving some life in her, as well as for humanity as their Professionsake, fell presently to act in order to her recovery. First, having caused her to be held up in the Coffin, they wrenched open her teeth, which were fast set, and powred into her mouth some hot and cordiall spirits: whereupon she ratled more then before, and seemed obscurely to cough: then they opened her hands (her fingers also being stiffly bent) and ordered some to rub and chafe the extreme parts of her body, which they continued for about a quarter of an houre; oft, in the mean time powring in a spoonfull or two of the cordiall water; and besides tickling her throat with a feather, at which she opened her eyes.[1]

Anne Greene was one of many unmarried women who were prosecuted for killing their children during this period, and her story is one of the strangest cases included in this study. As I have shown, the history of infanticide in the seventeenth century is a dark one and illustrates the way the law could be used to regulate sexuality. Laws were passed that specifically targeted unmarried women and made it easier to prosecute them for unchastity and bastardy. And as we have also seen, crime pamphlets played a vital role in spreading official ideas about crime and punishment, and, at least ostensibly, sought to inculcate proper values and behavior. The story of Anne Greene differs from the typical account of the unmarried infanticide, however, because she survives her execution. Her case is anomalous, too, because once she recovers, no attempt is made to execute her again, contrary to British law. According to Blackstone, "It is clear that if, upon judgment to be hanged by the neck till he is dead, the criminal be not thoroughly killed, but revives, the sheriff must hang him again; for the former hanging was no execution of the sentence, and if a false tenderness were to be indulged in such cases, a multitude of collusions might ensue."[2] There is little indication in the accounts why Greene was not hanged again beyond the fact that the governor and the justices of the peace "apprehended the hand of God in her preservation" and decided to grant her a reprieve (*Newes from the Dead*, 3). But, as I will show, she seemed to have greater symbolic (and monetary) value alive than she did executed. Given the enormous stigma attached to unmarried mothers, how, then, do early modern writers explain Anne Greene?

Because public execution provided a principal method by which the power of the state was confirmed, an "imposing demonstration of the state's might and authority,"[3] we would expect the pamphlet literature chronicling any execution to serve the same purpose and warn would-be wantons of the dangers of promiscuity. In this case at least, it does not. The pamphlet writers' usual purpose of illustrating the repercussions of crime and of reestablishing order seems thwarted by Anne's resurrection. Confronted with a criminal whose execution offers no lesson about proper female behavior because she survives her execution, these writers are much more interested in reconstructing Anne into proper womanhood. They "rewrite woman good," to paraphrase Sheila Delany.[4]

There are at least five versions of this story, one told by William Petty in his private writings and four accounts in the popular press: two brief news accounts in the *Mercurius Politicus;* the anonymous *Declaration from Oxford, of Anne Greene;* William Burdet's *A Wonder of Wonders;* and Richard Watkins's *Newes from the Dead.*[5] The earliest account of Anne Greene's botched execution is probably that told in two issues of the *Mercurius Politicus,* a weekly Interregnum newsbook edited by Marchamont Nedham. Published less than a week after the incident in December 1650, this account provides only a cursory treatment. Like the lengthier pamphlets describing the event, this version relates the incident as "a remarkable act of providence," but begins with the birth of the infant rather than the miraculous recovery. This account lacks most of the moralism of the typical crime pamphlet, and attempts to present the story in a matter-of-fact, straightforward way, thus only hinting at the complexities and contradictions that make this tale so fascinating. Nonetheless, it carefully emphasizes Anne's innocence (at least of murder) from the start, and looks forward to a more thorough account of the event "to the end that this great work of God may be fully and truly known, as becommeth so great a matter."[6] Never attempting to explain the miracle of Anne's survival, the writer nevertheless assures the reader of God's infinite wisdom and the order of the universe.

Two of the other versions in the popular press, William Burdet's *A Wonder of Wonders* and Richard Watkins's *Newes from the Dead* (both 1651), develop the narrative much more fully and provide a vivid example of the way the same event could be invested with different meanings.[7] Confronted with a woman who fails to fulfill the model stereotype of the good woman — the woman who is "chaste, silent, and obedient" — the writers must find ways to explain God's apparent beneficence toward her. They accomplish this in two very different ways: Burdet by virtually ignoring her sexuality and focusing on the injustice of her execution, and Watkins by denying her sexuality and reinscribing her into culture as a scientific and literary text.

Although it is clear from the beginning of both Burdet's and Watkins's accounts that Anne did not murder her baby but that it was stillborn, so great is the transgression represented by her pregnancy that she is condemned to die anyway. The explicit sexuality revealed by her pregnancy suggests that she is potentially disruptive. But both writers emphasize the injustice of this sentence. Burdet admits: "She was carried before a Justice, who upon examination, confessed, that she was guilty of the Act, in committing of the sin, but clear and innocent of the crime for murdering of it, for that it was born dead; . . . but after a short tryal, she was convicted for her life, and received sentence to be hanged on Oxford Gallowes."[8]

In other ways, Burdet's version of the story is typical of other crime pamphlets from the period and follows their pattern fairly closely in its rendition of crime, confession, repentance, and punishment. Burdet begins with a brief summary of the crime: Anne, very busy at work turning malt, suddenly feels ill and retires to "the house of office." There "a Child, about a span long sprung from her, but abortive, which much impair'd her health and strength" (1). Soon one of her fellow servants finds her uttering that she is "undone, undone, undone" (2).

From the start of the pamphlet Anne is portrayed as hardworking, a detail that immediately sets this narrative apart from other accounts of infanticide which seek to erase the everyday lives of their subjects. Rarely is mention made of work, family, or friends, a characteristic that further isolates the already marginalized woman. Here, on the other hand, Anne is clearly part of a community of servants who immediately respond to her cries for help. These details help to make her more sympathetic, along with the fact that there is no question here that she miscarried. Still, while there is no doubt that Anne is not guilty of murdering her baby, there is also no doubt that she is aware of the birth. Being fearful that a discovery will be made, she lays the baby in a corner and covers it with dirt and rubbish. But Burdet minimizes her guilt in this action by emphasizing the impossible situation she finds herself in: "Alas, alas! Mary, that ever I was born to live and die in shame and scorn," he portrays her as moaning. And he implies the injustice of her trial by pointing out that she was impregnated by "a Gentleman of good birth, and kinsman to the justice of the Peace" (2). Later, after telling of her resuscitation, he denounces her sentence, arguing that she was convicted without due and legal process by a corrupt and partial jury.

Burdet continues his narrative by offering the obligatory confession, but here the confession emphasizes Anne's contrition and innocence. Christlike, she meets her death asking God to forgive her prosecutors. Fixing her eyes on her executioner, she prays, "God forgive my false accusers, as I freely forgive thee." And her last words, according to Burdet, are "Sweet Jesus, receive my soul" (4). The pamphlet transforms her into a saint with at least some power and majesty. Yet even as she meets her death, Anne refuses to play her prescribed role completely and legitimate her punishment with the standard statement of wrongdoing. At the moment of her execution, the woman who has been cowed by the circumstances of her class and gender displays a glimmer of resistance. Of course, the designated purpose of the confession was often thwarted. The criminal might refuse to confess, meeting his or her death with curses and shouts, or even show up at the execution drunk. And not incidentally, the confession postpones the moment of death so the convicted might hold forth for much longer than intended in hopes of a pardon or simply to delay the execution.[9] The confession also grants a kind of authority to the criminal on the scaffold, giving her a voice and an audience to hear that voice. Although she does not admit her guilt in murdering her baby, Anne does repent her misspent youth and calls upon God to forgive her. Burdet could hardly create a more sympathetic heroine; thus the chastening spectacle of the scaffold is at least partially subverted.

Burdet spends little time on the resurrection, using it only to reaffirm "the poor Creature's" innocence and to illustrate the "great hand of God in this business." While Watkins's Anne is basically silent after she revives, Burdet depicts her extolling God, saying as she awakens, "Behold God's providence, and his wonder of wonders" (5). Unlike the justice who convicts Anne, Burdet is concerned not with policing sexuality but with showing how a good woman was unjustly prosecuted. Perhaps his pamphlet represents the popular press's reaction to what was clearly an unjust law. There is evidence that commentators from the period recognized the severity and potential injustice of the courts in cases of infant murder. For example, in his *Observations in Midwifery*, Percival Willughby discusses the case of a woman indicted for infanticide who was so mentally incompetent that she was unable to defend herself. The coroner spoke for her, using the size of the baby to argue her innocence. But to no avail: "the whole Bench saw that shee was a foole. It was in the Protector's dayes, and I feared that shee would have summum jus. The judg shewed the statute-Book to the jury. Neither judg, nor jury regarded her simplicity. They found her guilty, the judg condemned her, and shee was, afterwards, hanged for not having a woman by her, at her delivery."[10] By the eighteenth century even the courts seemed to recognize the potential injustice of the 1624 statute. Although unmarried women continued to be prosecuted under the law, they were treated more leniently, and most were acquitted. In some counties the conviction rate between 1620 and 1680 was as much as 53 percent, higher than the conviction rates for other kinds of homicide in the period; in the eighteenth century conviction rates dropped to 20 percent for women tried at the Old Bailey and were even lower in other parts of England.[11] By the beginning of the nineteenth century, the injustice of the law was more widely recognized. Thomas Percival, for one, pointed out that the statute making "concealment of the birth of a bastard child full proof of murder, confounds all distinctions of innocence and guilt, as such concealment, whenever practicable, would be the wish and act of all mothers, virtuous or vicious, under the same unhappy predicament."[12] The law was finally repealed in 1803. Burdet, too, seems uneasy with the statute. The crime pamphlet here, then, uses the repentance and confession of its wrongdoer not to set right a perverted social order, but rather to comment upon a perverted legal system. Ultimately, Anne's resurrection provides a vivid example of a victim's justified refusal to follow the script dictated by the authorities, even if that refusal was not consciously her own. In this case, as Burdet presents it, the intentions of divine providence supersede those of the state.

Far more interesting and complex is Watkins's version, *Newes from the Dead. Or a True and Exact Narration of the miraculous deliverance of Anne Greene*. Arguing that this "rare and remarkeable accident" had been "variously and falsely reported amongst the vulgar" (1), Watkins seeks to provide a faithful record of the event. Unlike Burdet, Watkins spends the bulk of his text relating Anne's recovery. As he does so, the narrative becomes the occasion for speculations on menstruation, pregnancy, and the viability of the fetus. Thus *Newes from the Dead* seems consciously different from other popular accounts of crime and wondrous events. Its serious, analytical tone and its focus on the scientific aspect of the miracle suggest a more learned audience than the typical crime pamphlet. Its overt purpose is neither to titillate nor to explicate providential justice, though it does both. Nonetheless, in its obsession with Anne's body and its reconstruction of her into a good woman, it reveals many of the same cultural anxieties and concerns of the other pamphlets.

With William Petty, the anatomist, as his obvious source, Watkins offers an extremely detailed account of the treatment of Anne's body and its reactions to the doctors' varied ministrations. The doctors examine and manipulate every part of Anne's body, tickling her throat, letting her blood, chafing her "extreme parts," and anointing her neck, her temples, and the bottoms of her feet with oils and spirits. And they note her every reaction: her sweat, pulse, and bowels; her bruises and blisters; her fever and swelling.

Watkins also records everything she eats and drinks, from the julep and cold beer that she drank on the 15th of December to the "part of a chick" that she ate on the 19th. The amount of detail here is remarkable for a news pamphlet, its pseudoscientific tone only thinly masking a prurient interest in the female body. Frances Dolan has argued that executions of women "downplayed the female body in order to highlight the divine comedy of the soul's release. Thus, the erasure of the condemned women's bodies becomes a means of avoiding the festive, unruly, carnivalesque possibilities of public executions . . . and instead represents these women as authoritative and virtuous in spite of their bodies, which are always disorderly because they are female."[13] Just the opposite seems the case here. The focus is almost completely on Anne's body, and her authority derives in large part from that body. While she may have averted a literal dissection by coming back to life, she seems figuratively dissected in Watkins's text.

The dissection of criminals in the name of scientific knowledge was increasingly practiced during the period, and the female body was all the more desirable because it was so rare. By following an execution with a public autopsy, legal authorities hoped to find an additional method of disciplining the body. The autopsy was conceived both as a deterrent to crime and as a way to reinstitute the recalcitrant body back into society once a crime had been committed. In death, at least, the body could serve the public good by imparting scientific knowledge.[14] (There was also some belief that the criminal body differed from that of ordinary people. An autopsy might reveal literal signs of that difference — a hairy heart, for instance — that would help explain criminality and make it less threatening.) By the eighteenth century the selling of dead bodies was a profitable business.[15] Anne's body seems similarly commodified and disciplined here. As Watkins himself remarks, "in the same Room where her Body was to have been dissected for the satisfaction of a few, she became a greater wonder, being reviv'd, to the satisfaction of multitudes that flocked thither daily to see her" (6). Once the doctors realize what a potential source of fame and profit Anne is, they decide to charge admission to those who want to see her: "they thought it a seasonable opportunity, for the maid's behalfe, to invite them either to exercise their Charity, or at least to pay for their Curiosity. And therefore (themselves first leading the way) they commended it to those that came in, to give every one what they pleas'd, her Father being there ready to receive it" (6). And later, after the pamphlet is published, Anne's body will be displayed for an even broader audience and will provide income for its author.

Only after the miracle is fully related and valued does Watkins turn to the crime: "And now, having done with the Sufferings, and the Cure, it will not be amiss to look back, and take a Review of the Cause of them" (6). In this portion of the narrative the pamphlet writer takes great pains to restore Anne to proper womanhood by arguing that she may not have known she was pregnant, thereby diminishing her guilt not just in the murder but even in the fact of having a baby out of wedlock. It is likely, Watkins argues, that Anne was unaware she was pregnant because she had "continual Issues which lasted for a Moneth together: which long and great Evacuation might make her judge, that it was nothing else but a flux of those humors which for ten weeks before had been suppressed; and that the childe which then fell from her unawares, was nothing but a lump of the same matter coagulated" (7). To relieve her of culpability, Watkins takes away her will and consciousness. Furthermore, he argues, the child was stillborn and not capable of being murdered.

Examining the fetus for viability, he finds that it was not a span in length, and its sex was hardly distinguishable; it had no hair and surely had never had life. In fact, Watkins conjectures, it rather seemed a "lump of flesh" than a "well and duly formed Infant" (6–7). Lacking direct witnesses to the birth, one of the primary ways for a woman to escape punishment according to the 1624 statute was to prove that the fetus was not viable. Court records throughout the seventeenth and eighteenth centuries provide examples of acquittals using pseudo-medical evidence to prove the premature birth of the child. For example, in the trial of a woman named Janet Todd, evidence of imperfect finger- and toenails and lack of hair forced an acquittal: "she did not go her full Time, the Child's nails not being in their full Proportion, and she having made Provision for its Birth, it was the Opinion of the Court, from the strict Examination of the Evidences, that it was Still-born, (as she affirm'd) and that she flattered herself with concealing her Shame, by carrying it off with so much Privacy: Upon the whole the Jury acquitted her."[16] Likewise, using her midwife and fellow servants to support his argument, Watkins posits that Greene's child was not viable, the miscarriage occurring not more than seventeen weeks after conception.

While Burdet speculates that the father was a gentleman and kinsman to the justice of the peace, Watkins actually names the baby's father: young Jeffrey Read, the grandson of Anne's employer. In naming her partner, Watkins hints at the sexual exploitation that we have seen was frequent between masters (or masters' sons or grandsons) and their female servants during this period. As further evidence of Anne's innocence, Watkins gives one additional fact only to dismiss it: "her Grand Prosecutor Sir *Thomas Read* died within three daies after her Execution; even almost as soon as the probability of her reviving could be well confirmed to him. But because hee was an old man, and such Events are not too rashly to be commented upon, I shall not make use of that observation" (7). It was her employer, Thomas Read, who initially brought the accusation of murder against her. God seems totally on Anne's side, smiting her false accuser dead while preserving Anne. But given his rational and scientific intent, Watkins seeks to minimize this point.

By mentioning the gentleman father of Greene's baby, both Burdet and Watkins seem to be criticizing a social climate that was increasingly concerned with hunting down fornicators and other sexual offenders, but that targeted such wrongdoers unequally. The kind of double standard embodied in the 1624 act was further codified in "An Act for Suppressing the Detestable

Sins of Incest, Adultery and Fornication," passed on May 10, 1650, just seven months before Greene's execution. In Keith Thomas's assessment, "This was an attempt, unique in English history, to put the full machinery of the state behind the enforcement of sexual morality."[17]Although the act was rarely enforced, it provided that a married woman convicted of being "carnally known by any man (other then her Husband) . . . shall suffer death as in case of Felony, without benefit of Clergy." Any man found guilty of having "the carnal knowledge of the body of any Virgin, unmarried Woman or Widow" was charged with the lesser offense of fornication and "shall for every such offence be committed to the common Gaol without Bail or Mainprize, there to continue for the space of three Moneths."[18] Adultery, then, came to be defined as a crime of women, not men. According to Thomas, the bastardy legislation of 1576 (which punished parents of bastard children chargeable to the parish and made whipping the usual penalty for women) and 1593 (which rejected whipping as suitable for men since it "might chance upon gentlemen or men of quality, whom it was not fit to put to such a shame") paved the way for the 1650 act.[19] Such drastic penalties regulating sexual behaviors were clearly based on class and gender. The unevenness of the law and the abuse of authority apparent in Greene's employer accusing Anne but not his grandson are reflected in the 1650 law as well. But neither Watkins nor Burdet develops this argument, although they both intimate it by calling attention to the class of the father.

Unlike most crime pamphlets of the day, Watkins offers no confession. The lengthy speech presented by Burdet is recounted in only the most general terms here: "after singing of a Psalm, & something said in justification of her self, as to the fact for which she was to suffer, and touching the lewdnesse of the Family wherein she lately lived, she was turn'd off the Ladder" (1–2). If, as I have suggested earlier, the confession serves the dual purpose of manifesting state authority and conferring limited agency and power on the criminal (what Foucault calls "two-sided discourses"),[20] that power seems deliberately suppressed here.

Although Anne is acquiescent and does offer the requisite gallows speech, there is no attempt in this account to record her actual words. We are told that after she revives, Anne sighs and talks to herself, and that she "fell into the like speeches as she had used in prison before the execution" (5, misnumbered page 6 in the pamphlet), but we never hear her speak. Anne's voice completely disappears in this account, a strategy consistent with Watkins's reconstruction of her. A good woman is a silent woman. In this representation, her hanging thus becomes a kind of purgation of her soiled body, and she is reborn as a maid. But in order for this transformation to take place, she must be totally ignorant of what has happened to her — before, during, and after her execution. As Frances Dolan phrases it, she is "an automaton, a machine that was temporarily turned off rather than a human agent struggling for life."[21]

Even more remarkable than Watkins's manipulation of his story in an effort to rewrite Anne's life are the dedicatory poems written by the students at Oxford that are appended to the narrative. (Actually, in the first edition of *Newes from the Dead*, the poems precede the narrative. But because the number of poems nearly doubles in the second edition — from fourteen pages to twenty-four — I shall use this edition.) That this eight-page narrative is overwhelmed with poetry seems significant. Anne becomes a conduit for the male poetic voice. Where the narrative presents Anne as a scientific text to be examined and understood, now she becomes a literary text. Earlier, her revival suggests male power and creativity; godlike, the scientists at the autopsy are credited with her resurrection. The poems, on the other hand, suggest another form of creativity and power as they resurrect her into art. As one overconfident student phrases it,

> For by this Historie
> The Author doth a Third Life to her Give,
> And makes her Innocence and Fame to Live.
> Her Life is writt here to the life: she fell
> At a cheap rate, when 'tis describ'd so well.

> For, th' Author's Pen's so good, that one would Die
> To be Reviv'd by such a History.
>
> (21, misnumbered page 11 in text)

Ironically, as Anne is silenced, the young student poets of Oxford find their voices.

The poetry is even more extreme in its reconstruction of Anne, making her into a kind of regenerate Eve or even a Christ figure:

> Now may the nine-liv'd Sex speake high, and say
> That here they fought with Death, and won the day.
> The *fatal Tree*, which first began the strife,
> Sided with them, and prov'd a *Tree of life*.
>
> (20, misnumbered page 10)

In other places it rewrites her as a martyr, depicting her as a virgin who, phoenixlike, rises "out of the ashes": "All's purg'd by Sacrifice: / The Parent slain, doth not a Virgin Rise?" (12) and "Rare Innocence! a Wench re-woman'd!" (14). Her restored maidenhood seems a greater miracle than her restored life:

> Mother, or Maid, I pray you whether?
> One, or both, or am I neither?
> The Mother died: may't not be said
> That the Survivor is a Maid?
>
> (16, misnumbered page 6)

And,

> She's a maid twice, and yet is not *dis-maid*.
> O Paradox! if truth in thee can lie,
> No wonder if the maid could live and die.
>
> (32, misnumbered page 22)

Given the extent to which Anne is sanctified in the course of the pamphlet, we might be tempted to read her pregnancy as comparable to that of the medieval female mystics, described by Caroline Walker Bynum, who endured bizarre bodily experiences: strange bleeding and lactation, mystical pregnancies, and even an incorruptible body in death.[22] She might even be compared to the Virgin Mary. Like Mary, she seems to have experienced a kind of manless conception, virginity remaining intact even after giving birth.

Anne's reconstruction as a kind of saint simply exaggerates the paradoxical status of the criminal both on the scaffold and in the pamphlet literature. Since both the saint and the criminal were exemplary figures — one a figure of all that should be emulated, the other of all that should be shunned — the two sometimes coalesce in this literature.[23] In fact, the process that identified the criminal with Christ and the saints reconciled the criminal with his executioners in a final act of atonement that served to legitimate the actions of the state by associating them with Christ and the saints and thereby with the will of God.[24] The association between the saint and the criminal is even more acute here; Anne's resuscitation re-creates her as a resurrected Christ. Yet the cultural process of atonement seems diverted precisely because the execution is unsuccessful. The incident actually disaffirms the power of the state, and explains the reason why this case must be examined so carefully by the pamphlet writer.

Yet not all poems included are poems of praise; the period's characteristic ambivalence toward women is evident here as well. As one of the student poets explains it, Anne Greene's story simply serves to exemplify the cunning and manipulative nature so characteristic of women:

> Admire not, 'tis no newes, nere think it strange,
> Twere wonder if a Woman should not change:
> They have mysterious wayes, and their designes
> Must be read backward still, like Hebrew lines.
> See, these with Death dissemble, and can cheat
> *Charon* himself to mak a faire retreat.
> Well, for this trick Ile never so be led
> As to beleive a Woman, though shee's dead.
>
> (18, misnumbered page 8)

Another poet seeks to show his wit as he puns on "morally light" and "light in weight":

I'll prophecy, Shee'l Lovers soone insnare
Without a Trope ther's Halters in her hayre.
Of the same cause here the effects doe fight,
One thing both hang'd and saved her, shee was *Light*.

(26, misnumbered page 16)

But these negative verses are the exception. Most of the poetry seems to anatomize Anne in order to reconstitute her as whole again: as a virgin. What is important here is the way that Anne's body provides an occasion for verse. As we have seen, this reconstruction is possible at least partially because of Anne's economic value. A shame to her household and community before her execution, she becomes a source of pride and an economic boon afterwards. Furthermore, she is a source of fame, both to the doctors who revived her and to the pamphleteers and poets who wrote about her.

And so, both writers would have us believe, she lived happily ever after. Indeed, a handwritten note in the Bodleian copy of *Newes from the Dead* suggests as much: "Anne Greene was portioned by the Students, married, had several children and lived about fifteen years after her Execution." With marriage and motherhood, she is completely reintegrated into the patriarchal structure. Thus Anne Greene is fully remade — and remaid — into a more socially acceptable version of womanhood.

The stories of Anne Greene provide a vivid illustration of the various ways the popular press used criminal accounts for different purposes. It is precisely because these texts are so ephemeral in nature that they can reflect the multiple anxieties and varying interests of early modern culture. In Anne Greene's miracle "the same story [is] two stories, with quite different cultural resonances and different implications for understanding the world."[25] And in this particular case the cultural implications of the narratives are especially evident, not just because this story was told so many times, but, even more interestingly, because of its connection to other traditional narratives. Anne Greene's story, especially as told by Burdet, seems to have its roots in the many "Miracles of the Virgin" written during the Middle Ages throughout Europe. The "Miracles of the Virgin" illustrate how Mary protected those who venerated her, criminal or not. In one of the tales of most significance here, Mary saves a thief who committed many robberies but who showed his deep devotion to her in constant prayer. When he was hanged for his crimes, the Virgin kept him alive for three days, seemingly by holding him up as he hanged. Later when the hangmen find him still alive after so many days, they try to kill him with a sword but Mary prevents it. Afterwards, they let him go free; he spends his remaining years as a monk in service to the Virgin.[26] These miraculous tales of divine intervention continued to be told in the popular pamphlets of the seventeenth century, but now, as we might expect, God replaces Mary and they serve as exempla of the rewards of Protestant piety. One such example occurs in a pamphlet entitled *A True Relation of Gods Wonderfull Mercies, in preserving one alive, which hanged five days, who was falsely accused* (1605?), in which an adolescent boy falsely accused and hanged for theft is preserved for five days when God places an invisible stool beneath his feet. As we have seen, the pamphlet literature frequently asserts the power of Providence, as Burdet does on his title page with the tag line "Behold God's Providence!" This melding of contemporary events with traditional narratives suggests the deep cultural significance of these stories. As Alexandra Walsham explains, "tradition and topicality coalesce. Accounts of ostensibly current events assimilate layers of ecclesiastical legend and historical myth."[27]

The way that these stories can be brought to the service of various cultural objectives becomes even more evident when we discover that virtually the same story was told in several French *occasionnels*, or canards, of the sixteenth century.[28] These French pamphlets relate an almost identical story of concealed pregnancy, unjust execution, and miraculous survival. The *occasionnels* concern a young servant, also named Anne (even more remarkably,

A Wonder of Wonders.

BEING

A faithful *Narrative* and true *Relation*, of one *Anne Green*, Servant to Sir *Tho. Reed* in *Oxfordshire*, who being got with Child by a Gentleman, her Child falling from her in the house or Office, being but a span long, and dead born, was condemned on the 14. of *December* last, and hanged in the Castle-yard in *Oxford*, for the space of half an hour, receiving many great and heavy blowes on the brests, by the but end of the Souldiers Muskets, and being pul'd down by the leggs, and was afterwards beg'd for an Anatomy, by the Physicians, and carried to Mr. *Clarkes* house, an Apothecary, where in the presence of many learned Chyrurgions, she breathed, and began to stir; insomuch, that Dr. *Petty* caused a warm bed to be prepared for her, let her blood, and applyed Oyls to her, so that in 14 hours she recovered, and the first words she spake were these; *Behold Gods Providence! Behold his miraculous and loving kindness!* VVith the manner of her Tryal, her Speech and Confession at the Gallowes; and a Declaration of the Souldiery touching her recovery. *Witnessed by Dr. Petty, and Licensed according to Order.*

William Burdet, *A Wonder of Wonders*, title page, shelfmark E621 (11). By permission of the British Library.

Anne des Grez, in one version), who is falsely accused of infanticide but who survives her hanging through the intervention of the Virgin Mary. The injustice of the sentence is more blatant in this case than in the English versions because this Anne is not pregnant at all. The daughter of Anne's master gives birth, kills her baby, and implicates Anne in the crime. Further, the association with Christ is even more striking: Anne remains on the gallows for three days and three nights before she is taken down and discovered to be alive. Roger Chartier argues that these narratives "came to be put in the service of Church authority at a time of bitter tensions and struggles" and function as anti-Reformation propaganda.[29] Likewise, the English accounts of Anne Greene can be read as serving authority. To those who might question the potential injustice of infanticide persecutions, the story provides assurance that God will intervene, but only on the rare occasions when the law blunders. In any event, the story of the hanged woman miraculously revived struck a cultural chord in both early modern England and France. Most significantly, the various versions of this event illustrate the way that female bodies provided important sites for re-negotiating ideas about society and culture.

Part 2: The Texts

Editorial Policy

As much as possible, my goal has been to make these texts accessible to the modern reader while maintaining their character. In transcribing and editing the texts in this collection, I used the earliest edition available on University Microfilms International, Ann Arbor, Michigan, with the exception of Richard Watkins, *Newes from the Dead*, where I used the second edition. Where the microfilm was illegible, I compared available copies from various libraries: the Bodleian, Folger, Houghton at Harvard, Cambridge, and British libraries.

Except for the main portion of the titles of the texts, spelling has been modernized, but I have retained archaic verb endings and obsolete words. Because proper names are often spelled several different ways in the same text, I have regularized the spelling of proper names throughout. I removed italics except where appropriate in modern practice. Punctuation has been added for clarity but because of the nature of the original texts does not always conform to modern grammatical rules. I added apostrophes for possessives and quotation and question marks where appropriate. I silently expanded abbreviations and changed "yt" to "that" and "then" to "than." I omitted foreign words and phrases when they were translated in the texts, except when they added significantly to the tone, as is the case with legal terms and in *A Hellish Murder Committed by a French Midwife*. Because early modern texts often use capitalization for emphasis, I retained the capitalization of the original texts, adding it only where needed for proper names or at the start of new sentences.

Most definitions are derived from the *Oxford English Dictionary*. Biblical quotes correspond to the Geneva and King James bibles.

A True Discourse

Of the practises of *Elizabeth Cald-well*, Ma: *Ieffrey Bownd*, *Isabell Hall* widdow, and *George Fernely*, on the parson of Ma: *Thomas Caldwell*, in the County of Chester, to haue murdered and poysoned him, with diuers others.

Together with her manner of godly life during her imprisonment, her arrainement and execution, with *Isabell Hall* widdow; As also a briefe relation of Ma. *Ieffrey Bownd*, who was the Assise before prest to death.

Lastly, a most excellent exhortorie Letter, written by her own selfe out of the prison to her husband, to cause him to fall into considera-tion of his sinnes, &c. Seruing likewise for the vse of euery good Christian. Beeing executed the 18. of Iune. 1603.

VVritten by one then present as witnes, their owne Country-man, *Gilbert Dugdale.*
(∵)

AT LONDON,

Printed by Iames Roberts for Iohn Busbie, and are to be sold at his shop vnder Saint Peters Church in Cornewell. 1604.

Gilbert Dugdale, *A True Discourse Of the practises of Elizabeth Caldwell*, title page, call number RB 60571. By permission of the Huntington Library, San Marino, California.

A True Discourse Of the practises of Elizabeth Caldwell,

Master Jeffrey Bownd, Isabell Hall widdow, and George Fernely, on the parson of Master Thomas Caldwell, in the County of Chester, to have murdered and poysoned him, with diverse others.

Together with her manner of godly life during her imprisonment, her arraignment and execution, with Isabel Hall, widow. As also a brief relation of Master Jeffrey Bownd, who was the Assize[1] before pressed[2] to death. Lastly, a most excellent exhortatory Letter, written by her own self out of the prison to her husband, to cause him to fall into consideration of his sins, etc. Serving likewise for the use of every good Christian. Being executed the18th of June, 1603. Written by one then present as witness, their own Country-man, Gilbert Dugdale.[3] (1604)

To the right honorable, and his singular good Lady, the Mary Chandois, R.A.[4] wisheth health and everlasting happiness

My honorable and very good Lady, considering my duty to your kind ladyship, and remembering the virtues of your prepared mind, I could do no less but dedicate this strange work to your view, being both matter of moment and truth. And to the whole world it may seem strange that a Gentlewoman so well brought up in God's fear, so well married, so virtuous ever, so suddenly wrought to this act of murder, that when your ladyship doth read as well the Letter as the Book of her own indighting,[5] you will the more wonder that her virtues could so aptly taste the follies of vice and villainy. But so it was, and for the better proof that it was so, I have placed my kinsman's name to it, who was present at all her troubles: at her coming to prison, her being in prison, and her going out of prison to her execution. That those Gentlemen to whom he dedicates his work witnessed may also be partakers in that kind, for the proof thereof, that your Ladyship and the world so satisfied may admire the deed and hold it as strange as it is true.

We have many giddy-pated Poets that could have published this Report with more eloquence, but truth in plain attire is the easier known: let fiction mask in Kendall green.[6] It is my quality to add to the truth, truth, and not leasing[7] to lies. Your good Honor knows Pinck's[8] poor heart, who in all my services to your Late deceased kind Lord never savored of flattery or fiction, and therefore am now the bolder to present to your virtues the view of this late truth, desiring you to think of it, that you may be an honorable mourner at these obsequies, and you shall no more do than many more have done. So with my tendered duty, my true ensuing story, and my ever wishing well, I do humbly commit your Ladyship to the prison of heaven, wherein is perfect freedom.

Your Ladyship's ever in duty and service,
Robert Armin

To the right virtuous, the Lady Marie Cholmsly and the right worshipful these Knights: Sir Thomas Houlcroft, Sir John Savage of Egerton, Sir John Egerton, Sir Peter Warborton, Sir Rowland Stanly, Sir Urian Leigh, Sir Thomas Aston, Sir Thomas Smith, Sir Thomas Savadge, Sir George Leister, Sir William Damport, Sir Thomas Stanly, Sir George Booth, Sir Henry Bunberry, Sir Hukin Beeston, Sir Richard Wilbrome, Sir Richard Brooke, Sir Richard Egerton, Master Peter Warborton Esquire, Master Thomas Wilbrom Esquire, Master Thomas Brooke Esquire, Master Richard Granesnor Esquire, Master Hugh Calmelie Esquire, Master Robert Cholmsly, Esquire, Master Ralfe Egerton of Ridly, Esquire, Master Thomas Marburie Esquire, Master Richard Brerton of Wetten Hall,

Esquire, and all the rest, as well Knights as Gentlemen then at the Assizes present, the true witnesses of this following history: your kind poor Countryman Gilbert Dugdale, engaged to you all in debt and duty, committeth this discourse with true and due commends, with continual prayers for your good health and successful fortunes.

Most endeared and right virtuous Lady, and you the rest of the right Worshipful these kind Cheshire Knights,[9] after my long being at Chester, in the time of this reported trouble, I in my melancholy walks bethought me of the strange invasion of Satan lately on the persons of Elizabeth Caldwell and her bloody lover Jeffery Bownd, together with that untimely actor Isabel Hall, widow. How that ugly fiend (ever man's fatal opposite) had made practice, but I hope not purchase, of their corruptible lives, and brought them to the last step of mortal misery. And then resolving with myself the great goodness of God in calling sinners to repentance, and withal, admiring his gifts in the penitent, I could no less than write my heart's trouble, as well to partake the world with my meditation as to make them wonder at this Cheshire chance; and thereby to plant or to engraft a kind of Fear by this way of example, how murder should hereafter bear any brain in sensible creatures, considering how the very stones shall betray the inward thoughts of massacre. All these considered, when I had coted[10] this wonder, thinking how incredulous our Nation is in things true, and how uncertain they are to believe fopperies[11] feigned, I could no less for the certainty hereof, but call you to witness of the proof, because since such an example was preferred unto us, that others, not eyewitness thereunto, might the rather assure themselves of the same. First, I knowing your general griefs for the fall of so good a Gentlewoman, and when no remedy could be to comfort such a godly soul, as well in her time of imprisonment as at the hour of her death, my own occasions also for that time considered, and being your true and natural Countryman, I could do no less but ostend[12] my duteous love to you all in this kind, desiring you to accept my poor mite.[13] Only considering this, the poor man's plenty is prayer to regrate[14] your worthy loves, and as truly as I live, that shall be no niggard; for that night wherein I lie me down and pray not for you all, let my rest be broad-waking slumbers, and my quiet, waking dreams; and that will be punishment more than I would enjoy for so regardless a good as I so late and so happily received. True it is that diverse reports passed up and down the streets of London as touching this act of murder, but how scandalously, as five murdered, three murdered by the means of six persons, which your Worships know is false. Only three murdered one; marry,[15] the intent was to him that now lives. Therefore being an ear-witness to this false alarum, it made me more diligent in the setting forth the truth, whereby GOD in his power might be known, Satan in his meaning no doubt overthrown, and the world's idle fabling by a contrary meaning known. For as it was, it was, and no otherwise, and thus it was, as your presences both at the examination, arraignment, and execution can justify; and how odious it is to hear any truth racked by slandering tongues, judge or imagine; only this, pardon my boldness, witness the right, accept my good will in the publishing; and so I commit you to God's protections.

Your poor Countryman, ever yours,
Gilbert Dugdale

The practice of Elizabeth Caldwell, against the life of her
own husband

I purpose,[16] God willing, to describe in brief, the life and death of Elizabeth Caldwell, late wife of Thomas Caldwell in the county of Chester, and daughter to one Master Duncalfe of the said county. A gentleman of very good sort, who fatherly and carefully trained up his daughter from her infancy — she being framed and adorned with all the gifts that nature could challenge, and wanting no good education — did in her tender infant years bestow her in marriage to the said Thomas Caldwell, giving her a good dower to her better preferring in the said marriage, with a yearly nuity[17] of ten pounds, to extend to her said husband and his heirs forever. And as the like matches do not often prove well, so this Caldwell, being young and not experienced in the world, gave his mind to travel and see foreign countries, which tended rather to his loss than profit, as also to the great discontentment of his wife, and other his friends, leaving her oftentimes very bare, without provision of such means as was fitting for her. And by these courses he did withdraw her affection from him, so that in the continuance of his absences, a young man, named Jeffery Bownd, a neighbor unto the said Elizabeth Caldwell, and she as I said before, enjoying all the excellent gifts of nature, set his affections abroach,[18] and being a man of good wealth, spared neither cost nor industry both by himself and others to withdraw her to his unlawful desire, and omitting no opportunity in this suit, though she a long time withstood their allurements. Insomuch that he feed[19] an old woman named Isabel Hall, late wife of John Hall, and preferred as an instrument to work her to an unlawful reformation, so that in process of time, with many earnest persuasions, they won this silly soul to their will; and having so done, the said Bownd's insatiable desire could not be so satisfied, but persuaded her of himself, and also by the said Isabel Hall, to yield her consent by some means to murder her said husband, the which she was, though drawn to the other, yet very unwilling to agree unto that. But by many and often assaults and encouragements, their persuasions did work with her, and took effect; the which being obtained, then were they as busy as before, devising which way to set their devilish and most hellish practices awork, preferring many devices for the accomplishment thereof. And she oftentimes entering into consideration with herself, what a damnable part it was, first to abuse her husband's bed, and then in seeking to deprive him of his life, was greatly tormented in her conscience, and diverse times, earnestly entreated them to surcease in this practice, laying before them the great and heavy punishments provided for such offenders both in this world and in the world to come. But their hearts being so deeply possessed by that filthy enemy to all goodness, that there was nothing to them more odious than such persuasions, still persevered in their former wicked inventions and drew her to associate them in this villainy, laying many plots for the performing of it. Amongst which Isabel Hall, as she was very expert in such like actions, being an ancient motherly woman and to all men's judgements in her outward habit was far from harboring such a thought. Yet as I was about to say, she advised Bownd to give a brother of hers, namely, George Fernley, five pounds, and she would persuade him that he should use some means to murder Caldwell. The which Bownd agreed unto, being that to him all her motions[20] were medicines, and for that her house was the place that Bownd and Elizabeth Caldwell did resort for their meeting place, and he having an intent to further this matter, caused this Fernley to be sent for and conferred with him. And he being a man slenderly furnished with means, agreed to this their motion, affirming that he would delay no time till he had effected their desire, though in my conscience he pretended nothing less but only to soothe them with fair words, for lucre[21] of the money. [Fernley] made a show to Bownd as if he were very diligent about the execution thereof, but still was prevented; in so much that Bownd entered into a great rage with the poor fellow, and swore most terribly if he did not dispatch his business with all expedition, he would lay him by the heels[22] for his five pounds.

Notwithstanding, he made delays so many, that the old fox, I mean Hall's wife, devised with herself of another course, and willed Bownd to buy some Ratsbane,[23] and she would minister it in Oaten-cakes, for that she knew Caldwell much affected them; and they being made, his wife would give them unto him, and so procure his speedy dispatch. Which device he very willingly consented unto, and used no delay in the matter, but presently repaired to a town in Cheshire called Knutsforth, there bought the poison, and brought it to Elizabeth Caldwell, and wished her to send it to Isabel Hall with all speed. Whereupon she received it, and instantly upon the receipt thereof, Hall's wife sent her maid to Elizabeth, and willed her to send the spice she spoke to her for. So the maid innocently went as her dame commanded her, and received the poison, and brought it to the said Isabel Hall, her dame, who presently did take it, and minister it, (as I said before) in oaten cakes. The which being done, she sent them to Elizabeth Caldwell, where she and her husband did sojourn; whereupon, being in the evening, she laid them in her chamber window. In the morning next ensuing, Caldwell, as his accustomed manner was, rose very early, and his wife still keeping her bed, he spied the cakes lie in the window, and demanded of her if he might take any of them. She answered, yea, all if he would, and thereupon he took some three or four of them, and went into the house, and called for some butter to eat them with, the which was brought him.

But let me tell you by the way, so soon as he was departed the chamber with the cakes, fear drove such a terror to her heart as she lay in bed, as she even trembled with remorse of conscience, yet wanted the power to call to him to refrain them, insomuch as he himself did not only eat of them but the most part of the folks in the house, children and all. Yet God bestowed his blessing so bountifully on them, as they were all preserved from danger, saving one little girl which could not so well digest them, which was a neighbor's child of six or seven years old, and coming in by chance for fire, to the which master Caldwell gave a piece of a cake and she ate it, and by reason she had been long before visited with sickness, she went home and died presently, while the rest by way of vomit were saved. But that which Master Caldwell did vomit up again, two dogs and a cat did eat, and they died presently also. Whether upon the force of that poison or no the child died, I cannot say, but well I know, they were all three brought within the compass of murder for the death of it, and were all executed at Chester for the same fact, as you shall hereafter understand.

Upon the death of this child, Elizabeth Caldwell was apprehended and brought before three Justices of the peace; namely, Sir John Savage, Sir Thomas Aston, and Master Brooke of Norton, where before them she truly confessed all their practices and proceedings from the beginning, even till that day. Upon which confession, Bownd and Isabel Hall were apprehended and brought before the same Justices, and examined as touching the murder, and they very stoutly denied all, affirming that they were not guilty to any such action, although her confession in her Examination did manifest against them, being laid to their charge. All which would not move them to acknowledge their fault, the devil having so great a command over them. Notwithstanding, they were all committed to the Castle of Chester, there to remain without Bail or Mainprize,[24] till they should be delivered by due course of Law, according to the tenure of warrants directed in such a case.

So the Assize approaching within few days after their commitment, their causes and trial for that time was rejourned,[25] till the next great Assizes held there. And whether it was by special means of Bownd made to the Judge or for that Elizabeth Caldwell was with child, I cannot truly say, but there they continued from that time, being a sennight[26] after Easter, till Michaelmas[27] following, during which time they were not admitted one to speak to another. And for Elizabeth Caldwell, from her first entrance into prison, till the time of her death, there was never heard by any so much as an idle word to proceed out of her mouth. Neither did she omit any time during her imprisonment, in serving of GOD, and seeking pardon for her sins with great zeal and industry, continually meditating on the Bible, excluding herself from all company, saving such as might yield her spiritual comforts, as learned Divines,[28] and such, the faithful servants of God. There was many of all sorts resorted to see her, as no fewer some days than three hundred persons. And such as she thought were viciously given, she gave them good admonitions, wishing that her fall might be an example unto them.

Thus the deceitful devil, who hath sometime permission from GOD to attempt the very righteous (as Job), was now an instrument to her sorrow, but her feeling[29] faith the more increased, and no doubt to her comfort, though in our eyes terrible: for indeed so it ought, being sent from God as an example to thousands. For where so many live, one or two picked out by the hand of God must serve as an example to the rest to keep thousands in fear of God's wrath and the world's terror. But see her constancy. All the time of her imprisonment, she used all possible means, both of herself, and by those good members that did visit her, to convert all the rest of the prisoners, which good work begun in her did take good effect, for she sent some days a dozen Letters to several Preachers to be resolved as touching her faith, and the want of a sound resolution that GOD had pardoned her offenses. Where the Lady Mary Cholmsly of Cholmsly amongst others, together with the comfortable relief of one Master John Battie (no doubt both God's Children), so relieved, as want never grieved her conscience, but that she continued in zeal, without grief of the world's offences both in soul and body: nay, not only her, but also to the rest of the prisoners. For note, that death never feared or daunted her, but only fearing she was not fully purged from her sins, till at the end, as by her words at her execution appeareth.

This foresaid Master Battie well deserves a due remembrance for his clemency and charity showed to that distressed and deceased poor soul, by whose good means, which in mere compassion by him extended, did not only receive comforts for her bodily relief, but also great satisfaction for her soul. He oft employed such industry to the Learned, both to repair unto her themselves, as likewise daily in sending unto her good and learned instructions. Surely he deserves to be registered in the hearts of all well-disposed persons, and his demerits (no doubt) will find restitution at the hands of him who is the Pay Master[30] for all such charitable deserts.

It is also to be noted, that after these three aforenamed persons had remained in prison all the whole Summer, at Michaelmas then ensuing the Assizes were held, and Elizabeth Caldwell had her trial, where she openly before the Judges, and the rest of the Worshipful Audience, acknowledged her offence; for the which she first demanded pardon at the hands of God, then of her husband, lastly of all the world. And desiring, as it was ever her prayer, that she might be as a Looking glass to all that either did see or hear of her fall, that by her they might see into their own frailness and the infirmities which are subject to the flesh. And having, as I said, acknowledged her guiltiness, was condemned. And by reason she was not then delivered of child,[31] still reprieved; and at the same Assize Bownd was indicted. And whether by evil counsel given him, or for his own obstinacy, I cannot truly report, but he would not answer to the Articles[32] objected against him, nor refer his cause to GOD and the Country, but stood mute, though the Judges very earnestly moved him to put his cause to trial: all which would not persuade him, and therefore, according to the Law, he was adjudged to be pressed, receiving his judgement on the Saturday, to be executed on Monday following. And for Isabel Hall, her matter that Assize was not called in question, which yielded her such encouragement that she was altogether regardless of the good of her soul.

But Bownd, ever before he perceived how he should speed,[33] pleaded to everyone whom he had any communion with of his innocence, till he saw no hope of life; then he, before two or three Preachers and others, did manifest the whole truth, and affirmed that flesh and blood was not able to endure the often assaults that Elizabeth Caldwell had of him and Isabel Hall, and upon the Monday about nine of the clock, was pressed: where to every man's judgement there present, he made a very penitent end, being heartily sorrowful for his offences, and very devoutly craved pardon of GOD and all the world, and so died (I trust) the true servant of Jesus Christ.

Then that night next after his death, Elizabeth Caldwell was delivered of a boy, which child is yet as I take it still living with another boy she had before her imprisonment, the which are at the keeping of Caldwell their father, and as it was generally reported, he made suit to the Judge to procure a warrant to have his wife executed within a certain time after her delivery. But how true it was that he made such means, I cannot truly affirm, but sure I am, a warrant was granted and sent the keeper for to have her executed within 13 days or thereabouts after she was delivered, the which was converted by reason the Constable of the castle did mistake the delivery of the warrant to the Sheriff till the date was out. Though she a sennight before the time had prepared herself only to receive the mercy of God and terror of death, yet it pleased God otherwise a while to prolong her days, which time given her, she did not vainly spend, but employ[ed] her uttermost endeavors to obtain mercy and forgiveness in such rare sort, as if I should describe the particulars thereof, it would not only be endless and tedious, but I doubt, to the hearers and readers, it would be thought incredible; for in her might be seen the true image of a penitent sinner as the like hath not often in these days been seen. God showing his glory so abundantly, working her penitency, as to me, and many more, was most admirable. For if she espied in any one, of what calling or degree soever, that they willfully or carelessly abused God's holy ordinances, she would reprove them for it and courteously entreat them to amend such and such abuses; though some disdained she should seem so to do, in regard of her own former offense, though indeed none might better do it than she, having smarted even at her soul for her sins. This is the frailness of our flesh; we only disdain not our afflicted brethren, but also their good admonitions. God of his mercy, I beseech him give us grace, that we may see into our fickle estates, and receive willingly any reproof that may tend to the good of our poor souls.

So by this means, as I showed you before, this Elizabeth Caldwell was still detained in prison till the next Assize following, at what time Isabel Hall was indicted as an actor in this murder and found guilty by the Jury, condemned, and executed. And Elizabeth

Caldwell also received the death of execution at the same instant, though my Lady Cholmsly, very worshipful and lovingly, made earnest suit unto the Judge for her reprieve till the Assize following, that which by no means would be granted. And she seeing her suit would not take effect, being very sorrowful, like a kind Lady, went unto Elizabeth Caldwell herself and showed her she could not therein prevail for her.

Indeed my Lady and others had an intent, if they could have got her reprieve, to have used means to the king for a petition, but seeing it would not be, Elizabeth dutifully yielded thanks unto her Ladyship and said she was very well content to receive the death ordained for her. My Lady departed, and she practicing her former exercises, I mean prayer, until such time as the keeper came and told her the Sheriff was come to the Gloverstone,[34] to receive her and the rest of the prisoners appointed for death; and she very cheerfully answered, "I trust in my God I am ready, and farewell to the Law. Too long have I been in thy subjection." And so departing the castle, taking leave with everyone, and from hence to the place of execution, she sometimes sung Psalms and used other godly meditations as was thought fitting for her by those Divines and godly Preachers, which accompanied her even to her death.

A Letter written by Elizabeth Caldwell to her Husband, during the time of her imprisonment[35]

Although the greatness of my offense deserves neither pity nor regard, yet give leave unto your poor sorrowful wife to speak unto you, what out of her own woeful experience, with abundance of grief and tears, she hath learned in the School of affliction. It is the last favor that I shall ever beg at your hands, and the last office that ever I shall perform unto you. And therefore dear Husband, if you have any hope or desire to be partaker of the joys of heaven, let my speeches find acceptance, and do not slightly esteem what I write unto you, but read these lines again and again, and lay them up in your heart, where I beseech Almighty God they may take deep root and impression. For my witness is in heaven, that my heart's desire and earnest prayer to GOD is that your soul may be saved. And if the loss of my blood or life, or to endure any torments that the world can inflict upon me might procure your true conversion, I should esteem it purchased at an easy rate. But since none can have salvation without true Reformation, both inward and outward amendment in changing the affection, words, and works from evil to good, which till you feel in your soul and conscience to be effectually[36] wrought, you have not repented. Defer not time, but call to God for grace of true Repentance, which may be found even in this accepted time, when the doors of God's mercy are open, that so he may have mercy on you, lest he give you over to hardness of heart that you cannot repent. And so you knock with the foolish virgins,[37] when the date of God's mercies are out, and then nothing but woe, woe, and vengeance. Therefore the longer you defer, the harder it will be for you to repent; and delays are most dangerous, for what know you how suddenly death may strike you, and then, as the tree falls, so it lies; that is, as you die, so shall you have, if in true repentance, joy; if in your sins, sorrow. Therefore saith Solomon, "All that thy hand shall find to do, do it with all thy power, for there is neither work, nor knowledge, invention, nor wisdom in the grave whither thou goest."[38]

O husband, be not deceived with the world and think that it is in your power to repent when you will, or that to say a few prayers from the mouth outward a little before death, or to cry God mercy for fashion sake, is true repentance. No, no, not every one that saith "'Lord, Lord,' shall enter into the kingdom of heaven, but he that doeth the will of my Father which is in heaven,"[39] saith our Savior. Late repentance is seldom true, and true repentance is not so easy a matter to come by, as the word doth judge. Do not presume on it, and so run on in your sinful course of life and think to repent when you list.[40] You cannot do it, for repentance is the rare gift of GOD, which is given but to a very few, even to those that seek it, with many tears and very earnestly with fervent prayers. None can better speak of it, for none better knows it than myself, my sorrowful heart hath smarted for it, and my soul hath been sick to the gates of hell, and of death, to find it. And to have it is more precious then all the world. Therefore cease not to pray day and night with the prophet. Turn thou us unto thee, oh Lord, and we shall be turned, and with Ephraim, "Convert thou me, oh Lord, and I shall be converted":[41] for except you be converted, you shall not enter into the kingdom of heaven.

And because none can be converted nor come unto Christ except the Father draw him,[42] never leave to solicit the Father of mercy to create a new heart, and renew a right spirit within you,[43] and call to remembrance the dissoluteness of your life. I speak it not to lay anything to your charge, for I do love you more dearly than I do myself, but remember in what a case you have lived, how poor you have many times left me, how long you have been absent from me, all which advantage the devil took to subvert me. And to further his purpose, he set his hellish instruments awork, even the practice of wicked people, who continually wrought upon my weakness, my poverty, and your absence until they made me yield to conspire with them the destruction of your body by a violent and sudden death, which God in his great mercy prevented. And on the knees of my heart, in the abundance of his compassion, I beseech him to forgive us all, and wash our souls in the blood of his Christ, and to open the eyes of your understanding, that you may see by my example, which the providence of God, for some secret cause best known to himself, hath appointed to come to pass. How weak and wretched we are, and how unable to stand of ourselves, when it shall please him to take his grace from us and to leave us to ourselves. Therefore good husband, as you tender the welfare of your soul, go no further on in your sinful race,[44] but turn unto the Lord, and so shall you have your soul alive. If you continue in your abominations and shut your ears against the word of Exhortation, you cannot have any hope of salvation, for the book of God is full of judgements against willful sinners, and mercy is to them that repent and turn.

Therefore I beseech you use no delay, defer no time, but presently be acquainted with the Scriptures, for they will lead you to eternal life: make haste, even before your hands part with this paper to search therein, that so you may truly understand the wretched estate and condition of those who, following the lusts of their eyes, wallow in all sensuality, and so heap up vengeance against the day of wrath, even heavy Judgements, no less than condemnation both of soul and body. As Solomon saith, "Rejoice, O young man in thy youth, and let thy heart cheer thee in the days of thy youth, and walk in the ways of thy heart, and in the sight of thine eyes, but know that for all things God will bring thee to judgement."[45] Remember he spared not the Angels when they sinned, but cast them down into hell, nor of the old world but eight[46] only escaped. The rest were drowned in their sins because they would not be warned. "Balthazar," saith Daniel, expounding the fearful vision of the hand's writing, when he was banqueting with his Concubines, "thou art weighed in the Balance, and are found light."[47]

These and many more are written for our admonition, upon whom the ends of the world are come; search for them, and I pray God you may be warned by them, and that you may seek the Lord now while he may be found, and call upon him while he is near. Behold now the day of salvation, even now, when he in mercy offereth himself unto us, by preaching of his word. Receive not these graces in vain, but redeem your time, and run unto the house of God, and there in great congregation, pour forth your plaint. With obedience hear the word of God, and endeavor to practice what you hear in your conversation, for the doers only shall be justified at the last day. The word must judge us, in this life it worketh effect, for which it was sent: it either converts or hardens. It is the favor of life unto life, or of death unto death. It is offered to all: to those that embrace it, it brings life; to those that will not be reformed by it, it brings death; to those that love and desire it, it is the quicking[48] spirit; to those that refuse it, it is the killing Letter. It is no special argument of God his favor unto any, unless they feel the power thereof working reformation in them; then it is the power of his spirit, the pledge of his blessing. Ignorance must not excuse you, for the Prophet saith, "My people languish for want of knowledge,"[49] and knowledge without practice leaves all men without excuse; for he that knoweth his master's will, and doth it not, shall be beaten with many strips.[50] Therefore make more conscience of the word of God than you have done, and love his Messengers, the Preachers that bring that glad tidings, for to love them is to love Christ, and to hate them, is to hate Christ. As our Savior saith, "He that despiseth you, despiseth me,"[51] and it is hard to kick against the prick.[52] And love the children of God that profess Christ Jesus, for hereby shall men know, that "you are my Disciples, if you love one another," saith our Savior.[53]

And for the Sabbath day, be ye assured that the Lord of heaven hath not in vain chosen it to himself, commanding us to Sanctify it unto his holy name. No, no, if ever we desired to be partakers of the spiritual Sabbath in heaven, whereof ours on earth is but a type and a figure,[54] then must we strive to keep the same Sabbath on earth as much as in us lies, which the Saints keep in heaven. They are at rest from those labors that mortality is subject unto and incessantly sing praises unto the Lamb; so should we rest that day from the labors of our calling and spend the whole day in hearing of the word preached, praising the Lord publicly in the great congregation, privately at home with our families, preferring such other holy exercises as may tend to the glory of God, the comfort of our souls, and the good of others, which we are bound to perform so straitly,[55] as that we may not that day be allowed to speak such words as concern of vocations. And howsoever it please the world to think of the great God of heaven, and of the sanctifying of the Sabbaths, yet be you assured he is a jealous God, and will visit sinners, and one seed of his word shall not be lost, but he will be glorified by it either in the salvation of those who in a good conscience willingly endeavor to sanctify them, or in the condemnation of those who willfully oppose themselves against his blessed ordinance to profane them, which is one of the crying sins of this land, wherewith the whole Kingdom is infected. And if there were not some few to stand in the gap,[56] for whose sake the Lord doth spare the rest, it had not been possible we should so long have escaped his heavy judgements.

O dear husband, the Lord hath long since taken his sword in his hand to execute his vengeance against all disobedient wretches who turn the Sabbath of the Lord into a day of wantonness, liberty, and licentiousness, and although in his great mercy he doth yet forbear to proceed to judgement, as it were in great mercy, waiting our repentance, yet there will suddenly come a day of reckoning, all together; and the wicked make the patience of our God an occasion to commit sin and profaneness. Yet let them know, the Lord will take vengeance on his adversaries and reserve wrath for his enemies, and though he be slow to anger, yet is he great in power, and will not surely clear the wicked though he defer the Sessions, yet they will come, and though he have Leaden feet, yet hath he Iron hands, though the fire light not upon Sodom[57] all the evening, yet it came. Do not therefore provoke the Lord any longer by your profaneness, for he is strong, ready to punish, and hath promised that the person that despiseth his word shall be cut off. Did he not command a man to be stoned to death for gathering a few sticks on the Sabbath day,[58] and is he not still the same God? Yes certain, his arm is not shortened if we willfully persist in our disobedience.

Six market days he hath given us to provide us necessaries for our bodies and but one hath he chosen for himself to be a day of holiness, which is the market day for the soul, wherein we should provide us of comforts for the whole week. The excellency and worth of this day is unspeakable to those that sanctify it. It is the badge and livery whereby they are known to be the servants of God; to those that profane it in spending the day in worldly pleasures, drunkenness, and filthiness, it is the certain badge and livery whereby they are known to be the servants of the devil. According to the sayings of the Apostle, "Know you not unto whomsoever ye give yourselves as servants to obey, his servants ye are, to whom ye obey, whether it be of sin unto death, or of obedience unto righteousness."[59]

"If my people will sanctify my Sabbath," saith the Lord, "it shall be a sign between me and them, that they may know that I am the Lord their God,"[60] and blessed are they who have the Lord for their God. So that to those that profane the Sabbath, the Lord is not their God, but the devil, and cursed are the people that are in such a case. Therefore dear husband, defer no time, put not off from day to day to turn unto the Lord. Neither be you deceived, for God is not mocked. The longer you run on, the more you set on the score,[61] and such as you sow, such shall you reap.[62] For the Lord hath said, "He that heareth my words, and doth bless himself in heart, saying, I shall have peace, although I walk according to the stubbornness of my heart, thus adding drunkenness to thirst, the Lord will not be merciful unto him; but the wrath of the Lord, and his jealousy, shall smoke against that man, and every curse that is written in this book shall light upon him, and the Lord shall put out his name from under heaven."[63] But unto them that repent, the Lord hath said, "When the wicked turneth away from his wickedness, that he hath committed, and doth that which is lawful and right, he shall save his soul alive."[64] You see the judgements of God are begun already in your house. Happy shall you be if you make a holy use of them; otherwise heavier may be expected, especially if you persist. In his mercy he hath spared you, and doth yet wait for your repentance. Do not you abuse his patience any longer, lest thereby you provoke him to proceed to execution against you, but embrace his mercy which is yet offered unto you; for which, that you may so do, I shall not cease to pray whilst I live to him who only is able to effect it, even the Lord of heaven, who sends us joyful meeting at the day of our Resurrection.

Your poor wife,
Elizabeth Caldwell

The words of Elizabeth Caldwell at the time of her death

First she desired that the Lord would give a blessing unto the speeches that she delivered, and they might tend to the converting of many of the hearers, and also she said, that the word of God did not give her any privilege and authority to sin, but that it was her own filthy flesh, the illusions of the devil, and those hellish instruments which he set on work. Yet notwithstanding, she ever had a detestation to those sins that she lived in, but she affirmed that she wanted grace to avoid them, therefore as she had given a great scandal to the word of God by professing and not practicing the same. Even so, she desired the great mercy of God to forgive her that sin, acknowledging that she stood too presumptuously upon her own conceit, and grew too proud, bowing and swearing that she would never do such and such things, but suddenly fell into the like again.

Therefore she gave Saint Paul's admonition unto every one, "Let him that thinketh he stands, take heed of a present fall."[65] Likewise, she exhorted all to the diligent observation of the Sabbath day, saying that one of her chief and capital sins was the neglect thereof, and although the world did reckon and esteem it a small matter, yet she knew it to be one of her greatest sins, wishing all people in the fear of God to make a reverent account of the Lord's glorious Sabbath. She complained much of adultery, and said it was that filthy sin which was the cause of her death, and was persuaded in her conscience that her afflictions was rather for that than any murder she ever committed. Notwithstanding, she yielded herself culpable in concealing of it, manifesting that in regard of her sins and iniquities, she deserved a thousand deaths, praying most earnestly unto God that herself might be a warning and example unto all there present, wishing them most earnestly to serve the Lord, of what degree so ever they were, if they were never so poor, but were forced to crave their living from door to door, which done, then were they happy creatures.

Then again, she admonished all to keep the Sabbath, to go to the church, and hear the word of God preached, for that was the only truth, and able to save their souls. But as touching Papistry, she ever hated it, knowing it contrary and flatly opposite against the truth of the great God of heaven, and his holy word, praying for the confusion and desolation of the great whore of Babylon, but most devoutly and sincerely, praying for the current passage of the Gospel of Christ Jesus throughout the whole world, to the converting of thousands, desiring that the very stones of the street might set forth the glory of God.[66] And withal, most religiously she prayed for the King's most excellent Majesty, and said she might call him her King while she lived, that his sacred and royal Person might be a bright shining lamp of God's glory in the advancement of the Gospel of Christ and the overthrow of popery and superstition in these his kingdoms and dominions. Then made known that she could teach as the Preachers, for they taught as they found it in the word, and she was able to speak from a feeling heart, very confidently affirming that her sins were the greatest reason of the dullness and hardness of her heart and the separation of God's mercies from her. And therefore she carefully advised all to beware of sin because it was hateful and odious in the sight of God and all reasonable creatures.

Concerning repentance, she spoke thus, that it was not in the power of man to repent when he list, but the only gift of God. Protesting before the Lord of heaven and earth that during the time of her imprisonment, being a full year and a quarter, she had sought the Lord with many bitter tears, with broken and contrite heart, to see if his Majesty would be entreated, and yet she found not such assurance as she desired, but avouched what she did was done in simplicity of heart. Whatsoever the world did other was censure. Moreover, saying that in the mercies and merits of Christ Jesus, she hoped her sins were pardoned, and said, "I believe. Lord, help my unbelief." Also she said that in the time of her imprisonment the Lord had been very gracious and merciful unto her, for many the faithful ministers and dear servants of Jesus Christ had recourse unto her, by whose means she had recovered great comfort, praising the Lord for the same; yet notwithstanding, the world most injuriously did deride, scoff, and mock them, which was most wicked and abominable, saying, that if there were forty and two children devoured for mocking the Prophet Elijah,[67] what then shall befall of them that do blaspheme the name of the great God of heaven, profane his holy Sabbath, speak evil of his word, and abuse his faithful Ministers. Therefore she desired all to turn from their sins, and to turn to the Lord by true and unfeigned repentance, praying very earnestly for her husband's conversion, and that her two children might have the fear of God before their eyes, and that the glory of God might appear in the conversion of prisoners, though it were with the loss of her own life, so infinite was her zeal.

Then she prayed the Lord that he would pardon all her grievous and heinous sins in the bloodshed of Christ Jesus, beseeching him to cleanse her from her secret sins, praying that she might be a Doorkeeper in the house of God and receive the meanest place of glory. Then, said she, that if the great and tall Leaders of the Church of God have fallen, as David, Solomon, and Manasseh, how then could she stand, being but a bramble and weak wretched woman. Therefore she exhorted everyone to depend only upon the Lord and not to stand upon their own strength as she had done. And greatly then desiring all the people to pray unto GOD for her, she called for her Prayer book, reading and praying zealously and devoutly to Almighty GOD with her eyes lifted up towards heaven. Which done, she requested that they would sing a Psalm, reading it herself, and singing with a good spirit, that afterwards she uttered that she felt the mercies of GOD, and her soul was much comforted; and [she] hoped that in the blood of Christ Jesus her sins were pardoned, and said she could not amend that which was past but was most heartily sorrowful for her former sins; saying, that if she should live yet many years, her desire would be in serving the Lord. Therefore she desired him upon the knees of her heart, that he would respect the will for the deed, and accept her poor desires, saying, "I suffer me yet once to recover my strength, before I go hence and be seen no more." Praying likewise for all those that ministered comforts unto her in her misery and distresses, that the Lord would bless them and continue them faithful unto the end.

Then forgiving, and asking forgiveness of all, making herself ready, saying her bodily death did not dismay her, concluding with these her last words, "Lord Jesus, receive my spirit." And so she left this miserable world, and died the true servant of Jesus Christ, the xviii day of *June*, 1603.

At the time of her death

Now yet again remember our old beldame[68] aforenamed, that uncharitable creature Isabel Hall, widow, being the only instrument of this timeless action, who standing on the Ladder and ready to suffer for her fact, did notwithstanding very stoutly deny everything that had been done in their late proceedings, nay and abjured it, had not Elizabeth Caldwell with affirmation of all inserted her confession in that behalf, Who with an easy repentance to the world's eye, ended her life. Whereby may be seen how strong the Devil in some actions is, that she by whose instigation all was done, both in the adultery and murder, would so impudently deny every particular, notwithstanding the trial of the cause both manifested by Judge and Jury. But thus we see the boldness of sin and the coldness of the truth, till God in mercy makes plain the truth of the one and the wonder of the other. All which tending to the example of others may move us to lively repentance, which not done, salvation cannot come, but truly effected, breeds both the comfort of the soul and body. To which comfort, God in mercy bring us for his son Jesus Christ his sake.

FINIS

The Adultreſſes Funerall Day:

In flaming, ſcorching, and conſuming fire:

OR

The burning downe to aſhes of *Alice Clarke* late of *V x-bridge* in the County of *Miadleſex*, in *Weſt-ſmith-field*, on *Wenſday* the 20. of *May*, 1635. for the unnaturall poiſoning of *Fortune Clarke* her Husband.

A breviary of whoſe Confeſſion taken from her owne mouth, is here unto annexed : As alſo what ſhe ſayd at the place of her Execution.

By her daily Viſiter H. G. *in life and death. And now publiſhed by Authority and Commaund.*

LONDON

Printed by *N.* and *I. Okes*, dwelling in *Well-yard* in lit-tle St. *Bartholmews*, neare unto the *Lame* *Hoſpitall* gate, 1635.

Henry Goodcole, *The Adultresses Funeral Day*, title page. By permission of the Houghton Library, Harvard University.

The Adultresses Funerall Day:

In flaming, scorching, and consuming fire: or The burning down to ashes of Alice Clarke late of Uxbridge in the County of Middlesex, in Westsmithfield, on Wednesday the 20th of May, 1635, for the unnatural poisoning of Fortune Clarke her Husband. A breviary[1] of whose Confession taken from her own mouth, is here unto annexed: As also what she said at the place of her Execution. By her daily Visitor[2] H. G.[3] in life and death. (1635)

Murder upon Murder:
Or, the Old Way of Poisoning Newly Revived

In the remarkable Act of Alice Clarke, performed upon her Husband Fortune Clarke, by her, poisoned on Ascension Day[4] last past. For which being arraigned, convicted, and condemned, she suffered by Fire in West Smithfield, upon Wednesday in Whitsun week,[5] being the 20th day of May, 1635. With the last words she delivered at the time and place of her Execution.

Great and stupendous are the works and wonders of the God Almighty, who only searches the hearts and reins,[6] and therefore perspicuously knows the very thoughts and strength of man. For be his vain apprehensions never so cunning to contrive, his policy to conceal, or his boldness to out-face[7] any nefarious act committed, yet his unfounded and incomprehensible Wisdom, which can be no way circumscribed, is able at all times, and upon all occasions, as well to publish, as punish it in the open eye of the world, of which, as well those times past, as these present, have, and do afford us remarkable Examples. I will begin with the Sin, before I proceed to the Fact.

A Murderer, the Latins call *Homicida*, from *homo* and *cado*, id est, *Hominem occidere*, To kill a Man. Now who the father of murder is, you may read in the Gospel of St. John, Chapter 8, Verse 44, where our blessed Savior speaking to the Pharisees, says, "Ye are of your father the Devil, and the lusts of your father Ye will do: He hath been a murderer from the beginning," etc. For the punishment thereof, read Genesis 9, verse 5: "For surely I will require your blood wherein your lives are, at the hand of every beast will I require it; and at the hand of man, even at the hand of a man's brother, will I require the life of man. Who so sheds man's blood, by man shall his blood be shed: for in the image of God hath he made man," etc. And Numbers 35: 31, "Moreover, you shall take no recompense for the life of the murderer, which is worthy to die, for he shall be put to death." That, for the punishment. Now for the execrableness[8] of the Sin. We find in Genesis 4:11, God speaking to Cain after the slaughter of his Brother Abel, after this manner, "Now therefore thou art cursed from the Earth, which hath opened her mouth to Receive thy brother's blood from thine hand." As also Deuteronomy 27: 24: "Cursed be he that smiteth his neighbor secretly: And all the people shall say, so he is."

If this monstrous sin be so heinous in the sight of God, betwixt neighbor and neighbor, or if committed by one stranger upon another, how much more horrid appears it in his eyes when the husband and Wife, who in the matrimonial Contract, are no more two, but one flesh, shall barbarously and treacherously insidiate[9] one another's life. According to that verse of the Poet, which I have late read thus paraphrased:

> All live on spoil, the guest is not secure
> in his Host's house, nor is the Father sure
> Protected by the Son: even brothers jar,
> True love and friendship is amongst them rare.
> The husband doth insidiate the wife

And she again seeks to supplant his life:
The rough-browed Step-dame her young stepson hugs,
Tempering for him (meantime) mortiferous[10] drugs:
The Son after the Father's years inquires,
And long before the day, his death desires, etc.

Such were the passages of those times there among the Heathens, when Christianity was not known, but that they should be so familiar and conversant with us is the more to be pitied and lamented.

In the flourishing State of Rome, there were many temperers[11] of poison, and these we called *Venefice*,[12] which word we apply to, and confer upon, Effascination,[13] Sorcery, and Witchcraft. Concerning which, the Civil Laws of the Empire thus speak, in the Cornelian Law,[14] that is, Let those be held guilty of capital offence, who by odious and abhorred Arts, as well by poison, as by magic spells and whisperings, shall kill any man. In which State are likewise included all such who shall publicly sell any evil Confections. From which Canon we may ground three several sorts of delinquents in this kind, which pass under the name of *Venificium*: the first Poisoners, the second Sorcerers, or Witches, the third these Apothecaries or Empricks,[15] who shall vend any mortiferous drugs, knowing that by them any man or woman's life may be insidiated and in this case now in hand, though the seller (as he hath apparently justified himself) may be excused, yet the buyer as the Law hath openly convicted her, so we may presume that she is legally condemned.

Now what the reason may be conjectured in these our latest, but worst days, that so many nefarious acts, equaling, if not far surpassing these perpetuated in former ages, should be new committed, as Catamatism,[16] Sodomitry,[17] Paracidy,[18] many headed murders and the like, I can give no other reason then this: the contempt of the fear of God and the neglect of his Sabbath.

But to leave off all foreign prodigious acts of the like horrid nature, Which as they are numerous, so they are manifest, in History and Chronology, and go no further than our own nation, and these latter days. Hath not one brother in the heat of Wine slain another in the Tavern? A Son transpierced[19] the very womb in which he was conceived and suffered for the fault upon the Gibbet?[20] A man in his drunkenness casts his knife upon his Wife, and missing her, pointed it into the breast of his innocent child, and killed him dead in the instant. Hath not the woman offered the like outrage upon her husband in her fury, and left him dead in the place, and suffered lately for it, for remarkable example?

Within the compass of fourteen months or there abouts, one Enoch ap Evans,[21] upon a small difference betwixt his brother and him, took the advantage when he was asleep, cut his throat first, and after his head quite off with his knife, and when the mother, hearing a bustling above, came into the room to hear the cause of such a noise, he prosecuted[22] her down the stairs, and afterwards cut off her head with an Hatchet, for which he was Apprehended, arraigned, convicted, condemned at Shrewsbury, and after, some distance from the place executed.

Since then, these grand Malefactors, who went commonly by the name of Country Tom and Canbery Besse,[23] their fearful murders upon three several Gentlemen, at three sundry times, the discourse of whose Actions, Examinations, Confession, and Sufferings, because they are already published to the view of the World, I will no longer insist upon, or make any Repetition of their heinous crimes to trouble the Reader. But to come nearer to the matter of this fact now in Agitation, I will only remember you of Mistress Arden,[24] who caused her Husband to be murdered in her own house at Feversham in Kent, the memorable Circumstances thereof deserving places in a most approved Chronicle, may be very well spared in the short discourse. As also of Mistress Page of Plymouth, who for poisoning her Husband suffered with her sweet-heart Master George Strangwich,[25] who had been before time betrothed unto her. Her husband being old, she young, by which may be apprehended the misery of enforced marriage. But not to tire your patience, I will only trouble you with the poor wretched creature, who last suffered in Smith-field in this kind, much commiserated, much lamented. Give me leave a little to insist upon her cause and compare it with this now in present.

Her injuries and harsh and unmanly usage, spurred on by the instigations of the devil, almost compelled her to what she did; which, as they would be scarce modest for me to speak, so they were almost beyond the strength of Nature for her to suffer. She being young and tender, he old and peevish, who not withstanding his clownish behavior and churlish comportment towards her, was seldom or never affording her a smooth brow or friendly countenance, used not only to beat her with the next cudgel that came accidentally unto his hand, but often tying her to his bed-post to strip her and whip her, etc.

But enough, if not too much of that; she, then weary of so wretched a life, which she would have been glad to be rid of, and loath in her modesty to acquaint any friend or neighbor with her desperate purpose, who perhaps, (nay no doubt) by their good counsel might have diverted her from so wicked a resolution, and the devil with all catching hold upon so fit an opportunity to work upon her weakness, she pondered with herself how she might end both their lives by poison; which having provided and prepared to the end, she first gave him part, and after resolved with herself to drink the rest. But better motions now coming into her thoughts, and she truly repentant of what she had done, finding the confection begun to work with him, fell down before him upon her knees. First acknowledging the fact, then humbly desiring from him forgiveness, with all, beseeching him to take some present Antidote to preserve his life, which was yet recoverable. On whom he sternly looking as he lay in that Agony gasping betwixt life and death, returned her answer in this manner: "Nay thou Strumpet and murderess, I will receive no help at all, but I am resolved to die and leave the world be it for no other cause but to have thee burnt at a stake for my death." Which having said, and obstinate in that

Heathenish resolution, he soon after expired. And this Relation I received from those of credit, who were well acquainted with the conditions of them both.

I know not how to parallel these two: Her of whom I made this Short discourse, or this miserable woman, who suffered by fire in Smithfield upon Wednesday in the Whitsun week last, being the 20th of May, Anno 1635, the passages of whose life, conviction, and death thus follows.

The Free and Voluntary Confession of Alice Clarke, 18th day of May, 1635, concerning the Death of Fortune Clarke, her husband at the time she was in Prison

A Just cause, all persons may conjecture, was given on her part, of great dissensions likely to arise between her Husband and herself, unto self-will thee to be so addicted, disobediently to request the company of one White, of whom often times her Husband had interdicted her his society and familiarity. Which acquaintance of theirs was begun before Clarke her Husband entered into Marriage with her, and therefore with no small difficulty could be forgotten, or shaken off, such former ancient entertainments. No admonitions or threats to either parties could prevail that proceeded from Clarke unto his wife or unto White of continual private meetings between them. Which Clarke perceiving, outrageously fell from words unto blows with his wife, the smart whereof she feeling, incontinently[26] begot in her heart dislike and resolution of revenge on her Husband Clarke for the same, a fit humor for the devil to work on, and to her old friend White, to give occasion, not of dislike, but content to put in practice what she intended, which he might easily perceive by many pensive declamations in private uttered between themselves of her Husband's unkind usage. The confirmation whereof appears by the words that proceeded out of her own mouth.

First, she confessed, because she often companied[27] with White that stirred up her Husband's just anger against White and herself.

Secondly, that unawares unto them both, her Husband, finding her and White shut up together privately in a Chamber in the house on Ascension Day last in the afternoon, was thereat so with fury enraged, that he did beat White going out of the doors, and after that, freshly fell foul upon her, and so cruelly added blow upon blow upon her body that the marks thereof were very visible on her body at this present. Her old Love, White, instantly takes this unto heart, and in a rage (as she said) uttered these words, "That it were better for one to be hanged, than to endure so discontented a life," and presently putting his hand into his pocket, he took out 4 Tokens, and gave them unto Alice Clarke, saying unto her, if he had more money, he would have given it unto her; which 4 Tokens so given unto her she went unto Uxbridge forthwith, and that afternoon bought a penny worth of Mercury of an Apothecary in Uxbridge, intending the same unto her Husband, with a further reservation, that if her Husband had not taken it, she would have administered the same unto herself, and so put an end unto all her sorrows, as she vainly supposed.

Thirdly, she said, that she was not the cause of her Husband's death because she gave not unto him the poison whereof he died, but he took it himself violently out of her pockets, which her Husband had rifled upon hope to find some chink or money there, but of such hopes he altogether was disappointed and deluded. Whether this be not a lame excuse, or strange delusion, I refer it unto the censure of the Judicious, and no further discovery of the fact could I get from her at that time.

She further said, that on Ascension Day her husband violently attempted to drown himself, which she prevented by her language upon him, but in short space afterwards, died that night of the Mercury taken by himself out of her pocket, as afore-said.

Fourthly, she seemed to be very much afflicted in conscience, that she was a year since gotten with Child by her Master, with whom she last dwelt with-all, who perceiving the same, with a small sum of money, matched her unto Fortune Clarke her Husband, about Allhallowtide[28] last, whom she could not love, or have any matter of maintenance, but relied upon her Master's former promises for the same; and he failing of giving her means, fell into folly and wickedness. A great clog unto such a man's conscience, if it be true, to seduce a woman unto his will and so leave her.

A Short Tract Upon the heinousness of poisoning

Though there be sundry sorts of Murder with their several degrees, as open, or secret, acted upon a friend, a stranger, or one's self, yet in my opinion, I know not any of them which contains so much villainy, neither including so many deep circumstances in them, as that of poisoning. That I think is the reason that there are so few examples of it in Holy writ, this way either being then not known, followed, or practiced; therefore, to describe the quality of it and to aggravate it, I must with you to consider these four things.

First, the *Duplicem modum*,[29] secondly, the *Duplicem effectum*:[30] *Modus Prior*,[31] the First Manner, *Deliberando, Meditando*,[32] Is an Act done by Deliberation, or Meditation, no ways carried and hurried by the violence either of will or of passion, but done upon a cold blood, and not seldom upon fixed resolutions.

Modus posterior, Celando, obtegendo,[33] by a secret intent to hide it and conceal it from God if it were possible, so it is to the Patient under the shadow of some Physic, or other medicine, colored with an outward show of honest intent, and as far as they can from the Public Magistrate; or else to make a distance of time, either to excuse themselves, or fly away from the hands of Justice. Though . . . [The first two lines of page B4 are illegible.] . . . changing, stupefying or absolutely breaking away the senses, and depraving the operative Organs of the soul and sometimes infecting all the principles of life as the head, the heart, and the liver, howsoever altering and overthrowing the frame and constitution of man's body in general and making him unfit for a preparation of himself for death, though it be upon him, so that without the special

Mercy of God, the party thus abused dies without either knowledge of his sins or repentance for them.

Secondly, *Effectus posterior, creaturarum abusus*,[34] the abusing of the Creatures contrary to the end of their Creation. They being brought forth for the use and health of Man's Body, by this means they are made deadly, nay this manner of killing any makes not only the prime Agents guilty, but infects and makes guilty others too, or at least, causes them to be examined strictly by the Magistrate. So that howsoever their good name for the present is blotted and blemished, and what more is, they have but two ways to comfort themselves: the first is the witness of their own Conscience's Integrity; the second, is the Judge's knowledge of their Innocence and Ignorance by a prudent examination of the fact perpetrated by all circumstances and suspicious Arguments. And in this kind, the Apothecary for selling, the Messengers for buying, the Composers of it, and the deliverers of it to the party stand in an hazard either of their lives, or fortunes, or both.

Laying aside all these together, I hope it will easily appear what heinous sin it is when it is thus committed, First, with Deliberation; Secondly, with Secrecy; Thirdly, with disabling the party to fit himself for mercy, and with the abusing the blessings of God and their own knowledge; and lastly, for bringing others into danger as well as themselves. Yet what is more, all this done under the Gospel, and often, as at this present, against one whose life, credit, goods, and good name the offender ought to cherish and maintain to the uttermost. So I may take up that saying of Jacob to his two Sons, "My soul come not into their secrets, neither be joined with their assemblies,"[35] nor have to do with their practices, whole conclusions are so deeply dyed with the blood of Innocents.

The Second Confession of Alice Clarke this 10th day of May, 1635, at the place of Execution, concerning the poisoning of her husband, Fortune Clarke

Physicians of the Soul ought to imitate those learned Physicians of the body, frequent visitations of those sick patients, whose diseases are desperate and inveterate, and sometimes it chances, that they must desire, necessity so requires, the advice and sound opinions of others, their Colleagues. Even thus it happened between this obdurate Malefactor and myself, who in Adultery was so Rooted and insensible of the heavy burden and most intolerable plagues ensuing for it. That at the first and second times of my visiting of her, little or no Repentance I found in her, or her heart to be touched for her most horrid clamorous crimes. This is apparent if you compare her first confession unto this; how different in truth, how improbable the one are unto the other. Nay, what she confessed on Monday, she was so far off to proceed in a further revealing of herself that what touched[36] her home, concerning her husband's death, she would have denied, though formerly confessed by her most confidently true.

I was thereupon enforced to hold her unto it and to extract the truth and try her spirit, called two of the Keepers of the Gaol, to her unknown, whom I appointed to observe and remember the speeches that passed between us, to verify them unto her face, which attestation both of myself, and of them, she would out-face, but could not.

Upon Wednesday morning on which she was executed, there assembled unto Newgate[37] multitudes of people to see her, and some conferred with her, but little good they did on her, for she was of a stout angry disposition, suddenly enraged if you began to touch her to the quick of her husband poisoning. Being that morning of her death accompanied and also assisted by diverse of my worthy, grave, and learned brethren in the Ministry, before and at the time of her Execution, for which I do most heartily thank them, but that God whose work it was, their reward for it with him is laid up in store. Like myself, they stood as men amazed to perceive that none of theirs or any other serious persuasions could for a great while prevail with her, joined in opinion with me, that she was no fitting guest for the Table of the Lord Jesus. Thereupon, I made as though I would have excluded her thence in denying the benefit of the holy Communion of the Body and Blood of Jesus Christ, inferring the benefit of the unspeakable bless by the worthy receiving of it by Repentance and Faith, and the most woeful malediction to all impenitent and unworthy receivers. Whereupon, it pleased God so to mollify her heart, that tears from her eyes and truth from her tongue proceeded, as may appear by this her ensuing Confession at the very Stake, where she was executed, unto M. Cordall, Sheriff of London, relating the same with as loud and audible a voice as possibly she could, that many others besides there present were also witnesses to such her ensuing Confession.

First she confessed that Henry White, who was arraigned as a party with her, consenting unto her Husband's death, did give unto her on Ascension Day in the afternoon, four brass tokens, advising her therewith to go and buy one pennyworth of Mercury, and give it unto her Husband, saying, if that her husband were dead, she should live more quietly and contentedly with him, and after such his death, that he the said White would marry with her; whereupon she went unto Uxbridge, and that afternoon bought the Mercury.

Secondly, she confessed that her Master got her with child a year since, which was her overthrow, and mediated for the Marriage between her and her Husband, whom she could not love, nor no way affect. By her Master's persuasion, who sent her up to London to be Married and paid the costs thereof, and further promised her maintenance during her life if she did condescend unto his desires, which were most unlawful, dishonest, and unchaste, before and after her Marriage with Fortune Clarke, her Husband.

Thirdly, she confessed, that one of Hillinden enticed her to run away from her Husband, with him beyond the Seas, and that she did lodge in that man's house, and lay with him a whole fortnight, and speaking unto him of her Husband, that she would not forsake him, he thereupon advised her to pop him up with white bread and milk, and to put something else into it to choke or stuff up his throat.

Fourthly, she confessed, for the Mercury which she bought, she intended it unto her Husband, but having no convenient opportunity to dispose of it, she put it into her sleeve, which her Husband, as she said, took it out of her hand, and then being over charged with drink he immediately swallowed it down, which she perceiving was thereat so perplexed, that she uttered these words unto her Husband, that he had undone both himself and her.

And here give me leave to note unto the World what a deal of comfort she found after she had disburdened her loaded conscience by confession. Being demanded at the same instant of her death, yea, or nay that after such her confession, she was by it the better prepared unto death, with comfort and willingness to suffer the same. She thus replied with hearty thankfulness unto God that she had better resolutions unto death then formerly she had, and by her countenance, which was very ruddy,[38] confirmed her inward new begotten cheerfulness, and that with hearty prayer and sweet tone of voice, surrendered her soul into the hands of the Lord Jesus, who will have mercy on whom he will have mercy, unto whom we all stand and fall.

Here is nothing contained in her confession, but that which is true, and what she uttered with her own mouth, which I was a witness of H. Goodcole.

FINIS

Murther, Murther.

Or,

A b'oody Relation how *Anne Hamton,*
dwelling in Weſtminſter nigh London, by
poyſon murthered her deare husband, Sept.
1641. being aſſiſted and counſelled
thereunto by *Margeret Harwood.*

For which they were both committed

to Gaole, and at this tyme wait
for a tryall.

Women love your owne husbands, as Chriſt doth the Church.

Printed at London for *Tho: Bates,* 1641.

*Murther, Murther. Or, A bloody Relation how Anne Hamton, ...
murthered her deare husband,* title page, shelfmark E 172 (7).
By permission of the British Library.

Murther, Murther. Or, A bloody Relation how Anne Hamton, dweling in Westminster nigh London, by poyson murthered her deare husband,

September 1641, being assisted and counseled thereunto by Margeret Harwood. For which they were both committed to Gaol, and at this time wait for a trial.

Women love your own husbands, as Christ doth the Church.[1] (1641)

A bloody Relation of Anne Hamton, who poisoned her husband at Westminster

Gentle Reader,

It is not my purpose to make thee now laugh, but if possible it be to be sad, not to rejoice but lament, not to be frolic,[2] but to dissolve into fountains of tears, because a daughter of Jerusalem[3] hath committed an abomination. Hearken to me you that be wives, and give attendance you which as yet are unmarried. Regard the words of Saint Paul which commands that every wife should love her own husband as Christ the church; not to be high-minded towards him, but humble, not to be self-willed, but diligent, not to be like a strange woman, which wanders abroad in the twilight to get a prey, but to be constant and loving to him. For why? Ye both be of one flesh.

A man must forsake his Father, Mother, Brethren, and Sisters to cleave to his own wife, and so likewise the wife for the husband.[4]

142

But I must tell of one who would never agree to any such pious matter.

Before I come to which relation, I cannot abstain myself from exclamation: let all the forests wherein fierce lions are contained be joined in one and privy search made to know if ever female did the male destroy. Oh no! For though by nature they be fierce and bloody, yet doth nature so much govern them that those which are couples, be linked in friendship, never disagree. Oh then, thou savage woman, why unto blood were thou addicted, as to destroy thy loving and kind husband, the relation of which shall be divulged throughout this universe.

In the parish of Saint Margaret's, Westminster, dwelt one Anne Hamton in the house of Margeret Harwood; this Anne Hamton had a husband, which like a loving man indeed delighted in nothing more but to see his wife pleasant; for he would often say, my wife being troubled, it behoveth me not to be at rest; she being pleasant, I ought to be joyful. But she, most unkind woman, was of a contrary disposition, for she at her own house would take occasion to be merry when the greatest mischief had befallen him. He was a very laborious man, but she, a light housewife. When he was working, she would be gossiping with one young fellow or another, or else with such women as were like to herself. Never was she more joyful than when she was out of her good husband's company. What her husband got by taking pains, she spent by taking her pleasure. His money being thus consumed and his goods wasted, he upon a time spoke to her after this manner.

"Wife, what do you mean to do? How dost thou intend to live? My money you spend, which I get hardly; my goods you waste. You never got the worth of a joint stool.[5] My company you hate, you must have better. O wife, wife, take counsel by me thy hitherto loving husband. Forsake that company which hate not thy body, but soul. Do not drink healths to thine own confusion, nor with so greedy an appetite swallow thine own destruction. Repent in time of thy wickedness lest when thou think thyself in security, the Lord doth cut thee off, and what will then become of thy poor soul? Love me, thy husband. Hate those which entice thee to wickedness; trust not to their smiling countenances, for in their hearts do lie hid nothing but abominations. If thou will (I say) have my love, hate such, or else never more think to enjoy that which as yet you have always had."

What harm was there in all this which he spoke unto her? But notwithstanding she forsooth took it in distaste, and giving him a scolding reply, she left the room, and went to her companion in mischief, Margeret Harwood, which was her Landlady, to whom she revealed the secrets of her heart, saying, that her husband was an enemy to good fellowship, and continually wrangled and brawled at her, because she affected it. In which she lied, for he always spoke in a very loving manner unto her, except she overmuch provoked him.

Moreover she said that she should never be in quiet until by some way or other she were shifted[6] of him.

The devil finding an occasion how to accomplish a mischievous intent, always makes use of it. He knows how to please everyone's wicked humor. Wherefore he tempted the Landlady with bloody cogitations, for she hearing her Ningle's[7] unjust complaint, she cried out that it was her own fault for letting such an abject villain to live: "Hang him, cut his throat, or poison him, for he is not fit to live upon the earth amongst good fellows." To condescend to whose counsel, she seemed very unwilling, but at length the devil got the better of her, and then she did agree to poison him. And for the same intent she went and got five drams[8] of poison, enough to have destroyed ten men, and mixed it amongst his food, which he no sooner had taken, but that he presently did swell very much, which she perceiving, did run to her Landlady, who asked her how much she had given him. She replied, "Five drams." "Well done," said she, "if five will not be enough, ten shall," and thereupon they went up to see him, but he was then burst. Then did they both dissemble a lamentable cry, which caused the neighbors to come in to see what was the matter, where they did behold such a woeful spectacle as was sufficient to exhaust tears from the driest eye composed of Pumice stone, for there did they see his nails quite peeled off, his hands did seem only like two great boils, his belly seemed as if hot irons had been thrust into it, his visage was so much defaced by the quick operation of the scalding poison, that had they not well known the body, they would have sworn it not to have been the man which they came to visit. They all easily perceived that he was poisoned.

A Chirurgeon[9] being sent for, ripped up his body, and found the poison lying about his heart. As also there was found poison in a paper in the window, the Chirurgeon, calling for a Venice glass,[10] put the same therein, which immediately broke the glass.

Wherefore they sent for an officer, and apprehended upon suspicion both his wife and Landlady, whose consciences cannot but confess that they washed both their hands in his innocent blood.

They are both in the Gatehouse prison of Westminster, nigh London, expecting a day of trial, which time will not be long; till when I rest. Then (gentle Reader) shalt thou have by God's permittance a more perfect relation.

FINIS

A

Hellish Murder

Committed by a

French Midwife,

On the Body of her

HUSBAND,

Jan. 27. 168$\frac{7}{8}$.

For which she was Arraigned at the
Old-Baily, *Feb.* 22. 168$\frac{7}{8}$. and
Pleaded *GUILTY.*

And the Day following received
Sentence to be BURNT.

LONDON,

Printed for *R. Sare*, at *Grays-Inn-Gate*, and published by
Randal Taylor, near *Stationers-hall.* 1688.

A Hellish Murder, title page, shelfmark Ashm. 739 (19). By permission
of the Bodleian Library, University of Oxford.

A Hellish Murder Committed by a French Midwife,

On the Body of her Husband, January 27, 1687/8.[1] For which she was Arraigned at the Old Bailey, February, 22, 1687/8 and Pleaded Guilty. And the Day following received Sentence to be Burnt. (1688)

Introduction

The late Barbarous Murder of Denis Hobry (what with Malice, Prejudice, Credulity and Mistake) has put more Freaks and Crotchets[2] into the Heads and Minds of the Common People than any Story of that size perhaps ever did in this World before. But as Fancy, Error, and Invention have No Bounds in the matter of Number and Variety, so with respect to the Quality of These Extravagances, it would be no less Frivolous, on the Other side, to Encounter the Passions and the Dreams of the Multitude with Formalities of Council and Reason. For the Exceptions are too Many to be taken Severally to pieces, and they are too Trivial (even all together) to be worth the while of a Serious Thought. And yet how Vain, and how Impossible soever, a Full and a Distinct Answer to so many Spiteful and Groundless Shams and Misunderstandings may appear to be; there is something yet to be done, methinks (though but in a Complement to Common Curiosity and Satisfaction); and the shortest way of clearing all Difficulties will be to Publish to the World a Plain and a Naked Narrative of this whole Affair, as it is Delivered and set forth in the Informations Themselves that have been given in Evidence upon This Cause, which I can the better undertake, for in regard that they have all pass'd through My Hands. This Course will settle all People Right that have a Mind to be set Right, and there's no better way in Nature to Rectify the Misapprehensions of Things than by setting forth Matter of Fact just as it *was*, which at the same time, serves to Prove unanswerably how it was *not*. Only a word or two of Introduction by the way.

Upon the first Rumor of this Horrible Murder, there were Two Journeymen[3] Joiners[4] taken up and Committed upon Suspicion of having laid the Body where 'twas found, but they prov'd themselves upon Inquiry to be very Honest Men. 'Tis true They passed that way. They were seen thereabouts; Witnesses Examin'd; and Unhappy Circumstances enough for a Ground of Jealousy. But afterwards, upon the Seizure of the Midwife, and unquestionable Proofs against her (beside her Own and her Son's Confession), the Coroner's Inquest Met, according to an Adjournment, and sat upon the Body, February 8, 1687, where they acquitted Mary Pottron and the Two Joiners, but Mary Hobry (the Midwife) was found Guilty of the Murder of Denis Hobry, as Principal, and John Defermeau (the Midwife's Son) was found Accessory after the Fact.

At Hicks Hall, Mary Hobry had a Bill[5] found against her, February 22, 1687, for Petty Treason[6] and Murder, as Principal; and on her Arraignment the same Day at the Old Bailey, she Pleaded *Guilty*, but the Court with all possible Tenderness, let her know the Danger and the Consequence of her Confession, and offer'd her yet the Liberty to Depart from her Plea and take her Trial, if she thought fit; but she still Persisted in her Confession.

There was, after this, Another Bill found at Hicks Hall on the same Day against Denis Favet and John Favet (Frenchmen and Brothers) as Accessories before and after the Fact; and likewise against John Defermeau (the Son of the said Midwife) as Accessory after the Fact.

Upon their Trial at the Old Bailey, they were All found *Not Guilty*. But the Matter had such a Face, however, that the Court thought fit to put the Two Brothers to find Sureties[7] for their Good Behavior.

The Woman's Confession has Prevented the Public Notification of the Foulness of the Cause that would otherwise have been made by a Printed Account of the Trial, so that it remains only to supply that Disappointment by True Copies of the Following Informations, which would have been the Foundation at last (in case she had put herself upon her Defense) for the Court to Proceed upon.

Midd. & West. } The Information of James Richards of the Parish of St. Margaret's Westminster, Victualler,[8] taken upon Oath, February 3, 1687/8.

Saith, That this Informant being in Company about Four or Five o' Clock in the Afternoon, Yesterday, with Mr. Yard, and another Person, there was a Discourse about the Dead Body that was lately found; whereupon Mr. Yard was saying that there was a Friend of his missing and that he was afraid. This was the Man, having heard his Wife Often say that she would Murder him, or Dispatch him, or to that Effect. This Informant thereupon putting it to the said Mr. Yard if he could make good what he said; Whose Answer was, that he could make it good. Upon which, this Informant advis'd the getting of an Officer to Apprehend the Woman. The Third Person Answering, that tomorrow morning would be time enough. But this Informant said, it was a Case would bear no Delay, and that therefore he was resolv'd to Inform with all speed, to which they Agreed. And this Informant going then out of the Room, Mr. Yard follow'd, and told this Informant that the Thing was too true, and that the said Woman had told him as much, but Promised within some few Days to tell him more. Upon this, the Informant got a Constable and went as an Assistant to the Apprehending of the Woman, whom they found at a House in Phoenix Alley, and so she was taken into Custody and Committed.

James Richards.
Jurat' Die & Anno Supradict coram me,[9] Roger L'Estrange.

Midd. & West. } The Information of Philip Yard of St. Martin's in the Fields, Cook, taken upon Oath, February 3, 1687/8.

Saith, That this Informant becoming known to the Family and to the Person of Denis Hobry in Paris, many years since, and having of late been several times in his Company here in England, where his Wife (a Midwife) was present, became also known to the said Midwife, whom this Informant hath heard within the Compass of Two months last past (speaking upon a modest Recollection of his Memory) menacing and reviling the said Denis Hobry more then Forty several times, Calling him "Dog," "Drunken Villain," and other the Foulest Words of Reproach. And saying over and over upon several Occasions, "I must kill him, and will kill him, though I be Hang'd for 't," speaking the words in French, "C'est un Chien; C'est un Ivrogne," &c. "Il faut que je le Tue, quoique Je devrais être pendue."

And saith particularly, That upon Thursday in the last Week about Two or Three o' Clock in the Afternoon, being at the House where her Daughter lodges, the said Midwife took occasion to fall into a Violent Passion against her Husband and broke out into Passions of Threatening to Kill him in manner as above recited.

And saith, That on the Day mentioned in the Paragraph next above, the wife of Hobry, breaking into Violences of Discourse as abovesaid, desired this Informant to take No Notice of anything she had said, whatever should happen. This Informant demanding what she meant by that Thing that he was not to take Notice of, She replied, of her calling her Husband Ill Names and the like.

And saith, That Three or four days after what is abovesaid, This Informant went to the Lodgings of the said Hobry and Asked where he was. They made Answer they had not seen him for several Days. This Informant reflecting at that Time upon the Bloody Menaces of this Woman toward her Husband of the Thursday before, And that this Informant could hear no Tidings of the said Hobry among All his Acquaintance, This Informant had an Apprehension within himself, that she might have done him a Mischief.

On Wednesday Morning, being the Next Day, this Informant went again to the Lodging of the said Hobry to Inquire after him, and hearing no News of him yet, this Informant Advis'd them to open the Door for fear he might have carried some of the Goods into France. But the People of the House would not open the Door because the Midwife that Lodg'd there had the Key.

This Informant went the same Day to the Lodgings of the said Midwife's Daughter, where the Mother there waited for an Opportunity of speaking with her in Private, and took the Occasion at last to go out of the Lodgings with her and walking in the Street. This Informant said after this manner to the said Midwife, "Hark ye. You spoke dangerous Words th' other day concerning what you'd do to your Husband. Have you done as you said you would? For the People have been looking everywhere after him, and there's no such Man to be found. I hope 'tis not the mangled Body that they talk of to be murder'd." "No," says she, "'tis not that Body." This Informant said further to her, "Why, how could you go to Work to Dispatch a Man that you are not able to Grapple with?" "Oh," says the Woman, "he put me hard to 't, but I won't tell you today; 'tis not a thing to be talk'd of in the Street." This Informant replying, "Why, We speak French; Nobody understands us." "Well!" says she, "Let it alone for Five or Six Days, and I'll tell you." This Informant pressing her again to tell him, till she Swore she would not.

And saith, That the said Midwife going toward Phoenix Alley in Long Acre, where this Informant left her, she the said Midwife said to this Informant in French, "Bouche Close"; or in English, "Not a Word."

Philip Yard.
Jurat' Die & Anno, Supradict coram me, Roger L'Estrange

Midd. & West. } The Information of Julian Coze, of the Parish of St. Anne's Westminster, Gardener, taken upon Oath, February 9, 1687/8.

Saith, That being in Company upon Thursday Last in the Evening with one Yard, a Frenchman, he the said Yard told this Informant that he would never see the Parisian more (speaking of Denis Hobry). This Informant asking him What made him say so? To whom Yard replied, that Hobry's Wife had told him as much.

Whereupon this Informant, reflecting upon the manner of speaking and upon Hobry's being from his House for some time, and no News of him, He, this Informant, propos'd the charging of a Constable with her, which was done that Night accordingly, and this Informant was Assistant to the Seizure of the said Mrs. Hobry.

Julian Coze.
Jurat' Die & Anno, Supradict coram me, Roger L'Estrange.

Midd. & West. } The Information of Henry Fuller, of St. Margaret's Westminster, taken upon Oath, February 17, 1687/8.

Saith, That being told by James Richards, a Victualler, in Long Ditch, that there were Two Frenchmen at the said Richard's House that were speaking something about the Murder'd Body, and that one of them said, the Woman, suspected for the Murder, had as good as Own'd it. This Informant being in the Office of a Constable, agreed with the said Richards to go to the Lodgings of the said Woman and Apprehended her upon the Suspicion. Whereupon, This Informant, and the said Richards, taking one Philip Yard along with them and another Person then in the Company, went to the House where the said Woman Lodg'd, but missing her at Home, went according to Direction to the Last in Phoenix Alley, where they took her into Custody. This being betwixt Eleven and Twelve at Night, upon the Second of this Instant February. And not finding a Justice of Peace up, Deliver'd her up to the Gate House[10] 'till next Morning.

Hen. Fuller.
Jurat' Die & Anno *Supradict coram me*, Roger L'Estrange.

The Information of Christopher Austin, of St. Paul's Covent Garden, Shoemaker, taken upon Oath, February 3, 1687/8.

Saith, That being the Servant of John Izember (or some such Name), a Shoemaker living at the Golden Shoe in Phoenix Alley, Long Acre, the Mistress of this Informant being ready to fall in Labor, sent her Prentice Richard to a French Midwife, living in Castle Street, to come and Assist her. The said French Midwife coming to the Mistress of this Informant, and she not presently falling in Labor as she expected, she desir'd the Midwife to stay that Night with her, for she did not know how things might fall out. The Midwife stayed accordingly, and went away the next morning; this was some Day last Week, but this Informant did not remember what part of the Week. The Midwife aforesaid came several times after this to inquire how it was with this Informant's Mistress, and particularly, came Last Night to the House, and Supp'd there, and desir'd to Lodge there because she did not know what Occasion there might be for her. This Informant's Mistress agreeing that she should be there that Night, The Midwife went accordingly to Bed toward Eleven o' Clock. There came a Constable to the Door, just about the Watch, crying "Eleven," when Richard, this Informant's Fellow Prentice, Ask'd Who was there. To which, no Answer being return'd, this Informant called again and again, "Who's there? If you do not Answer, you shall not come in." Upon this a Frenchman asked in English, if Madame, meaning the Midwife, was within, but this Informant did not remember the Name. Upon this, the said Richard above-spoken of, spoke in French to the French Midwife, and told her that somebody call'd for her to go to a Woman's Labor; whereupon the Midwife went up to this Informant's Mistress to fetch the Keys. So this Informant's Mistress went down along with the Midwife, the said Midwife desiring that Richard might go along with her and carry a Light. Upon this, the Boy got up, and the Midwife opened the door, a Frenchman entering first, and bidding the Constable to come in; who, upon coming in, show'd his Staff, the Midwife seeming Surpris'd. Hereupon, one of the Frenchmen asked the Midwife Where her Husband was. Who Answered that she left him in Bed last Thursday. The Frenchman Answering, that if she left him in Bed, it was with his Arms and Legs cut off. The Midwife, upon these Words, deliver'd up herself before they laid Hands on her, and Desir'd them to make No Noise but to go Civilly along with her. This Informant's Mistress Then did bid Richard ask what the Matter was. To which, a Frenchman made Answer, that he would swear that she walk'd up and down the Room when she had Cut off one Limb and then Cut off the rest in her own Bed. Upon giving an account hereof to this Informant's Mistress, the Constable Commanded the Frenchman Last above mention'd to Assist in Carrying her away, This Informant's Mistress giving order for a Piece of Link[11] to Light them along. And upon Discourse among them, the Frenchman that Spoke of what he could swear, told the Midwife that he was taken upon Suspicion, and that if he were Call'd, he must Impeach her and tell the Truth. The abovesaid Richard, speaking to This Informant of some Blood in the Bed, by which it was discover'd.

And saith, That this Prentice, Richard before spoken of, said to This Informant, That This Murder, if 'twere Twenty Year, would be found out at Last, and This in the Hearing of the Midwife, who made No Answer. And the said Richard told this Informant further, That his Master saying in the Hearing of the Midwife, that if he knew who it was that did it, he would be the first that should tell on it, adding that he never heard of such a thing in his Days. Hereupon the Midwife said she saw the Limbs brought from the Savoy[12] in a Sack.

This Informant's Mistress, upon the hearing of the Story, gave Hard words to the Midwife, and call'd her Villain, saying if she had Imagin'd such a Thing she should never have come within her Doors.

And moreover, that the Prentice abovemention'd told This Informant that he Heard the said Frenchman say that she had formerly Threatened to kill her Husband.

The Mark of C., Christ. Austin.
Jurat' Die & Anno Supradict coram me, Ro. L'Estrange.

Midd. & West. } The Information of Richard Kirkham, Servant to John Izember, Shoemaker of the Parish of Covent Garden, Taken upon Oath, February, 1687/8.

Saith, That a French Midwife passing by the Name of Madam Defermeau came Last Night to the House of This Informant's Master, stayed Supper there, and was to have Lodg'd there; and

That This Informant heard his Mistress say, That the said Midwife desired she might stay there All Night, being Under some Disappointment at home.

When the Key of the Street Door was Taken out, and About the Hour of Eleven, there was a knocking at the Door. And an Inquiry after a French Midwife, Naming the Person, and This Informant said she was There. And upon Further Discourse, the Person at the Door said he came from one Mrs. Richards in Shandois Street. The French Woman Scrupled at going to Strangers, but however she would Fetch the Key. And being come down, and one of the Persons that knocked being let into the House, the French Midwife would have had this Informant to go before to see what was the matter. This Informant went to the Door then, with one Richards, being one of those that knocked at the Door, who immediately made a Sign, and a Constable and two others came in; and upon their Entry, One asked, which it was? To which, a Frenchman, one Yard, replied, "This is the Woman," pointing to the Person. Whereupon the Constable show'd his Staff, and took her into Custody. This Informant's Mistress being Frighted at this, Ask'd What the matter was? To which the Midwife replied, "Quelque Drollerie"; or in English, "Some little Waggery."[13] This Informant's Mistress pressing more and more to know the Bus'ness. And somebody asking the Midwife Where her Husband was? She made Answer, that she had not seen him since the Thursday before, when she left him in Bed. And being asked, If she had not seen him since? She said, "No," and in French, that he was a Vagabond, and she knew nothing of his ways, or to that Effect. It was Replied, She must find him out: And her Answer was, How should she find him out, that did not see him once in six Months? One of the Frenchmen made Answer that he would be found. His Informant's Mistress asking thereupon (as mistrusting the Bus'ness), Where he was, or what was become of him? Some One of the Frenchmen replying that he was dead, and cut in pieces, and that by her own Hands, in her own Room, and in her own Bed. This Informant's Mistress speaking furiously to her, "Traîtresse! Que vous ayez

Commis un Crime si Noir! Traitress that thou art, to be Guilty of so black a Crime!" "No, Madam," says she, "I am Innocent." And so they Carried her away; and at Parting, "Well," said this Informant's Mistress, "I believe I shall never see you more."

The Mark of R, Rich. Kirkham.

Jurat' Die & Anno Supradict coram me, Ro. L'Estrange.

Midd. & West. } The Information of John Izember, of the Parish of St. Paul's, Covent Garden, taken upon Oath, February 3, 1687/8.

Saith, That this Informant hath known a French Midwife by the Name (to the best of this Informant's memory) of Defermeau, for about five years last past, she having laid[14] this Informant's Wife of several Children.

And saith, that about Ten or Twelve days since, the Wife of this Informant sent for the said Midwife, being, as she thought, ready to fall in Labor. The Midwife came accordingly, and the Wife of the Informant desired her to stay all Night to see the Event of that Illness. She stay'd, but the next morning this Informant's Wife finding herself better, the Midwife went away, but came day by day afterward to Inquire how 'twas with her.

And saith, That the said Midwife came Last Night to the House of this Informant, saying that she did not care for lying at home that Night; and so she Supp'd with this Informant, whose Wife told him that she had agreed she should Lodge there that Night. About Eleven o' Clock, the Midwife came up to the Informant's Wife and ask'd her for the Key of the House, saying that there was somebody knock'd to call her to a Woman's Labor, but she did not know the Voice, and had a mind to see who it was. This Informant's Wife thereupon going down with her to open the Door. After which, this Informant's Wife told this Informant, that the Midwife said, "I do not care to go Alone with that Man," speaking of one of the Company. "Pray let your Servant go along with me." Upon this, a Frenchman that was already Enter'd the House call'd in the Constable. And this Informant, upon the Subject matter of the

Clause, refers himself to the Testimony of his Wife, from whom this Informant had the Relation.

Jean Izember.
Jurat' Die Anno Supradict. coram me, Ro. L'Estrange.

Midd. & West. } The Information of Mary, the Wife of Tobias Hope, of the Parish of St. Martin's in the Fields, Sawyer,[15] taken upon Oath, February 3, 1687/8.

Saith, That a French Midwife, of whose Name this Informant cannot give a perfect Account, Lodg'd in the House of the Informant for about Three Months last past. And that within the Compass of that time (but the precise time uncertain), a Person that the said Midwife said was her Husband came and Lodg'd with her and went (as this Informant was told) into France, about a Month or Six Weeks since (to this Informant's best memory). And that he return'd again to the House of this Informant about Three Weeks since, and that this Informant hath not taken Notice of his Lodging in the House for about Ten or Twelve Days since.

But that some time last Week, this Informant Asked the said Midwife how it came to pass that he did not Lodge in the House, and where he was? The Midwife's Daughter, in the Presence of the Mother, telling this Informant that he heard there was a Warrant out against him, and he durst[16] not come, saying further, that he was to go with a Lord into New England for Three Years. And the Daughter saying that her Husband did Work for that Lord, and that her Husband would give the said Midwife's Husband Thirty Shillings to clothe him, and 'twould be a good Riddance of him. The Daughter Adding, that the Mother should keep out of the Way till he was gone. And the Mother likewise came Yesterday morning to the House of this Informant, and said, that Now he was gone, for which she was Glad with all her Heart, and that she came now to Lodge there again.

And saith, That the Midwife and her Daughter came to this Informant's House upon Last Tuesday morning, and paid this

Informant Eight Shillings in part of Rent, and the Mother desir'd this Informant put her off 'till Saturday, and she rested contented.

At the Time next above mentioned, this Informant Asked the Midwife and her Daughter, whether they had seen the murder'd Body. The Midwife replied, No, No, she did not love any such Sights. The Informant taking Notice of a very outrageous Quarrel betwixt them, Advis'd the Woman to have a care what she did to her Husband, being afraid it might go further. The Informant refers herself upon the Particulars above, to the best of her Memory.

The Mark of Y, Mary Hope.
Jurat' Die & Anno Supradict coram me, Ro. L'Estrange.

The Information of Elizabeth Beech, the Daughter of Mary Hope above-mentioned.

This Informant saith upon Oath, That the whole matter in the above-written Information of her Mother is true to her Knowledge.

And saith, that there is a Lock put on to a Back Door of a Low Room where the Midwife Lodg'd, which had only a Bolt before, and that this Informant knew nothing of it till this morning.

The mark of E, Elizabeth Beech.
Jurat' Die & Anno Supradict coram me, Ro. L'Estrange.

Midd. & West. } The Information of Marie Anne Rippault, the Wife of Claude Royer, of the Parish of St. Giles's in the Fields, Goldsmith, Taken upon Oath, February 20, 1687/8.

Saith, That This Informant was told about a Fortnight or Three Weeks before the Murder of Hobry was spoken of, that the said Hobry was returned out of France; about which time, the reputed wife of Hobry came to the Lodgings of This Informant and Discoursed to This Informant in the Presence of this Informant's Mother to the Effect following: "Mon Coquin de Mari est encore Une fois Revenu de France"; and in English, "This Rogue My Husband is come back out of France again. My Cousins are stark mad upon't, but we have Complotted,[17] or laid our Heads together, how to get quit of him." This Informant replying, "Why, what will You do? How will you get quit of him?" The other making Answer, "You shall hear more of That 'ere it be Long." And so she went her way.

And This Informant being Interrogated if she had had any Discourse formerly with the Wife of Hobry concerning the Cousins before spoken of, she made This Answer, That the said Wife of Hobry, having Assisted This Informant about five or six Months since in the Office of a Midwife, among other Discourses said to This Informant to the Purpose following, "These Cousins of Mine are good Husbands, and Industrious Men, and there are enough would Marry them, but we will keep them to ourselves, for Myself and my Daughter" (who both of them had Husbands at the same time). This Informant Asking her how she could think of Marrying Those Young fellows to her Self and her Daughter when they had Husbands already? The Wife of Hobry replying, "Oh Never Trouble yourself for that: *J'ai des ruses de diable pour nous en défaire*"; In English, "I will find out as many Tricks as the Devil himself but we'll get quit of him." This Informant being at that Time Indisposed did not recollect anything further Material in that Discourse.

But This Informant said further, That the Wife of Hobry came to This Informant's Lodgings upon Thursday next after the finding of the Body, about four or five a Clock in the Afternoon, with the Younger of the Two Cousins before spoken of, whose Name, as This Informant remembers, is Favet. This Informant asking the said Woman, "He bien! vous vous êtes défaites de votre Mary"; In English, "Well! You have got quit of Your Husband then?" The Woman Answered, "Oui." And the Yong Favet (or Cousin) stood a little while, Pale, and Surpris'd, but recovering Himself: "Oui," dit il, "nous l'avons envoyé aux Maroquins; & quand il reviendra il nous apportera des Diamants"; In English, "Yes," says he, "we have sent him into the Indies, and when he comes back again he will bring us Diamonds; speaking the words Smiling, and in a way of Raillery.[18] And hereupon, the Wife of Hobry and Young Favet being about to go away, This Informant ask'd them whether they were going? The Woman made Answer, "We are going Home," speaking of the House where Hobry Lodg'd.

And further saith, That upon Thursday above mentioned, about Eleven or Twelve at Noon, the Mother of This Informant said to her to This Effect, "Here has been This Morning the Wife of Hobry, who tells me that she is now got quit of the Rogue her Husband, and that she has sent him away to the Indies." This Informant's Mother Asking her How she had sent him away to the Indies? She said, That they had made him Drunk with Brandy, and put him on Board, and that the Elder Favet had lent her Two Guineas[19] to give to the People to say Nothing of it. Hobry, Pursuing her discourse how she had told her Two Cousins that she should be the ruin of them in Taking their Money, To which she receiv'd for Answer, That if she got but quit of her Husband, they could earn more Money.

And This Informant called also to Mind that she hath heard the said Hobry say, several Months since, many Times, That she would be the Death of her Husband, and that she had it several times in her Thoughts to Strangle him and put him into a Common Shore[20] near at hand to her Lodgings, but that it was too Little, for she had Measur'd it; and she was Resolv'd to Cut him in Pieces, or to Dispatch him some other way.

Marie Anne Rippault.
*Jurat' Die & Anno Supradicto coram m*e, Ro. L'Estrange.

Midd. & West. } The Information of Joan Rippault, of the Parish of St. Giles's in the Fields, taken upon Oath, February 20, 1687/8.

Saith, That she hath many times heard the Wife of Denis Hobry exclaim against her Husband, calling him Drunkard, and Lewd Names; and that within the Compass of Five or Six Months last past, she this Informant hath heard the said wife of Hobry say (meaning her Husband) that she would kill him, and that she has had it in her head to Kill him, and cast him *dans l'Égout*, that is to say, in the Common Shore, but that upon measuring the Passage, she found it was too narrow for him.

And saith, that the said Wife of Hobry, telling this Informant at a time uncertain (but since Hobry's last Return out of France), that the Villain her Husband was now return'd out of France, and that her Little Cousins (speaking of the Two Brothers that passed under the Name of Favet) were very much troubled at it; but saying withal, speaking of the Two Brothers, "We have been advising together how to get rid of him."

And saith, that upon Thursday, in the Week when the Body was said to be found, the said Wife of Hobry came alone to this Informant in a Low Chamber, saying after this manner to her, "My Daughter has bid me come and tell you something concerning my Husband." This Informant asking what it was, the other replied, "I have sent my Husband to the Indies, and I have given Fifty Guineas to put him abroad, and to send him away." This Informant asking her if she had so much Money; she replied, Yes, she had gathered it together, saying over and above, That a Kinsman of Hobry had help'd to make him drunk, and so got him abroad. "And without the help of Hobry's Kinsman, I could have done nothing. I borrow'd two Guineas more of *Le Grand* Cousin for People to keep Hobry quiet in the Ship if he should be troublesome." Pursuing this Discourse and saying further, that she told the Two Brothers this drawing of Money from them would be their Ruin. To which one of them replied, "Get quit of your Husband, and we can get more Money."

And further, that the Wife of Hobry came toward the Evening to the Lodgings of this Informant, with the Younger Favet in her Company, to whom the Daughter of this Informant said somewhat to this purpose, "Well! You have got clear of your Husband then?" The Wife replying, "Yes, we have sent him for the Indies," and the Younger Favet, saying thereupon, "We have sent him to the Maroquins to look for Diamonds."

Joan Rippault.
Jurat' Die & Anno Supradict coram me, Ro. L'Estrange.

The Information of Claude Poullet of Long Acre, Enamel Painter, taken upon Oath, February 20, 1687/8.

Saith, That about five Months since, this Informant heard the

Wife of Hobry talking Bitterly against her Husband to Mademoiselle Marie Anne Rippault, among other matters, in Words to this Effect, "I have had it several Times in my Thought to Strangle that Husband of mine, and to throw him into the Common Shore before my Door, but I have taken measure of this Place, and I find it is too little to receive the Body, unless I should cut him all to pieces. But I must do it some other way."

C. Poullet.
Jurat' Die & Anno Supradict coram me, Ro. L'Estrange.

Midd. & West. } The Information of Margaret Vasal, of the Parish of St. Anne, Westminster, taken upon Oath, February 6, 1687/9.

Saith, That Yesterday was Sennight,[21] Dame Hobry, a Midwife, came after Mass to the House of this Informant, being formerly known to this Informant, and ask'd to Dine with her, For she was loath to go home to Dinner because there was somebody she had no mind to see. She stayed Dinner, and told this Informant that she was going into the Country the next day to lay a Lady of Quality; this Informant telling her she would lose those in Town that had occasion to make use of Her. Hobry Answering, That would make amends for all. Hobry had at that Time a little Office of our Blessed Lady[22] in her hand, and thereupon told her, this Informant, that it was the first Present that Hobry had made her, upon which Words she fetch'd a Deep Sigh, and told this Informant, that her Husband had threaten'd to Dispatch her in Three or Four days.

After this, "Ah my dear Lady," says she, "I know you well enough to be a Person that I may trust my Life in your hands." This Informant asking her immediately, "How your Life? Pray will you explain yourself. You Fright me. What's the matter?" "Well," says Hobry, "Upon pain of Eternal Damnation, lift up your hand, and promise you'll never discover it, but keep it as secret as if 'twere under the seal of Confession." And fetching a deep Sigh, "I have murder'd that miserable man," she cried. This Informant calling out to her, "Miserable Wretch, what have you done?" and bid her be gone. She would have nothing to do with her. Hobry crying out, She was Lost, She was mad, and other Words of Desperation; this Informant seeming not to believe her. Hobry told her that she had strangled him with his Cravat.

Hobry told this Informant further that the Landlady of the House came into her Chamber and ask'd if it were not a Shame that her Husband should be abed at that time of day. Hobry telling the Landlady that he had been out Late and bid her let him lie asleep, whereupon the Landlady went away.

And further, Hobry told this Informant that she had declar'd the Murder to her Two Cousins and begg'd their help to carry him away, but they told her that for the whole World they would have nothing to do in't. And upon this, Hobry went away crying.

And that upon Thursday Last about Nine in the Morning, Hobry came again to this Informant, and this Informant spoke softly to her, "O thou wretched Creature, art thou not content to murder thy Husband, without cutting him to pieces!" Hobry replying to this Informant that She had not cut him to pieces. And in Proof of it, she said, That This was a Lord, with several Rings upon his Finger, and his Head was found in the Park. But she said further, that she had caus'd him to be Buried by two of his Particular Friends, and that the doing of it cost her Fifty Pieces, and there was an End of him. But for her own Part, she was a lost Woman.

This Informant told her, 'twas impossible for her to Bury her Husband and nobody to take Notice of it, for she could not carry him out alone. But she said, "Yes," he was Buried, and that in Three or Four days she would tell her where he was Buried.

Margaret Vasal.
Jurat' Die & Anno Supradict coram me, Ro. L'Estrange.

Midd. & West. } The Information of James Lorraine, of the Parish of St. James, Westminster, Surgeon, taken upon Oath, February 3, 1687/8.

Saith, That about Three Months since, this Informant had some Discourse with a French Midwife, and ask'd her what was become of her Husband. She made Answer, she would give a good deal to have him Drown'd or Kill'd.

And further, that on this Last Wednesday he went to the House where the said Midwife Lodg'd, and missing of her Husband, left a Chalk upon the Door of Direction, where Denis Hobry might come to this Informant; and according to the Appointment of the above-said Direction upon the Door, the Wife of the said Hobry came to this Informant, of whom the said Informant inquired, What was become of her Husband? Who Answered, That he was afraid of an Arrest and dared not show himself. This Informant Answering, that he would show him where he would be safe and try to make up the Bus'ness; the said Midwife Answering, that she would bring him Word the next morning. On Thursday morning (Yesterday) the said Informant met her at Chapel, who asking again after her Husband, received for Answer, That he was gone to the Indies, and he should never see him more.

This Informant ask'd her this Morning before two of his Majesty's Justices of Peace, what was become of her Husband? She said She could not tell him, but Such a One would give him a particular Account of it, mentioning a Person, whom this Informant took to be Yard.

And saith, That this Informant being Interrogated if he knew any Mark about the Body of Denis Hobry to Distinguish him particularly from another Man. This Informant saith, That he remembered that he had a Scar upon One Hand, and since the Delivering of the said Evidence, He, This Informant, hath been to see the said Body and Limbs where they lay Expos'd, and told Sir Robert Clark, one of his Majesty's Justices of the Peace, with the Officer that show'd the Body, and other Persons that were there Present, that if This was the Body, and Those the Limbs of Denis Hobry, there would be found a Scar upon such a Part of the Hand; and upon the Sight of the Limbs, there was a Scar to be seen upon the right Hand, as This Informant had told Sir Robert Clark and Others before, who likewise saw the said Scar with This Informant.

J. Lorraine.
Jurat' Die & Anno Supradict Coram Nobis,[23]
Ro. L'Estrange, Pet. Lugg.

Midd. & West. } The Information of Anthony Matson, Beadle[24] of the Duchy-Liberty[25] in the Strand.

Saith, That by the order of Mr. Thomas Harris, High Constable of the Hundred[26] of Oswalston, This Informant caused Night Men[27] to come and search the House of Office[28] belonging to the House of Mr. Defresneau, near Exeter-Change, where this Informant attended accordingly and saw the taking up of a Head out of the said House of Office, in a Cloth, about a Fortnight since, which This Informant Carried to his own House and there Caus'd it to be Wash'd, and afterward by the order of the High Constable Carried it to a Body at St. Giles's Bone-House.[29] This Informant having had the said Head in his Custody all the While, from the taking it up to the Delivery of it to the said Bone-House.

Ant. Matson.
Jurat' Die & Anno Supradict Coram Me, Ro. L'Estrange.

Midd. & West. } The Information of Giles Malvault &c. And Mary Hope, Taken upon Oath, February 6, 1687/8.

They say Jointly and Severally, that having been up at St. Giles's Church together to see the Head of a Man that lies there Exposed, They These Informants Declare that they knew the Person of Denis Hobry, Reputed the Husband of a French Midwife, and that they Know That to have been the Head and Face of Denis Hobry.

Giles Malvault, The Mark of Mary Hope.
Jurat' Die & Anno Supradict Coram Me, R. L'Estrange.

Midd. & West. } The Examination of Mary the Wife of Lewis Pottron of the Parish of S. Giles's in the Fields, taken February 3, 1687/8.

That she, this Examinate, was at the House of Mr. Hope, where her Father and her Mother lodged, upon Wednesday last, and her Mother likewise in Company, she and this Examinate going thither together. And that this Informant went thither to pay some Money owing for Rent, there being Twelve Shillings due, and Eight Shillings paid. And this Examinate saith, That she was not there Yesterday.

And saith, That this Examinate went to the House of the said Mr. Hope upon Monday last in the Morning, and that her only Business was to see her Mother and that there was no Discourse of her Father.

And saith, That upon Tuesday, the Mother of this Examinate was about Noon (as this Examinate remembers) at the Lodgings of this Examinate, telling this Examinate That there was a great Noise in the Street about a Dead Body that was found, saying, It was a sad thing; and this Examinate answered, That she had heard of it too. And that this is all the Examinate remembers of the said Discourse.

And saith, being interrogated, If she, this Examinate, ever spoke of her Husband's allowing Thirty Shillings to her Father-in-Law Hobry to buy Clothes or to that Effect, and that if the Money were lost, it would be a good Riddance. This Examinate saith, That she said nothing to that Purpose.

And this Examinate being asked if she gave her Opinion for her Mother not to appear 'til her Father-in-Law was gone, This Examinate positively denied her having said anything to that Purpose.

And saith, being interrogated, When she last saw her Father at his Lodgings at Mr. Hope's, That it was upon Sunday last Sennight.

And being interrogated, If ever she saw her Mother in any other Lodging when she lay from Home, saith, That she hath not heard where her Mother Lodged at any time since her lodging with Mrs. Hope, but only once or twice, as she believes, in Phoenix Alley.

The Mark of X, Mary Pottron.
Die & Anno Supradict coram me, Ro. L'Estrange.

Midd. & West. } The further Examination of Mary Pottron, February 5, 1687/8.

Saith, that this Examinate hath several times heard her Father-in-law Denis Hobry, say to this Purpose, That he would be the death of this Informant's Mother. And hath likewise heard her Mother say, That Denis Hobry had often threatened it, but that this Examinate never heard her Mother speak of any purpose she had to kill her Husband.

And saith, That this Examinate hath not seen the Dead Body of her Father; neither was she any ways Consenting or Privy to any Violence upon him, but that she hath observed her Mother to be very much Disordered in her Mind for about a Week last past. And that she, this Examinate, asking her Mother what she ailed, received for an Answer, She was not well.

And being interrogated, If she, this Examinate, knew one Matthew Darney, a Joiner, or one David Foster, a Joiner also, She, this Examinate, made answer, That she knew neither the One nor the Other.

The Mark of X, Mary Pottron.
Capt'[30] *Die & Anno Supradict coram me*, Ro. L'Estrange.

Midd. & West. } The Examination of John Defermeau, Servant to Martin Dubois, of the Parish of S. Clement's Danes, Weaver, February 3, 1687/8.

Saith, that upon Monday Morning last, the Mother of this Examinate came to his Master to have him Home with her, to speak to one that she could not understand, this Examinate's Mother not understanding English; and about Nine or Ten o' Clock, this Examinate went with his Mother to her Lodgings, but the Man she spoke of did not come.

This Examinate stayed at his Mother's Lodgings about half an Hour and went then to Covent Garden, where this Examinate stayed 'til Seven or Eight o' Clock at Night, where he spoke to no Body, but about that Hour returned Home to his Mother's, and saw his Mother, and stayed about a quarter of an Hour, and then went and lay under a Stall over against the Rose Tavern all Night. About Seven o' Clock in the Morning, he went again to his Mother's, where he saw his Mother, and saw his Sister also that Morning, meeting her in New Street in the Strand.

Capt' Die & Anno Supradict coram me, Ro. L'Estrange.

Midd. & West. } The further Examination of John Defermeau, Servant to Martin Dubois, &c. February 5, 1687/8.

Saith, that the Mother of this Examinate (Mary Hobry) hath said several times That she was afraid her Husband would Kill her and that he Threatened her several mornings when he had been all night at a Debauch.

And that upon Monday last, the Mother of this Examinate fetched him from his Master's home to her Lodgings, where she told this Informant that his Father was dead, and he must help to carry him away, showing the Body (as it lay upon the Bed) to this Examinate, who said he would not help her, and ask'd her, why she did such a Thing? Whereupon she said to this Examinate, as at other times, That she was continually in fear of him, and asked this Examinate what she should do with him. And hereupon this Examinate offer'd to go away, but she hindered him from going out, and then she would have this Examinate help her to Quarter the Body, which this Examinate refused and did not so much as touch it, but went away into the next Room, his Mother saying she would do it herself then. So she took a Knife, and afterwards brought the Head into t'other Room, where this Examinate was. Going back again, and cutting off the Legs, the Arms, and the Thighs and bringing them into the Room one after another, this Examinate pressing to be gone, but she bade him stay and not leave her alone. After this she put the Body in a Rag and took it up with her Petticoat, and, after several Refusals to help and go along with her, This Examinate went with her at last, she saying she was loath to go alone, upon which she went away with the Body into Parker's Lane, and there threw it behind a Dunghill.

After she was rid of the Body, she went back and took the Thighs and carried them to the Savoy and put them into the House of Office, and from thence returning, she carried the Legs and Arms to the same place, this Examinate going along with her.

And after that, she went back for the Head, and propounded the putting of it into a Common House of Office. This Examinate telling her that he was afraid to meddle with it, his Mother replying, That if she should be taken, he would be in no danger because he did not touch it. From thence she went back again and went to Bed.

This Examinate being Interrogated, Whether he ever heard how his own Father came by his Death and whether his Mother had ever been Question'd about it? He made Answer, That he hath heard it said by some that he died of a Wound; by others, that he died of a Natural Death; but never heard any thing of it Charg'd upon his Mother.

And saith, That upon Monday last this Examinate asked his Mother if his Sister knew of his Father's being Dead, who made Answer, Yes she did. And saith, That he knew not any such Person as Matthew Darney, or David Foster.

The Mark of X, John Defermeau.
Capt' Die & Anno Supradict coram me, Ro. L'Estrange.

Midd. & West. } The Examination of Mary Hobry, of the Parish of S. Martin's in the Fields, taken February 4, 1687/8.

Saith, that this Examinate was Married to Denis Hobry about four years since, and that after the Solemn Marriage of the Church, he the said Denis Hobry, with Curses and Imprecations[31] denied the said Marriage and cast all sort of Infamous Reproaches upon this Examinate. This being the occasion of all his Outrages, because this Examinate would not submit to a compliance with him in Villainies contrary to Nature. In the miserable Condition above spoken of, this Examinate liv'd for the space of Three Months, under Beatings and Revilings, going every day in danger of her Life.

This Examinate being brought to a Desperation by this miserable Usage, retir'd into a Private Chamber and left him, living very close for a matter of Four Months. When her said Husband going into France, she appeared abroad[32] again, and followed her Affairs. This continued for about Two Years, he being most of the time in France.

After this Examinate had been Two years Married, and Suffered and Parted as above, her said Husband came Three or Four times to her, making large Promises how good a Husband he would be and how kindly he would live with her, and in fine, desir'd that by all means they might live together again, declaring that he had Confess'd his Sins to Almighty God, and that he would be another Man. To which this Examinate yielded, upon Condition that he should declare the same before a Priest and Two Witnesses, and own That this Examinate was his Lawful Wife, which Declaration was Made and Sign'd before Father Gaspar and Enter'd in Writing upon a Register.

This Examinate had not been above two or three days with him again before he began to use her as formerly and continued his Ill usage for a matter of two Months upon the same Subject and Occasion as formerly. About that time he went away into France, and carried all away that he could, to the wearing Clothes and Necessaries of this Examinate. After Three Month's stay, he returned again, and upon the same Instances and Promises as before, this Examinate submitted to accompany with him again. And this way of Life this Examinate led from time to time, till this last unhappy Separation; her Husband continuing in the same way still of Leaving her and Coming again and using her Ill.

This Examinate finding herself in this hopeless Condition, and under frequent Temptations of putting some violent end to her Misfortunes, she rather chose to make Trial if she could prevail upon him to agree to a Final Separation, and pressed it upon him several times with great Earnestness; and he still refused it with Outrages of Language and Actions, telling this Examinate he would be the Ruin of her.

This Informant finding herself without Remedy, in a Distraction of Thoughts, and under the Affliction of Bodily Distempers contracted by her said Husband's dissolute Course of Life, her Frailty was no longer able to resist the Temptations of dangerous Thoughts; sometimes this Examinate was thinking to go into some other Part of the World and leave him; and other while she was tempted to think of Extremities either upon her Husband or upon Herself and often told her Husband plainly, That she would Kill him if he followed that Course. This Examinate having lamented her Condition to others of her acquaintance, and telling them she was not able to live this course of Life, and that Mischief would come on't at last. But after all these dangerous Words and Menaces, this Examinate upon Recollection bethought herself of the Horridness of the Sin, and by God's Grace was diverted from executing so wicked a Resolution.

And saith, That this Examinate was transported about two or three Months since to that degree of Rage and Impatience that she took a Knife once with a Resolution to Kill her Husband, but retracted and did not go forward with it. And that she took the same Desperate Resolution again, a matter of fifteen Days after, proposing both times to do it in the Night, but by the Grace of God she was then again restrained.

And saith, That she this Examinate told her Husband in the morning, both these times, the Resolution she had taken over Night to Kill him in his Bed, but he made slight of it and told this Examinate she durst not do it.

And saith, That on the very Evening before this Examinate's Husband went last into France, this Examinate spoke to her Husband to this effect: "Hobry, you are now going into France. Pray bethink yourself and lead a better Life; for when you come back again, if you Treat me as you did formerly, I do not know what Extremities you may Provoke me to." Whereupon he promis'd this Examinate with dreadful Oaths that he would be a good Husband to her.

The Husband of this Examinate returned out of France, and came to this Informant's Lodgings about three Weeks since, when this Informant received him after the following manner, saying to him, "Hobry, you are welcome, and pray you will change your course of Life now that we may live Comfortably together." "Yes," saith he, "upon condition you will put me in Clothes, and furnish me with what I want." (He having got Money in France and spent it to the last Farthing.) This Informant told him she could not supply him at that Rate, for Times were hard, and she had much ado to Live and pay Honest Debts. This Examinate's Husband replying to this effect, "If you do not do as I say, I will be a worse Husband to you than ever I was." This Examinate told him she did not know what she should do with him for his Barbarous Usages had made her Mad. And his way was so often as he asked anything of this Informant that she could not supply him with, he would abuse her, and say he would make her repent of it. And this Examinate hath been told by one Yard that her Husband said in his hearing, That he would be the Destruction of her. This was the Course of Life this Examinate led, till this Thursday last was Sennight, upon which day this Examinate had no Thought of offering any Violence to her Husband, but went to Bed about her usual hour, Ten o' Clock, leaving the Fore door open for him when he should come home.

About Five in the Morning, the Husband of this Examinate came in, outrageously in Choler, and more than half Drunk. This Examinate was asleep, till her Husband Waked her with a heavy Blow with his Fist upon her Stomach, and said to her, "What! you are Drunk?" This Examinate Answering, "No, you are Drunk. You'd never come home at Five o' Clock in the Morning else; you have been among base Company." He made Answer, "I have been among Bougres[33] and Rogues that have made me Mad, and you shall pay for 't." Whereupon he gave this Examinate another violent Blow upon the Breast. With That, this Examinate turn'd from him and fell a weeping. And this Examinate declared in the Presence of Almighty God That she had not as yet any Purpose or Thoughts of attempting upon his Life.

While this Examinate was weeping, her Husband took her in

his Arms and Press'd her so hard that she could not fetch her Breath and that the Blood started out of her Mouth. Immediately upon this, he attempted the Forcing of this Examinate to the most Unnatural of Villainies and acted such a Violence upon her Body in despite of all the Opposition that she could make as forced from her a great deal of Blood. This Examinate crying out to her Landlady, who was (as she believes) out of distance of hearing her. This Examinate told him, "I will immediately Rise and Complain to the Neighbors." Whereupon he took her Forcibly by the Arm and threw her down on the Bed, being before sitting up to rise; and after this, Bit her like a Dog &c. — this Examinate saying to him, "Am I to lead this Life forever?" "Yes, and a worse too, ere it be long; you had best look to yourself," and upon these words he fell asleep.

Upon this Respite the Examinate lay in Torments both of Body and of Mind, thinking with herself, "What will become of me? What am I to do! Here am I Threatened to be Murder'd, and I have no way in the World to Deliver myself, but by Beginning with him," and immediately upon these Thoughts, this Examinate started up and took one of his Garters, which was *de Ficelle*, or Pack thread,[34] put it double about his Neck *et la noua en serrant de toute sa force*, and so tied it, and drew it as hard as she could, *de sorte qu'il en est tout Étranglé dans un quart d'heure, sans beaucoup de Résistance.* Insomuch that he was Choked with it in a Quarter of an hour, with little resistance. The Body rested there till Monday, only this Examinate took off the Pack thread within a Quarter of an Hour after his Death and in hopes that he was not yet Dead, repenting with all her Heart that she had been guilty of such a Heinous Sin, and tried Brandy to bring him to Life again.

Upon Monday Morning, January 30, 1687/8 this Examinate went to the House of Monsieur Dubois, living in the Strand, to desire him he would give leave for the Son of this Examinate to go home with his Mother, upon occasion of speaking with an English Man that this Examinate could not Understand, her Son speaking both French and English, the Youth being an Apprentice to the said

Dubois, and of Age, Thirteen Years and an half. This Examinate took her Son with her home to her Lodgings, in Expectation of the Englishman before spoken of, who did not come.

This Examinate fetched her Son on purpose to have his Assistance about the conveying away of her Husband's Body; and this Examinate told her Son of a great Calamity that was fallen out, which the Child was very much surprised at, and being showed the Body, ready to sink down at the Spectacle. But this Examinate put the Boy to an Oath forty times over to say nothing of it, and he swore he would be torn in Pieces first. And asked this Examinant, "Mother, What will you do? Shift for yourself, and go out of the Land, for if you are once taken you'll never get off." This Informant answering, She had no Money for a Voyage, and she could think of no way better than to cut off the Quarters and disperse the Parts in several Places, so as People should not know whose Body it was. Besides That, she herself could carry them off and dispose of them much better, her Son saying that he was afraid to meddle with the carrying of them.

This Examinate hereupon, about Four or Five that Afternoon, having taken a Resolution of cutting off the Quarters to make it more Portable, took a Knife, and first cut off the Head, after that the Arms, and then the Thighs, and last the Legs, some Drops of Blood coming from the Neck, but very little or none at all from the rest.

The Quarters being cut off by Eight in the Evening, or thereabouts, this Examinate bethought herself how to convey them away, and first took up the Body which she put into a Piece of Linen and carried it before her in her Petticoat. The Examinate passed through Castle Street into Drury Lane, and thence into Parker's Lane, and so among the Dunghills, and there left it, her Son following to give notice if any Body came.

The Body being thus disposed of, this Examinate, with her Son, went back and took the Thighs in a Linen Cloth. This Examinate carrying them likewise, and her Son following in like manner, as before; and this Examinate threw them into a House of Office at the Savoy, and immediately went back with her Son again and fetched the Legs and the Arms, her Son following her to the Savoy again and put them also into the House of Office.

The Quarters being carried away, as above, and only the Head remaining, this Examinate advised with her Son, What they should do with the Head? who advised her to throw it into the Water. But this Examinate was then afraid it would be found and known. And said, She would rather cast it into the House of Office of a Friend of hers, meaning Defresneau, a Fringe-Maker, over against the Savoy, to which Place she went accordingly, her Son following her, and cast it into the second House of Office, there being two belonging to the Place.

And saith, That upon Tuesday Morning last, Mary Potter (or Pottron), the Daughter of this Examinate, came to this Examinate's Lodgings, and in Discourse said something to this Purpose, "What is become of Hobry, where is he? Yard says he is gone for the Indies." This Examinate made Answer, That she had not seen him for Four or Five Days. The Examinate put her Daughter off at first, but came soon after to tell her the Truth of the Matter.

And saith, That this Examinate, thereupon, told her daughter the whole Truth of the Matter, as is reported above; her said Daughter ready to fall down at the hearing of it and transported with Astonishment, asking this Examinate, What they should do to keep it Private. This Examinate charging her to say nothing of it, and the Daughter replying, That she would be burned first, but that if it were any other Person than her Mother, she would discover it herself, but since her Mother was concerned, she would never open her Lips of it.

And this Examinate being interrogated, How it came to pass that she, this Examinate, being of the Communion of the Church of Rome, came to throw the Quarters of her Husband into a House of Office at the Savoy, which was a way to bring so great a Scandal upon the Religion she professed, by laying the Murder at the Door of the Professors of that Religion? This Examinate made Answer, That she had no Thoughts in what she did as to that Matter more than to part the Limbs and the Body, and hoped the Water might carry them away.

And being interrogated, If any other Person whatsoever, beside the Persons herein named, was privy to this Practice upon her Husband, or assisting to the Conveying away of the Body, this Examinate answered, That there was no Person privy to the Secret nor any Person assisting to it besides the Persons within mentioned.

Jo. Ridley. Mary Hobry.
Capt' Die & Anno Supradict coram me, Ro. L'Estrange.

I have heard the Information of Mrs. Mary Hobry, consisting of Two Sheets and one Page, read in English, and have signed the Papers, and do hereby declare, That I have truly Expounded them in French to Mrs. Mary Hobry, according to the best of my Knowledge.

Jo. Ridley.

J' avoue que ce qui est écrit sur ces deux feuilles de Papier, & une page, est véritable; selon ce que Monsieur Ridley me L'a expliqué, en Français.

Marie Hobry.

Postscript

Here's a Just and Punctual Account of all the Informations in the Cause of Mary Hobry; and I do here Appeal to the Informants themselves, That I have dealt Candidly and Conscientiously both in the Publishing and in the Taking of them. Nay, to prevent the uttermost Spite of Envy and Calumny, they had almost all of them, as many Witnesses to the Fairness of them as the Room would hold, where I took them. And so far from Extorting any Evidence, That the Mother's and the Son's were purely Confession. The Woman, 'tis true, was examined in Private, for fear of any un-seasonable Discovery of what she might declare. But before I put so much as one Question to her, I rendered her so particular an

Account of the Points in Evidence against her that she gave herself for Lost, without any Hope either of an Acquittal or of a Pardon, and so frankly told me from Point to Point the whole Series of the Narration, as it is here set down. But still that which stuck with other People, stuck with Me: That is to say, How all this could be done without Complices?[35] Now the Boy's Story lay as yet in the Dark, and his doubling in his Tale gave manifestly to understand, That there was a Mystery still Undiscovered. He denied all upon Friday. Upon Saturday, his Mother declared herself. Upon Sunday the Boy denied all again, 'till upon the Hint given him of his dining with his Mother, her drawing the Curtain of the Bed and showing him the Body of his Murdered Father upon that Monday when the Body was quartered, He fell a Weeping and told an orderly Story, without any Mincing of Matters, from the very Act of quartering him, to the disposing of the Body, the Limbs and the Head, into those Places where they were afterwards found. This Relation of his is so agreeable to his Mother's in the Order and Manner of it, that it is almost impossible to be False. And to anyone that considers the Bulk and Weight of the Trunk of an ordinary Man, without either Head, Arms, Thighs or Legs, a Woman's carrying such a Burden in the Truss of her Petticoat will be found no greater a Wonder than he shall see ten times over in one Day's Walk betwixt the Old Exchange and Westminster.

In the Woman's Story, I have done all the Right that Honestly I could to the Compassionable Condition of an Unhappy Wretch, but without Extenuating the Horror of Wickedness. I have, since that time, Inquir'd into the Humor and Character of the Husband, and his Acquaintance report him at all hands to have been a Libertine and Debauchee to the Highest Degree, but Drunk or Sober, without any Malice. This is, in fine, an Impartial Report of the Case. It falls to the Midwife's Lot to Suffer Alone, but if she had stood her Trial, so that the Evidence against her had been left to take its Course, it would not have gone much better with some of her Companions than it did with the Miserable Creature herself.

The End.

A pittileſſe Mother.

That moſt vnnaturally at one time, murt
two of her owne Children at Aɕon within ſixe miles f
London vppon holy thurſday laſt 1 6 1 6. *The ninth of May*
Beeing a Gentlewonan named *Margret Vincent,* wife of
Mʳ. *Iaruis Vincent,* of the ſame Towne.
With her Examination, Confeſſion and true diſcouery of a
proceedings in the ſaid bloody accident.

Whereunto is added *Anderſons* Repentance
was executed at Tiburne the 18. of May being Whitſon-Eue.
Written in the time of his priſonment in Newgate.

A pittilesse Mother, title page. By permission of the Houghton Library,
Harvard University.

A pittilesse Mother. That most unnaturally at one time, murthered two of her owne Children

at Acton within six miles of London upon holy Thursday[1] last 1616, The ninth of May, Being a Gentlewoman named Margret Vincent, wife of Mr. Jarvis Vincent, of the same Town. With her Examination, Confession and true discovery of all the proceedings in the said bloody accident.[2]

Whereunto is added Anderson's Repentance, who was executed at Tyburn[3] the 18th of May being Whitsun-Eve.[4] Written in the time of his prisonment in Newgate. (1616)

How easy are the ways unto evil, and how soon are our minds (by the Devil's enticement) withdrawn from goodness. Leviathan,[5] the Archenemy of mankind, hath set such and so many bewitching snares to entrap us that unless we continually stand watching with careful diligence to shun them, we are like to cast the principal substance of our reputation upon the wrack of his ensnaring engines.[6] As for example, A Gentlewoman, ere now fresh in memory, presents her own ruin among us, whose life's overthrow may well serve for a clear looking Glass to see a woman's weakness in: how soon and apt she is won unto wickedness, not only to the body's overthrow but the soul's danger. God of his mercy keep us all from the like willfulness.

At Acton, some six miles westward from London, this unfortunate Gentlewoman dwelled, named Margret Vincent, the wife of Mr. Jarvis Vincent, Gentleman, who by unhappy destiny marked to mischance, I here now make the subject of my Pen and publish her hard hap[7] unto the world, that all others may shun the like occasions by which she was overthrown.

This Margret Vincent before named, of good parentage, born in the County of Hartford, at a town named Rickmansworth, her name from her parents Margret Day, of good education, graced with good parts from her youth that promised succeeding virtues in her age, if good luck had served; for, being discreet, civil, and of a modest conversation, she was preferred in marriage to this Gentleman Mr. Vincent, with whom she lived in good estimation, well beloved and much esteemed of all that knew her for her modest and seemly carriage, and so might have continued to her old age had not this bloody accident committed upon her own children blemished the glory of the same.

But now mark (gentle Reader) the first entrance into her life's overthrow, and consider with thyself how strangely the Devil here set in his foot and what cunning instruments he used in his assailments.[8] The Gentlewoman, being witty and of a Ripe understanding, desired much conference in religion, and being careful as it seemed of her soul's happiness, many times resorted to Divines[9] to have instructions to salvation (little thinking to fall into the hands of Roman[10] Wolves as she did) and to have the Sweet Lamb, her soul, thus entangled by their persuasions.

Twelve or Fourteen Years had she lived in marriage with her husband well beloved, having for their comforts diverse pretty children between them, with all other things in plenty, as health, riches, and such like, to increase concord, and no necessity that might be hindrance to contentment. Yet at last there was such traps and engines set that her quiet was caught and her discontent set at liberty. Her opinion of the true faith (by the subtle sophistry of some close Papists) was converted to a blind belief of bewitching heresy, for they have such charming persuasions that hardly the female kind can escape their enticements, of which weak sex they continually make prize of and by them lay plots to ensnare others, as they did by this deceived Gentlewoman. For she, good soul, being made a bird of their own feather, desired to beget more of the same kind, and from time to time made persuasive arguments to win her husband to the same opinion, and deemed it a meritorious deed to charge his conscience with that infectious burden of Romish opinions, affirming by many false reasons that his former life had been led in blindness, and that she was appointed by the holy Church to show him the light of true understanding. These and such like were the instructions she had given her to entangle her husband in and win him if she might to their blind heresies.

But he, good Gentleman, ever deeply grounded in the right Faith of Religion than to be thus so easily removed, grew regardless of her persuasions, accounting them vain and frivolous, and she undutiful to make so fond[11] an attempt, many times snubbing her with some few unkind speeches, which bred in her heart a purpose of more extremity. For having learned this maxim of their Religion, that it was meritorious, yea and pardonable, to take away the lives of any opposing Protestants were it of any degree whatsoever, in which resolution or bloody purpose she long stood upon, and at last (only by the Devil's temptation) resolved the ruin of her own children, affirming to her conscience these reasons: that they were brought up in blindness and darksome errors, hoodwinked (by her husband's instructions) from the true light, and therefore to save their souls (as she vainly thought) she purposed to become a Tigerous Mother, and so wolfishly to commit the murder of her own flesh and blood. In which opinion she steadfastly continued, never relenting according to nature, but casting about to find time and place for so wicked a deed, which unhappily fell out as after followed.

It so chanced that a discord arose between the two towns of Acton and Willesden about a certain common, bordering between them, where the town of Acton as it seems having the more right unto it, by watching defended it a time from the others' Cattle. Whereupon the women of the same town, having likewise a willingness to assist their husbands in the same defense, appointed a day for the like purpose, which was the Ascension Day last past, commonly called Holy Thursday, falling upon the 9th of the last passed month of May, which day (as ill chance would have it) was the fatal time appointed for her to act this bloody Tragedy, whereon she made her husband fatherless of two as pretty children as ever came from a woman's womb.

Upon the Ascension Day aforesaid, after the time of Divine service, the women of the town being gathered together about their promised business, some of them came to Mistress Vincent, and according to promise desired her company, who, having a mind as then more settled on bloody purposes than country occasions, feigned an excuse of ill at ease, and not half well, desired pardon of them, and offering her Maid in her behalf, who being a good, apt, and willing Servant was accepted of, and so the Townswomen, mis-doubting[12] no such hard accident as after happened, proceeded in their aforesaid defenses. The Gentlewoman's husband being also from home, in whose absence, by the fury and assistance of the Devil, she enacted this woeful accident in form and manner following.

This Mistress Vincent, now deserving no name of Gentlewoman, being in her own house fast locked up, only her two small Children, the one of the age of five years, the other hardly two years old, unhappily brought to that age to be made away by their own Mother, who by nature should have cherished them with her own body, as the Pelican that pecks her own breast to feed her young ones with her blood.[13] But she, more cruel than the Viper, the envenomed Serpent, the Snake or any Beast whatsoever, against all kind[14] takes away those lives to whom she first gave life.

Being alone (as I said before) assisted by the Devil, she took the youngest of the two, having a countenance so sweet that might have begged mercy at a tyrant's hand, but she regarding neither the pretty smiles it made nor the dandling before the mother's face, nor anything it could do, but like a fierce and bloody Medea,[15] she took it violently by the throat, and with a Garter taken from her leg, making thereof a noose and putting the same about her Child's sweet neck, she in a wrathful manner drew the same so close together, that in a moment she parted the soul and body, and without any terror of Conscience, she laid the lifeless Infant, still remaining warm upon her bed, and with a relentless countenance looking thereon, thinking thereby she had done a deed of immortality. Oh blinded ignorance! Oh inhuman devotion! Purposing by this to merit heaven, she hath deserved (without true repentance) the reward of damnation.

This Creature not deserving Mother's name, as I said before, not yet glutted,[16] not sufficed with these few drops of Innocent blood — nay, her own dear blood bred in her own body, cherished in her own womb with much dearness full forty weeks — not satisfied, I say, with this one murder, but she would headlong run unto a second and to heap more vengeance upon her head, she came unto the elder Child, of that small age that it could hardly discern a Mother's cruelty nor understand the fatal destiny fallen upon the other before, which as it were, seemed to smile upon her as though it begged for pity, but all in vain. For so tyrannous was her heart, that without all motherly pity she made it drink of the same bitter cup as she had done the other. For with her garter she likewise pressed out the sweet air of life and laid it by the other upon the bed, sleeping in death together, a sight that might have burst an iron heart in sunder and made the very Tiger to relent.

These two pretty children being thus murdered without all hope of recovery, she began to grow desperate and still to desire more and more blood, which had been a third murder of her own babes had it not been abroad at Nurse[17] and by that means could not be accomplished. Whereupon she fell into a violent rage, purposing as then to show the like mischief upon herself, being of this strange opinion, that she herself by that deed had made Saints of her two children in heaven. So taking the same garter that was the instrument of their deaths and putting the noose thereof about her own neck, she strove therewith to have strangled herself; but nature being weak and flesh frail, she was not able to do it. Whereupon in a more violent fury (still animated forward by instigation of the Devil), she ran into the yard purposing there in a pond to have drowned herself, having not one good motion of Salvation left within her.

But here, good Reader, mark what a happy prevention chanced to preserve her in hope of Repentance, which at that time stayed her from that desperate attempt. The maid, by great fortune, at the very instant of this deed of desperation, returned from the field or Common where she had left most of the neighbors, and coming in at the backside,[18] perceiving her mistress by her ghastly countenance that all was not well and that some hard chance had happened her or hers, demanded how the Children did. "Oh Nan,"[19] quoth she, "never, oh never, shalt thou see thy Tom more," and withal gave the maid a box upon the ear, at which she laid hold upon her Mistress, calling out for help into the Town, whereat divers[20] came running in and after them her husband, within a while after, who finding what had happened, were all so amazed together that they knew not what to do. Some wrung their hands; some wept; some called out for the Neighbors. So general a fear was struck amongst them all that they knew not whether to go nor run, especially the good Gentleman her husband, that seeing his own Children slain, murdered by his Wife and their own Mother, a deed beyond nature and humanity, in which ecstasy of grief at last he broke out in these speeches: "Oh Margret, Margret, how often have I persuaded thee from this damned Opinion, this damned Opinion, that hath undone us all." Whereupon with a ghastly look and fearful eye, she replied thus, "Oh Jarvis, this had never been done if thou had been ruled and by me converted, but what is done is past, for they are Saints in heaven, and I nothing at all repent it." These and such like words passed between them till such time as the Constable and others of the townsmen came in, and according to law carried her before a Justice of the peace, which is a Gentleman named Master Roberts of Willesden, who understanding these heinous offenses rightly according to law and course of Justice, made a Mittimus[21] for her conveyance to Newgate[22] in London, there to remain till the Sessions[23] of her trial. Yet this is to be remembered, that by examination she voluntarily confessed the fact, how she murdered them to save their souls and to make them Saints in heaven, that they might not be brought up in blindness to their own damnation. Oh willful heresy, that ever Christian should in Conscience be thus miscarried! But to be short, she proved herself to be an obstinate Papist, for there was found about her neck a Crucifix, with other relics[24] which she then wore about her, that by the Justice was commanded to be taken away and an English bible[25] to be delivered her to read, the which she with great stubbornness threw from her, not willing as once to look thereupon nor to hear any divine comforts delivered thereout for the succor of her Soul.

But now again to her conveyance towards prison, it being Ascension Day and near the closing of the evening, too late as then to be sent to London, she was by Commandment put to the Constable's keeping for that night, who with a strong watch lodged her in his own house till morning, which was at the Bell in Acton where he dwelled, who showing the part and duty of a good Christian with diverse other of his Neighbors, all that same night plied her with good admonitions, tending to repentance and seeking with great pains to convert her from those erroneous Opinions which she so stubbornly stood in. But it little availed, for she seemed in outward show so obstinate in Arguments that she made small reckoning of repentance nor was a whit sorrowful for the murder committed upon her children but maintained the deed to be meritorious and of high desert.

Oh that the blood of her own body should have no more power to pierce remorse into her Iron-natured heart, when Pagan women that know not God nor have any feeling of his Deity will shun to commit bloodshed, much more of their own seed. The Cannibals that eat one another will spare the fruits of their own bodies; the Savages will do the like; yea, every beast and fowl hath a feeling of nature and according to kind will cherish their young ones. And shall woman, nay, a Christian woman, God's own Image, be more unnatural than Pagan, Cannibal, Savage, Beast or Fowl? It even now makes a trembling fear to beset me to think what an error this unhappy Gentlewoman was bewitched with, a witchcraft begot by hell and nursed by the Romish Sect, from which enchantment God of heaven defend us.

But now again to our purpose, the next day being Friday and the tenth of May, by the Constable Mister Dighton of the Bell in Acton with other of his neighbors, she was conveyed to Newgate in London, where lodging in the Master's side,[26] many people reported to her, as well of her acquaintance as others and as before, with sweet and comfortable persuasions practiced to beget repentance and to be sorry for that which she had committed. But blindness so prevailed that she continued still in her former stubbornness, affirming (contrary to all persuasive reasons) that she had done a deed of charity in making them Saints in heaven that otherwise might have lived to destruction in hell, and likewise refused to look upon any Protestant book, as Bible, Meditation, Prayer book and such like, affirming them to be erroneous and dangerous for any Roman Catholic to look in. Such were the violent opinions she had been instructed in, and with such fervency therein she continued that no dissuasions could withdraw her from them, no, not death itself, being here possessed with such bewitching willfulness.

In this danger of mind continued she all Friday, Saturday, and Sunday. The Sessions drawing near, there came certain Godly Preachers unto her, who prevailed with her by celestial consolations that her heart by degrees became a little mollified and in nature somewhat repentant for these her most heinous offenses.

Her soul a little leaning to salvation encouraged these good men to persevere and go forward into Godly labor, who at last brought her to this opinion, as it was justified by one that came from her in Newgate upon the Monday before the Sessions, that she earnestly believed she had eternally deserved hell fire for the murder of her children and that she so earnestly repented the deed, saying, that if they were alive again, not all the world should procure her to do it. Thus was she truly repentant, to which (no doubt) but by the good means of these Preachers she was wrought unto.

And now to come to a conclusion as well of the discourse as of her life. She deserved death, and both Law and Justice hath awarded her the same, for her examination and free confession needed no Jury; her own tongue proved a sufficient evidence, and her conscience a witness that condemned her. Her judgment and execution she received with a patient mind; her soul no doubt hath got a true penitent desire to be in heaven, and the blood of her two innocent Children so willfully shed (according to all charitable judgments) is washed away by the mercies of God. Forgive and forget her, good Gentlewomen. She is not the first that hath been blemished with blood nor the last that will make a husband wifeless. Her offense was begot by a strange occasion, but buried I hope with true repentance.

Thus Countrymen of England have you heard the ruins of a Gentlewoman, who if Popish persuasions had not been, the world could not have spotted her with the smallest mark of infamy but had carried the name of virtue even unto her grave. And for a warning unto you all, by her example, take heed how you put confidence into that dangerous sect for they surely will deceive you.

FINIS

[Although the pamphlet seems to end at this point, an additional eleven page ballad is attached. This portion, in roman type as opposed to the black letter of the primary narrative, is entitled "Andersons Repentance who, was executed at Tiburne the 18 of May being Whitson even, 1616." In it the speaker bemoans his dissolute life and asks God's and the king's forgiveness. Since this section has no connection to the story of Margret Vincent, I have omitted it.]

Blood for Blood,

OR;

JUSTICE EXECUTED

FOR

Innocent Blood-Shed.

Being a true **Narrative** of
that late horrid Murder, committed by *Mary Cook*, upon her
own and only beloved Child, with
several remarkable paſſages, preceding the fact, as alſo what was
moſt worthy obſervation, during
her Impriſonment, and at her Execution, faithfully communicated
for Publique Satisfaction.

By *N. Partridge*, and *J. Sharp*.

With a Sermon upon the ſame occaſion.

With other Spectaters and Vi-
ſiters whilſt in Priſon, and at her
Execution.

LONDON,
Printed for F. *Smith*, at the *Elephant* and *Caſtle* without *Temple-Bar*; and D. *Newman*, at the *Chy-
rurgions-Arms* in *Little-Brittain*. 1670.

Blood for Blood, title page. By permission of the Syndics of
Cambridge University Library.

Blood for Blood, Or: Justice Executed For Innocent Blood-Shed

Being a true Narrative of that late horrid Murder, committed by Mary Cook, upon her own and only beloved Child, with several remarkable passages, preceding the fact, as also what was most worthy observation, during her Imprisonment, and at her Execution, faithfully communicated for Public Satisfaction. By N. Partridge, and J. Sharp, With a Sermon upon the same occasion. With other Spectators and Visitors whilst in Prison, and at her Execution. (1670)

To the Reader[1]

Courteous Reader,

Here is at length now exposed to public view this brief but true Narrative of that ever to be abhorred cruelty of M. C. in murdering her innocent Babe, which we humbly submit to thy favorable censure and charitable interpretation.

Two reasons especially have drawn it forth:

First, to fulfill the will of the poor creature which was executed, who had an earnest desire at the place and time of her execution to have given glory to God by confessing her sins, accepting her punishment, and giving warning to all the numerous spectators of the evil of sin and the danger of eternal wrath, but natural strength failing her, wished some of us in the Cart[2] with her to have manifested the same then. But the noise of the multitude was such that it could not be done conveniently. Some days passed after before any thoughts were stirred up in us to publish anything of this nature, during which time some of us could have little rest,

189

apprehending some neglect might be imputed unto us, in a business, which for ought we knew might be for general good.

As we would not cover over with gilt or paint rotten Wood or Copper, neither would we bury under dirt the least grain of pure Gold; therefore, we have not taken upon us to pass any judgment upon the dying state of M. C. but leave it unto him who sees and looketh into the hidden man of the heart and weigheth both sins and repentance in the balance of the Sanctuary,[3] and to the judicious Reader, who we hope will measure what is spoken by her and of her by the rate of Christian charity; and as we apprehended in her whilst living great fear and yet greater hopes, so we leave her now dead, hoping that her application to the blood of Christ was sincere (as discovered more at large in the following Narrative), the which blood speaks better things than the blood of Abel. His precious blood crying to God for mercy may outcry the loud cry of the innocent blood shed by her for vengeance.

The second reason was, That this (through the blessing of God) might be a word in season[4] both to the Professors[5] and profane persons in this day of Satan's violent temptations; to Professors, because we find by daily and sad experience, the Devil setting upon those richly laden with choice treasures, with furious assaults. To them therefore speak we (or rather the Lord), look well to your foundation; secure your principles, live in the daily exercise of those rooting graces — humility, self-denial, and repentance — and then grow up in the nutritive graces — faith, hope and love — and to crown all, let integrity and uprightness preserve thee, and so persevere unto the end, the Lord helping thee to set up his watch tower in thy heart. Continually natural reason and common providence may prompt thee to secure and watch thy outward estate, but grace alone instructs thee how to keep thy heart were thy heart danger-free from enmity without and treachery within. Thou hadst then a Plea for the abatement of thy soul's intention herein, but whilst a danger of surprise by both remit no diligence, show me that man or woman whom the impudence of sin and Satan doth not sometimes charge and assault. But if such a one cannot be found, be convinced of thy need of the Divine breastplate, which will not only put temptations back, but force the tempter to surcease his assaults; or if so impudent, notwithstanding, will yet enable thee to shake them off (as St. Paul did the Viper from his hand)[6] unhurt.

And to the profane, that they by reading this sad relation as the consequences of sin (and the awakening Sermon thereunto annexed) may come to know themselves and their unsafe condition whilst in their unregenerate state, and the Spirit of God working with it, they may be thereby provoked to consider their ways and amend them before the day come wherein sinners shall cry out, "Who among us shall dwell with devouring fire? Who shall abide with everlasting burnings? For the day of the Lord will burn as an Oven, and sinners shall be as stubble." Oh! therefore it is to warn them to flee from the wrath to come, and in the bowels of our Lord Jesus to beseech thee to look their faces in the glass of God's Law and to continue therein and be a doer of the work.

And now Reader, because the cry of blood reacheth unto the Heavens and calleth for a narrow search and inquiry from thence that justice may take place and vengeance from God may be executed to answer the nature of the crime committed, the sin of blood being of that deep dye in the eyes of God that he hath left in his written Word no City of refuge to fly unto for the outward part of the offender, though sought, if possible, with tears of blood. Yet it is his Law unalterable, "Whoso sheddeth man's blood, by man shall his blood be shed," Genesis 9:6. Weeping, wailing, and gnashing of teeth will not here prevail, nor can create a door of hope; witness the case of poor Butler and Savage,[7] who wrung their hands for sorrow, smote upon their breasts, and with thousands of bitter sighs cried, "Oh! That I had not done this wicked Act. What, to murder my innocent friend? It makes me so far from desiring life or refuge here that I am not meet nor worthy to tread any longer upon God's earth nor yet to live in the society of men or to be seen above ground or die a natural death upon my body, but must call for justice, justice, justice, and that in a violent way, it may be executed upon me to send me as speedily as is possible from off the earth I have so defiled by so dreadful a sin as this my

Murder was." And no marvel but the offender if touched with a thorough sense of this dreadful crime must and will cry out for speedy and public justice to be done upon him in the sight of the Sun. While the Law of God is so far from giving respect in this case to the Judges of the earth that he will punish not only particular persons, but Families, yea Cities and Kingdoms too, where justice for this bloody crime is omitted or remitted; and when the Magistrate hath done his Office, so dreadful in God's eye is this foul Crime that after sentence and execution hath removed the Offender from the society of men, except deep sorrow and unfeigned repentance, bitter sighs, lamentable cries, and above all, the blood of a Savior doth mediate to the appeasing wrath, the same Offender must be given up into the hands of Devils to be tormented with fire and brimstone. Whereas St. Mark saith, "Their worm shall never die, and their fire shall never be quenched."[8]

Therefore Reader, if Murder speaks thus loud with God and man, no doubt but City and Country will ring of it, and Oh, that the cry of this, even of this (that a Mother should forget her tender Babe, as not only to neglect it, but the worst of evils to murder it; yea, to bathe as it were her hands in her child's blood). We again pray and say, Oh, that it might, if possible, reach to the ends not only of England but the earth to beget a reverence to God, a dread to sin, and a continual praying and watching over our hearts and lives; and to bespeak warning to all, that none henceforward upon themselves, their child, or neighbor, shall entertain a thought to do this abominable thing that God so hates.

In a word, there is nothing in the world, the flesh, or the devil can suggest (how taking soever with thy sensual affections, or however backed with arguments of pleasure or profit or secrecy) but this Narrative and Sermon may teach thee to retort upon the suggester, "How can I do this wickedness and sin against God, or hearken to this lying vanity and forsake my own mercy?" Oh, that when you find your hearts at any time a vain sinful thought arise or lust conceive in thee, thou wouldst dash it in pieces against the spiritual rock Christ and oppose enticements unto the secretest evils. That the eye of God sees thy most retired thoughts and actions whilst yet unhatched and in the shell are open and manifest to him. Fearing that the portion is too large already, to conclude in order to the spiritual and eternal advantage of your soul, we leave this short warning and small expedient in your hands; and if it may further that end, we have our aim and let God have the sole praise.

A more full account of the life and death of Mary Cook, taken by several Eye and Ear Witnesses most conversant with her from the hour she did commit that horrid Murder upon her Child, till she was laid in the grave

The subject of our present Narrative being a horrid Murder, Before we come to the sad and Tragical matter of Fact, give us leave in a few lines to open the heinousness of this sin, the dangerous consequences of it, and what means ought to be used for the preventing of it.

No Sin committed against the Commandments of the second Table[9] cryeth louder to God for vengeance and unto Man for Justice than the shedding of innocent blood: "And the Lord said unto Cain, What hast thou done? the voice of thy Brother's blood cryeth unto me from the ground," Genesis 4:10; Revelation 6:10.[10]

1. God will not stop his ears from the cry thereof; nay, he seemeth to speak as if he could have no rest until he be avenged on the Murderer.

    1. Because it is a sin against his express Commandment: "Thou shalt not kill," Exodus 20:13.

    2. Because it is the defacing of God's Image in which man is Created: "Whosoever sheddeth Man's blood, by Man shall his blood be shed." Why? "For in the Image of God made he Man," Genesis 9:6. Now to raze the King's Picture or great Seal is High Treason.

2. Man ought not to stop his Ears from the cry of innocent blood because there is no way to purify the Land from the guilt of innocent blood but by executing Justice upon the Blood-Shedder.

You shall take no satisfaction for the life of a Murderer: "So you shall not pollute the Land wherein you are; for the blood defileth the Land, and the Land cannot be cleansed of the bloodshed therein, but by the blood of him that shed it," Numbers 35:33.

Now as above said, God's Commandment is expressly, "Thou shalt do no Murder."

1. Murder lies either in the Omission of Duty in doing good to myself or my Neighbor with respect unto Soul or Body whereby I may procure his welfare.

2. In practicing evil against myself or Neighbor, whom I am commanded to love as myself, and to avoid all cruelty and unmercifulness against him.

A word or two of Soul-Murder

Soul-Murder is dreadful, though minded but by a few in the World, the greater pity.

1. When a people perish for want of plain and faithful preaching: "If thou warn not the wicked, and he die in his sin, his blood will I require at thy hand." Ezekiel 33:8.

2. When Parents and Masters of Families neglect their Duties to the souls of those that are committed to their charge, mind not to teach Children and Servants to know God, and to train them up in the nurture and admonition of the Lord, to stir them up to read and hear God's holy Word, and to hallow God's Holy day to sanctify it, and themselves to the Worship and Service of their God, whereby they might come to know God, and Jesus Christ, which is Life Eternal, Deuteronomy 6:6–7.

May not we take up a lamentation for the excessive Remissness in this Duty. Youth for the most part suffered upon the Lord's day to take their pleasure as if it were a day only for play. Sad will the charge be of such Masters and Parents at the last day!

And those Children and Servants that are Sons of Belial[11] will under no Yoke, but refuse to receive instruction and turn away from or stiffen the neck against reproof, shall die without remedy, and his Soul's blood required at his own hand, Proverbs 1:29.[12] But so much shall suffice to be spoken of Soul-Murder or Omission of Duty to the Soul. So I may murder myself or Neighbor by willful neglect of doing good to myself when I shall refuse either Food or Physic which God hath ordained for the preservation of natural Life or Health.

The principal thing is to open Murder, as it lieth under the practice of Evil against myself or Neighbor, which is done sometimes secretly, sometimes openly.

1. Secretly, when I am angry with another without cause, or that it exceeds the cause, either for time or measure. When passion sinks deep in the heart it becomes devilish; so that there should never be anger in our breasts where sin against God is not the cause; otherwise, you sin in being angry and give place to the Devil, Ephesians 4:26–27. If you be angry only for some injury done to yourself, you may easily find pride at the Root, and if not timely prevented, revenge will be the Fruit.

> Question: But how shall I prevent it?
> 1. Lay those manifold offenses done by thee against God into the Balance against those offenses or injuries men do against thee and that may be one way to abate hate, Titus 3:2.[13]
> 2. No provocation can be given to thee but by God's permission, for the trial and exercise of thy Graces and Virtues; Therefore David said, "Let Shimei Curse."[14]
> 3. Avoid all kindling or blowing up the flame of passion in thy own breast; put and keep at a distance all that combustible stuff that would take fire. Be not a Companion of the Gamester, the Drunkard, or the froward in Spirit.
> 4. Consider that anger resteth in the bosom of Fools. So much fury, so much folly, Ecclesiastes 7:11.[15]

2. When it causes envy to rise in my breast against my Neighbor: Herein the Devil was a Murderer for that he envied our first Parents' happiness, the melioriety[16] of their estate, he being fallen himself.

And Cain being of that Seed, he envies Abel because accepted of God before him.

Now this springeth from the want of true Love and from over-much Self-love, for love envies not, 1 Corinthians 13:4. "And he that hateth his Brother for that good which is in him for which he should love him is a Murderer," 1 John 3:5.[17]

Now Satan takes the advantage to kindle the Fire and Fuel and make it boil over and break forth in action, either against others or ourselves in Revenge, and injuring our neighbor in desire or purposes of Revenge, as Esau said in his heart, "The days of mourning for my Father are at hand, then will I slay my Brother Jacob for the Blessing,"[18] not considering whose propriety it is to Revenge Wrong, Romans 12:19.[19]

And hence proceeds actual Murders against our Neighbor or ourselves, sometimes secret, by giving or taking poison or giving way to Temptation of that kind.

Sometimes open, by laying violent hands upon ourselves or others.

1. Upon ourselves, A Sin so heinous in the sight of God that he Commands if a Beast slay a Man, the Beast was to be stoned to death, although he had neither Law nor Reason to restrain him. How much more Man whom God hath endowed with a Reasonable Soul and bounded with a Righteous Law, Exodus 21:28.

Now this is so much the more evil by how much the nearer and stronger the bonds are by which God and Nature binds us to preservation, whether the Bonds of Consanguinity or Affinity,[20] but most Monstrous and Unnatural of all is to lay violent hands upon ourselves, to whom I am bound by all Bonds to love and preserve. Therefore for one to rend in sunder his own Soul and Body is very dreadful, breaking all Bonds of God and Nature, and for ought man can judge, plunging themselves into Hell without Remedy, there being no space betwixt Sin and Death for Repentance, and certainly no Murderer hath Eternal Life in him, 1 John 3:15.

Now, what is the cause? Find out that, and you have half the cure.

> 1. No one layeth violent hands upon themselves but pride is the root of it, discontented with God's wise providential disposal, when persons choose and resolve not to be at all because they may not be what they would be themselves, not submitting themselves to what God will have them to be.
> 2. Unbelief and impatiency, want of faith in God to keep him in a quiet waiting upon the wise Governor of all things to work a good issue for us out of troubles.

2. None lay violent hands upon others but for want of retaining the knowledge and awe of the all-seeing and sin-revenging God in their hearts; as you may read at large, Romans 1:28–31.[21]

Now to prevent both,

1. Beg earnestly of God to write his Law in thy heart and to put his fear in thee and keep thee in a meek and quiet frame of spirit.

2. If at any time differences do arise that may by Satan or thy own heart be blown up to passionate revenge, do these few things.

> 1. If two constructions can be made of a word, or gesture, or action, be sure to make the best. It is a note of a wicked person to invent evil if he may construe it unto good.
> 2. Be as ready to forgive as you would be forgiven yourself, either of God or man.
> 3. Seek, yea, pursue peace until you overtake it, 1 Peter 3:8–9, 11.[22] "If it be possible, as much as lieth in you, live peaceably with all men; avenge not yourselves, but rather give place unto wrath," Romans 12:18–19.
> 4. Carefully maintain a noble spirit of sympathy with any when under temptation or oppression. Could we obey that blessed rule to do as we would be done unto, Galatians 6:1–2,[23] it would abate anger, prevent revenge and murder; which is

to the matter of fact. Now we shall proceed to give you the relation with the aggravating circumstances which accom-panied
this heinous, and we think almost unparalleled, murder.

The person which committed this murder was one Mary Cook,
the wife of T. C., living since the late dreadful fire in Clothfair,
near Smithfield in London, who was about the age of 37 years and
had been married to her said Husband near 12 years, by whom she
had eight children. And by the relation of many creditable persons
who have known her of a child, have given this character of her:
That she was of a very civil and sober life and conversation, living
in the neighborhood very inoffensively. But also, that she was of a
very melancholy temper, which is the Anvil that the Devil delights
to forge upon; for now Satan makes use of all advantages against
her to increase her melancholy, blowing up in her mind great
discontent with her present condition; so that as her affection unto
it decreased, so her affliction in it increased; insomuch that
common business became a burden and fears arose in her as to
wants, that in fine, she fancied death less bitter than life; and now
the Devil having thus far prevailed is not wanting to put her upon
such temptations as might speed her ruin.

1. Then the Devil stirs her up to revenge, and this as she hath
related since, did give her a kind of secret content, and this
temptation prevailed much with her; for being asked that morning
she committed the fact, what might be the reason of it, one answer
was, That she had been a fortnight sick and weak, and no one took
care what she wanted. Thus through temptation she prefers revenge
before temporal safety and eternal peace.

2. The Devil prevailed with her to keep his secrets and counsel
for she discovered her affliction to none that might pray with or
for her or could give suitable counsel to her and help to bear her
burden; by which means she, struggling in her own strength, until
at last she concluded there was no hope of amendment of her
condition or ease to her troubled mind but by death.

3. Temptation by which the Devil prevailed upon her was to grow mindless of hearing God's holy Word preached, or read the Scriptures, or to perform public or private prayers. This had prevailed so high that the morning she gave that fatal blow, she confessed for months together she had not been at Church to hear God's Word taught, neither had been much (if at all) troubled for her backwardness or neglect therein. Thus did she at once provoke the Devil to bend his bow against her and left herself destitute of those special remedies to avoid his keen and dreadful arrows.

4. Temptation was her self-murder; and this she did with great liking embrace, being more concerned how to bring it about with speed and secrecy than either to discover it or prevent it.

And first, she resolves of drowning herself; to promote which design she goes into a solitary place in the fields, walking to and fro like a distracted Woman, but could not find where to pitch the best conveniency for her purpose, still wandering about until God in his good providence at last met her with some suitable acquaintance, which prevented the Devil's temptation from having success at this time.

Some time after this, now above a year and quarter a gone, she is put upon another device to her own destruction, namely, to hang herself, for which purpose she had gotten two long skeins[24] of silk and in her own cellar was preparing to act this sad tragedy. But a kinswoman going into the cellar and seeing her stand in the corner told her Uncle, the Woman's Husband, who ran down and found the skeins of silk in her hand, demanding what she was doing. She then told him her intentions if he had not prevented her. He got her up and went and fetched her father unto her, and they together endeavored to persuade her. Then her Husband knocked down all the nails and hooks in the cellar to prevent her for the future.

But it is here worthy of consideration to all that shall read this sad story whether upon giving up themselves under this assault to fasting and prayer with deep humiliation before God might not have proved an effectual means to have cast out this kind of Devil.

For the Devil sets upon her again to be her own Executioner and to cut her own throat; for which purpose she gets a knife and whets it sharp and sets it to the hollow of her throat and makes a small scar, causeth some blood to issue; but whether from the bluntness of the point of the knife, or the failing of her spirits, it would not enter, whereupon she put the knife into her skirt, hoping to take another opportunity to accomplish her design upon herself, still keeping the Devil's counsel, and consulting with him and her own evil heart, who never left hurrying her with temptations until he had prevailed upon her.

Now at last the habit of wicked devices had so taken root in her that she thirsted and as it were was impatient till some way or other her own life was brought to an end; for on the 5th of February last past, her Husband being for some hours absent (and as she apprehended, neglected his business at home, she grew full of discontent,), who coming in, and saying, "Mary, I must go out again." She answered, "If you do, I will cast the child into the fire." But his compliance and stay prevented this. Yet still the Devil pursues her like a roaring Lion seeking to devour her, for that night a great pressure of melancholy discontent overwhelmed her to a restlessness of body and spirit much like them in Deuteronomy 28[25] who in the evening wished that it were morning and in the morning, Oh, that it were evening. So that in the night, when her Husband was in bed and asleep, she took the child out of the cradle down into the Kitchen, which when her Husband awaked and missed, he knocked. Whereupon she brought up the child and laid it into the cradle and came to bed. But he could get no satisfactory answer why she took down the child, but she lay until the morning, which when it approached, being February 6th, the Lord's day, whether any discomposure happened betwixt her Husband and her because his better days' garments were not laid out ready for him, or what it was God knows, but the sequel was dreadful, for all contributing together, fills her brim-full with resolution to some horrid and speedy execution. For soon after she arose and had made

her fire one story lower, she takes her knife and whets it sharper
and makes the offer to her own throat as before is hinted, but the
Husband having knockt twice to have her come up to give him his
better clothes, and she not coming, he arose, put on his every days'
clothes, and came upon her, and very probably prevented her
execution of herself. He asking her why she came not up when he
knockt, she gave him no answer but slips up the stairs into the
chamber where the Babe lay in the cradle. And now the Devil puts
her upon a fresh consultation what should become of the child,
which she so dearly loved, after she was dead. Upon this she
concludes she had better rid that of life first, and then all her fears
and cares for it would be at an end, and so she should put an end
unto her own miserable life, which was so burdensome unto her.
The which temptation for want of having the fear of God in her
heart, she gave way unto, and sitting down by the cradle, asked
the innocent Babe about two years and one quarter old, "Betty,
Wilt have thy breakfast?" Unto which the Babe answered, "Ey,"
crying "Aha, aha," as it used to do when it was pleased, and put
forth her hand to stroke her Mother. But she, laying aside all
Motherly Bowels,[26] took the Babe out of the cradle, set her on her
lap, took the knife out of her skirt, laid her left hand upon its
face and chin, and with the other hand, cut her throat at one stroke
in a ghastly manner to behold, then threw it from her upon the
hearth.

This relation she gave herself but the day before her execution
with this doleful reply: That when she did that barbarous act, the
child gave one shriek and fetched three or four dreadful sighs and
so became the Mother's sinful sacrifice; which sighs she mentioned
with much dejection of spirit, saying nothing like that gave her
fresh grief and trouble for she was followed with the imagination
that she heard its doleful sigh still.

Thus having given the fatal blow, she stamped with her foot for
her Husband, and as an amazed Woman, half dead, cast herself
down upon a low seat, with her bloody hands on each side covered

with part of her upper garment, and her head leaned against a Chest of Drawers did thus with an affrighted countenance repose herself. And it is worthy of note that with the violence of the act when she cut her Babe's throat, both her hands was so colored with blood that she could not endure the sight of them. The terror of this fatal stroke made such a seizure upon her conscience with the reflection of that doleful sight, her child lying before her eyes, with its heart-blood running out. Immediately upon this, her Husband approaching at the Chamber door, saying, "Wife, what is the matter you so hastily knock with your feet?" [She] dolefully replied, she had given the child its breakfast. No sooner had she spake, but he beheld with an afflicted spirit his Babe lie bleeding on the ground, at which amazement broke out into such lamentations as occasioned both Lodgers and Neighbors to approach. The Chirurgeon[27] being mentioned to be sent for, to which she replied, "You may save that labor, for I am sure I have killed it." Now the doleful report of this dreadful act did soon spread itself, upon which both neighbors and strangers press in; amongst others, some of the relaters of this bitter story providentially going that way was invited upstairs where they found the bleeding Babe but newly dead, the Father wringing his hands and shedding multitude of tears, like a man so amazed as half distracted (God forbid but we should give him his due). His behavior to appearance did express that with a lamentable resentment he received this sad news.

The Mother when she had done this act was exceeding stupid,[28] though much was said to her and prayers performed with her and such Scriptures laid before her of the dreadfulness of the sin and punishment due for it both in this life and without repentance in the life to come. Yet she could not shed one tear, and being demanded why she had done this and spoken to to behold her dead Babe — how it lay murdered upon the ground before her eyes, being murdered by those hands — she then appeared not relenting at all, but said, it was done because she was weary of her life, her Relations slighting her, and lest that child being most in her affection should come to want when she was gone, she killed it first, knowing that way would also bring her to her desired end. This with many other passages not here so convenient to mention (because of the survivors) of the like nature was also uttered. But now appears Constables and other Parish Officers who caused her narrowly to be searched for fear of knife or any cord being found about her lest she might therewith take the like advantage to destroy herself the next opportunity. Her garters being then given up, but nothing else of danger found about her. Being told it was feared she would also kill herself, answered, she should not do so; and being demanded whether she was sorry for what she had done, replies, she could wish she had not done it, but now it was too late. Then being demanded whether she was willing to be prayed for, said yes, for she could not pray for herself. So being desired to go down to her knees and hold up her eyes and hands, readily did, but could neither weep nor sigh at that time. When her hour was come to be carried before the Justice, she did without any appearing remorse either in carriage or countenance make ready herself: took her rings from her fingers; caused a pair of silver clasps to be cut from her Scarf; gave her Husband the several keys of Trunks, Chests or Boxes, telling him which particular key was for such and such a use, in so unconcerned a manner, to all appearance, as if going only to take some long journey, which verily in charity lead us to believe she was so overwhelmed with melancholy as one bereft of senses. Being carried before Sir William Turner and being demanded whether she had killed her child, replied, "yes." Then being asked why, replied, she was discontented, and thought her Husband and Relations did not love her. Being again demanded why she thought so, assigned no cause, but that she did believe so; upon this her bloody knife and both her bloody hands was exposed to view and her full examination taken in which she lays the actual guilt wholly upon herself, clearing all others as to fact and privacy there unto. And indeed with such dejection of countenance and temper of carriage did demean herself that she became the pity of all or most spectators. After the Justice had told her of the greatness of the crime and what from men she must expect as punishment for the same, with serious and compassionate advice to the blood of Jesus Christ for remedy, did thus conclude: "and the God of heaven have mercy on your soul." After which her examination was read to her, which she owned as her act and deed. Being asked whether she could write her name, answered "no." "Then sign it with your mark,"[29] said the Justice, which she did, by making a cross instead of her name, the application of which gave thoughts to some standers by that sure providence guided that bloody hand to sign her temporal death with a cross that her eternal life might as assuredly be saved by the Cross. Then was she conveyed to Newgate; but going along, suddenly turned back, looking at her Relation, used these words, with a doleful countenance: "O, if you had been more careful to look after me, you might have hindered me from doing this." The application we commend to whomsoever concerned and thought it very meet to be inserted that such a word from a dying woman might not die with her. Then being told by one afflicted for her that now "you are going to Prison and from thence must be conveyed to the Judgment seat of men, and there receive Sentence of death, and from thence be sent to the Judgment seat of God. What think you of it? I pray for your soul's sake consider it; there is now but a little step between you and eternity." To which she replied: "O, I wish I had not done this, but I am willing to die, only afraid of my soul." "Well," replied the party, "there is virtue enough in Christ's blood to wash your scarlet sins white." "I," saith she, "but I cannot yet repent, my heart is so hard." "If you cannot repent, do what you can in order to repentance by lifting up your heart, your eyes, and your hands continually to God; for you say you believe there is a God, and if you can but speak few words, employ them that way to beg him to give you repentance, and to soften your hard heart. Remember the poor Publican[30] who smote upon his breast, saying, 'Lord, be merciful to me a sinner.' Will you do what you can?" "Yes, I will." "You say you wish you had not done this Murder and that is one step to repentance; therefore, labor to groan more after this, and to that end shall I put up Bills[31] this day, as your desire, that God's people may pray for you." "Yes, very willingly I desire that," &c. Now did she arrive at the Prison, and so with her Mittimus[32] was delivered into the hands of the Keeper, who with great expressions of pity received his Prisoner and desired God would have mercy on her soul.

Of her behavior in the time of her Imprisonment and other Passages very useful for every Christian that desires to be kept from being guilty of the like Fact

She no sooner cometh to Newgate, but the noise of this cruel Murder spreads abroad and several reports went as to herself and what should be the causes of that barbarous Act.

1. That the Devil appeared in a personal shape unto her and told her she must either destroy herself or her Child.

2. That the day before she went to see one of her other Children at Nurse and would have sent the Nurse forth that so she might have killed that Babe.

3. That she was under trouble of mind about Religion with many other things.

Which for satisfaction to ourselves and others and clearing the truth of Gospel-profession as being inconsistent for any true work of the Spirit of God in the conviction of a sinner to leave the soul, having begun in the Spirit to end in the flesh. Some of those Ministers which went to visit her in the Prison made more than ordinary diligent search into these things. And as to the first report she said, there was no appearance unto her but the violent Temptation of the Devil and her own wretched and sinful heart giving way to the Temptation.

And as to the second, she confessed she went to see her Child at Nurse upon the Saturday before, but it never entered into her heart to conceive a thought of doing that Child any hurt.

And as to the third, her answer was, That there was nothing of any Religious Concernment in it, but it was that great Discontent which she had conceived in her mind grounded upon her apprehension of exceeding unkindness of her Relations unto her, although she had never been undutiful unto them. But very sparing she was in accusing any but herself. And it is not the design of this Narrative to accuse them, only to desire they may call to mind and lay to heart and repent of their neglect of duty towards her, wherein they shall any of them be conscious unto themselves of remissness. And that all others who shall read this sad Relation may take warning thereby so to discharge their relative duties that they may not expose their Relations unto Temptations, and so when a separation cometh, either violent or natural, they have cause to mourn all their days for their own and their other men's sins.

But as to herself, the sense of her great sin and guilt lay with such weight upon her conscience that Satan used his utmost endeavor to drive her into despair of ever obtaining mercy; it being his usual method to present God *all mercy* to allure men to commit sin, and afterwards to present God *altogether severity* to drive the sinner into despair of God's mercy in the pardon of their sin.

A great wound lay upon her with respect unto her dear Babe whom she had so inhumanly destroyed: Whether her Fact might not hinder the Child's Salvation? Much care and pains was taken so to speak as might not in the least extenuate the sense of her guilt and yet to open a door of hope unto her that the eternal state of the Child might be safe (not withstanding her great wickedness) through the riches of God's grace, which showeth mercy unto whom he will show mercy, that 18th of Ezekiel, verse 24[33] being read unto her.

But still she sadly bewailed the horridness of her sin, wishing often, Oh that she had had more Grace! For, if it were to do again, she would submit to a thousand deaths rather than to commit that sin. And her sore trouble now was that her heart was so obdurate that she could not mourn as she should and desired to do, and begged that all good people would pray for her. And being asked what she desired us to pray unto God for, for her, her answer was that God would give her a broken and penitent heart.

She also sadly lamented her distraction by reason of her evil company in the Room with her that hindered both her meditations and addresses to God. Oh it is sad dwelling in the Tents of Kedar[34] and a sore evil to leave our great work to do until the last, not knowing what hindrance we may meet with. It is inconvenient to cast up our Accounts in a crowd and hurry of business.

Ever and anon she would sadly bewail her want of the light of God's countenance; and it was not to be wondered at that she was so much in the dark having committed such a gross sin against the light of Nature. Iniquity separates betwixt us and our God and causeth him to hide his face that it is rarely if ever they recover it. Though he may in mercy pardon the sin, yet he may justly cause the sinner to go mourning and with broken bones to the grave.

The Sessions now came on, and upon the 21st of February she was arraigned and indicted at the Old Bailey[35] and cast for her life.

Upon the Petition of her husband, she had a week's time granted her to prepare for her death, and being sentenced on Wednesday the second of March to die in Smithfield over against Clothfair Gate, where she formerly lived when she committed that horrible murder.

During this time, much pains was taken with her continually by skillful and faithful Physicians for her Soul's recovery out of the snare of the Devil, who had carried her captive at his will; and several Books of Mr. Baxter's[36] and other Books suitable to her present condition were brought her to read, which she seemed diligently to improve her time in, together with the holy Scriptures.

March 1, being the day before her Execution, one Mistress R. H. had an earnest desire to see her and to watch with her that night, and through God's mercy it was of great use unto her for her comfort who had now but a little time to live.

That day being asked, If a pardon for life or a pardon for her sin were equally presented to choose one, which would she choose? She answered, If her heart did not deceive her, it would be the pardon of her sin. O her sin, her sin! Her blood-guiltiness lay with weight upon her! But still she cried out she could not find her heart in that broken and believing frame which she desired it should be in.

On the same day great pains were taken with her to help her understanding and apprehension both as to the nature of true Repentance and saving Faith. To which she with more than former freedom answered, That as to Repentance opened unto her, she hoped God had given her a sight of her sin and a desire to be truly humbled for it; it was her wound she was no more wounded and that she did desire to forsake sin with abhorrence and to loathe herself for her sin, to lay her mouth in the dust, and yet to look up unto the Lord Jesus, if so be she might find mercy.

And as to her Faith, she said, God had convinced her that her own righteousness was but unrighteousness, even as a filthy menstruous[37] cloth, and therefore desired out of the sense of her own nothingness and utter emptiness to go out of herself and to rely upon Jesus Christ alone for Righteousness and Salvation.

Then several Scriptures were read unto her and pressed with earnestness upon her, amongst many others, that in Mark 5:25 and forward, concerning that Woman which had a bloody issue, who said in herself, "If I may but touch the hem of his garment, I shall be whole."[38] Much was spoken unto her from this, wherewith she was observed to be very much affected, tears trickling down more than usually, and with earnestness said, "O that I could believe!"

That evening before she suffered, her Husband's long absence from her gave her occasion to suppose that endeavors were using for a Reprieve or a Pardon for her at which she did rather express dislike than to be well pleased, saying she had rather choose to die than to continue in that place with that wicked company, it being a Hell upon Earth, if any such were; and that she was not at all concerned about a Pardon from Man, could she but obtain a Pardon from Christ, it was that she most desired. Nevertheless, for her better preparation for death, she could have wished a little longer time, but she was willing to die if that could not be obtained.

That night she took a little rest for the supporting of nature, but it was judged she slept not above half an hour; but some time was spent by herself, her Husband, and Mistress R. H. in prayer and reading. She herself taking her Bible, read the fourth chapter of Matthew,[39] and wept much in the reading of it, saying, "The Lord Jesus was tempted, but he was God-man, and the Evil-one found nothing in him and so could not prevail against him: but I, a vile wretch! Temptation no sooner came and assaulted me but I was overcome by it; a wicked woman that I am to give way to that roaring Lion!

Then reading Isaiah 44:22 ("I have blotted out as a cloud thy transgressions, and as a thick cloud thy sins: return unto me, for I have redeemed thee") broke out again with tears, saying, "Oh! What grace is this! What, my sins! What a Redeemer to such a great sinner as I have been!" Then turning further unto Isaiah 54:7–8 ("I will have mercy upon thee, saith thy Redeemer"). "See," saith she, "here is Redeemer again!"

Her Husband, a little before morning, asked her how it was with her. She answered, "Not so well as to boast, nor so bad as to be altogether dejected."

When morning came, she dressed herself that she might be in readiness when called, but seemed a little impatient to lose so much time in dressing her body when she had so little to improve for her soul which lay at stake. Several both Ministers and other Christian friends waiting to go up unto her when she was ready; one of them desiring to know how it was with her this morning. She answered that she was now entering upon the borders of Eternity, but Oh, what should she do, she wanted the light of God's countenance! Whereupon both awakening and comforting words were spoken unto her; and then a little time was spent in prayer to

God that he would please graciously to direct us so to speak unto her as might advance his Glory and effectually administer comfort unto her Soul. In prayer she was seen to melt very much. And having ended that duty, as God did direct, the words of God were spoken unto her, and she was desired to speak what was upon her heart for our comfort who had been laboring for the Lord with her.

But she being silent for a little space but observed to have some conflict in her soul by the tears which fell and sighs which broke forth, It was again propounded unto her, Whether she found not a secret persuasion that God was able to pardon her great and manifold sins but also very great fears, whether he were willing yea or no?

Whereupon she broke forth into a fuller passion of tears, saying, "O Sir, you speak the very thoughts of my heart. God hath convinced me of the All-sufficiency of his Grace, that though my sins be as Scarlet as Crimson, he can make them white as Snow, as Wool. But O to know whether he will or no, that lieth as my great fear." Whereupon endeavors were used to encourage her to hope in God's mercy, who had testified his unwillingness that any soul should perish; and that he took no pleasure in the death of sinners but rather desired their return that they might live. Also the Lord Jesus graciously invited sinners, yea the greatest of sinners, under the heaviest load and burden of their guilt and filth, being weary of their load, to come to him that they might be saved and find rest, and had promised that who ever came unto him though at last (if in truth) he would not cast them out; and that he had sent his Ministers to beseech sinners to be reconciled unto God; and that we came in his Name and Authority to deliver that his Message unto her.

Therefore the Question was put unto her, Whether she was willing to accept of mercy from Christ, and to take Him upon his own terms. Unto which she answered, with a seemingly altered countenance as to cheerfulness, Yea, she was willing, and desired with her whole soul to be sanctified throughout by Jesus Christ and washed in his Blood as ever she desired to be justified by his Righteousness or saved by his Death.

Then it was judged expedient to leave her a little retired that she might improve a few minutes in secret betwixt God and her own soul, desiring all the company to withdraw, saving her Husband and Mistress R. H. And after a little space of time, she desired we would come up again, and apprehending her in a pretty good frame, willing to resign up herself now unto the Lord, what time the Officers could spare (for now the time drew near) was spent in fervent prayers and tears unto God with and for her. In the close, being desired to tell us what returns God had graciously given to all our endeavors with her, She said that the Lord had brought her to that resolution that although she might not sensibly lie in his bosom yet she would penitently lie and die at his feet; and if she perished, she would perish there.

When she came to the place of Execution, she seemed to have a mixture of fear and hope in her, wringing one by the hand, said, "O, what shall become of me now if my heart have deceived me hitherto!" Some words being spoken unto her, she encouraged herself again in the freeness of God's grace and the fullness of mercy that was in Christ for poor penitent sinners.

After earnest Prayers put up unto God for her and seasonable Counsels given her by Mr. Ordinary[40] and some others, she went upon the Ladder,[41] having before expressed an earnest desire to have spoken to the people, but wanting strength she entreated us to declare to the Spectators and to all the World That she desired to justify the Lord in all his righteous proceedings against her, and that she died justly for her great sin; and earnestly begged that all that saw or heard of her untimely end would take warning by her deplorable fall to take heed how they gave way to Satan's Temptations.

Being upon the Ladder, a convenient time was left her to commend her soul unto God. And that she might not be surprised before she was ready was desired to give a sign when she had done;

and she with the same foot where with she stampt for her husband to tell him of her horrid fact which she had unnaturally done, stamped upon the round of the Ladder to give notice she was now willing and ready to die for the same: whereupon the Executioner did his office.

Many other passages might have been inserted, but because we are not willing to make this Narrative swell too large, we shall omit them.

O that this sad Execution may cause all that hear to fear and do no more so presumptuously. Deuteronomy 17:13.[42]

How apparent is it that the Devil goeth about like a roaring Lion seeking continually whom he may devour! And how much the more need have all the children of men to be upon their diligent watch and to be earnest and fervent in prayer to God that they may not be overcome with his temptations.

"Yea, let him that thinketh he standeth, take heed lest he fall."[43]

Let it be your care to check every temptation at the entrance of it. Consult not with flesh and blood; give no place to slavish fears; admit of no consultations with the Devil, lest he prove too hard for you. Give not way to sinful anger for therein thou giveth place to the Devil. And let all sinners know that if they do evil, sin lieth at their door; if they resolve to continue in their sin, then their sin will assuredly find them out; but if they break off their sins by works of righteousness, repent, and return to the Lord, iniquity shall not be their ruin.

Some passages omitted in the former Narrative

About ten of the clock the morning she suffered, the Officer told her Now they were ready to go with her to Execution. At this many strangers that were with her did both with prayers and tears commend her condition to God, she desiring they might continue the same to her end. 'Tis worthy of note to all that shall read her manner of deportment at this time: She went down the stairs in so unconcerned a manner as though she had not been the person to suffer, but rather a spectator, for while many that knew the bitter cup she was to drink could not cease from deep discomposure, she seemed as a person free from such fear or torment as commonly attends those that have such an hour of trial to undergo. At the foot of the stairs she had some half an hour's repose by reason a Cart was not ready. In this intermission did many hearts yearn toward her Eternal condition, telling her now there was but one step more between her and that. Then she asked how she might know Jesus Christ died for her? It was replied, He died for sinners, yea the greatest of sinners; and she knew she was one, and a chief one; and that in the 5th of Romans, verses 6–8 it is said, "He died for the ungodly," even the worst of people, and the Scriptures did nowhere exclude her by name from benefit in Christ's blood. And in 1 Timothy 2:3 it is charged that prayers and supplications be made for all; and in verse 4 the reason is rendered, for God would have all to be saved, and come to the knowledge of his Truth.

About this time came the Officer with a Rope, and it is worthy of note how she then did behave herself. He makes a noose before her eyes (enough to daunt any beholder, much more the person for whom it was making), then he takes her right arm and puts the Rope over that, then over her left, and so ties it with a knot at the middle of her back; she all this while attentive to what was spoken by the persons who came in love to visit her, appearing without change of countenance or terror of spirit. And indeed, excepting the guilt of Murder that lay on her conscience, her constant carriage was more like a Lamb going to the slaughter than a Murderer going to the Gallows. By this time the Cart was ready, which she ascending, then told us Nothing troubled her like that she should bring such dishonor to God by this sin, wishing with all her heart that all that did behold her might take warning by her miserable estate how they lived in this World.

Now she is come within sight of the Gibbet[44] on which she must in a very short time suffer death; and then the Executioner came and undid the Rope from where it was tied about her in the Prison, and taking off her Handkerchief, bares her neck, ties the Rope about it, fitting the knot to her right ear, at which (to the admiration of some present) she was not in the least terrified nor changed in her countenance. Mr. Ordinary now comes to pray with her, and gave her many useful exhortations. Then did Mr. P. also pray with her in a most earnest manner, as the last vocal prayer that was ever like to be put up unto God for her. Then did we all present take our farewell of her, beseeching God in this needful moment not to reject her in this miserable and low estate, which without his mercy and pardon must perish to all eternity. Then did Mr. P. as a close of all beseech her look up to a gracious God as her last and only refuge and carry with her these words to Execution, "Into thy hands, O Lord God, do I commit my Spirit."[45] Then did we lead her by the hands to the Ladder, where she was placed a convenient distance from the ground, and the Rope fastened to the Gibbet, while thousands of Spectators beholding her with a general compassion, to whom we signified her desire was to have the benefit of all their prayers. Upon which, with one consent they uncovered their heads and lift up their hands, using this expression, "The Lord have mercy on her Soul." Then she had near a quarter of an hour's repose to herself upon the Ladder, and though her hands were tied together, yet she was observed often to move them upwards in her private prayer.

Then we begged her to remember to the last that God was a very gracious God and to give us some sign of his goodness to her at her departure if she found it so. Upon which she replied with such a comfortable answer as gave us occasion to give thanks to his Name. And now to the glory of God's mercy be it spoken, and to the deterring all from Evil by her fall and to the encouragement of sinners to repentance that they may find mercy, as we trust she hath done; for now hath she to our joy (much exceeding our sorrow) ended her life in Smithfield, near Clothfair Gate, upon the 2nd of this instant March 1669, with her hands lifted up to God in a most fervent manner while sense remained, which was about half a quarter of an hour; and she continued upon the Gibbet about three-quarters more. Then was her Body taken down and conveyed to the same room her dear Child was by her killed in; and on the next day after in the evening she was buried in Great St. Bartholomew's Churchyard, being accompanied by a great many Neighbors and Strangers to perform their last office of love for the dead that had given them no other cause while living but in this great transgression.

FINIS

FAIR WARNING

TO

Murderers of Infants:

BEING AN

ACCOUNT

OF THE

Tryal, Codemnation and Execution

OF

Mary Goodenough

AT THE

Affizes held in *Oxon*, in *February*, 169¼.

TOGETHER

With the Advice fent by her to her Children, In a Letter Sign'd by her own Hand the Night before fhe was Executed.; with fome Reflections added upon the whole: Printed for the Publick Good.

LONDON:

Printed for *Jonathan Robinson*, at the Sign of the *Golden Lyon*

Fair Warning to Murderers of Infants, title page, call number Rb 64625. By permission of The Huntington Library, San Marino, California.

Fair Warning to Murderers of Infants:

Being an Account of the Tryal, Codemnation and Execution of Mary Goodenough at the Assizes held in Oxon, in February, 1691/2.[1]

Together With the Advice sent by her to her Children, In a letter Sign'd by her own Hand the Night before she was Executed; with some Reflections added upon the whole: Printed for the Publick Good. (1692)

It would grieve a Man to think how many's Curiosity will tempt them to buy this Paper; how few's Consideration will lead them to make useful Application of it to themselves; How many more will, through a vainly censorious Wit, charge the Publishing this Letter as a Trick to pick Pockets; how few's Wisdom will conduct them to fall in with the direct Tendency it hath to enrich and ennoble their Minds; while most, it is to be fear'd, read such things with no more concern than Persons in Health read Quack Doctors' Bills and make no better use of them. Yet he that hath an Ear to hear let him hear. This Letter speaks by strong Consequence at least to the highest concerns of Mankind in general. It lays open Men's greatest Mistakes about and misconduct of them. Oh that they were wise, that there were in all that shall read an heart to consider this. In this Letter is wrap'ed up most suitable Persuasions to the Youth of these Kingdoms to consider thoroughly of and engage themselves heartily in their Baptismal Covenant. It gives an awakening Alarm to negligent Parents to instruct their Children in and conduct them diligently into the Paths of Heavenly Wisdom lest they deeply mourn at last (as this poor Woman did) their fatal Cruelty to their Children's Souls. This Letter suggests a Warning to Adulterers and Adulteresses to repent of and forsake their Crimes, lest God bring them to repent by open shame, as he did this poor Creature, or suffer them to go on in a covert way to Hell. It's a Cry after the Backsliders in heart, those who have had strong Convictions, taken up good Resolutions, and follow'd them for a while, with a course of Amendments, but are return'd with the Dog to his Vomit.[3] That they return to God from whom they have fallen, lest he in Judgment give them up to commit enormous Sins, to fall under dismal Punishments, yea, the most dismal of all, final Impenitency. Here's a discharge to all their Hopes of the Favor of God and everlasting Life, who are but formal, hypocritical, heartless Pretenders to Religion, till their Hearts are renew'd as well as the Face of their Conversation reform'd. And who amongst the dissolute, profane, and profligate part of Mankind can say but here's a most passionate Cry to them that break and shake off the fatal Chains wherein the Devil is leading them down to the Chambers of Eternal Death? In short, there's that in this Letter which may lead all to the most intimately acquainting themselves with their own Mortality. There's that by which all Persons may determine whether they belong to the Kingdom of Light or that of Darkness: the Letter of a Dying Person's Trial of the Truth and Life of her Repentance, Faith, Love and Obedience. Reader, will you not use what you have bought? Do you know all this Letter tells you already? Oh be persuaded now to fall a doing it. Will you censure it as being above these Children? Oh cast it not away as if it were below you; it was calculated as a Guide to them through their Lives. Will you charge it as too wordy? Oh confuse not your charge by making it appear there are not Words enough to persuade you to become Pious. Well, when the Testament of our Dying Jesus, nay, his last charge in that Testament, "Do this in Remembrance of me," prevails so little with Christians, what Effects shall we hope for from the words of a Dying Malefactor recommending him to the World she had so lately left? Yet canst not thou, Oh God, that causes Gibbets[4] to preach, make the most Refractory of Rebels hear?

You that will not hearken to Moses and the Prophets, Christ and his Apostles, will you not hear, though one is here raised from the Dead, a living Witness to the great truth they taught? Was she not dead in Trespasses and Sins? Was she not made alive to God through Jesus Christ, think you, before she died to Nature? Hear her then, Christ Jesus, by her, that your Souls may live. Open thou the Ears, Oh God, that are dead to the Voice of Charms. Is not Judgment thy strange work! Oh, then Reform Multitudes by the Chastisement of this one Criminal, who will otherwise by their Rebellions run themselves into great Misery in this World, if not also into everlasting Misery in the next. Well, whether any Person that reads this Letter will give a practical regard to it or no, this is certain, it will harden where it does not soften. They are a Degree nearer Hell by refusing who don't advance towards Heaven by embracing its Instructions. And if ever they repent, their sight of this Counsel will yield them a most bitter Reflection; or if they never repent, this reflex Advice will add to the Smart of their Eternal Vexations in the World they're passing to, of Horror and Despair.

As to that man who had the first and principal hand in this Woman's and her Infant's Tragedy, I would desire some Neighbors (supposing he'll scarce take pains to read this) to ask him seriously some such Questions as these: Whether he did not act the Devil's part when he tempted this Woman as Satan our Savior to purchase a Supply for the cravings of her Nature by a Crime tending to the Ruin of her soul? Whether he that serves the Devil in his Life and repents not is not like to fall into his Condemnation and merciless hands at Death? Whether he believes God has commanded "Thou shall not commit Adultery"? If he does not, whether he believes, or can prove the Christian World Fools, or Madmen, who also thus believe it? Whether God had not own'd this Command, as often in History, so now by avenging the Breach of it in this his fellow Criminal's Death? This were easily argued, tho' she was Condemn'd at man's Bar[5] for another Crime. But if he believes God has forbidden Adultery, whether he thinks God will always bear with him in the violating the plain Letter of his Laws? Whether he that being often reproved hardens his heart shall not suddenly be destroy'd, and that without Remedy? Whether he does not flatter himself with a secret Thought of future Repentance? Whether it be not his best and may not happen to be his only time to repent now? Or if he has no thought of Repentance, how he can think to dwell with devouring Flames or everlasting Burnings?

And as to the Neighborhood of this poor Woman, if the Judgments of God abroad in the World should teach the Inhabitants of the Earth Righteousness, surely then this Judgment of God fallen upon one amongst you, whom you knew, with whom you convers'd, is now clearly design'd by God to teach you Righteousness. Think it not a Warning to you against the particular Crimes for which she died only. Tho' I dare affirm it positively, you are not secure of yourselves that you shall not commit the Crimes or worse than those for which she died till you get your Hearts renew'd and chang'd, as she had showed you in the Trial of herself. No, nor are you then secure of avoiding the commission of such enormous Crimes, but in your close walking with God and through Faith on Jesus, receiving continual Supplies of Grace and Strength from him to resist Temptations. Did not David commit Adultery and Murder?[6] Was not this Woman as Religious as most of you? Did not she seemingly outgo[7] many of you? Will you not be warn'd by her Fall then not to content yourselves with a Form of Religion without the Power of Godliness? But I would chiefly apply myself to you on the behalf of her poor destitute Children. The Law of the Nation exacts from you the care of their Bodies. Does not the Law of God under several Penalties require you to take care of their Souls? Are not their Souls more valuable than their Bodies? Are not you become as Parents to these poor Orphans? The case of Orphans and Bastards is deplorable. Parishes indeed take care to place them out where they may learn a slavish way of living at the cheapest rates, but seldom consider whether they'll be carefully instructed in the Fear and piously conducted in the ways of God where they have plac'd them; a Cruelty indeed (Oh, monstrous) many religious Persons are guilty of towards their Children. The best Trade and most knowing worldly Master is all their inquiry.

Will you be so cruel to these Children's Souls? Know if you be, their Blood will God require at your hands. But whilst I speak to all, I'm afraid lest none will think themselves concerned. Are there none amongst you that have devoted yourselves to Christ Jesus in an everlasting Covenant and Love him in Sincerity? I apply myself to you in Christ's words, "Feed these his Lambs." Of such little children as those of this Woman's with you are the Kingdom of Heaven. Are they not Christ's Members whilst they are yet devoted to him in Virtue of their Mother's Faith? Will not God reward your labor of Love towards them? Will they not be Blessings to the Families, to the Town they shall live in, and an Honor too, if you endeavor to bring them up to the Practice of their Mother's Precepts? Take care her Children learn to read, learn the Catechism; read to them, and press upon them this their Mother's Last Will concerning them. Don't stick at a little charge or trouble to do them good. Will anything please you but the good you have done with what you had when you come to die? Will anything displease you than but that you have done so little! And I beg leave to mind you of an Obligation, which however to you it may seem small or none at all, yet by God perhaps is accounted no small one upon you, to be kind to those poor Children. Who knows how far your Uncharitableness hiding yourselves from your own Flesh from this poor Woman's Wants contributed to the strength of that Temptation which brought her to that Sin and Punishment which have left these Children Motherless. It was for want of Bread, she said. If her Modesty did make her asham'd to beg, did not her meager Look, her starved Children, her meanly furnished House and Table beg from you? Should you not have answered this silent Prayer by Charity? Though you did not do it as then, show your Repentance now in showing a more bountiful and constant Kindness to her Children. This way God has left open for you. I wish all Parishes might by these Considerations be brought more narrowly to inspect the State of their poor Neighbors and consequently to administer to them. Some noisy poor are maintain'd in their Idleness, whilst other modest poor are starv'd in the midst of their Labors.

In short, from this Woman's Crime and Punishment may we be brought firmly to believe "Except we repent, we shall all likewise perish." May they that think they stand take heed lest they fall. May all hear and fear, and do no more wickedly.

An Account of the Trial, Condemnation and Execution of Mary Goodenough, at the Assizes[8] held in Oxon, in February 1691/2

Mary Goodenough Widow, aged about 40 years, liv'd at Bradwell in the County of Oxon. Being in great Poverty and Straits, even to the want of Bread for her and hers, she was seduc'd by a neighboring Baker (reported Infamous for like Practices with others) through his Promises of some Allowance towards her necessary Maintenance to the commission of Adultery with him who was a married Man. She becoming with Child by him, conceal'd it to her time of Travel,[9] which, when she fell into, she also conceal'd under pretense of Sickness till on the 3rd day, two or three Neighbors suspecting the matter, came to her, and upon search presently discovered by her Breasts, etc. that she had had a Child. Upon their charging it, she immediately own'd and directed them to the Infant, which lay wrap'd up in a Blanket at her Feet in the Bed dead. She had a Son about seven years old and a Daughter about eleven, whom she shut out of the Room in the time of her Labor. The Daughter told the Neighbors she heard her Mother cry out. About Ten days after her Travel, she was brought to Oxon, committed Prisoner to the Castle, and toward the end of February, being about a Month after her Commitment, she was brought forth and Tried before Judge Ayres, at the Assizes there. The Witnesses (who were Neighbors above mentioned) depos'd the Matter of Fact, as above declared; and she acknowledged the Purport of it, and particularly that she call'd not out for Help, as also with relation to the Child afterwards, That it perish'd for want of suitable Help and due Attendance. So that upon the whole Matter, she was justly Convicted of Murder and receiv'd Sentence of Death. Together with which, when the Judge pronounced it, he told her with a most becoming Concern and judicious Piety to this purpose, That she had committed Murder, where even Nature, as well as the Laws of God and of the Land, one would have thought, should have bound up her Hands and so had drawn the deepest Charge of Blood upon her Soul; that from Man's Law nor God's, there was no escape for her natural Life; quoting her that Passage, "He that sheds Man's Blood, by Man shall his Blood be shed"[10] and the Statute Law of this Realm to her Case. Yet in Answer to her vehement Cries for Mercy from him, he directed her to God as being gracious, merciful and ready to forgive the Guilt of that and all her Sins, which would bind her over to a great Tribunal and more dismal Sentence; and persuaded her to apply herself to the Blood of the Everlasting Covenant, which could wash out the deepest Stains and dissolve the strongest Guilt of her Sins. Whilst she lay under Sentence of Death, she was with Care and Diligence attended by the Ordinary,[11] Mr. Blackbourne (Minister of Cairfax in Oxon), to her last hour; he instructed her in the way of Salvation, frequently pray'd with her, and gave her the Sacrament on the Sabbath Day, which was the very day before she died, she giving good Evidences of her Repentance. She was also during this time visited by the Nonconforming Minister[12] in Oxford, who from the Wednesday before her Death had daily Conferences with her. In her three first Conferences, he most industriously applied himself to lead her into an affecting Sense of the Sinfulness of her Nature, the Sinfulness of her every Sin, to bring her to an humbling Reflection upon all the Sins of her past Life before God, as also to show her the fearful Consequences of an unpardon'd, unrenew'd State, still interweaving the comfortable Doctrines of the Gospel. One particular result of these Conferences was her sending for him on the Friday before she died and acknowledging with great Remorse that she had been convinc'd of her Duty towards God by the Famous Mr. Birch, late of Burford, and had resolved on those Convictions to live more Piously, and accordingly endeavored it. But in some process of time had baffled them and returned to her former Remissness in Religion, Forgetfulness of God and of her Soul, &c.

In the two last Conferences, the Minister proceeded to make more particular Application to her concerning her closing with the Offers of Pardon and Salvation on the Terms and Grounds of the Gospel Covenant, which she profess'd her Readiness to embrace. But he admitted it not without the most trying Search he could possibly make into the Nature and Grounds of her profess'd Consent that she might not be imposed upon as to her Eternal Estate. She answer'd the most trying Questions with great Sincerity and to the great Satisfaction of the Minister, who also pray'd with her at these Conferences. Most of the Prisoners attended usually whilst he discours'd her, and it was hop'd, some of them to good purpose. The Night before she died she was observably more Cheerful in her Countenance, more Free and at Liberty in her Speech, and more Satisfied in her Condition than ever she had showed before. She said she had been under Clouds and Darkness, but God had vouchsafed her the Light of his Countenance. She Blessed God that had caus'd her Iniquities to find her out, else, said she, "I might have gone on in my Sin, smother, smother, till I had fallen into Hell." And this she did with Signal Demonstration[13] that she had a cheerful and sensible Feeling of what she said. When she was asked what she would have pray'd for her, she answer'd "greater Assurance of God's Love," but Blessed God for good Hopes through Grace. To the Pious Advice and Fervent Prayers in this her Letter to and for her Children, I am persuaded none of the Bystanders can from their Hearts witness any less than that she gave her Heart as well as Hand the Night before she was Executed. This was her own Project and Desire, and she did then most Solicitously beg of God that he would give her a Mouth of Courage to say something that might be for his Glory and the good of their Souls who should come to see her die. And when she was put upon writing to the man who had drawn her into this Wickedness and Shame, she was more than willing, nay, seemingly desirous to have something writ to him. Though she said she fear'd he was so hardened in that Sin, it would reclaim him. And though he neither came to see nor sent to her, neither took any manner of Care of or showed any Pity towards her after she was in this Distress. But want of time prevented a Letter to him. When she came to the Gallows in the Castle Yard at Oxon, at about 6 of the clock on Monday Morning, being the 7th of March, 1691/2, she said or did little there but died, only begged of the People to be warn'd against her Sins by her shameful and untimely End. And indeed, without a Miracle almost, it could not be expected she should say much more for she must needs be in great Confusion and Surprise, who in less than Two Month's time was Committed, Tried, Condemn'd and Executed for her Crime. Besides, she seem'd never to have had any great Faculty or Freedom of Speech; and further, the Fatigue and hard Fare of a Prison to one that kept the Two Thirds of her Lying in Month[14] there had mightily weakened her and impaired her Spirits; though she declar'd to one that carried her some Victuals, she ate them out of Conscience, Looking upon it as a Duty required of her by God to support her Nature for the short space of time she had to live. In short, though she died without such outward Demonstrations of it as some have done, yet there are few or none that saw the last Scenes of the last day of her Life but must own she appeared to have a great Abhorrence of Sin, a strong Love to Holiness upon her Heart, and a sincere Desire to propagate them both in others. Her Character amongst her Neighbors was a Quiet, Honest, Civil, Harmless, Poor Woman's, yea, Religious too, before this Fact. And thus you have seen what was necessary to lead you clearly into this her following Letter of Advice to her Children and to Recommend it to you as being the Advice of a Dying Penitent.

My Dear and Loving Children,

It is no small addition to my Troubles that I cannot see and speak to you before I go hence and be no more in the Land of the Living, especially considering how wanting I have been towards you. I would most willingly have endeavored to do that for you at my Death which I have hitherto neglected. I am now forced to take this way of Writing and to beg the help of another Hand, my own Hand being as my Heart is, trembling, and my confused Head incapable of expressing what I desire to impart to and impress upon you. I leave nothing in this World with so much Grief and Trouble as you my poor Children, and it greatly aggravates my Sorrow that my Sin shortens my time with you in this World. As I have heinously sinned against God and my own Soul, against him whose Body and her whose Bed I join'd in defiling and against the Life of that unhappy Infant which I took not care to preserve, So have I also offended against you, my Dear Children, whom through my own Default,[15] I am forced to leave to the wide World e're you are fit to live in it and to leave you under a Blot to be reproached, it may be, with that which is not your Fault but Unhappiness. But as to this, I'm less concern'd if you shall but make a good use of it, endeavoring to humble yourselves under that mighty Hand of the Just God, which falls so heavy even upon you through me. Consider this your Affliction is righteous with God since you also were born in Sin, and that it may by your due Improvement be a means of greatest good to your Souls. That which is my greatest Trouble with reference to you is that I have not only conceiv'd and brought you forth in Sin but have neglected the means I should have used for the changing of you from Darkness to Light and bringing you from under the Power of Satan unto God. And though I have indeed brought you to Baptism, therein professing to give you up to God the Father, Son, and Holy Spirit to be his true and faithful Servants and to engage you by that Solemn Vow against the World, the Flesh, and the Devil, Yet I have not instructed you about that Engagement nor call'd upon you to perform it. Had I consider'd how much I myself stood oblig'd to God in my Baptism and by my farther Resolutions upon sometime hearing of my Duty from Mr. Birch, I had never fallen into the Depths of Sin which have brought me into the Depths of Misery that at present cover me. 'Tis now my last time to call and your last time of hearing me call in the Land of the Living; this Call is accented to you with Groans and Sighs from the deepest bowels of a Dying Parent. 'Tis a Call to which God and all good Men witness to be your Duty, yea to which your own Consciences will witness to be so. If you diligently listen to them and do not stifle and harden them by sinning against them, 'tis a Call to the performance that I have laid you under, the most Solemn Vow and Oath to Almighty God to perform in your Baptism. 'Tis a Call of both of you, so as soon as ever you come to understand yourselves, to sign or take upon you your parts of that Baptismal Covenant which you are brought under, according to the Direction given you in Page 155 of the Reverend Mr. Allein's *Sure Guide to Heaven*,[16] which I herewith send you that you may have all the Blessings of that Covenant for your Heritage in this Life and the all-sufficient God for your everlasting Portion. If you take not upon you this Covenant so soon as you ripen in Understanding but should go on to neglect it to your Lives' end, I testify to you both, that your Baptism will prove no other than a strong Band to tie you faster to everlasting and aggravated Misery. And take notice, this Call to you to this your Duty is from one who feels every Sin cut deeper into her Soul by its having been acted against such a Vow so early laid upon me, so reasonable, so beneficial a Vow. A Vow, which had I kept, would have kept me from those Sins which now as Spears pierce my Heart and are the poisoned Arrows that drink up my Spirits. A Vow, which if kept by you, will sweeten the bitterest Miseries of your Life, yea, the most harsh and terrifying Embraces of the most painful and lingering Death. A Vow which ought to curb all your sinful Inclinations and to constrain you to all virtuous and religious Conversation in the World. A Vow which greatens all the Sins that the World count little, though they will not so account them I'm sure when they come either to repent of or suffer for them eternally. In short, it is the Vow upon you, in force of which, I conjure you both deeply to consider and diligently to observe this my Dying Charge, that you may live eternally.

Let not the Devil cheat you of your Youthful days with the Promise of a long Life to come wherein you shall serve God and save your Souls. Let him not cheat you with the fair outside of Profit, Pleasure, Ease or Esteem in Sin; no, nor with the hopes of Secrecy, Impunity, or the hopes of an after and late Repentance.

This last, believe me, is most difficult to attain, most dangerous to trust to. And as to Secrecy and Impunity in Sin, both of which were promis'd me by the Father of Lies, behold how I enjoy them whose Crimes are brought forth and punish'd in the sight of the Sun; and then depend on them if you can or dare. 'Tis a Mercy I bless the God of Grace for, that I enjoy'd them not. Believe God's Word, which tells you a Companion of Fools shall be destroy'd. Be you so wise for yourselves as to be Companions of those that fear the Lord, whilst you shun all idle Company, or loose or profane, with more care, because more dangerous than Persons infected with the Plague. The former will corrupt your Souls, the latter do but threaten the corrupting of your Bodies. I charge you as you will answer it at the Tribunal of the great God that you get and labor to understand the Catechism I herewith send you — Two Questions at least every Week out of them, that the Elder of you teach it to the Younger, whilst you are together. Hence shall you learn what God would have you be, believe and do the Ten Commandments, Lord's Prayer and Creed, being there. Thus shall you not be destroy'd for lack of Knowledge, which want highly greatens my present Misery. I farther charge you that you read some part of God's Word daily, diligently and reverently in your Bibles, since according to that Word, you must finally be Judg'd. I charge you to keep the Lord's Day holy to the Lord, spending it in publicly hearing God's Word where most soundly and affectionately Preached. And in privately reading and meditating on that Word and in Prayer because God has promis'd great Blessings to those who keep that day from polluting it. And because your religious Conversation all the Week depends much, that I say not altogether, upon this, I charge you that you pray to God devoutly and fervently on the Mornings and Evenings of every day at least, confessing the Sins of your Natures and the Sins of your Thoughts, Words, Deeds, begging God's Pardon and his Renewing Grace that you may amend and grow fitter every day you live for Heaven when you die. Beg also in your Prayers God's Protection, Provision, Guidance and Blessing, as those who are sensible that on him you depend for

Life and Breath and all things. Renounce particularly in your Prayers the Black Sins for which I die, and pray to God that he will not farther visit them upon you; yea, "Watch and Pray, that you enter not into Temptation"[17] to them. Be content with what Condition God shall assign you in this World. Be sure you Love your Neighbors as yourselves; do nobody the least Injury in Thought, Word or Deed; yea, Love Your Enemies, even those I charge you, who, you may think had the first hand in your poor Mother's Death, whom with all the World, I do now heartily forgive. Set a Watch before the Door of your Lips against all Swearing, Lying, Idle Talking, or Foolish Jesting, Slandering or Censuring any that you offend not with your Tongues. See that you be diligent in whatsoever Employment God shall assign to you for the gaining a Livelihood in this World; obey those that shall have Rule over you, as Masters, Mistresses, &c. in all things Lawful, for the Lord's Sake. And beg time from them, yea, Redeem time by your Diligence from their Business, wherein you may serve God every day. Shun all unjust ways of getting, tho' for the Supply of mere Necessity. In a word, get God's Commands into your Heads and hide them in your Hearts that you may not sin against him. Remembering always you are not of yourselves sufficient, so much as to think any good thing as of yourselves, but believe it upon my sad Experience (who fail'd and fell by trusting to my own strength for performing the good Resolutions I took up). Without Christ you can do nothing. That all your Sufficiency is of God whose Spirit and Grace you must therefore beg as you would do Bread when you are ready to starve of your Parents. Since Christ hath told you if Parents though evil give good Gifts to their Children, how much more will not your Heavenly Father give the Spirit to them that ask it and continue asking it? Oh Children, would you live happily and die so take the Advice of your Dying Mother. Would you not have it to say at last, How have we hated Instruction and despised Reproof? Would you not have God laugh at your Calamity and mock when your Fear cometh? Oh then, take my Advice as here given you. Would you be Blessings to your Generation, the Love of

Good Men, the Delight and Care of Heaven. Read then, over and over. Ponder and Practice my Advice. Bind these my Precepts on your Heads, Hands and Hearts; an Ornament of Grace they will be unto you, even as Chains about your Neck and Bracelets on your Arms. Oh what a Peaceful, Happy and Joyful Life had I led if I had ever chosen these ways of Wisdom, these ways of Pleasantness which I mark you out! Oh what an Honorable Death should I have died, what a Sweet, Flourishing and Blessed Memory should I have left behind me; whereas now, Woe is me, my Life is going out like the Snuff of a Candle, cut off in the midst of my Years; the Proud Waters are come in unto my Soul. Oh what would I now give, Ten Thousand Worlds surely if I had them, that I had led my Life as I am persuading you, the Dear Fruit of my Womb, to lead yours! Oh had I my past Life again, would I barter it away for Toys, for Vanity or sinful Pleasures? Should the World or the Devil again impose upon me as I find they have done? No, surely No. Yet alas, had I kept the Precepts I have recommended to you from my Youth upward, as exactly as I would beg of you to keep them or as you would wish you had kept them, did you stand in my present Circumstances, yea, allowing these Precepts to contain a perfect Rule of Life, yet would there be one thing lacking and chargeable upon me, even a Satisfaction for the Guilt of my Sin in and from Adam. Nor can my present Prayers, Tears, Penitent Confessions, Promises of future Obedience, &c. expiate that Guilt, much less atone for all the Violations of God's Laws through my past Life. Oh no, I must have the Righteousness of the Lord Jesus to cover my naked Soul withal before the Bar of God in order to my Acceptance and Salvation. Where's any room then, my Children, for that vain Conceit, think you, that Persons may be too diligent, exact or abounding in the Way and Works of God? When you have done all, must you not own yourselves unprofitable Servants? But oh, how much short of the whole will you fall when you do all you can of whatever I have counseled you! Believe me then, (for 'tis undoubted Truth) never any repented of too much Diligence in God's Service whilst they liv'd, much less when they came to die. Oh, that I

could draw forth the present earnest Pantings of my Soul before
you! Sure they would put your Souls into the like or better motion.
Hear Children the Prayers of your Dying Parent for her own Soul,
which she puts up with infinitely more Earnestness if it were
possible that she could pray for her Release from the present Chains
she wears, the Dungeon she lies in, the Shame and approaching
Death she is to undergo. Yea, hear the Prayers, and pray them whilst
you live, which your Dying Mother makes for you; not for Riches,
Preferment, Esteem, Ease or Plenty in this World. No, let the World
enjoy the Gods they dote on. May you my Children (who are born
with Souls naked before God and so ought to be asham'd) have the
Clothing of Christ's Righteousness to cover your sinful Nakedness.
May you who have Souls expos'd to the Wrath of God for the Sin
of your Natures and the Sins of your (but as it were) newly begun
Lives have Christ's Righteousness as Armor against the second
Death, Armor of Proof to keep off all furious Discharges of God's
Law upon you. May you who have Souls miserably poor by Nature,
void of all saving Knowledge and Grace, which are the true Riches,
have your Souls made Rich by Christ Jesus with his Gold tried in
the Fire, Rich in Faith, Rich with all the Graces of his Holy Spirit
dwelling richly in you, Rich in the Love of God manifested to your
Souls, and Rich through Christ's Purchase, in your being united to
him, having a sure Reversion of Eternal Glory. These mighty
Blessings may you seek after; may God give you them early. Had I
look'd after them as I advise you now to do, I might once more
easily have attained and secured them; I might have had the Life
and Comforts of them through my Life. Oh that I may not now
fail of these Blessings at Death! Alas that I have driven it to this
doubtful Point! God and Christ waited on me with their Offers
ever since and are ready always to bestow them upon you, if you
are but ready to receive them. Well, shall I show you the way
wherein you are to seek these Blessings, wherein seeking ye shall
find, yea, wherein only seeking, I hope myself to find them, why
truly 'tis in the way of Repentance and Faith on the Lord Jesus
Christ. The World think they can as easily Repent and Believe

almost as I can write the Words, but alas! They'll find themselves desperately mistaken if they don't alter their Minds, mistaken to their endless Ruin.

Oh, how hard it is for me to believe my Heart, which was but some Weeks ago in deep Love and League with Sin and with this World, to be now absolutely, unalterably, irreconcilably set against all Sin and set fixedly to mortify its Members to this World! My Heart once flatter'd me, the Change was wrought, but alas! 'twas but a Cheat. And do not I now want the issue of some time and trying Temptations to prove to me whether its present Pretensions to a Change be true or no? Oh my Children, don't think of delaying to begin Repentance till the time comes of Sickness or of Death, when most begin it indeed, but its odds whether one in an Hundred of them ever end it to a long Eternity. Every day you delay it, every Sin you commit, renders it more difficult to attain. Every Delay draws on the Curse of God, provoking him to give you up to a Judicial Hardness. Begin this great Work betimes, which you'll see occasion never to break off till your Lives' end. Who would be so Mad as to have the whole Volumes of their Accounts of Sins to call over, when they should have nothing to do but die? Lament your lesser Sins now that you may not have greater hereafter to lament. Lament your Budding early Sins, 'tis the way wherein you are likely to prevent gross and more grown Sins; resist the first springings of every Motion of Sin in your Thoughts, that's the way to prevent its growing into sinful Thoughts and yet more sinful Actions. Oh, that I had thus us'd myself to fight against my Lusts, surely through Almighty Grace, I could not have been thus miserably soil'd by them, surely I should have been more than Conqueror. When now, alas! Behold what Shame covers me; I am Contemn'd, the Scorn of Bad Men, and a Scandal to the Good; and now whither shall I cause my Shame to go? Well for all this, I once thought I had repented. Beware then, rest not in Sorrow for some single Sin alone; rest not in present Pangs of Grief for or hasty Resolves against Sin in general. Pray, Strive, and wait upon the Grace of God in God's way to have your Hearts deeply touch'd with Shame and Sorrow, for with the loathing of your natural Aversion from God and what is good. Labor to see an evil in Sin greater than all you can suffer for Righteousness' sake. Labor to feel it an intolerable Burden, which therefore you are glad to throw off on any Terms and by which you are brought to admire God's Terms of Pardon through Christ.

I needed a Savior, Christ Jesus, as soon as I was born, and so did you; yea, and every day you live, your need of him greatly Increases. Is it too soon to look after an Interest in him? Or can you do without it? You have an Interest in Christ if you unfeignedly consent to have him on the Terms in your Covenant of Baptism (for which, see Mr. Allein's Book again, Page 135). But Oh Fool that I was whilst I was Well, at Ease, in Business; I saw no need I had of a Savior. Or if I thought I wanted him upon the sight of some affrightful Sin or in some serious Fit, I took him for that time and banished him again when I had done with him. I thought I could have him with a wet Finger[18] almost. A Lord have Mercy upon me! An outward Reformation, some cold Prayers now and then, going to Church, repeating my Creed: I thought I could have serv'd my turn of Christ without any cordial Affection or sincere Consent. I was for having him with the World and my Sins, or when I could have these no longer. But these Shadows are fled away; now the Deceit lies plain. Christ Jesus is indeed to be had without Money and without Price; but I must give up myself to him, if I will have him; and that's no Price neither, for I am myself the Purchase of his Blood, though I have unjustly detain'd it from him. Now I am convinced I must Love, Honor, and Obey Christ Jesus, and so must all that will receive him to the saving of their Souls. And oh, Blessed Jesus, how can I be sure that I love thee now, who a while since, lov'd not thy Ways, nor thy People, for the sake of thine Image on them nor thy Laws the Image of thyself, who was for the most part of my Life doing those Works which thou came to destroy? How can I assuredly know that I Honor thee, who lately slighted and trampled under Foot thy Blood, the Blood of the Covenant, condemn'd the Methods of thy Government, despis'd in my Heart

the Mean and Garb of thy Subjects, even the chief Glories of thy
Person, whilst on Earth, viz. thy Deep Humility, Extensive Charity,
Heavenly Mindedness, Readiness to do thy Father's Will,
Faithfulness to advance his Glory? Thy Submission and Prayerful-
ness to him, thy Patience, thy Purity of Heart and Life, thy strong
Faith even under strong Hunger. These I despis'd, in that I
endeavor'd not the Practice of them, nay, practic'd contrary to them.
How know I, in short, that I Honor thee now, who know to my
Sorrow, a while since, I prefer'd Sin, my Name, yea, the Devil in
Disguise, before thee? Oh, my Lord, how know I that I now have a
fix'd and unalterable Disposition to obey thee, when before I came
into this Prison, yea, before I came into these condemned Circumstances, other Lords had Dominion over me, my Practice was quite
contrary to thy Commands? What, have I learn'd the Christian
Exercise and Discipline so soon? Learn'd habitually to deny myself,
that always us'd to please myself, even to the Refusal of myself to
thee? Have I learn'd to Watch and Pray in good earnest that I enter
not into Temptation, whose Aim and Endeavor was chiefly for
Profit, Pleasure or Esteem in this World before? What! have I learn'd
to resist the Devil that never understood his way of Fighting, his
Baits and Snares before? Have I learned to despise all this World
for Christ Jesus, that could not a while ago deny a lustful Thought,
sinful Word or Action for thee? How do I forsake this World for
thee, from which I'm forced by the Punishment of my Sins against
thee? Have I learn'd to believe all thou sayest practically that scarce
a while since could give any reason why I believed any of it
historically? Oh Good God! What a Change is this! Who amongst
my Neighbors will believe it's wrought in my Heart? Or how can
I believe, at least, how can I be assured of it? Only the Almighty
Grace of God can effect and the Spirit of God assure this Change.
Thus, thus it must be with me and everyone before they die, if
ever they be admitted into the Kingdom of Glory. Did the World
know and believe this, would they not be startled at it? But who
hath believed this Report? Children, will you also be numbered
amongst the Deceived, and at the next Remove, the Damned

Multitude? Oh be Wise, be Instructed, Kiss the Son of God, lest he be Angry and ye Perish from the way when his Wrath is kindled but a little. Blessed are all they who place a rightly grounded Trust in him. Oh learn betimes to Love, Honor, and Obey this Lord that has Redeemed you with his Precious Blood shed upon the Cross, his Meritorious Righteousness; learn to hear and know his Voice. He speaks to you in your Bibles, by Faithful Ministers, by your own Consciences, by his Spirit, by Sound Christians, if you seek to get into their Company, their Houses, yea, their Hearts, by inquiring of them concerning his Will. Nay, sure he calls you by your Dying Parent now to come to him that you may have Life, to prefer him before this World, before childish Sports and Vanity. Oh, my Aching Heart for you, my Yearning Bowels[19] towards you. What a World of Snares and Wickedness have you to pass through? What a Life probably of Labor, Contempt, and Poverty to undergo, and of Persecution too, if you will live Godly in Christ Jesus? What a Subtle Devil to resist, Cunning and Malicious to cheat and destroy you? To whom shall I leave you, to whose Care and Conduct? You have been sometime without a Father on Earth, shortly you'll be without a Mother too. Will you not seek a Father in Heaven? Oh choose Christ Jesus. He'll be a Friend, a Portion, a Guard, a Guide, Honors, Pleasures, all things; yea, even more and better than all things to you, in him God will be your Father. Oh, Blessed Trinity in Unity! Wilt thou accept my (I hope now unfeigned) Dedication of these my poor Children to thee? Oh Son of God, wilt thou be their Savior from Sin and from Eternal Death? Oh Blessed Spirit, wilt thou early Enlighten, strongly Incline, and powerfully Enable them to choose God for their Portion, Jesus for their Prince and Savior, thy Word for the Rule of their Life? Shall my Unworthy Prayer be heard on the Account of my Savior for these my Distressed Children? Oh then I'll no longer call them forsaken, no, nor think them so; the Lord is their Shepherd, they shall not want. Well, had I my Life again, my Tender Hearts, would I not again Travel in Birth with you till Christ were formed on you? Were you not Happy, think you, if you were in such a case? Will you not be happy, Children, if your God be the Lord? Well then, as you love your Souls, Pray daily, Early, Earnestly, that you may be Renewed in the Spirit of your Minds. Pray till you find a Return of your Prayers. Pray till you can understandingly and truly say you need no more Grace, no more Aids against Corruption, no more Help in Religious Duties, no more Wisdom and Resolution to contest against the Devil, who will be always Tempting you; then I'm sure you'll from this time to your latest Breath on Earth, and in all likelihood, till you breath Praises in Heaven. If you pray aright, pray earnestly; believe those Honest Christians that tell you there are Joys in Religion above the Joys of Harvest; not to the Formal, Sluggish, Inconstant, Trifling Christian, I believe, but to the Diligent. Must you not work in this World to maintain you? Will you not work for Eternity much more? With what words shall I Excite you? Will not my Death, my Doubts, my Danger of Everlasting Death excite you? Oh I exceedingly Fear and Tremble, lest your hard Heart should bar out or despise my wholesome Counsel; how oft has Heaven Thundered in my Ears, and yet I, dead in Trespasses and Sins, arose not to call upon my God? I started indeed once in my dead Sleep, but the World, Flesh, and Devil soon Lulled me asleep again, faster than I was before, on the Pillow of Carelessness and Security. Now by waking Pains I pay for that Lethargic Sleep.

Come, cast a Look with me into Eternity; see if that will move you. Oh, that I could leave you the Eyes wherewith I now see; but use your own, I mean the Eyes of your Mind, to look into Eternity. Such Thoughts will Instruct and make you Wise; Thoughts of your Temporal Death may stir you up to lay hold on Everlasting Life. Keep Death always in view of your Minds, so whenever it seizes, it shall not surprise you.

If you shall fear at anytime henceforward, when you are reading this Paper that I'm gone to the Blackness of Darkness forever, where God is only known by the Vengeance which he Executes, where the Damned drink Eternally of Rivers of Flaming Brimstone, and keep Company with Spiteful Friends in endless Despair, Will you not be afraid to follow, though it were a Mother to that Eternal

Prison? Or how can I bear the Thought that you should come to share, yet not alleviate, but sharpen Torments before Intolerable? To Curse my former Negligence towards you and your own Neglects of my present Advice in so doleful a Place, in such dreadful Company forever? Oh take Heed. Better, Ten Thousand times better, a Millstone were hang'd about your Necks, and you cast into the Depths of the Sea. But if you can believe from this Copy of my Mind that I'm gone to Heaven, the place of Everlasting Joys, will you not take my foregoing Advice, wherein I have mark'd you out the Strait and Narrow Way, thither? Oh if you do, who can tell the Joys shall attend our Meeting in those cheerful Regions that never know a Storm nor so much as fear a Cloud? Blest with the most Healthful, Refreshing Airs of God's Countenance, Water'd with the Rivers of Pleasures that flow at his Right Hand: Oh how shall we there Rejoice Eternally together!

Oh that I could prevail with you to Meditate some time every day upon Eternity! Your Mother in a few Hours will be swallow'd up therein; will not that draw your Thoughts a little thither? Oh that you might be Haunted, as it were, wherever you go with the Thoughts of Death and Eternity. I see Death marching towards me every Hour and Moment, and is it not thus marching towards you and all the World, whether they Eat, Drink, Sleep or Play? I see my Judge seated on his Throne; will he not be yours likewise, having Eyes as a Flame of Fire, which will pierce into all the Secrets, both of mine and your Hearts and Actions? I see methinks, my own Conscience unfolded and as it were, compar'd with God's Omnipotence, where all I have done in the Body is Recorded; and is there not in Heaven a Register kept of your Actions too? I hear the Devil as it were, charging all my Sins against me at God's Bar, Asserting my Services to his Interest, and putting in an High Challenge to me as his own. Will he not serve you so think you, if you serve him? I would think I hear on the other side the Blood of Jesus pleading for my Ransom from Eternal Death and Hell, as being made a Penitent Believer. This is all the Life I have in Death. Will you not want it at your Deaths? May you not have it in your

Lives? In short, I see as it were, Hell naked before me and Destruction without a Covering. I see Heaven fill'd with Crowned Martyrs, Triumphing Saints, and Shining Angels all swallow'd up in the Light and Love of the Glorious Jehovah. And now what Hope and Fear fills my Head and Heart? I can't certainly determine which is my Place and what my Portion. I liv'd neglecting to determine this great Point; 'tis just if Heaven suffer me to die doubting of it. And will you dare to do so? Can you like to die so? Oh now a World for such a Repentance as I could be assur'd I should never repent of were I to live in this World again; as that I should hate Sin in my very Soul, and burn it up with Jealousy and Indignation. Oh for such a Love to God and Holiness, as I could be assur'd, if I were to love on Earth again, would carry me through the Force of contrary Examples, through the Fires of raging Persecution, through the deepest Waters of Affliction, through the strongest Contradictions of my own Corruption to Love, Serve, Honor, Fear, Obey, Trust, Reverence, Desire, Delight in the Living God. Then would I welcome Death in its closest Attack and most dismal Shape; yea, I would leave this World with a more cheerful Heart than ever I bore in it through my whole Life. My Dear Children, that I have any Hopes now of Pardon of my Sin, Peace with God, and Everlasting Life is owing to the abundant Riches of the Glory of God's Grace. Oh, take you heed of Sinning that Grace may abound; if you do, you may come to rue it forever. But go I must hence, whether I hop'd or no; Time draws to a Close, and calls me to bid you a long Farewell. Farewell my Dear Children. May your Souls be bound up in the Bundle of Life. I commend you to God and to the Word of his Grace. May the very God of Peace Sanctify you wholly and preserve you Blameless in Body, Soul, and Spirit to the Second Coming of the Lord Jesus. Amen, Amen.

Sign'd with my own hand,
Mary Goodenough

Postscript

I am in this Paper a Witness to you my poor Orphans of your Duty and Danger. Oh, force me not in as a Witness against you by your Carelessness and Obstinacy at the Great Tribunal whither I am now called, and where you must shortly appear. Read this Paper, or get it Read to you by my Neighbor Thomas Bolt, or Mrs. Mary Rose, or such other as will teach you to Understand and Improve, not to Contemn and Neglect it. Read it over, or a good Part of it every Lord's Day. Be not ashamed of my Dying Confessions or Advice, for they are the best Remains of your Dying Mother, the only Legacy she has to leave you, and if well Improv'd, they will indeed yield you a Goodly Heritage.

FINIS

The Bloudy Mother, title page. By permission of the Houghton Library, Harvard University.

The Bloudy Mother

Or The most inhumane murthers, committed by Jane Hattersley upon divers Infants, the issue of her owne body: & the private burying of them in an Orchard with her Arraignment and execution. As also, The most loathsome and lamentable end of Adam Adamson her Master, the unlawful begetter of those unfortunate Babes being eaten and consumed alive with Worms and Lice. At East Grinsteed in Sussex near London, in July last, 1609. (1609)

To the Reader

You have here no translated wonder, no far fetched matter, no English lie, to pass for an outlandish truth, but a true relation of that that many tongues can witness to those that ambiguously shall stand to withstand it. If it is brought not with it that probability that it doth, I could not blame any that should have a jealousy or mistrust of the certainty of it; for we have had some pieces that have had fair stamps, but the stuff has been counterfeit. But this I cannot suspect can be suspected by any (after they have read it). For first, the nearness of the place where these cruelties were executed; secondly the time; thirdly the rumor hath been spread of it; and lastly the names of those that at the bench gave evidence against them, persons (for the most part) of good sufficiency, yet living, cannot but enforce a belief in any that have sense to censure upon such manifest marks of verity.

Such it is, as mothers with wet eyes, and Fathers with grieved hearts may receive: for with the chief of many precedent soul-confounding mischiefs, this may stand to show (with terror) the bloody and most dangerous events of lust and such libidinous living.

Tho. Brew.[1]

The bloudy Mother, Or The most inhumane murders of Jane Hattersley upon diverse infants, being the issue of her own body

Happy is that man whom other men's harms make to be wise. Happy, and thrice happy is he indeed: but such is the folly of men in this our unhappy age, that though they see the most heavy and lamentable ends of thousands of hell-charmed malefactors yet they will not learn good from their ill nor to be wise by their folly.

Sin, like a subtle and most cunning adulator, comes upon us with a fair look and a tongue full of most fine words and phrases, promising all happiness and sweet content at his entrance; and with that promise hastily gets to the heart of man, where having once got firm footing, he stays, till the most bitter and tormenting contraries of his promises even kill the heart he takes hold on.

O how happy is he that seeing the foul ends of folly and ungracious actions afar off, fears least the temptation and thought, which was the Embryoa[2] of that evil, insinuate, and creep into his heart; and fearing praise for assistance to him that helps, whosoever calls upon him for help. One coal of fire is easily quenched when many are hardly or never extinguished till they have confounded the matter they light on. So sin, while 'tis but a spark, with easy opposition may be expelled [from] the heart and mind of man, but suffered to feed upon the fuel Satan casts in and so to go forth and spread it-self in furious flames will be the dire fall and confusion of his sufferer.

What heavy ends follow light beginnings, we may easily see & not go far to find them; for alas, the multiplicity of sin shows it in every corner. As for example: many there be that amongst their cannes,[3] half cannes, and most unhealthful healths, have fallen from ordinary & familiar conference to high and opprobrious speeches; from such words, to blows; from blows to stabs; so in blood and hemp[4] have made an untimely and heavy division of their souls and bodies.

Some entering into play, thinking at the entrance upon nothing but the ordinary end — upon some petty, ridiculous, and most childish occasion — have entertained anger and in that madness (for in-deed it is so) one has been sent to his grave and the other to the gallows.

Some taken in the strong entangling net of a beauteous look have so labored for their maintenance and security in that most dangerous pleasure that they have drawn upon themselves an unexpected reward, for the reward of their labor has been the horror of their consciences, the grief of their friends, and the shortening of their own days with shame and bitterness.

Thus much have I said to excite men at the very beginning and entrance of sin to behold it with an eye of perfect judgement and thoughts of a heavenly temper that this Serpent, with an Angel's forehead and devil's tail, may not be suffered to creep in to his confounding labor.

But now to my bloody and heavy subject: In Sussex, in a town called East Grinsteed, dwelt one Adam Adamson, a man that for his years, place, and sufficiency in estate of living was in good account and reckoning amongst his neighbors. But men can but see as men. The eye of man cannot pierce or pry into the thoughts and intent of man; neither can it give the heart intelligence but from outward behavior and working. And therefore right easily may the judgements of men be deceived, for most common it is for man to seem that he should be and be that he should not be: so deceiving (as I said) the honest conjectures and judgements of men by a false and adulterate appearance, as in this Adam Adamson is apparent. For with a show of honesty and good dealing he covered a mass of dishonest and putrefied cogitations; amongst which, the most rank and corrupted, were of lust.

He had a wife, but the vigor and strength of lust carried his love from her to a servant he kept, who was as fit for his thoughts (in affability and easy yielding) as if she had spent an apprenticeship in a house of such trading as trains such as she to such damnable service and employment.

So much he doted upon this Strumpet that all the love and kindness that was fully due to his legitimate bedmate, she was mistress and commandresse of: what she commanded must be performed; what she requested, must be provided; and what she was displeased with, to please her must be removed. Her will was Adamant[5] and his Iron, which followed the attraction of hers to the very uttermost of her pleasure. And often to make her the more prone and apt to his will, he would promise her when his wife died to make her his wife: which promise so wrought in her mind that she thought every day a year till she might see the last gasp of her Dame.

So long were these thoughts suffered, without a gracious resistance, that they grew to that strength that they stirred her to show the foulness of them in action. But the Lord so guarded the innocent wrong'd wife of Adamson that she could not have the power to perform her devilish purpose.

Six weeks she bore poison in her purse to spice her dame's drink withal, in which time she made many fair (or rather most damnable foul) proffers, but all were most strangely and admirably frustrated by the will of the almighty searcher of hearts and reins,[6] who saw and prevented every wicked and ungodly attempt of hers. When she saw that she was so oft and so strangely prevented, she resolved to give over that purpose, and in that resolution, she threw her poison into the fire and burnt it.

Many years did this old Lecher maintain this young Lena[7] in this obscure and most foul sin, in so thick a cloud of secrecy as the devil makes fit to help those that labor in the business that is sweet & pleasing to him, for ten or twelve harvests have they reaped the most wicked pleasures of their ungodly lust. In which time, the full number of the babes they have had cannot be known, but three she confessed, besides one that is yet living.

Of the first of her loads of woe and shame (being by Adamson turned off,[8] for that he suspected she made another partner with him in his loathsome libidinous sin), she lay in the house of one Goodman[9] King, who with his wife ignorant of her ignominious course of living and present estate of body, had entertained her very kindly.

But as she deceiv'd them, she deceiv'd many, for she so cunningly blinded the eyes of people in the time that her sin must needs appear with loose lacing, tucking, and other odd tricks that she used, that to the very instant minute of her delivery, none could perceive she was with child.

This Goodman King and his wife (as thrifty persons use to do) left their bed early every morning, and Jane to lie by it at her pleasure.

It chanced so one morning, being thus left alone, that a neighbor's wife, coming to speak with goodwife King, found her in hard travail with child: which (with an astonished mind) perceiving, she presently ran to King's barn, where she found him at his labor.

To him she very hastily, as half affrighted with that she had seen, told all, desiring him to call his wife and go home. He presently left his work and went with her, and before they came to his door they met his wife, then altogether going hastily home. They met this common & most impudent bastard bearer coming out of the doors with the pretty infant, that even that minute was come from her polluted womb into this world and that then should have been tenderly laid and lovingly looked unto, most carelessly wrapped up in her apron, intending (as we may boldly imagine) in some impious and execrable sort to have made it away.

But that intent was by the blessed will and pleasure of God most happily prevented by these persons.

Very kindly at first, considering her case, they desired to see what she had in her apron; but Jane knowing the peril of it, told them she had nothing there but a few foul clothes she had looked up to have washed, and so would have past by them.

But they by no means would suffer her to pass; insomuch that she fell to striving with them for passage.

In this strife, the poor infant, so unnaturally laid by his most unnatural mother, in a pitiful shriek did, as it were, tell his preservers that she told a wicked and villainous untruth.

They hearing the cry of the infant, violently took it from her, and after they had it, with kind usage requested her to show the womanhood that in that case was requisite, and not to shame herself, and being a scandalous imputation upon her sex, by her obstinacy and stubborn wildness.

After many honest and fair persuasive speeches, they got her in a doors and laid her in her bed, Goodwife King very carefully tended her, and mistrusting she would do some mischief to that unhappy issue of her loins, she nightly lay with her.

Five or six nights she was her bedfellow, in which time she perceived in her no intent of evil against the infant, so that then she made bolder to rise from her then at the first she used to do.

But (oh grief to relate it) she was no sooner out of the house, but this shame of women took that from her sweet infant that all honest mothers strive with all tender, loving, and diligent industry to preserve and maintain.

With that hand that should have tenderly fed it and giv'n it that should have maintained the breath, the more than Tigerlike stopped the breath. O cruel mother, O grief to mothers, O wretch most wicked, unworthy the name of a mother.

Mothers have hearts of wax that melt and consume in the heat of sorrow that comes by the wrong of their children and eyes that like full fountains in abundance of tears show the grief and anguish they suffer for the least wrong their children suffer.

But this wretch had a heart of steel and eyes of marble so indurate that no motion of heaven or spark of humane pity could be seen or perceived in them.

Long this woman (though too long) stayed not in the business she went to, but returning she found a heavy object: the babe by his mother breathless, with the mouth of it all soiled with foam that rose by her violent wringing.

This sight struck her with such a strange and excogitable[10] amazement that she could not perfectly tell whether she saw that she saw or no, but felt as if her senses had lost their power and operations: for she knew she left the child perfectly well, and to see it so suddenly dead (for she was not an hour absent), she lamentably wondered.

This honest woman marvelously incensed against her by the death of the infant, presently ran and fetch'd the constable and other neighbors to see that eye-wounding spectacle, but before she (with them) could return, this most wicked of all precedent wickedness had so wrought upon the child to cleanse and trim it, that there was no sign of such a hand as is minister to a hell-hardened heart to be found upon it: so that the babe (ignorantly) taken to be ignorantly overlaid[11] (for so Jane boldly and deeply swore it was) was without any great ado, there buried. Goodwife King presently giving her such things as were hers, except a gown she stopped for some arrearages[12] of money due for some matter, turned her out of her doors.

Jane presently, notwithstanding the spleen of her master in his jealous humor, went unto him, & after a few fair words and kind promises, was as strongly possessed of his filthy affecting favor and friendship as ever she was before: where with a face artificially set, dissembling, she made a very sore complaint of very great and grievous abuse offered her by Goodman King and his wife, and how they kept her gown from her.

These words of hers stirred the blood of Adamson so strongly (in which he showed the strength of the love he bore her) that presently he got them jointly arrested, and so wrapped them (as I may say) in the law, and wrought upon that wrapping, that in revenge of his harlot, like a man utterly void of all sense or feeling, either of the joys of heaven or woes of hell, he did utterly undo this poor couple.

As soon after this as nature will suffer, mistrusted to be with child, she was searched by women,[13] and found to be so: yet against them all with bitter and vehement oaths, she stood in it they wronged her and were ignorant in that knowledge in giving that judgement upon her, swearing she was as clear from that state or the cause of it as she was in her cradle.

But within a while after (as great breakers[14] use to do), she stayed least in sight, for the space of four or five days no neighbor could have a sight of her: all which time, she lay to be delivered of the load that made her load her soul with perjury in Adamson's house.

This unfortunate fruit of lust and unlawful pleasures was no sooner born, but by the hand of the bloody mother it was murdered, and by the cunning of the cruel father, most secretly buried in a grave of his own making by the side of a Box tree in his orchard, which orchard not long after he sold to one Edward Duffield. Which done, she presently (to wipe off the stain of suspicion) crept from her bed (the bed that honest women cannot step from so lightly, neither if they could would, in decency and womanhood) to her ordinary walkings.

She was (I say) presently seen abroad again well, and so lusty, as if she had no such strength-abating pang as was justly suspected, and she truly suffered to have made her carry a contrary appearance.

But common it is that such common pieces can bear it out better than true and lawful bearers of children can.

Adamson upon this, cunning in their villainy emboldened (to cast this and other such like rubs[15] out of the way of their wickedness), impudently like a true brazen fac'd founder,[16] opposed himself against her searchers and all such as muttered in suspicion against her, with peremptory speeches, oaths and threatenings, which carried such a show of innocence and cleanness, that for that time he carried himself clear from the danger due to so foul and most vile a transgression.

The shame of her previous offending, a third time grown to ripeness, she was laid in her old receptacle of sin (Adamson's house) very privately; to which in it upon the time of her pain in that business came one Fraunces Foord, the wife of one John Foord, a neighbor, to buy bread, who hearing some low depressed cries and groans from Jane, thinking she had been diseased by some ordinary infirmity, went up: but she was no sooner entered into the room where Jane lay, but Jane very suddenly (fearing she would betray her) requested her to go down into the parlor to get her nekercher,[17] which Foord's wife did; and when she had done (mistrusting no such thing, as they feared she would find), went up again to her chamber, but ere she could get to the top of the stairs, the chamber door was shut against her by the wicked woman that was hir'd by her and her master to keep her in that case and to keep that wickedness forever concealed. This Goodwife Foord, thus withstood in her kindness, marveled, but made no words about it, yet mistrusting she knew not what, she went not down but stayed and peeped through the keyhole of the door: through which she saw Jane (very warm wrapped) set in a wicker chair by her bed's side with a look betraying very great debility and faintness of body. And not far from [her] was a good fire to comfort her and to make ready such things as might comfort her.

Yet nothing mistrusted Foord's wife that she sat then groaning under the Annual or yearly woe[18] of a woman.

But long she stood not thus, ere she heard the weak shriek of a new born infant and saw in the hands of the keeper a bole-dish,[19] in which was the afterbirth of a child and other perspicuous and evident tokens of a child born at that instant.

Having seen this, to keep it from their knowledge, she very easily went down the stairs, and after a little stay, hearing the chamber door open, up again, and suddenly (to prevent another prevention) into her chamber. And there (without any show of anything that might betray her knowledge) she stood talking with Jane half an hour: in the time of which conference, her eye and ear were busy to find that she saw through the keyhole, but she could neither see what she had seen nor heard what she had heard. For all was most cunningly cleared by her cunning keeper.

This child, as by manifest and probable circumstances appeared at her trial, Adamson (after they had by most vile and inhumane violence taken the breath from it that but then it had received) in the dead of the night (friend to rape & murder) buried in an unknown grave as the former.

And this villainy, as the former, he with his countenance as opposed against the weak words of Foord's wife by reason of want of greater proof than her own speeches, he easily passed over, and they slept as securely for all this start in their horrible uncleanness as before.

Still progressed this most graceless, audacious, and impudent beast (too bad to bear the good name of woman) in this sin with all impudency.

This Chimera[20] with a Lion's upper part in boldness, a Goat's middle part in lust, and a Serpent's lower part in sting and poison.

Not long after this (for there were no greater Interims between their great bellies than must needs be), the maturity of her womb showed itself again in swelling, which with a greater circumspection than before was looked into. Many eyes attended it to see the event and find the events of former.

But she perceiving she was so narrowly pried into, fearing they would find that they sought for (her foresaid villainy) she left her master's house and went to Darking to one Crab a Tailor, who had married a sister of hers, & in his house she was delivered of a child, which was put to nurse to one Thomas Ellis, who tenderly tended it.

There she was too far from the murdering hand or cunning brain of her master to serve it as she had served his fellows: nay this babe had such blest fortune that instead of the cruelty his poor brethren or sisters had from his lawless begetter, he had kindness and comfort, for he allowed the nurse a good cow to give her milk that the allowance of the child might be the better.

Many great bellies had she besides these here spoken of, but the unhappy loads of them could never be seen: by which we may justly think and perfectly in reason, know, that there were many more murders than are in these leaves laid open. For (as I have before said) for the space of ten or twelve years this wicked couple continued undetected in these abominable sins of lust and murder.

Many times did Adamson with his own tongue give cause of suspicion, for three or four times, as Edward Duffield wrought in his Orchard (which I have before said was Adamson's), he was earnestly requested and sometime straightly charged not to dig near the Box tree. He not mistrusting such a thought as raised that prohibition, marveled; yet not knowing what to make of it, let it pass without any further thinking upon it.

But see the goodness of the fear of every secret; within a small time after this (upon what occasion I know not) Adamson & Jane were at high words and very bitter revilings passed from one to another. In which windy battles, Jane called her master murderer in the hearing of many neighbors, and that not once or twice, but iterated and re-iterated it, very freely & boldly; and to this added, that there was that yet hidden that would hang him. And that there was a tree in Duffield's orchard, which if it could speak, would send him to the gallows.

These words in the vehemency of anger she uttered, for thus it pleased him that made Balaam's Ass[21] to speak, that beast, to make the beast speak to open the way to their destruction: for hereupon Edward Duffield took diverse of his neighbors and (remembering that many times he had been warned not to dig near the Box tree) went then and digged about it to see if there were any such thing as they suspected should be by her speeches.

Small digging serv'd to betray their wickedness, for he had not digged a full foot deep ere he found many small bones; which bones, not long after before Justices and men of account, were proved (to bar all opposite objections) by the skill of a cunning and very expert Anatomist to be the bones of a child.

Upon this (in a word) Adamson and his servant Jane were apprehended & sent to Horshan gaol some ten or twelve miles from Grinsteed; but Adamson, upon bands[22] and good security to answer all that might be objected against him at the Assizes,[23] was in a little time from thence released and had his liberty to walk about his business.

Jane lay not long there neither; she was upon bonds from thence released too: but her bonds were the bonds she was bound in & her release but a remove from thence to the King's bench[24] in Southwark, where while she stayed, she wanted nothing, for he that had been kind and liberal to her in the time of her liberty did not forget her in the time of her captivity.

But that he did at the first was in love, the last in policy: for all he spent then upon her was only to win her confidently to deny the words she had spoken & to clear him in her speeches; as for herself, he had her perform upon it, without fear or doubting he would get her pardon.

But to prevent that and all hope of it, she was removed from thence to Kingston, from thence (to omit tedious recital) to Grinsteed again. And there again Adamson as before (for contrary to orders in that case instituted, whether by purse or policy I know not, he had access unto her in the gaol) labored hard with her to unsay all her dangerous words against him; and to say that she was to say at the Bench to the demands of the Judges for his clearing & acquitting & withal told her that in so speaking well in his behalf, she should help herself in that danger.

And moreover (for like waves one upon the neck of another came words of inducement from him) if the worst should come that might, he would save her with the King's pardon.

And to make her belief and resolution the stronger, he told her if she did not do as he counseled her there was no less to be expected by her than death, and backed it with this reason: that the least syllable uttered in way of confession would frustrate the pardon he should purchase and make it to be of no force or virtue.

Thus, as since her execution hath been found, did he very cunningly and as closely work upon her simplicity, and offered his wishes in her most wicked and impious credulity. For she, believing all he spoke and making no doubt of the performance, with a face set to the highest key of impudency, was at the Bench very ready in the lesson he had taught her; so that he was by the Jury acquitted, but she condemned and adjudged to the gallows, which sentence (presuming upon her master's promise) she heard with an undaunted heart.

To be short, she was according to her judgement, upon or about the first of July 1609, carried to the place of execution, where still expecting the pardon Adamson told her should come to the gallows and save her, she was as stout and fearless, as if she had been but (like a stage player) to act the part in jest.

But when she had stayed so long she might stay no longer from the halter, her heart began to fall and fear to rise, yet remembering that he had said a word in confession should frustrate her pardon, which (not withstanding) in the last minute of her breath she expected (and fearing so to prevent it) she would say nothing but in that fear and hope of life. Even in the rope she gave the hangman six pence to cut her down quickly: for she (simple wench) thought verily though she were turned off,[25] before she could be half dead the pardon would come & save her in that heavy gasping. But her belief was vain, and her vain hopes were deceived, for as she deserved, she there died.

But now you have with the eyes of your understanding seen the most just and deserved end of her, turn them again to Adamson, who presently after her execution fell into a most miserable, grievous, and lamentable consumption.

Worms' meat we are all in death, but he in life was (by the just judgement of God, which God makes us all have an eye to) a prey to these despicable and devouring creatures, which had entrenched themselves in many parts of his body to the bone, and minutely, and so mercilessly, with eager appetites fed upon his afflicted flesh, as though he had been laid only out but for one meal to be devoured.

Lice in great multitudes tormented him. No shift in linen nor other costly shift in trimming, picking, & anointing could decrease the innumerable number of them, and so loathsome a savour[26] came from his body that those that went to see him could not stand to give their eyes satisfaction for the grievous and odious strength of it. But turning as disdainfully in the offence (or grievance of that sense) as from the infecting stench of carrion, they would leave him ere they could well look on him.

Thus for the space of half a year lay he most grievously tormented, in which time, he spent much money for a happy restoration or recovery, but all his cost was lost, for alas, *Cum deo pugnare, grave est*: there is no striving against the will of God.

All his means were wasted and consumed, for he never left consuming till he was consumed to skin and bone, and so lamentably ended his days about the beginning of November last.

If we look well into this lamentable end of his, we shall find a lesson worth the looking into, and that is this: that though he could by money and friends some false color and covering prevent his defect from the hands of men, yet the Lord would not let him pass this world without a punishment, that like the Sun burst out through the fogs & clouds of his dissembling and privy[27] contriving to show the world that he was not the innocent man that he would have seemed to be.

Many that have wit to shift[28] and craft to cover think themselves wise, but the Lord knows they are fools & so makes their end show them. But to that we cast not an eye, but (alas) being set in the race of our own ruin we run (like the O-nagrie,[29] or Wild Ass of Mauritania), with such dexterity and strength, that till we are breathless we stop, not till we are breathless indeed: for till our breath leaves us, we leave not sinning. O could we imitate him as well in the path of piety, We should have heaven in our bosoms. I mean such consciences as (after this life) would assure us of the everlasting beatitude of Angels.

An exhortation

If the Apostle Peter illuminated by the spirit of God, in his time determined the consummation of the world to draw nigh, and like the Lord of Hosts his loyal Herald proclaimed thereupon to all the faithful: "Now the end of all things is at hand"; If godly Cyprian[30] many years after, justly thought and taught that the end of the world did hang over his head; If sweet Lactantius[31] sighed in spirit & said it could not lack above two hundred years, and holy Jerome[32] (that observed a journal & watched the hours of his life) had so certain a persuasion of the suddenness and nearness thereof that he ever seem'd to hear the sound of the Trump[33] of the latter day, sounding this heavy note in his ears: "Arise ye dead and come to judgment," all no doubt incited thereto and guided by the holy Ghost, certes[34] we have the great and good cause that live in these later and dangerous days steadfastly to believe for many causes, and especially these three, that the second coming of Christ cannot be far off.

First, for that all the prophesies of the Patriarchs and Prophets, of all the ancients, yea, and of the Jews themselves, who yet idly and ignorantly expect another Messiah, so concordantly agree with this our after age, that the Orthodoxes so long since deceased may seem now to live and behold the state of the days instant.

Secondly, for that all those prodigies and tokens foretold by our Savior in the Gospel are now universally fulfilled in the world and authentically import an universal dissolution of the world.

Thirdly, for that in the same place our Savior promises to shorten those days; and surely if (as there he promised) for his elects' sake those days were not shortened, scant any flesh should be saved; for if we narrowly look on the course of time, the manners of men, the starting up of false Christs, the uprise of counterfeit Prophets, the contempt of Religion, and untowardness of all things, we shall assuredly find that this our old writhen[35] world is altogether like to unfruitful and dry stubble or chafe, apt for nothing, but to be consumed with fire, or as the Apostle Peter saith, "The heavens and earth that now are kept by the same word in store and reserved unto fire against the day of judgement." Lord it is time, yea it is full and due time (if it were thy blessed will and pleasure) that thou come to judgement. Come thou *Alpha* and *Omega*, thou first and last, come Lord Jesu, come quickly: For sin overfloweth, Iniquity aboundeth, Faith faileth, Hope fadeth, Love freezeth; instead whereof Paganism, Despair, and Murder are founded, and generally wickedness flourisheth and virtue falleth.

But omitting all the rest, this willful murdering of Innocents is judged a most heinous iniquity in the sight of God and amongst all good men counted principal of those sins, whose lamentable clamors ascend up before the majesty of God, & incessantly yell out, greedily thirsting for revenge.

Let us therefore take warning by those Cruel, bloody,
and libidinous bad livers, whose horrid sins calls vengeance
from heaven: and let us desire almighty God to
hasten the latter day to the comfort of his elect
and glory of his most holy name
Amen.

The names of the witnesses.
Master Andrew Sackvill
Edward Paine.
George Drury.
Steven Price.
And Edward Duffield in whose orchard the bones of the murdered Infants were found.
Goodwife King
Goodwife Foord
Goodwife Paine
Goodwife Pulman
Goodwife Kent.

FINIS

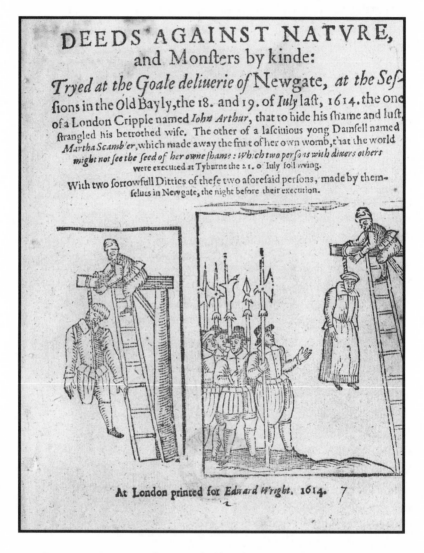

DEEDS AGAINST NATVRE,

and Monſters by kinde:

Tryed at the Goale deliuerie of Newgate, *at the Seſ-*
ſions in the Old Bayly, the 18. and 19. of *Iuly* laſt, 1614. the one
of a London Cripple named *Iohn Arthur*, that to hide his ſhame and luſt,
ſtrangled his betrothed wife. The other of a laſciuious yong Damſell named
Martha Scambler, which made away the fruit of her own womb, that the world
might not ſee the ſeed of her owne ſhame : which two perſons with diuers others
were executed at Tyburne the 21. o Iuly foll wing.

With two ſorrowfull Ditties of theſe two aforeſaid perſons, made by them-
ſelues in Newgate, the night before their execution.

At London printed for *Edward Wright.* 1614. 7

Deeds Against Nature, title page, shelfmark 4° L.68 Art (7). By permission
of the Bodleian Library, University of Oxford.

Deeds Against Nature, and Monsters by kinde:

Tried at the Goal delivery[1] of Newgate,[2] at the Sessions[3] in the Old Bailey,[4] the 18th and 19th of July last, 1614, the one of a London Cripple named John Arthur, that to hide his shame and lust, strangled his betrothed wife. The other of a lascivious young Damsel named Martha Scambler, which made away the fruit of her own womb, that the world might not see the seed of her own shame: Which two persons with diverse others were executed at Tyburn[5] the 21st of July following. With two sorrowful Ditties of these two aforesaid persons, made by themselves in Newgate, the night before their execution. (1614)

Is it not a marvel that fire falls not from heaven to consume an infinite number of worse than savage natur'd people in this land, when vile wretches, whom God hath marked with his secret brand of secret purpose, so impiously attempt things against nature, as for example (which God grant it may so prove for our amendment), here remained amongst us in this City a deformed creature, an unperfect wretch wanting the right shape and limbs of a man though in form and visage like unto one of us. This decrepit creature (as I said) named John Arthur, lived and maintain'd himself with the charity and devotions of alms-giving people, and by his lame and limbless usage purchased more kind favors than many others of his base fraternity: money and means being easily gained by a few beggarly observations, as a wretch graceless and unthankful for God's blessings thus bestowed upon him, made no good use thereof, but spent the same in the service of the Devil, as in blasphemy, swearing, drunkenness, and such like, all damnable sins and such as be the nurses and breeders of others. This aforenamed Cripple, being on a time in the middle of his drunkenness heated with lust, fell into familiarity with a certain woman of his own condition, who purposing to live as he did, upon charity and good men's alms, and seeing good benefit to come by his lameness, unto who many people grew willing to give, promised to be his associate and his companion and wife to beg with him. Many days and months spent they together, continually abusing the gifts of charity and wasting away the same with drunkenness in the by-places and suburbs of the City, which is evermore the receipt of such begging vagabonds and disordered livers, instruments of the devil prepared still for deeds of mischief. This Cripple, having not one good thought of God's grace, so lusted after his begging companion that he obtained the daily use of her body and continually committed to that sin of lust & shame, making a practice thereof in the contempt of God's Laws, that the eye of heaven could no longer wink at them, but with a clear sight see their base wickedness; yea, more than base in that a deformed lump of flesh, and no perfect creature should thus abuse the seed of generation and now and then in the fields and highways commit such beastly offenses. But God, we see, hath iron hands and will at last strike heavily, as he did upon these two shameless malefactors. For the Cripple in time surfeiting[6] upon this his shame and growing weary of this hated offense, as all people will do being not lawfully married, began to cast her off and to loath her company, though he himself might be thought the more loathsome, which she (abused woman) perceiving and knowing herself to be but his strumpet, challenged of him the promise of marriage and so importuned him thereunto by his former vows and promises and that heaven would otherwise call his perjured oaths to account, all instigations of the devil, and subtle policies to draw them both to destruction. Her importunate suits to marriage so troubled his mind, bred such a rage in his heart, that a purpose came into his mind to rid her away by some untimely death, a motion no sooner set on fire, but the devil was ready to bring more fuel and never rested till it was all on a flame. So upon a night, a time fitting for such a dark deed, the Cripple enticed her forth into the fields near Ilsington, where secretly at the Brick Kils, the lodging place for rogues and nightwalkers, he renewed his former familiarity and with a dissembling kindness persuaded her to lodge there with him all night, which she, mistrustless woman, consented to, and little misdoubting his devilish intent, laid her down upon a pallet of straw by him to sleep, which as a token of hard misfortune suddenly possessed her. The Cripple, perceiving all secure and silent, and now thinking to be rid of the shame thus daily following him, took this woman's own girdle and putting the same slyly about her neck, where though nature had denied him strength and limbs, yet by the help of the devil, which always adds force to villainy, he made means in her sleep to strangle her and to take away her life, as it were suddenly without repentance. Therefore, all people by this example ought still to be prepared for death, for he comes as a thief in the night and gives no warning. Who would have thought such an outcast of the world, such a lame deformed creature, not able of his own strength to help himself, should have power to take away another's life? But the devil, we see, is cunning and will still make the simple his strongest assisters, and those that be the most weakest to be of the vilest thoughts. But to conclude, the cripple, blinded thus with his own shame, had that ignorant opinion of the discovery hereof that he thought the world too simple to look into his life and his decrepit carriage would keep away all suspicion and that no man would think a lame creature could be able to do so wicked a deed, but graceless varlet, as he was, too much flattered in his own opinion. The Devil, as he was first beginner of his sin so was he last end of his shame, for the same morning the woman was found thus murdered, and being seen the night before in his company, [he] with slender examinations confessed the fact. Where for the same he had his trial at the Sessions by a Jury of twelve men and his execution at Tyburn in the sight of many hundreds of men, woman, and children, which accounts him to be a Monster by kind and the doer of a deed against nature.

Like unto this viper of our age, we are to place in Our discourse another Caterpillar[7] of nature, a creature more savage than a she wolf, more unnatural than either bird or beast, for every creature hath a tender feeling of love to their young, except some few murderous-minded strumpets — women I cannot call them, for a woman esteems the fruit of her womb, the precious and dearest Jewel of the world, and for the cherishing of the same will (as it were) spend her life's purest blood. Where, contrariwise, the harlot (delighting in shame and sin) makes no conscience to be the butcher of her own seed, nay, the Image of God created in her own body, and now and then in the conception makes spoil of the bed of creation before it can receive true form. Therefore for an example likewise, cast your eyes upon this other monster of nature, which was a lascivious, lewd, and close strumpet, a harlot lodging privately near Bishopsgate in Bedlam at a kinsman's house of hers, which little suspected this her unwomanly carriage. But shame long raked up in the ashes of secrecy, though close smoking, will at last break forth into open flame. So this graceless wanton (spending her youth in lascivious pleasures, as many a one does in and about this City) happened to prove with child, & having no husband to cover this her act of shame, and withal fearing the disgrace of the world, by a devilish practice sought to consume it in her body before the birth. But not prevailing (as God would have it), she was forced by nature to deliver it alive to the world and so was made the unhappy mother of a man-child. Unhappy I may name her, for her own hand made her unhappy. To our purpose, her lusty body, strong nature, and fear of shame brought an easiness to her delivery and required in her agony no help of a midwife, which among women seems a thing very strange, for not so much as the least child in the house where she lodged had knowledge of her labor, nor hardly was she thought to be with child so closely demeaned she herself. But the devil, we see, adds force unto wickedness and puts a kind of strength to nature in that kind, otherwise had she been discovered in the childbirth.

Consider this the Child being born with shame: she by it made a scandal to her acquaintance, renewed the remembrance of her passed sins, and presented present shame unto her grieved thoughts, which troubled cogitations by the persuasions of the Devil put her in mind violently to make it away and to give it death before the body had well recovered life. Whereupon taking the poor tender babe as it were new dropped from the mother's womb, and not like a mother but a monster, threw it down unto a loathsome privy house, therein to give it an undecent grave, and as she thought thereby make to herself a riddance of a further Infamy; but God is Just and will reward shame where it is deserved, and such unnatural deeds let them be acted in deserts, in the caverns of the earth where never light of day nor Sun shines, yet will they be discovered and brought to the world's eye. So happened it with this harlot. When all fear of suspicion was past, she safely delivered, the Child in the privy smothered, and in the world no notice taken thereof, yet in the end was it thus most strangely discovered. The Tunnel of the aforesaid vault or privy ascended up into the next neighbor's house, as in many places they do, where by chance (as God had ordained) dwelled an untoward lad that, in taking delight in knavish pastimes, took a cur Dog then living in the house and carelessly threw it down the Tunnel into the vault where the murdered infant lay, and taking no regard thereof, interred the Dog to remain there wailing and crying for food the space of three days and nights. During which time the yelping of the dog much disquieted the neighbors and so troubled the dwellers there abouts that they could not sleep a nights for the noise, but especially the good man of the house, who grieved to see a dumb beast so starved and for want of food thus to perish, like a kind natur'd man caused the privy to be opened and the poor cur taken up, which proved by God's Justice the only discoverer of the aforesaid fact. For in taking up the dog, they were woeful witnesses of the sweet Babe lying all besmeared with the filth of that loathsome place. The sight whereof caused no small amazement, especially to the good man of the house, who with diligent care (as his duty was both to God and his country) and that all such inhumane deeds might be brought to light, made it known to the Magistrates, which likewise with Christian care caused a certain number of substantial women to make search of suspected persons and of such who were like to be the murdered Infant's mother, or murderer, amongst many other loose livers and common harlots, of which number these by places have too many, the more is the pity. This aforesaid murderess came to the touch,[8] where upon examination, she confessed the child to be born with life, and herself not worthy of life, and so pleading guilty, she was brought to her trial and for the same arraigned and condemned by the assize[9] in the old Bailey the 18th and 19th of July last 1614, and hath suffered death at Tyburn the 21st, following as an example, that God, either by beasts of the field, fowls of the air, fishes in the seas, worms in the ground, or things bearing neither sense nor life will by one means or other make deeds of darkness clear as day, that the world may behold his high working powers, and that no malefactor can escape unpunished, though his deeds be as secret as the works of hell, beyond the thought of human imagination. Convert us from sin, great God of Israel, so that we never be endangered with the like persuasions, which God in his mercy grant. Amen.

The Cripple's complaint in the Dungeon at Newgate

Me thinks I hear a doleful sound,
Within this dungeon under ground:
Prepare thyself (poor soul) to die,
For so the Bellman's[10] voice doth cry.

And Beggars all come ring my knell,
The Cripple now bids all farewell:
Both Crutches, Scrip,[11] and patched gown,
Wherewith I begg'd from town to town.

Though limbs I want and could not go,
Yet was my mind not pleased so:
But had my faults, as others have,
Which brings me thus unto my grave.

In vain delights I spent my days,
And wronged my fortunes many ways:
The alms that good men gave me still,
I wasted to content my will.

For heaven had marked me out for shame,
Whereto I did my courses frame:
And as I was misshaped by kind,
Deformed also was my mind.

For by that sweet enticing sin,
My sudden downfall did begin:
Wherein I set my heart's delight,
On wanton women day and night.

At last when I love's pleasures prov'd,
I hated her whom late I lov'd:
And sudden loathing, soon begun
Ashamed sore, of follies done.

And still desired to end the life
Of her, I promised to make Wife:
For love so gained can never last,
No sooner done, but love is past.

Then as my shame I hated her,
And would her death no time defer:
But arm'd with wroth[12] in dead of night,
I trained[13] her from all people's sight.

That never more my follies great,
To my disgrace she should repeat:
Nor say unto the world, that I
Had liv'd with her most wantonly.

For in the fields we two alone,
With weeping tears and bitter moan:
She crav'd amends for my amiss.
To make her Wife as reason is.

But I refus'd that honest course,
But did an act of sad remorse:
To end her shame with mine as then,
I did exceed the deeds of men.

The devil my helper at that hour,
For he as then had strongest power:
Nor by his means I could not faint,
Though I was lame and limbs did want.

My heart with furious rage possessed
About her neck her girdle cast,
And forced so away her life,
Rather than make her married wife.

Never like deed by Cripple wrought,
For pleasures being too dearly bought,
Both old and young, both rich and poor,
Make never maid a common Whore.
     For doing so my life I lose,
With burdens of repentant woes,
For wanton loves are wretched things,
And with them still much sorrow brings.
     Adieu vain world, the Cripple cries,
In this my life much wonder lies:
That born a lame deformed wight,
Should thus take pride in love's delight.

Martha Scambler's Repentance

Poor I, The poorest now on earth,
May well accuse my cause of birth:
Not being born I never had known,
     This guilt that hath me overthrown.
Woe worth the cause of sin and shame,
Which stains my credit and good name:
Woe worth the trains which still are laid,
Whereby we women are betrayed.
     When I was won to follies' will,
And took delight in doing ill
No thought I had of pleasures past:
But still my youth did vainly waste.
     Till at the length my womb did breed,
A substance of unlawful seed:
Which I supposed a shame to be
(God knows) unto my friends and me.
And to prevent the world's disgrace,
I sought to find a secret place,
My shameful burdened womb to ease,
That way which did my God displease.
I, when my hour of labor came,
To bring to light this fruit of shame,
No Midwife's help at all I sought,
But soon my own delivery wrought.

The Babe being born and in my arms,
I should have kept it from all harms,
But like a Bear or Wolf in wood,
I wished it smothered up in blood.
Whereat strange motions without fear,
From hell to me presented were,
And bade me bury it in a Vault,
For none alive did know my fault.

And so my credit and good name,
Should take no spot of black defame:
And I as pure and chaste should be,
From such a crime as any she.

My soul then blinded by the Devil,
Bid me consent unto this evil:
Where I full soon thereto agreed,
To act a more than woman's deed.

The loathsome Jakes[14] received my child,
Which all misdoubts and fear exiled
For being tumbled down therein,
There well might end my shame and sin.

But God, this deed more dark than night,
In wondrous sort did bring to light,
For by a Dog the Child was found,
As it was thrown therein to drown'd.

Three days and nights with yelping cry,
It troubled much the dwellers by,
Which caus'd them to release him thence,
And so found out this vile offence.

For which I surely now must taste
Rewards for my offences past,
And die for that accursed crime,
That makes me monster of my time.
Both maids and men, both young and old,
Let not good lives with shame be sold,
But bear true virtues to your grave,
That honest burials you may have.

FINIS

Natures
Cruell Step-Dames :

O R,

Matchleſſe Monſters of the Female

Sex; *Elizabeth Barnes*, and *Anne Willis*.

Who were executed the 26. day of *April*,
1637. at Tyburne, for the unnaturall murthering of their owne Children,

Alſo, herein is contained their ſeverall Confeſſions,
and the Courts juſt proceedings againſt other notorious
Maleſactors, with their ſeverall offences
this Seſſions.

Further, a Relation of the wicked Life and
impenitent Death of *Iohn Flood*, who raped
his own Childe.

Printed at London for *Francis Coules*, dwelling in
the Old-Baily. 1637.

Natures Cruell Step-Dames, title page. By permission of the Folger
Shakespeare Library.

Natures Cruell Step-Dames: or, Matchlesse Monsters of the Female Sex;

Elizabeth Barnes, and Anne Willis. Who were executed the 26 Day of April, 1637 at Tyburn,[1] for the unnatural murdering of their own children. Also, herein is contained their several Confessions, and the Court's just proceedings against other notorious Malefactors, with their several offences this Sessions. Further, a Relation of the wicked Life and impenitent Death of John Flood, who raped his own Child.[2] (1637)

A Narration of the Diabolical seduction of Elizabeth Barnes, late of Battersey in the County of Surrey, widow, mercilessly to murder Susan Barnes, her own natural child

A Whole month, as she confessed in the public hearing of diverse persons of good repute, this Savage continued with this hellish fire kindled in her breast, violently at the last breaking forth into the unnatural deprivation of the life of the fruit of her own womb. The subtle serpent Satan, that thus long time has possessed her, put into her mind the manner how to put in execution her diabolical, execrable intention on the innocent child without its least suspicion, as you may perceive by the sequel of the History. To entice the child unto its slaughter and to go abroad with her, she provided [on] the 24 day of March last 1637 very early in the morning, an Apple Pie, a Herring Pie, Raisins of the Sun, and other fruits which she carried with her, accustomed baits used by loving Parents to quiet and still their children in their unquietness, but this creature otherwise, to destroy her child by that means. These things being thus prepared beforehand, and the child beholding them, did set an edge on its affections[3] willingly to accompany her cruel mother in her travel towards her long home.

The innocent Lamb and ravenous Wolf both spend out the day together with joyful expectation, the one willingly endured the travel and heat of the day to go to be placed with a kinswoman of hers, as was pretended, but alas, this was but flattery to shed innocent blood. Towards the evening of the same day, these her alluring kind of deadly junkets she brings with her child into a Wood called Wormewall Wood, being in the parish of Fulham in the County of Middlesex, some four miles distance from the place where she dwelt; being there in secret and covered with darkness, she feigned unto the child this excuse, saying, that she was very weary and was not able to go any further, but must upon necessity stay a while, there to rest and ease herself, the which the poor child, as she said, most lovingly entreated her to do, being also glad of such repose. Being set down together, she took out of her basket, the Pies, and fruit, and sets them before the child for to eat of them, which did so.

Thus having eaten of such things formerly provided for it, being tired with going so far a journey, it being but of the age of eight years, afterwards sweetly fell into a fast sleep, which was very opportune for her mother's accursed design, for that same night about the hours of xi and xii, she drew out of her sheath a knife, and with that knife barbarously did cut the throat of the child. Soon after this bloody fact being done by her, her eyes were opened that she beheld her miserable condition, and that, that by her bloody hands had been done, that could no way be again undone. She resolved beforehand how to dispose of herself after the fact committed. For she carried with her the instrument of her own death, as she did the child's; for it a knife, so a halter wherewith to end her own life, and attempted it, but had not power to lay violent hands on herself, being mercifully thereof prevented by the all-powerful hand of heaven. After this first attempt, as she said, she was strongly set on again by the Devil to drown herself, but that prevailed not against her, but forthwith broke out then into a great passion, as it were a fountain of tears, humbly and heartily imploring Heaven's mercy and forgiveness for her bloody crying-fact.

Her guilty conscience will no way permit her to rest or show her any place of refuge for safety, but according unto that saying of the Psalmist it falls upon her: "Evil shall hunt the wicked person to overthrow them,"[4] and so it did, to the full satisfaction of all the beholders. For whether does this affrighted Creature run or flee suppose ye, but even unto the gates of Justice, crying, as it were there, for Justice to be rendered according to her demerit? From the wood she flees into Kensington, and there hides herself all in straw, in the Barn of one Disney. And being there found, suspicion of this murder was laid unto her charge, which she confessed to his wife and servant, and afterwards she was carried unto Master Pen, a Justice in that Town, unto whom she confessed the same fact.

This fact being rumored abroad, I went unto Newgate[5] to visit this miserable delinquent, who at my first view of her matronlike aspect induced me to enter into present discourse with her to prevail if I could possibly to find out the cause that moved her unto such unheard of cruelty. She answered me again, none but the Devil alone tempted her thereunto, and with tears fast trickling down her cheeks, desired myself with the rest that stood by to pray unto Almighty God to take mercy on her poor sinful soul, to save that from hell.

A second time I urged her to discover the cause of that fact and disburden her conscience, and somewhat then fell from her, thus saying, that she had spent all the estate she had upon one that pretended love unto her, and being by that means become poor and indebted, knew not what would become of her, but instantly resolved on this desperate course, leaving such deep impression in her mind with the continuance of time in not disclosing of it that the temptation and resolution waxed daily stronger and powerfully wrought on her. Being demanded what she thought should become of her after the fact done, thus replied, that she attempted to hang herself, but had not power, nor doubtless could not have such a hard heart to kill the child had it been but awake, as it was asleep. For that time I departed from her, and freshly the third time endeavored to discover more but could not, but constantly she adhered to her former confession, no whit varying.

Serious advertisements unto all good Christians, and cautions
by this ignorant sinful woman's sudden downfall

If this woman's house had been set on fire, doubtless she would have made such an outcry in the streets that all her neighbors must of necessity rise and add unto her all help possible to quench the fire. Her heart was here set on fire by hell. Musing to perpetrate mischief, her tongue is silent and mouth is shut when it should have been wide open to cry aloud unto God for grace and mercy and to crave the help of the effectual prayers of God's holy Ministers and Congregations of his Saints here on earth to deliver her out of the snare and bondage of Satan, whom she voluntarily obeyed. If a limb had been broken, she would not rest satisfied till a Chirurgeon[6] had been present for to cure her. If she had fallen suddenly desperate sick for fear of death, hastily they post and run to seek for a Physician; but her soul is sick and draws nigh downward into Hell. What care or cure of that? Where was God or his Ministers thought of all this while? Blessed Saint Paul, so soon as the Viper seized on his hand, shook it off immediately into the fire: a whole month this venomous Viper, Murder, lodged in her heart. God, prayer unto him, and hearing of his Word all this while was laid aside. Cunning, deluding Satan sat likewise on her tongue, as he took seizure on her heart, that he tied fast, not able to pray, which might have prevailed against him. Devout Prayer is his scourge, and faithless faint-hearted people only give place unto him and sink down at his feet.

The Devil is but a weak faint-hearted Coward. "Resist him," saith the blessed Apostle, "and he will fly from you."[7] This kind of evil spirit, saith our Savior Christ, cannot be cast out, but by fasting and prayer. Our blessed Savior Jesus Christ in the disconsolate time of his most bitter passion on the Cross for our sakes, to encounter Satan, to comfort himself in that great Agony he was in, and to get the Conquest of that grand captain of all mischief, prayed unto his heavenly Father in the Garden, inculcates frequently this duty unto his distressed followers, "Watch and pray," and joins the necessity of it, "least ye fall into Temptation."[8] Is a weak child able to stand in the way of a Lion stirred up unto fury and rage? No whit possible. Much less is a sinful weak man able to grapple with the powerful strength of sin and Satan; and therefore pray that power may be given unto you from above to resist the least of whose temptations ye are no ways able to resist of yourselves. 1 Peter 5:8: "Be sober, and watch for your adversary the Devil, as a roaring Lion walketh about, seeking whom he may devour." *Diabolus non dormit*;[9] the Devil is not idle, neither sleeps nor slumbers, but watches to take his advantage, seeks which way unawares to rush in suddenly upon poor souls. By lamentable late experience, Satan has foiled many. Witness those weekly bills of casualties for London and Middlesex. The Devil, although he is impudent and potent, the holy Apostle in the ninth verse shows a means there to abate his pride who resist in the faith.[10] A faithful Christian makes him to fly, fear, and quake. In the first of Samuel Chapter 17, verse 40, there is mention made that David chose him five smooth stones out of a brook; with one of them he slew Goliath.

Learned Physicians apply various medicines unto the nature of the disease, but unto Christians only one Sovereign medicine as an Antidote is prescribed against all manner of malignous[11] diseases: the only remedy is medicine of Prayer. The healthy man prayer preserves alive; the sick man Prayer restores health. In time of war prayer is the victorious Conqueror. In the time of Peace prayer is the infallible Defender of King and people, in health and propriety. Saint James Chapter 5 verse 15: "Sins are promised to be forgiven, and the prayer of a righteous man avails much if it be fervent." As the foot by paces carries the body, so the soul is carried up unto Heaven by Prayer; therefore let thy prayer ascend up unto thy God daily that he may send down the dew of his holy Spirit into thy soul. Satan is cast under thy foot when thou raise up thy soul toward Heaven by Prayer. Two manner of ways there are that man may climb up unto the top of Heaven's holy hill, namely meditation and prayer; meditation is prayer's handmaid. Meditation instructs what becomes the soul to do; prayer supplies what is wanting unto the soul.

Good King David in the 5th Psalm, verse 3 made a promise unto Almighty God, and what was it? "My voice shalt thou hear betimes, Oh Lord, early in the morning will I direct my prayer unto thee, and will look up."

We are of the Lord Jesus commanded this chiefly (to pray) that of him unto whom the secrets of all hearts are manifest, we may receive openly a heavenly Reward of our Prayers offered in secrets. To conclude this, as the Psalmist advised, "Pour out your prayers before him, without which no minute of the day can be happy unto us." I will commend unto your daily meditations and practice that replete zealous Collect[12] prescribed to be read in the second Sunday in Lent, and the Lord give a daily blessing to those that do embrace the instruction.

The last caution is the neglect of God's Minister in not repairing unto him

Sin is like a spot in a garment. At the first it may be easily expunged, but by continuance, it gathers more and more soil unto it, making it so difficult that it frays the garment into pieces before it can be clean. Ignorant people behold their sins through the spectacles of their own fantasies; they extend or extenuate their sins as they please, thereby deceiving themselves; some make sins lesser and others greater than they are, and it cannot otherwise possibly be because they are not able to judge of the difference, being ignorant and unlettered, than a blind man can distinguish colors.

A stumbling block into this women's way the Devil casts, not to go unto her Minister unto whom the Almighty GOD had given the pastoral Cure of her soul to reveal her mind unto him, for fear of revealing it again. What does GOD intrust us with your dear souls? And will not you trust us with your filthy sins? To discover them, to disburden your heavy laden consciences, will you not make nice to show a noisome foul ulcerated body, and show the place where it pains you most to the chirurgen, to have thereby ease, and be too, too curious in the matters of your soul? Your abominable sins let them alone untouched, or not confessed at all, which by confession may be lessened, and people made wary to walk more circumspectly, and the heinousness of sin being set before men's eyes may deter them from committing of them again. Beloved, a weak slight and subtlety in the Devil that withholds the poor pensive sinner from his ghostly comforter (Confession), what then? Oh no, by no means, I will not do it; he will reveal me. Will you not blush for shame nor hold it no blemish to harbor wicked thoughts in your hearts, which GOD knows and sees, and in the open day of the world exorbitantly commit them, and is this a greater offense to confess them and to turn from them, judge ye? Our aim of the Church of England is not such, as that of Rome, to creep into men's secret hearts, to hold them in awe, but discover their sins, to save that way their souls. And as for disclosing of such kind of persons, let me advise them not in the least manner to doubt our secrecy; we have learned better and desire our Auditors to be otherwise persuaded of us. Whether is God or men wiser? The holy Spirit advises unto this duty of Confession; by that means you lessen sin in you and cast out the Devil. Christ cured none but those that showed their disease and believed his power. By confession of sin the way for the Lord Jesus is prepared, and by the prayer of the faithful Minister unto God for the poor penitent sinner, his sins are forgiven him, Satan cast out, and his soul better armed against his future strong temptations. King David resolved, saying, Psalm 38, verse 18: "I will confess my wickedness, and be sorry for my sin."

The step that we set towards Heaven after we have fallen into sin is the unfeigned confessing of our downfall by sin. Saint Luke chapter 15 with the prodigal, "I will go to my father, and say unto him, Father, I have sinned against Heaven and thee."[13] Psalm 15: "Against thee only have I sinned, and done evil in thy sight," at last he prays, "O cleanse thou me from my secret faults, there is none whole in my body or soul by reason of sin."[14] 32 Psalm, verses 5–6: "I will knowledge my sin unto thee, and mine unrighteousness have I not hid. I said, I will confess my sins unto the Lord, and so thou forgave the wickedness of my sin." These were the ensuing comforts and favors of God to the sinner; remission of sins for confessing of them. Read the 5th Chapter of James, verse 6: "Acknowledge your faults one to another, and pray one for another, that ye may be healed."[15] Our blessed Savior, when he sent his Disciples into the world, as he gave them a Commission for to preach, so likewise power over unclean spirits to cast them out. In a word, he gave them power of sins in the total lump: "Whosoever sins ye retain" (saith he) "they are retained, and whosoevers sins ye remit, they are remitted."[16] What greater comfort could Christ pronounce then say, "Son, thy sins be forgiven?" And how did the Jews disdain at those words, saying, "Who can forgive sins, but God only?" Christ readily replied, and gave them a token of the truth thereof, by the peraliptick[17] man to rise up and walk before them, "That ye may know the Son of man has power to forgive sins here on earth, I say unto thee, Arise, take up thy bed, and walk."[18] The chief way to obtain mercy at God's hands for sins past is to acknowledge the offenses done. And the sinner is not readier to confess his wickedness, but God is as ready again for to forgive them. God knows all things, yet the voice and confession of penitent sinners he regards and expects. If a sinner be at any time silent, he is but the Devil's Secretary.

The Confession of Elizabeth Barnes, the 26 of April, 1637, at the place of Execution

During the time that she was in prison, she concealed her Adultery, that she was begot with Child by him on whom she had wasted her estate and deluded with hopes of Marriage. His name, as she said, was Richard Evans, a Tailor dwelling in Battersey in the County of Surrey, upon whose conscience lies very heavy his false dealing with the poor woman. I wish that he may heartily ask God and the world forgiveness for his impieties in public. Through whose deceits and flatteries, this poor creature's ruin was occasioned. And so much for Elizabeth Barnes.

A Relation of Anne Willis, the manner of the murdering of her own Child, confessed by her at the place of Execution

Upon an Inquisition of one of the Coroner's Inquest, for the County of Middlesex, upon the view of the body of her Bastard child, taken out of a vault in Rosemary Lane by Tower Hill, by her therein thrown, being by the Jury made, returned unto the Coroner of Murder. Warrants were immediately sent out unto all parts for the apprehending of the said Anne Willis, who upon the seventh day of March, 1637, was taken and brought before Sir Thomas Jaye, unto whom she confessed the fact: That the Child was borne alive; there was two upon oath justified it that she said it was alive. Oh, cruel Monsters of that tender Sex. "Can a woman forget the child of her womb?" Isaiah 9.[19] Heaven's infinite compassion is compared unto the Mother and Infant, the near tie between them, and the entire care of mothers over their children! When I lift up mine eyes towards the Heavens and again cast them down to the earth, Birds and Beasts, me thinks, do rise up in judgement against these unnatural cruel Beasts in women's shapes. The Swallow flies high and in the towering Trees, Churches, and Houses build their Nests to Preserve their young ones out of danger; the Sparrow watches alone on the House top, as careful what it had hatched and brought forth. Beasts, such as Lions, Wolves, Tigers, and Foxes, have secret caves and woods where they hide their young to preserve and foster them alive: But these bloody dogs degenerate from them. O let therefore the memorial of them perish.

A Relation of John Flood, late of St. Giles in the Fields, for the committing of a Rape on the body of his own natural child, being under the age of ten years

This man was most notorious and generally reported to be of a most dissolute conversation. The fact which was laid unto his charge, fully proved by the Testimony of diverse grave and sober Matrons, which searched the Body of the Child, and said, she had been abused by a man without all question. The Honorable Judges before whom this heinous fact was tried inquired to find out the Actor of so horrid a deed. The Child on whom it was done produced nor accused any other person but Flood her own father and related very confidently the manner of their carnal knowledge of each other, to the full satisfaction of all that heard her, that none but he could be the man. Being demanded the reason why she did not immediately reveal that her Father had to do with her, she answered, That she dared not speak of it again unto anybody, because her father said, If she should at any time tell what he did unto her, the Devil would presently tear her in pieces. This the child averred unto the Court before his face at the time of his Trial.

What Flood said at the place of Execution

As he impudently denied the Fact at the time of his Trial, he persevered to the instant of his death of the denial of the fact, with many fearful imprecations of judgements and renunciation of God's mercies if he were any ways guilty. In great passionate hot terms he broke forth against his wife, on this wife saying, That three years she was conspiring to work his downfall, which now by her was effected. And thus this barren Tree at the Tree of execution stood and fell.

The Confession of Joane Burs, taken before Sir James Cambell, Knight, the 8 day of April 1637

She said that the Saturday before Christmas last, her Master having given her sharp correction for the stealing away of a Runlet[20] of Wine and expending it out in the company of Lewd creatures lazing about the City, in revenge unto her Master and Mistress, she went and bought Mercury and put it into a Posset[21] and gave it unto them both for to drink, which did endanger their lives. But blessed be God, are both yet alive. And for that exorbitant Fact, [she] was by the Court fined, and remains in the Gaol to this present. Being demanded why she did so unto her Master and Mistress, She stood mute. But it was justified unto her face at her Trial, that these words should proceed out of her own mouth: That if her Mistress were dead, she might afterwards have better Clothes. And to her Master she did it because he did beat her so cruelly. But observe in this silly Girl a passage worth note, Who, perceiving the Mercury to work violently on her Mistress, brought some thereof in a Paper and showed it unto her Mistress, saying, that doubtless her Master had put something into the Posset that made her so sick; craftily intending by this, to cast off all suspicion from herself; but that fastened it upon her, as just cause there was. And so much for that.

The Confession of Anne Holden, before Sir James Cambell, the 16 Day of March 1637

The said Anne Holden confessed, as it was in the Court read, That last Night was seven weeks, she being lodged in the house of John Atkins at Colebrooke, was delivered of a Child. Nobody being with her, which said child she threw into a Ditch on the Backside of the said House, because it should not be known nor seen. But she was spared her Trial because she is to be removed unto Buckingham, there to be tried upon another Murder.

Lastly, there is one Notorious Bawd Rebecca Smith, who dwelt at the Seven Stars in Whitecross Street, convicted for a Bawd, who according unto her deserts, is to be Carted[22] about the City, and thence ought to be banished.

FINIS

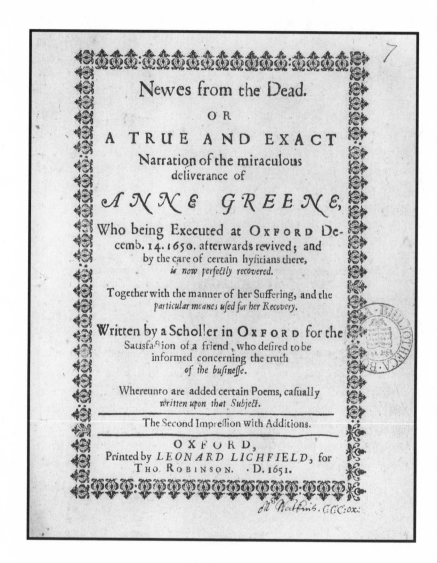

Newes from the Dead.

OR

A TRUE AND EXACT

Narration of the miraculous
deliverance of

ANNE GREENE,

Who being Executed at OXFORD Decemb. 14. 1650. afterwards revived; and
by the care of certain hysicians there,
is now perfectly recovered.

Together with the manner of her Suffering, and the
particular meanes used for her Recovery.

Written by a Scholler in OXFORD for the
Satisfaction of a friend, who desired to be
informed concerning the truth
of the businesse.

Whereunto are added certain Poems, casually
written upon that Subject.

The Second Impression with Additions.

OXFORD,
Printed by *LEONARD LICHFIELD*, for
THO. ROBINSON. ·D. 1651.

Newes from the Dead, title page, shelfmark Wood 516 (7). Reproduced by
permission of the Bodleian Library, University of Oxford.

Newes from the Dead. Or a True and Exact Narration of the miraculous deliverance of Anne Greene

Who being Executed at Oxford December 14, 1650, afterwards revived; and by the care of certain physicians there, is now perfectly recovered. Together with the manner of her Suffering, and the particular means used for her Recovery. Written by a Scholar in Oxford for the Satisfaction of a friend, who desired to be informed concerning the truth of the business. Whereunto are added certain Poems, casually written upon that Subject.

The second impression with additions. (1651)

Newes from the Dead [1]

Here happened lately in this City a very rare and remarkable accident, which being variously and falsely reported amongst the vulgar (as in such cases it is usual) to the end that none may be deceived, and that so signal an act of God's mercy and providence may never be forgotten, I have here faithfully recorded it, according to the Information I have received from those that were the chief Instruments in bringing this great work to perfection.

In the house of Sir Thomas Read at Duns Tew in Oxfordshire, there lived a maid named Anne Greene, born at Steeple Barton in the same County, being about 22 years of age, of a middle stature, strong, fleshy, and of an indifferent good feature; who being (as she said) often solicited by fair promises and other amorous enticements of Mr. Jeffery Read, Grandchild to the said Sir Thomas, a

279

youth of about 16 or 17 years of age, but of a forward growth and stature, at last consented to satisfy his unlawful pleasure. By which act (as it afterward appeared) she conceived, and was delivered of a Man-child, which being never made known and the Infant found dead in the house of office,[2] caused a suspicion that she being the mother had murdered it and thrown it there on purpose to conceal both it and her shame together. Thereupon she was immediately taken into examination and carried before several Justices of the peace in the Country. And soon after, in an extreme cold and rainy day, sent unto Oxford Gaol, where having passed about three weeks more in continual affrights and terrors, in a place as comfortless as her condition, she was at a Sessions[3] held in Oxford, arraigned, condemned, and on Saturday the 14 of December last, brought forth to the place of Execution, where, after singing of a Psalm & something said in justification of herself, as to the fact for which she was to suffer and touching the lewdness of the Family wherein she lately lived, she was turn'd off the Ladder,[4] hanging by the neck for the space of almost half an hour. Some of her friends in the meantime thumping her on the breast, others hanging with all their weight upon her legs; sometimes lifting her up and then pulling her down again with a sudden jerk, thereby the sooner to dispatch her out of her pain: insomuch that the Undersheriff, fearing lest thereby they should break the rope, forbade them to do so any longer. At length, when everyone thought she was dead, the body being taken down and put into a Coffin was carried thence into a private house, where some Physicians had appointed to make a Dissection.[5] The Coffin being opened, she was observed to breathe, and in breathing (the passage of her throat being straightened) obscurely to rattle, which being perceived by a lusty fellow that stood by, he (thinking to do an act of charity in ridding her out of the small relics of a painful life) stamped several times on her breast and stomach with all the force he could. Immediately after, there came in Dr Petty[6] of Brasenose College, our Anatomy Professor, and Mr. Thomas Willis[7] of Christ Church, at whose coming, which was about 9 o'clock in the morning, she yet persisted to rattle as before, laying all this while stretched out in the coffin in a cold room and season of the year. They perceiving some life in her, as well for humanity as their Professions' sake, fell presently to act in order to her recovery. First, having caused her to be held up in the Coffin, they wrenched open her teeth, which were fast set, and poured into her mouth some hot and cordial spirits; whereupon she rattled more than before and seemed obscurely to cough. Then they opened her hands (her fingers also being stiffly bent) and ordered some to rub and chafe the extreme parts of her body, which they continued for about a quarter of an hour; oft, in the meantime, pouring in a spoonful or two of the cordial water, and besides tickling her throat with a feather, at which she opened her eyes, but shut them again presently. As soon as they perceived any heat in her extreme parts, they thought of letting her blood; & no sooner was her arm bound for that purpose, but she suddenly bent it, as if it had been contracted by a fit of the Convulsion. The vein being opened, she bled about five ounces, and that so freely that it could not easily be stopped. All this while her pulse was very low, but otherwise not much amiss. Her arm being bound up again, and now and then a little cordial water poured down her throat, they continued rubbing her in several places, caused Ligatures[8] to be made in her arms and legs, and then ordered her to be laid in a bed well warmed. Then they caused her neck and also her temples to be anointed with confortative[9] oils and spirits, and so likewise the bottoms of her feet, and upon this she began to open her eyes and to move the lower parts of her body. About this time came in Mr. Bathurst of Trinity College, and Mr. Clerke of Magdalen College, whose advice and endeavors were then and all the time afterwards concurrent with those of the other two above mentioned. Then they applied a plaster to her breasts and ordered an heating odoriferous Clyster[10] to be cast up in her body to give heat and warmth to her bowels; after that, they persuaded a woman to go into bed to her and to lie very close to her and gently to keep rubbing of her.

After all which she seemed about noon to be in a sweat. Her face also began somewhat to swell and to look very red on that side on which the knot of the halter had been fastened.

Whilst the Physicians were thus busy in recovering her to life, the Undersheriff was soliciting the Governor and the rest of the Justices of Peace for the obtaining her Reprieve, that in case she should for that present be recovered fully to life, she might not be had back again to Execution. Whereupon those worthy Gentlemen, considering what had happened, weighing all circumstances, they readily apprehended the hand of God in her preservation, and being willing rather to cooperate with divine providence in saving her than to overstrain justice by condemning her to double shame and sufferings, they were pleased to grant her a Reprieve until such time as her Pardon might be completely obtained.

All this while she had no sooner opened her eyes, but presently she shut them again, and being call'd upon to try whether she could hear or speak, there appeared no sign that she could do either. Soon after, they made trial again, bidding her if she understood them to move her hand or open her eyes. Whereupon she obscurely opened her eyes. The Physicians, fearing least her face might swell more & more and a Fever come upon her by reason of the former suffocation, took from her right arm about nine ounces more of blood and then ordered her a Julep[11] and other cordial things to be administered upon occasion, and so left her for that night. And about two hours after she begun to speak many words intelligible.

On Sunday the 15th about 8 in the morning they return'd and found her much amended, being able to answer to any question propounded unto her. She then complained of her throat (but not much of any other part), whereunto they ordered a Cataplasm[12] to be applied; then she complaining of drought, a Julep was offered her, which she first took with difficulty and at last refus'd; warm beer being given her, she disrelished it, but of cold she drank and thanked them.

All this while, she lay often sighing and talking to herself, as if she had been still to suffer. About noon she felt an extreme soreness in her breast and sides, but there appeared nothing discolored or like a Contusion. That night they ordered her a Clyster & a Cataplasm to be applied to her breast and sides, with other means to prevent what evil might ensue by reason of contus'd blood, and so left her to rest. About 9 of the clock she laughed and talked merrily, looking fresh and of a good color: being a little feverish, her tongue not furred nor clammy.

Monday the 16th, they found that she had taken some rest and her fever not much increas'd; they then took from her left arm about six ounces of blood more. She fainted not, but talked very cheerfully, complaining somewhat of her neck, stomach, and throat.

But before they let her blood, having first caused all to depart the room except those Gentlemen that were of the Faculty, they asked her of her sense and apprehension during the time of her suffering: she answered, that after she put off some of her clothes, bequeathing them to her Mother (which was early in the morning before her execution) and heard someone say that one of the prisoners was let out of the chain to put her to death, she remembered nothing at all that had been done unto her, and that she knew not when her fetters were knock'd off or how she came out of prison or that she had been upon the Gallows. Neither could she remember that any Psalm had been sung or that she said anything there, notwithstanding those that were present do testify that she spoke very sensibly. Only about a fortnight after, she seemed to remember something of a fellow wrapped up in a blanket, which indeed was the habit of her Executioner.

It is observable also, that when she came to herself again, she fell into the like speeches as she had used in prison before the execution: seeming there to go on where she had so long time left off, like to a Clock whose weights had been taken off a while, and afterwards hung on again.

That night she was fomented[13] about the sides and other contused places, her neck being very sore, especially on the right side, where it was all black, and began to blister. There appeared also diverse spots of settled blood on her right cheek.

Tuesday the 17th in the morning they found her pulse slow, but very unequal; her tongue not very dry nor rough. The night before she slept well; in the morning she arose, but her head was so light that she could hardly stand upright. She now complained of pain beneath the pit of her stomach; she complained also of a deadness in the tip of her tongue, thinking she had bitten it in the time of her suffering. She call'd this day for some bread, which she did eat, being first toasted and moistened in beer. At night when they visited her again, the pain of her neck and throat was decreased; the spots of settled blood about her cheek and neck lessened, but the deadness of her tongue still remained. That night she slept six or seven hours, and on the 18th in the morning had no fever; her pulse was much amended; all Symptoms lessened; the pains in her breast seemed to descend into the region of the belly, being (as 'twas conceived) not in the bowels, but only in the musculous outward parts.

The 19th she was up, and did eat part of a chick. All Symptoms decreased: yet could she not go without the help of somewhat to uphold her. Her neck still sore, but mending. The deadness of her Tongue lessened. That night she slept well. About four or five days after, being hard frosty weather, there appeared a blackness over the lower part of her right arm and upon her flanks on the same side, which by degrees waxed yellow and in four or five days vanished.

By this time, the care of the Physicians was well over. The pains in her breast and side when she drew in her breath, as also the inequality of her pulse (which caused a suspicion of a contusion and extravagated[14] blood spilt on the Lungs) being now fully ceased. The deadness of her tongue and soreness of her neck quite gone. There remained only a giddiness in her head when she walked or stirred her body, which in a short time likewise left her. And now being able to walk about the town, eat, drink, and sleep as well as before this accident had befallen her, she had liberty to repair (and is since gone) unto her friends in the Country, taking away with her the Coffin wherein she lay as a Trophy of this her wonderful preservation.

Thus, within the space of a Month, was she wholly recovered; and in the same Room where her Body was to have been dissected for the satisfaction of a few, she became a great wonder, being reviv'd, to the satisfaction of multitudes that flocked thither daily to see her.

One thing more I had almost forgotten; that when the numbers of people still pressing into the house began to be too impetuous, and the Physicians had obtained of the Governor to have a Guard plac'd at the door, yet because those of the better sort could not altogether be denied admission, they thought it a seasonable opportunity for the maid's behalf to invite them either to exercise their Charity, or at least to pay for their Curiosity. And therefore (themselves first leading the way) they commended it to those that came in to give every one what they pleas'd, her Father being there ready to receive it. After a few days the Governor (a Gentleman as much to be belov'd for his Courtesy, as he is honor'd for his Prudence) coming himself to see her did not only contribute to her in a liberal manner, but also improved his charity with many pertinent and wholesome instructions. By this means there was gathered for her to the sum of many pounds: whereby not only the Apothecary's Bill and other necessaries for her Diet and lodging were discharged, but some overplus remained towards the suing out of her Pardon.

And now, having done with the Sufferings and the Cure, it will not be amiss to look back and take a Review of the Cause of them, as matter of fact for which she suffered, which (as I have said) was the supposed murder of her own Infant.

There are two things very considerable alleged on her behalf, and that may seem to clear her Innocence as to that business.

The first is, that the Child was abortive or stillborn and consequently not capable of being murdered. The other, that she did not certainly know that she was with child, and that it fell from her unawares as she was in the house of office.

As for the first, it is evident that the child was very unperfect, being not above a span[15] in length, and the sex hardly to be distinguished, so that rather seemed a lump of flesh than a well and duly formed Infant. The Midwife said also that it had no hair and that she did not believe that ever it had life. Besides, her fellow-servants do testify, that she had certain Issues[16] for about a month before she miscarried, which were of that nature (Physicians say) as are not consistent with the vitality of a child: the eruption of which Issues came on her after she had violently labor'd in skreening of malt.[17] Lastly, it is not likely that the Child was vital, the mischance happening not above 17 weeks after the time of her conception.

For the second that she might not know certainly that she was with child, it is not improbable, for she was not ten weeks without the usual Courses[18] of women; before she had those continual Issues which lasted for a Month together, which long and great Evacuation might make her judge that it was nothing else but a flux of those humors which for ten weeks before had been suppressed, and that the child which then fell from her unawares was nothing but a lump of the same matter coagulated. As for the pain, it must needs be different in such cases from that which accompanies the timely fruit of the womb, and by reason of those Issues coming from her, for so long continued a time before she could not have those throes and passions at the time of her abortion as women in travel[19] are subject unto.

Add to all this, that at her Trial she ingeniously confessed as much as was alleged by the witnesses, and continued in the same assertions, not only before, but at her Execution, the last supposed minute of her life; and the very first words after she came to herself again (which certainly were not spoken with design, or purpose to deceive) confirmed the same.

There is yet one thing more which hath been taken notice of by some as to the Maid's defense: that her Grand Prosecutor, Sir Thomas Read, died within three days after her Execution, even almost as soon as the probability of her reviving could be well confirmed to him. But because he was an old man, and such Events are not too rashly to be commented on, I shall not make use of that observation.

It may perhaps be expected by some (and 'tis pity I can give them no better satisfaction) that I should here relate some story (like those of Orpheus or Aeneas[20] in the Poets) of what fine visions this maid saw in the other world; what celestial music or hellish howling she heard; what spirits she conversed with; and what Revelations she brought back with her concerning the Present Times or the Events of things to come. But for such matters the Ballad makers must rest contented. Since she (as you have heard) was so far from knowing anything whilst she was dead, that she remembered not what had happened to her even when she was yet alive. Her spirits at that time being either so fixed or benumbed with fear as not to admit of any new Impressions, or otherwise so turbulent and unquiet, as presently to discompose and obliterate them. As we often see, it fares with men that are buzz'd in the head with drink, or transported with madness, who, though they seem sensible enough of every present object that moves them, yet after they recover can own but little of what they did or said before.

Having here done with the Story, I cannot but reflect upon the generous attempt of those Gentlemen that freely undertook and have so happily performed the Cure. That while they missed the opportunity of improving their knowledge in the dissection of a Dead body, they advanced their fame by restoring to the world a Living one, who now (deservedly) accounts it her happiness to have fallen into such courteous and skillful hands: not only for their successful endeavors used in her Recovery, but for being a means to vindicate her from that foul stain of Murder, which, in most men's judgments (and, perhaps, Heaven itself also bearing witness) was so harshly charged upon her.

[There follow a series of poems by Oxford students. In this edition, the poems, in both English and Latin, overwhelm the text, numbering over 50 and adding 24 more pages to the text. I include only a selection of these here to give the reader a sense of their character. The signatures are reproduced as they appear in the original text.]

On She which was hang'd and afterwards Recover'd

Orpheus, to fetch his Wife, did go
A voyage to the Shades below
('Twas more than many a man would do:)
The bloodless Ghosts did weep (they say)
and Pluto[21] groan'd, as He did play;
Yet She came back but Half the way.

Now we have seen a stranger sight;
Whether it was by Physic's might,
Or that (it seems) the Wench was Light.
But sure 'twill spoil her Marriage day,
For who so hardy to assay
Such an immortal Virbia?[22]

Wives may deceive, and do their best
To counterfeit in all the rest;
Only let them not Die[23] in jest.
        Hen. Perin Gen. Com. of Trin. Coll.

Why Ate,[24] dost thou Double thus thy Smart?
Not suffering Her to Live, nor to Depart?
Physicians straining to Repair what Loss
The Judge inflicted, Multiply the Cross:
Death wrote Her Martyr; but from Rest to Come
Back through such Pains, is Second Martyrdom.
Yet she these cruel Miracles sustains,
Rival Enrolled in Proserpines[25] both Trains;
And seated on Fates Tropic, doth survey
With either Eye the Courts of Night, and Day.
So Phoebe's Orb[26] in th' Equinox appears,
With Oblique Looks viewing two Hemispheres:
Thus Eagles, when They to the Confines Fly
Of th' Atmosphere, dwell not in Air, nor Sky:

Such, Pyrhha's[27] Unripe Issue, is display'd,
When it was yet half-Carcass, and half-Maid.

Pluto with Juno[28] here might Presents claim,
While Dirge, and Carol Consort forth her Name;
That Pantomime should Act these Obsequies,
Whose Face Parti-per-pale[29] both Laughs, and Cries:
For She Triumphs in Tragicomic shrouds;
As Rainbows glister, yet in Weeping Clouds:
Or as a Protean Picture's different Site
Here shews Democritus, there Heraclite.[30]

Straight from her Urn this Unchang'd Phoenix[31] rose,
Offspring Herself, and Midwife to her Throes:
And Antedates by this Mysterious Birth
Her Resurrection: Born-again from Earth.
Hippolytus[32] Revived in every Part,
But 'twas by Magic, or Poetic Art:
Sibylla[33] Saw, then Left the Ghosts below;
But She did In, not From the Body Go:
The Shades[34] sent back Eurydice[35] to Day,
But Fainting She Return'd fierce half the Way.
This Wonder surmounts All: See, here is bred
Posthumous Life ev'n when the Mother's dead.
Part Died before, part Survived after Breath;
The Embryo's Birth's Abortive, and Her death.
Orpheus, and Aesculape[36] were here Outvied,
'Cause both their Arts Concenter'd in one Guide.

Suiters Courage, All's purg'd by Sacrifice:
The Parent slain, doth not a Virgin Rise?
Forgetful She did Gallow Lotos Try,[37]
And Lethe[38] taste: Let All cry Amnesty.
For who can think her Guilty, whom the Tomb
Does thus declare unworthy of her Doom?
Whom Law, whom Physic could not kill, whose Date
Soldiers Repriev'd, Three Committees of Fate?
If ye doubt still, her Dying Words Receive:
How e're, Distrust her Risen must Believe.
   H. B. Coll. Om. Anim.

On the She that was Hang'd, but not Executed

Rare Innocence! a Wench re-woman'd! see
What the small Sophs[39] say to this Fallacy.
Up to the ears in death, and 'scape! no kind
Was thought more fit then to tie up her Wind.
Women in this with Cats agree, I think,
Both Live and Scratch after they have tip't the Wink.[40]
Henceforth take heed of trusting Females. She
That 'scapes Welsh Parsley,[41] Soldiers take for me.
    H. B. Soc. N.C.

On one dead by Law, but reviv'd by Physic

Come Sophister,[42] distinguish, you that call
Restor'd Privation Supernatural.
To solve your Ignorance, come view in one
An Antedated Resurrection.
Some rigid ones perhaps this act will spell
With the strange letters of a Miracle:
But know, Physicians have a larger Call,
Apollo and Physic are collateral.
Think not Physicians Atheists, since they do
Profess Divinity, and Practice 't too.
    J. Hutton Fell. of New Coll.

The Woman's Cause put to the Lawyers

Mother, or Maid, I pray you whether?
One, or both, or am I neither?
The Mother died: may it not be said
That the Survivor is a Maid?
Here, take your Fee, declare your sense;
And free me from this New Suspense.
    Joh. Watkins, Eq. Aur. fil. Coll. Reg.

Thou shalt not Swing again: come clear thy brow,
Thou hast the Benefit o'th' Clergy now;
Nor is thy Neck-Verse[43] writ in Blood, which might
Confound thy Thoughts, as it must needs thy Sight.

Thus when Apollo keeps th' Assizes,[44] then
Women are sav'd by Book, as well as Men.
   Strange Wench! what character may fit thee best,
    That still canst live, though Thou art Hang'd and Prest?
     Rob Mathew, Fellow of New Coll.

To the Physicians

To raise a Pyramid unto your skill
Were to mistrust experience, and still
Think Death a Giant, whose vast grip could span
And squeeze to nought both memory and man.
Ye are not mortal, nor need fear to die:
To conquer Death is Immortality.
Ye have done that. Marble may serve to hide
Its own dust now, or tell who should have died:
There is no other use for't. And thou Death
Vaunt not henceforth 'tis with Thy leave we breath.
Th'art vanquish't quite, and this thy Mulct[45] shall be,
To write Probatum[46] to their victory.

Admire not, 'tis no news, n'ere think it strange,
T'were wonder if a Woman should not change:
They have mysterious ways, and their designs
Must be read backward still, like Hebrew lines.
See, these with Death dissemble, and can cheat
Charon[47] himself to make a fair retreat.
   Well, for this trick I'll never so be led
   As to believe a Woman, though she's dead.
    Rob. Sharrock, Fellow of New Coll.

Thou more than Mortal, that with many lives
Hast mock't the Sexton, and the Doctors' knives:
The name of Spinster thou mayst justly wed,
Since there's no Halter stronger than thy Thread.
   To the same.
Thou, thine own Clotho,[48] that knew'st not to feel
The darts of Death, yet wore'st no Buff,[49] nor Steel:
If with such Art thou canst thy Distaff rule,
The Soldiers all to thee shall go to School.
   Dan. Danvers, Coll. Trin. Alum.

On the Death and Life of Anne Greene

What Cable-thread twin'd thee thy happy fate,
That it outlasts thy own life's destin'd date?
Was thy Harmonious Soul strung so-so well,
As break it could not, stretched to a Miracle?
Did'st thou indent with Rigid Atropos[50]
To los't a while, and then to quit the Loss?
As cast-off Habits, when hang'd by a space,

Regain their Fashion and their pristine grace.
    Lo, here's life's Gemini, two lifes in one!
Or th' fame in'ts Tropical Reversion!
Time after Stylo novo[51] inchoated![52]
From the first Sun a Parely[53] created!
A strange Appendix after Finis[54] fixt,
Or Funis[55] rather: Death and Life co-mixt!
A Posthume Act after Catastrophe!
Or Antedating of the Latter day!
    Death's Puzzler! Self-survivor! thy strange fate
Does contradictions Legitimate.
Entwisted Miracles constellate here,
And complicated Wonders Co-insphere.[56]
Thy uncouth Paradox Resuscitation
Tempts to believe, that from a pure Privation
Nature's propension[57] signs a free Regress
To pristine Habit; tempts even to confess
Plurality of Souls in One, since Thou
Can'st prodigally one to Death allow,
Another keep thyself; whilst both maintain
Castor and Pollux-like[58] alternate Reign.
    That Belgian Headsman, whose rare artful hand
Could slice off heads, and they yet seem to stand,
Had he thee Execut'd, had sham'd his skill,
When finding thee not dead, but living still.
Perillu's Torturing Engine[59] had but been
A Very Bull, had'st thou first entered in.
Their Law would have some plea, were it to thee,
Who first the Malefactor Hang, then see
Where 'twere a just and equitable Cause,
Whether not consonant unto the Laws.

Strange Sophister! that grant'st to Destiny
The Premises, conclusion dost deny;
Dar'st yield to Suffer Death, but not to Die.
    Joh. Aylmer, Schol. of New Coll.

So sportive, Atropos?[60] what, must we see
Some Hocus-tricks? the thread of life to be
Asunder cut, and yet entire remain?
A Body-banished soul recall'd again?
Now may the nine-liv'd Sex speak high, and say
That here they fought with Death, and won the day.
The fatal Tree, which first began the strife,
Sided with them, and prov'd a Tree of life.

Another

Death, spare your threats, we scorn now to obey;
If Women conquer thee, surely Men may.
How came this Champion on I cannot tell,
But I n'ere heard of one came off so well.
    Pet. Killigrew, Eq. Aur. fil. Coll. Reg.

Hippolytus[61] was dead, and (as the strain
Of Poets tells) was made a Man again.
Poetic Figments are turn'd Truths, for we
Have seen a Dead Maid's Palingenesy.[62]
He twice a Man; She twice a Maid: 'Tis brave;
She had one Life to Loose, and one Save.
Or else it was our Logic Died, not she:
For from Privation a Regress we see.
Let's not admire then Bacon's Brazen Head,[63]
When we see one that speaks, and yet was Dead.
You that so much for new Inventions give,
Observe a way, found out, by Death to Live.
Cats have for every Muse a life: but She
For every Grace; For by this History
The Author doth a Third Life to her Give,
And makes her Innocence and Fame to Live.
Her Life is writ here to the life: she fell
At a cheap rate, when 'tis describ'd so well.
For, th' Author's Pen's so good, that one would Die

To be Reviv'd by such a History.
   Rich. Glyd, Fell. of New Coll.

For certain, she was dead! yet then
The reason how she lives again,
Is that which so much puzzles men.

Sure when her soul this clay forsook,
Towards Pluto's court her way she took,
And came unto th' infernal brook.

It drank so deep of Lethe[64] there,
She had forgotten whatso'ere
She had suffer'd in her life time here:

Arraign'd by Minos,[65] straight denied
That she before a Judge was tried,
Or sentenc'd on the Gallows died.

No other way was left to win
Her to confess her shame and sin
But send her back to learn't again.

Entering her body straight, 'twas grown
So rack't and torn, that 'twas not known,
Not yet believ'd to be her own.

This neck was Halter-gall'd, nay more,
These sides and breasts with strokes were sore,
And Hers were nothing so before.

Her legs (she's sure) had shackles on,
And wonder's finding These have none;
Herself and they were lost and gone.

Thus what she suffer'd last, was now
The lesson she first learn'd to know,
Else no account can pass below.

If she learn't well, and not constrain
Herself to act it o're again,
She may pass safe through Pluto's reign.
   John Dwight, Ch. Ch.

Are Fates grown kind? have they thus chang'd their (doom
From Murtherers to supply the Midwifes room?
Or were they not o'erpowr'd, since Life had spun
Two strings unto her bow, and Death but One?
    Tho. Ireland, Ch. Ch.

To the Hangman

Come Flesh-Crow, tell me, what's the cause that you
Rigor to men, to Women Favor show?
Your Office you have not perform'd, 'tis plain:
See, here's the Wench you hang'd, alive again.
Yet, for this once, I'll clear you; it was not
Your slack rope saved her, nor your fast-loose knot.
Her fatal halter she (to the end the strife)
Untwisted spun into a thread of life.
    Ed Norreys Eq. Aur. fil. Coll. Reg.

Wonder of highest Art! He that will reach
A Strain for thee, had need his Muse should stretch,
Till flying to the Shades, she learn what Vein
Of Orpheus call'd Eurydice[66] again;
Or learn of her Apollo, 'till she can
As well, as Singer, prove Physician:
And then she may without Suspension sing,
And, authorized, harp upon thy String.
Discordant string! for sure thy soul (unkind
To its own Bowels Issue) could not find
One Breast in Consort to its jarring stroke
'Mongst piteous Female Organs, therefore broke
Translations due Law, from fate repriev'd,
And struck a Union to herself, and liv'd.
    Was't this? or was it that the Goatish Flow
Of thy Adulterous veins (from thence let go
By second Aesculapius[67] his hand)
Dissolv'd the Parcae's,[68] Adamantine Band
    And made Thee Artist's Glory, Shame of Fate,
    Triumph of Nature, Virbius,[69] his Mate.
      Christ. Wren, Gent. Com. Wad. Coll.

Had I been tongue-tied, nor as yet had said
An Infant word, but kept my mouth a Maid,
This would have cut those Ropes, this to rehearse
Had Midwife prov'd to an Abortive verse,
Despightful Embryo in secret plac't
By Her, by thee She's publicly disgrac't.
Such blows o' the breast the standers-by her lend
As those that force tir'd Jades[70] to' th' journey's end.
Had but a modest soul that under gone
T'would soon for shame have quit its Mansion.
Yet she's not dead, nor is her glass quite run,
Although her Thread be cut her life's not spun.
She lives and hath recal'd her wonted strength,
Nor is her life made short by her neck's Length.
I'll prophecy, She'll Lovers soon ensnare
Without a Trope there's Halters in her hair.
Of the same cause here the effects do fight,
One thing both hang'd and sav'd her, she was Light.
    Walter Pope e Coll. Wadh.

Search for a pleasant now delight,
    To celebrate her birth's day's right.
It is a birth when after Death
    The body gains his former breath.
O! who'll pay him that dig'd the pit?
    The hungry grave hath lost a bit,
And yet still gapes, alas! I fear
    Death it self will be buried there.
She's sick, and melts in her own woe,
    The female Sex should cheat her so.
(That she could not deceive the same,
    In whom the first deceit found game.)
Either Physic conquers Death,
    Or Physicians coin new breath;
Or Atropos hath lost her knife:
    This was a hanging to the Life.
O! Wench reform in thy new age,
    Write Virtue in this second page:
The first shows Characters of Vice,
    O! live well once, who livest twice.
        Theodore Wynne Fell. Com. Fes. Coll.

Jugglers we have seen cut a Thread, whole: Thy Line
Of life was so: just such a Trick was Thine.
Hocus Pocus, fast and loose, dead and gone,
Here again: Women have more tricks than one.
    Hen. Capell Armig. Coll. Winton.

What hath the Law its power lost
Since th' English tongue hath it engross't?
Or did old Juno[71] own a spite
To Fate, and it for to requite
Sit cross-leg'd charming Her alive,
And hence Death prove so Abortive?
Sure Venus was in th' Horoscope,
When She was struggling with the Rope:
And kept out Death from entering in,
To show that Cupid cannot sin.
If so? then might She well escape,
Love suffers not a second rape.
Strange Beast! what all her Riders fling?
Could not Death rule Her in a string?
    Sam Christopher of S. Joh. Coll.

Justice would cut, but Fate unedg'd the knife,
Unravel'd the vex'd thread, and repriev'd life,
Bade the astonish'd Sisters spin more years,
New-cloth their Distaff, and lay by their Shears.
    Wonders long since were in their Sepulcher,
    Yet did One miracle revive with Her.
        Joh. Hall, Eq. Aur. fil. Coll. Reg.

Notes

Notes to Chapter 1

1. Thomas Bodley, *The Letters of Sir Thomas Bodley to Thomas James, First Keeper of the Bodleian Library*, ed. G. W. Wheeler (Oxford: Clarendon Press, 1926), 222, quoted in Alexandra Halasz, *The Marketplace of Print: Pamphlets and the Public Sphere in Early Modern England* (Cambridge: Cambridge University Press, 1997), 1.

2. Karen Newman, *Fashioning Femininity and English Renaissance Drama* (Chicago: University of Chicago Press, 1991), 146.

3. Jean Howard, "Feminism and the Question of History: Resituating the Debate," *Women's Studies* 19.2 (1991): 150.

4. George Orwell, *The British Pamphleteers*, ed. George Orwell and Reginald Reynolds, vol. 1, *From the Sixteenth Century to the French Revolution* (London: A. Wingate, 1948), 15, quoted in Halasz, *The Marketplace of Print*, 17.

5. Frances E. Dolan's book *Dangerous Familiars: Representations of Domestic Crime in England 1550–1700* (Ithaca: Cornell University Press, 1994) offers the most vivid and successful example of the juxtaposition of "popular" and "elite" texts. Dolan's analyses have helped me rethink my ideas about pamphlet literature, and my own analysis is greatly indebted to hers. Joy Wiltenburg's *Disorderly Women and Female Power in the Street Literature of Early Modern England and Germany* (Charlottesville: University Press of Virginia, 1992) is the first extended treatment of these texts and presents an excellent overview of the subject. Other shorter studies are also important and illustrate the growing interest in this area: Betty S. Travitsky, "Child Murder in English Renaissance Life and Drama," *Medieval & Renaissance Drama in England: An Annual Gathering of Research, Criticism and Reviews* 6 (1993): 63–84, and "'A Pittilesse Mother'? Reports of a Seventeenth-Century English Filicide," *Mosaic* 27.4 (1994): 55–79; and Garthine Walker, "'Demons in Female Form': Representations of Women and Gender in Murder Pamphlets of the Late Sixteenth and Early Seventeenth Centuries," in *Writing and the English*

Renaissance, ed. William Zunder and Suzanne Trull (New York: Longman, 1996), 123–39, to name a few. For a discussion of literacy, see Adam Fox, *Oral and Literate Culture in England, 1500–1700* (New York: Oxford University Press, 2000). For a discussion of the spread of religious ideas, see Peter Lake, "Deeds Against Nature: Cheap Print, Protestantism and Murder in Early Seventeenth-Century England," in *Culture and Politics in Early Stuart England*, ed. Kevin Sharpe and Peter Lake (Stanford: Stanford University Press, 1993), 257–83; Peter Lake, "Popular Form, Puritan Content? Two Puritan Appropriations of the Murder Pamphlet from Mid-Seventeenth-century London," in *Religion, Culture and Society in Early Modern Britain: Essays in Honour of Patrick Collinson*, ed. Anthony Fletcher and Peter Roberts (Cambridge: Cambridge University Press, 1994), 313–34; and Alexandra Walsham, *Providence in Early Modern England* (New York: Oxford University Press, 1999). See Malcolm Gaskill, *Crime and Mentalities in Early Modern England* (New York: Cambridge University Press, 2000), for a discussion of the way crime narratives of various kinds help to recover popular ideas and attitudes in the early modern period.

6. Katherine Usher Henderson and Barbara F. McManus do include two crime pamphlets (and one witchcraft pamphlet) in *Half Humankind: Contexts and Texts of the Controversy about Women in England, 1540–1640* (Urbana: University of Illinois Press, 1985) and Zunder and Trull include two in *Writing and the English Renaissance*, but not enough of these texts have been reproduced to give an idea of their variety and richness as cultural resources. Neither *Half Humankind* nor *Writing and the English Renaissance* includes the texts in their entirety. Joseph H. Marshburn and Alan R. Velie also edited a volume of crime pamphlets and ballads, *Blood and Knavery: A Collection of English Renaissance Pamphlets and Ballads of Crime and Sin* (Rutherford, N.J.: Fairleigh Dickinson University Press, 1973), but their collection does not include any of the pamphlets edited here.

7. Adam Fox, "Ballads, Libels and Popular Ridicule in Jacobean England," *Past and Present* 145 (1994): 48.

8. Tessa Watt, *Cheap Print and Popular Piety, 1550–1640* (New York: Cambridge University Press, 1991), 3.

9. David Cressy, *Literacy and the Social Order: Reading and Writing in Tudor and Stuart England* (New York: Cambridge University Press, 1980), 72.

10. Fox, *Oral and Literate Culture*, 8–9.

11. Lake, "Deeds Against Nature," 259.

12. See, C. Dobb, "Henry Goodcole, Visitor of Newgate 1620–1641," *Guildhall Miscellany* 4 (1955): 17–21. Peter Linebaugh suggests that the ordinary of Newgate stood to make even more by publishing these accounts. See "The Ordinary of Newgate and His Account," in *Crime in*

England, 1550–1800, ed. J. S. Cockburn (Princeton: Princeton University Press, 1977), 250.

13. Lake, "Deeds Against Nature," 262.

14. I derived this number by looking at Hyder E. Rollins's *Analytical Index to the Ballad-Entries in the Registers of the Company of Stationers of London* published in *Studies in Philology* 21.1 (1924): 1–324. Of the 56 entries Rollins indexes under various murder categories from 1569 to 1640, 17 treat husband murder, 5 infanticide, 2 the murder of husband and child, and only 1 the murder of a nonfamily member. While these numbers are not representative of actual cases because several of the more notorious stories are retold over and over, they do give some idea of the popular fascination with murderous women during the period. I took the suggestion for this analysis from Betty S. Travitsky, "Husband-Murder and Petty Treason in English Renaissance Tragedy," *Renaissance Drama* 21 (1990): 176.

15. J. S. Cockburn, "The Nature and Incidence of Crime in England 1559–1625: A Preliminary Survey," in *Crime in England 1550–1800*, ed. J. S. Cockburn (Princeton: Princeton University Press, 1977), 49–71. Surveying assize records, Cockburn points out a high incidence of domestic crime in the period, but three-quarters of the victims in marital murders were wives (57).

16. Since Joan Kelly's influential essay "Did Women Have a Renaissance?" scholars have debated whether women actually experienced an increase in power. Although I do not wish to enter into that debate here, it does seem that with the shift toward a more capitalistic economy that occurred during this period, women became more visible (and hence, more threatening) as they moved out into the marketplace as consumers, truck farmers, brewers, and occasionally as shopkeepers. For a discussion of the preoccupation with female rebellion brought about by changes in the social and economic order, see Susan Dwyer Amussen, "Gender, Family, and the Social Order," in *Order and Disorder in Early Modern England*, ed. Anthony Fletcher and John Stevenson (New York: Cambridge University Press, 1985), 196–218. For the counterargument that women were more economically powerless than in earlier periods, see Keith Thomas, *Religion and the Decline of Magic: Studies in Popular Beliefs in Seventeenth Century England* (New York: Scribner, 1971), 520–26, 568–69.

17. Christina Larner, "Crimen Exceptum? The Crime of Witchcraft in Europe," in *Crime and the Law: The Social History of Crime in Western Europe since 1500*, eds. V. A. C. Gatrell, Bruce Lenman, and Geoffrey Parker (London: Europa, 1980), 69–70.

18. Ibid., 68.

19. For additional discussion of this analogy, see Lawrence Stone, *The Family, Sex and Marriage in England, 1500–1800* (New York: Harper & Row, 1977), 27–29.

20. Natalie Zemon Davis, *Fiction in the Archives: Pardon Tales and Their Tellers in Sixteenth-Century France* (Stanford: Stanford University Press, 1987), 4.

21. Francis Bacon, "The Advancement of Learning," in *Critical Theory Since Plato*, ed. Hazard Adams (New York: Harcourt Brace Jovanovich, 1971), 193.

22. E. Jane Burns, *Bodytalk: When Women Speak in Old French Literature* (Philadelphia: University of Pennsylvania Press, 1993), xv.

23. Dolan, *Dangerous Familiars*, 5.

24. Parker, "A Warning for Wives, By the example of one Katherine Francis, alias Stoke, who for killing her husband, Robert Francis with a pair of Sizers, on 8 of Aprill at night, was burned on Clarkenwell-greene, on Tuesday, the 21 of the same moneth, 1629," in *A Pepysian Garland: Black-Letter Broadside Ballads of the Years 1595–1639, Chiefly from the Collection of Samuel Pepys*, ed. Hyder E. Rollins (Cambridge: Cambridge University Press, 1922), 304.

25. Witchcraft is another gender-based crime of this period but is beyond the scope of this volume. Because witchcraft pamphlets are readily available, I have not included any of these texts in this volume. Two of the more interesting discussions of witchcraft as social control are Alan MacFarlane, *Witchcraft in Tudor and Stuart England* (New York: Harper & Row, 1970), and Christina Larner, *Witchcraft and Religion: The Politics of Popular Beliefs* (New York: Blackwell, 1984).

26. Elizabeth Tebeaux and Mary M. Lay, "The Emergence of the Feminine Voice, 1526–1640: The Earliest Published Books by English Renaissance Women," *JAC, a Journal of Composition Theory* 15.1 (1995), <http://jac.gsu.edu/jac/15.1/ARTICLES/4.htm> (July 31, 2002).

27. T. E., *The Lawes Resolutions of Womens Rights: or, The Lawes Provision for Woemen. A Methodicall Colection of such Statutes and Customes, with the Cases, Opinions, Arguments and points of Learning in the Law, as do properly concerne Women* (London, 1632), 6, reprinted in *The English Experience: Its Record in Early Printed Books Published in Facsimile*, no. 922 (Norwood, N. J.: Walter J. Johnson, 1979).

Notes to Chapter 2

1. Leon Radzinowicz, *A History of English Criminal Law* (London: Stevens & Sons, 1948), 628.

2. J. S. Cockburn, "The Nature and Incidence of Crime," 57.

3. *Holinshed's Chronicles of England, Scotland, and Ireland, in Six Volumes*, vol. 3 (New York: AMS Press, 1965), 1024. Holinshed also includes another of the more notorious cases of husband murder that caught the attention of the pamphlet writers, the infamous case of George

Sanders (1573), a murder that like Arden's provided the material for a drama from the period, *A Warning for Fair Women*. See volume 4, 322–23. Stow also mentions Sanders's case, as does T. E. On Holinshed's inclusion of the Arden story, see Catherine Belsey, *The Subject of Tragedy: Identity and Difference in Renaissance Drama* (New York: Routledge, 1985), 129–31.

4. T. E., *The Lawes Resolutions of Women's Rights*, 6.

5. Dolan, *Dangerous Familiars*, 27–28.

6. Ibid., 28.

7. For an examination of women as litigants in equity and church courts, see Tim Stretton, *Women Waging Law in Elizabethan England* (Cambridge: Cambridge University Press, 1998); on women's roles in slander suits, see Laura Gowing, *Domestic Dangers: Women, Words, and Sex in Early Modern London* (New York: Oxford University Press, 1996); on women suing for property, see Amy Louise Erickson, *Women and Property in Early Modern England* (New York: Routledge, 1993).

8. Carol Z. Wiener, "Is a Spinster an Unmarried Woman?" *American Journal of Legal History* 20.1 (1976): 27–31.

9. See for example, Susan Dwyer Amussen, *An Ordered Society: Gender and Class in Early Modern England* (London: Basil Blackwell, 1988), and David Underdown, "The Taming of the Scold: The Enforcement of Patriarchal Authority in Early Modern England," in *Order and Disorder in Early Modern England*, ed. Anthony Fletcher and John Stevenson (Cambridge: Cambridge University Press, 1985), 116–36.

10. Belsey, *The Subject of Tragedy*, 130.

11. John Dod and Robert Cleaver, *A Godlie Forme of Household Governement* (London, 1598), 88, quoted in Linda Fitz, "'What Says the Married Woman?' Marriage Theory and Feminism in the English Renaissance," *Mosaic* 13.2 (1980): 5.

12. This is one of the primary arguments of Frances E. Dolan's invaluable study of the popular literature of the period, cited above.

13. T. E., *Lawes Resolutions*, 4.

14. Ibid., 206. T. E. goes on to suggest the complexities of assigning culpability by pointing out those occasions when a wife is not accountable for felonious crimes: "And note, if a Feme Covert steale anything by cohertion of her husband, this is not felonie in her."

15. Margaret Doody, "'Those Eyes Are Made So Killing': Eighteenth Century Murderesses and the Law," *Princeton University Library Chronicle* 46.1 (1984): 58.

16. Actually, the penalty for husband murder was greater than that for wife murder. Since a woman condemned for murdering her husband was considered guilty of petty treason, a crime against the state as well as the household and thus a far more serious crime than murder, she could be punished by burning at the stake. More commonly, murderers were hanged. For further discussion of petty treason see Travitsky, "Husband-

Murder," 171–98, and Frances E. Dolan, "The Subordinate('s) Plot: Petty Treason and the Forms of Domestic Rebellion," *Shakespeare Quarterly* 43.3 (1992): 317–40.

17. Belsey, *The Subject of Tragedy*, 190–91. See also Belsey for a more complete discussion of the contradiction concerning accountability, 153–54.

18. *Murther, Murther. Or, A bloody Relation how Anne Hamton, dweling in Westminster nigh London, by poyson murthered her deare husband* (London, 1641), 2. Page numbers cited hereafter in the text. I have chosen to retain the original spelling and punctuation of these texts in my discussion of them.

19. Dod and Cleaver, *A Godly Form of Household Government* (London, 1614), sigs. L 4–5, quoted in Kathleen M. Davies, "Continuity and Change in Literary Advice on Marriage," in *Marriage and Society: Studies in the Social History of Marriage*, ed. R. B. Outhwaite (New York: St. Martin's Press, 1981), 67.

20. The handling of household goods seems a particularly troublesome matter in the prescriptive literature. In Gouge's list of wifely duties, for example, he includes at least ten sections devoted to the wife's management of the family's material possessions. "Of wives particular Duties," in *Of Domesticall Duties* (London, 1622), 293–304. Reprinted in *The English Experience: Its Record in Early Printed Books Published in Facsimile* 803 (Norwood, N.J.: Walter J. Johnson, 1976).

21. "Anti-housewife" is Diane Purkiss's term. See her "Women's Stories of Witchcraft in Early Modern England: The House, the Body, the Child," *Gender and History* 7.3 (1995): 414.

22. Goodcole wrote pamphlets on three types of transgressive women: *The Adultresses Funerall Day* (on husband murder); *Natures Cruell Step-Dames* (on infanticide); and *The Wonderfull Discoverie of Elizabeth Sawyer, a Witch, late of Edmonton* (on witchcraft).

23. Henry Goodcole, *The Adultresses Funerall Day: In flaming, scorching, and consuming fire* (London, 1635), sig. A3v. Page numbers cited hereafter in the text.

24. Henry Goodcole, *Natures Cruell Step-Dames: or, Matchlesse Monsters of the Female Sex; Elizabeth Barnes, and Anne Willis. Who were executed the 26 day of April, 1637* (London: Francis Coules, 1637), 16.

25. Belsey, *The Subject of Tragedy*, 191.

26. Thomas Deloney, "The Lamentation of Master Pages Wife of Plimouth," in *The Roxburghe Ballads*, vol. 2, ed. Charles Hindley (London: Reeves and Turner, 1874), 191–92.

27. The murder of M. Page is told in *Sundrye Strange and inhumaine Murthers, lately committed* (London, 1591). STC 18286.5

28. On forced marriages, see Joan Larsen Klein, "Women and Marriage in Renaissance England: Male Perspectives," *Topic* 36 (1982): 23.

29. William Heale, *An Apologie for Women, or An Apposition to Mr. Dr. G. his assertion . . . that it was lawfull for husbands to beate their wives* (London, 1609), 30. Reprinted in *The English Experience, Its Record in Early Printed Books Published in Facsimile,* 665 (Norwood, N.J.: Walter J. Johnson, 1974). T. E. is more ambivalent, arguing first that it is permissible for a husband to beat his wife because "there is some kind of castigation which Law permits a husband to use." He argues that the husband may do "bodily damage" but only as it "appertaines to the office of a Husband for lawfull and reasonable correction." Anything more, however, and he notes that the wife can sue him for bodily damage if he hurts her (128). For discussions of wife beating during the period, see Susan Dwyer Amussen, "'Being Stirred to Much Unquietness': Violence and Domestic Violence in Early Modern England," *Journal of Women's History* 6.2 (1994): 70–89, and Margaret Hunt, "Wife Beating, Domesticity, and Women's Independence in Eighteenth-Century London," *Gender and History* 4 (1992): 10–33.

30. Heale, *Apologie,* 6.

31. The rejection by the lover who encouraged the murder occurs quite frequently. For other examples, see *The Tragedy of Master Arden of Faversham* and *The trueth of the most wicked and secret murthering of John Brewen* (London, 1592).

32. Such is also the case with Mary Goodenough, a destitute widow with two children, discussed below. In a futile attempt to provide for her family she exchanges sexual favors with a neighbor in return for "necessary maintenance." Soon becoming pregnant, she does nothing to save the baby's life when it is born and is found guilty of infanticide in 1692. The author of the pamphlet admonishes her neighbors for their negligence: "If her Modesty made her ashamed to beg, did not her meagre Look, her starved Children, her meanly furnish'd House and Table beg from you?" *Fair warning to Murderers of Infants: Being an Account of the Tryal . . . of Mary Goodenough* (London, 1692), 4.

33. *The trueth of the most wicked and secret murthering of John Brewen, Goldsmith of London, committed by his owne wife through the provocation of one John Parker* (London, 1592), often attributed to Thomas Kyd, reprinted in *Illustrations of Early English Popular Literature,* vol. 1, ed. J. Payne Collier (New York: Benjamin Blom, 1966), 14.

34. Gilbert Dugdale, *A True Discourse Of the practises of Elizabeth Caldwell . . .* (London, 1604), sig. Bv. Page numbers cited hereafter in the text.

35. Frances E. Dolan, "'Gentlemen, I have one more thing to say': Women on Scaffolds in England, 1563–1680," *Modern Philology* 92.2 (1994): 171.

36. "*The Source of* Arden of Faversham," in *The Tragedy of Master Arden of Faversham,* ed. M. L. Wine (London: Metheun, 1973), 149.

37. *A Hellish Murder Committed by a French Midwife, on the Body of her Husband* (London, 1688), pages hereafter cited in text; *A Cabinet of Grief: or, the French Midwife's Miserable Moan for the Barbarous Murther Committed upon the Body of her Husband* (London, 1688); "A Warning-Piece to All Married Men and Women, Being the Full Confession of Mary Hobry, the French Midwife" (London, 1688); and *Epilogue to the French Midwifes Tragedy* (London, 1688), attributed by Wing to Elkanah Settle.

38. At one point, the narrative specifically associates the murder with her religion. The examiner asks her how she "being of the Communion of the Church of Rome, came to throw the Quarters of her husband into the House of Office at the Savoy, which was a way to bring so great a Scandal upon the religion she professed, by laying the Murder at the Door of the Professors of that Religion?" (36).

39. "The Discontented Married Man," quoted in Elizabeth Foyster, "A Laughing Matter? Marital Discord and Gender Control in Seventeenth-Century England," *Rural History* 4.1 (1993): 13.

40. Adrian Wilson, *The Making of Man-Midwifery: Childbirth in England, 1660–1770* (Cambridge, Mass.: Harvard University Press, 1995), 26–31. Willughby, quoted in Wilson, 30–31.

41. Dolan, *Dangerous Familiars*, 34. Bracton, quoted in Barbara J. Baines, "Effacing Rape in Early Modern Representation," *English Literary History* 65.1 (1998): 76. Baines's article provides a good overview of the complexities of rape law within the period and the ambiguities surrounding issues of consent.

42. T. E., *Lawes Resolutions*, 390. It is true that women were given more agency in rape cases as the seventeenth century progressed and the courts began to focus more on the issue of consent and changed the definition of the crime. Matthew Hale, for instance, redefined rape as "the carnal knowledge of any woman above the age of ten years against her will, and of a woman-child under the age of ten years with or against her will" in *The History of the Pleas of the Crown*, quoted in Miranda Chaytor, "Husband(ry): Narratives of Rape in the Seventeenth Century," *Gender and History* 7.3 (1995): 395. Ironically, once the law began focusing on consent it simultaneously gave women agency and turned the fault back on them. Questions of the victim's innocence then became paramount (396). For additional discussion of consent, see Baines, "Effacing Rape," cited above.

43. Dolan, *Dangerous Familiars*, 34–35.

Notes to Chapter 3

1. Christopher Newstead, *An Apology for Women: or Women's Defence* (1620), in *Renaissance Women: Constructions of Femininity in England*, ed. Kate Aughterson (New York: Routledge, 1995), 116.

2. Travitsky, "Child Murder," 64. See also Travitsky, "The New Mother of the English Renaissance: Her Writings on Motherhood," in *The Lost Tradition: Mothers and Daughters in Literature*, ed. Cathy N. Davidson and E. M. Broner (New York: Frederick Ungar Publishing, 1980), 33–43; and Patricia Crawford, "The Construction and Experience of Maternity in Seventeenth-Century England," in *Women as Mothers in Pre-Industrial England: Essays in Memory of Dorothy McLaren*, ed. Valerie Fildes (New York: Routledge, 1990), 3–38.

3. Deborah Willis, *Malevolent Nurture: Witch-Hunting and Maternal Power in Early Modern England* (Ithaca, N.Y.: Cornell University Press, 1995), 17.

4. Mary Beth Rose, "Where Are the Mothers in Shakespeare? Options for Gender Representation in the English Renaissance," *Shakespeare Quarterly* 42.3 (1991): 308.

5. On the false association of midwifery with witchcraft, see David Harley, "Historians as Demonologists: The Myth of the Midwife-witch," *Social History of Medicine* 3.1 (1990): 1–26. On the professionalizing of childbirth assistance and the concomitant replacement of midwives with male doctors, see Adrian Wilson, *The Making of Man-Midwifery*.

6. *The Murderous Midwife, with her Roasted Punishment* (London, 1673), 2–3.

7. Valerie Fildes, *Breasts, Bottles and Babies: A History of Infant Feeding* (Edinburgh: Edinburgh University Press, 1986), 189.

8. Elizabeth Clinton, *The Countesse of Lincolnes Nurserie* (Oxford, 1622), 13. Reprinted in *The English Experience, Its Record in Early Printed Books Published in Facsimile*, no. 720 (Norwood, N.J.: Walter J. Johnson, 1975).

9. *A True Relation of the Most Horrid and Barbarous Murthers Committed by Abigail Hill of St. Olaves Southwark, on the persons of foure Infants* (London, 1658). See also *Concealed Murther Reveil'd* (London, 1699), a broadside that relates the drowning murder three years earlier of an infant by her nurse, who was frustrated by the baby's crying.

10. Marina Warner, *Monuments and Maidens: The Allegory of the Female Form* (New York: Atheneum, 1985), 283. See also Jacqueline T. Miller, "Mother Tongues: Language and Lactation in Early Modern Literature," *English Literary Renaissance* 27.2 (1997): 177–96.

11. Crawford, "The Construction and Experience of Maternity," 7. *The True Discripcion of a Childe with Ruffes*. London, 1566.

12. L. Lemnius, *The Secret Miracles of Nature* (London, 1658), 9–10, quoted in Crawford, "The Construction and Experience of Maternity," 7.

13. Vives, *Instruction of a Christen Woman* (London, 1529), quoted in Rose, "Where Are the Mothers?" 301.

14. Newman, *Fashioning Femininity*, 61.

15. For a fuller discussion of malevolent nurturing, see Deborah Willis, *Malevolent Nurture*.

16. Deborah Willis, "Shakespeare and the English Witch-Hunts," in *Enclosure Acts: Sexuality, Property, and Culture in Early Modern England*, ed. Richard Burt and John Michael Archer (Ithaca, N.Y.: Cornell University Press, 1994), 99.

17. John Knox, *The First Blast of the Trumpet Against the Monstrous Regiment of Women* (Geneva, 1558), quoted in Rose, "Where Are the Mothers?"303.

18. R. W. Malcolmson, "Infanticide in the Eighteenth Century," in *Crime in England, 1550–1800*, ed. J. S. Cockburn (Princeton: Princeton University Press, 1977), 192.

19. Elizabeth Jocelin, *The Mothers Legacie to her Unborne Childe* (London, 1624), Sig. Bv.

20. Travitsky, "Reports of a Seventeenth-Century English Filicide," 60.

21. *A Pittilesse Mother* (London, 1616), A2v. Pages cited hereafter in the text.

22. Travitsky, "Reports of a Seventeenth-Century English Filicide," 60.

23. *Bloody Newes from Dover* (London, 1647), n.p.

24. For a discussion of the various controversies surrounding baptism during the period, see David Cressy, *Birth, Marriage and Death: Ritual, Religion and the Life-Cycle in Tudor and Stuart England* (New York: Oxford University Press, 1997), 97–194.

25. Cressy, *Birth, Marriage and Death*, 101.

26. See Patricia Crawford, *Women and Religion in England, 1500–1720* (London: Routledge, 1993).

27. "The Distressed Mother, or a Sorrowful Wife in Tears" (London, 1690?).

28. There is some discrepancy in the accounts about the number of children Cook had. *The Cruel Mother* reports that she has three, two boys and one girl.

29. N. Partridge and J. Sharp, *Blood for Blood* (London, 1670), 9–10. Pages cited hereafter in the text.

30. See Audrey Eccles, *Obstetrics and Gynaecology in Tudor and Stuart England* (Kent, Ohio: Kent State University Press, 1982), 76–77.

31. Coppélia Kahn, "The Absent Mother in *King Lear*," in *Rewriting the Renaissance*, ed. Margaret W. Ferguson, Maureen Quilligan, and Nancy J. Vickers (Chicago: University of Chicago Press, 1986), 34.

32. For a discussion of pregnancy as disease, see Eccles, *Obstetrics and Gynaecology*, and Lori Schroeder Haslem, "'Troubled with the Mother': Longings, Purgings, and the Maternal Body in *Bartholomew Fair* and *The Duchess of Malfi*," *Modern Philology* 92.4 (1995): 438–59.

33. *The Cruel Mother* (London, 1670), 5.

34. Marilyn Francus, "Monstrous Mothers, Monstrous Societies: Infanticide and the Rule of Law in Restoration and Eighteenth-Century England," *Eighteenth-Century Life* 21.2 (1997): 139.

35. Francus, "Monstrous Mothers," 139.

36. Michael MacDonald, *Mystical Bedlam: Madness, Anxiety, and Healing in Seventeenth-Century England* (Cambridge: Cambridge University Press, 1981), 84.

37. Dolan, *Dangerous Familiars,* 148.

38. Although Michael MacDonald points out that married women were likely to be pardoned as insane for the murder of their children, such is not the case here, *Mystical Bedlam,* p.13ff. Although English law held that a person *non compos mentis* should not be charged with a felony for homicide, records reveal several cases in which psychologically disturbed women were successfully tried, convicted, and executed for these crimes. See Keith Wrightson, "Infanticide in European History," *Criminal Justice History* 3 (1982): 2.

39. Francus, "Monstrous Mothers," 141.

40. Rose, "Where Are the Mothers?" 307. Dorothy Leigh expresses the early modern view on female desire: "You of yourselves shall have no desires, only they shall be subject to your Husbands." *The Mothers Blessing* (London, 1616), 37, quoted in Rose, 303.

41. *Fair Warning to Murderers of Infants* (London, 1692), 1. Pages cited hereafter in the text.

42. Margaret Ferguson, "A Room Not Their Own: Renaissance Women as Readers and Writers," in *The Comparative Perspective on Literature: Approaches to Theory and Practice,* ed. Clayton Koelb and Susan Noakes (Ithaca, N.Y.: Cornell University Press, 1988), 97.

43. Rose, "Where Are the Mothers?" 307.

44. Kristen Poole, "'The fittest closet for all goodness': Authorial Strategies of Jacobean Mothers' Manuals," *Studies in English Literature* 35 (1995): 72.

45. On the collapsing of public/private space in mothers' advice books, see Elaine V. Beilin, *Redeeming Eve: Women Writers of the English Renaissance* (Princeton: Princeton University Press, 1987), 247–85. As Beilin explains, "While the role of loving mother instructing her children may seem to be a safe persona for a woman writer, instead it highlights the conflict between private and public status, and since publicity always endangers chastity and modesty, ironically a mother who wrote threatened the essence of her womanly virtue" (266–67).

46. Dolan discusses the necessity for public confession and notes the omission here in "'Gentlemen, I have one more thing to say,'" 169.

Notes to Chapter 4

1. William Gouge, *Of Domesticall Duties*, 507.

2. J. A. Sharpe, "The History of Crime in Late Medieval and Early Modern England: A Review of the Field," *Social History* 7.2 (1982): 200. Sharpe conjectures that accusations of infanticide throughout Western Europe may have resulted in more executions than the witch craze.

3. T. E., *The Lawes Resolutions*, 6.

4. Henderson and McManus, *Half Humankind*, 55.

5. Joseph Swetnam, *The Arraignment of Lewd, Idle, Froward and Unconstant Women*, in Henderson and McManus, *Half Humankind*, 204.

6. Michael Dalton, *The Countrey Justice* (London, 1618), 210. Reprinted in *The English Experience: Its Record in Early Printed Books Published in Facsimile*, no. 725 (Norwood, N.J.: Walter J. Johnson, 1975).

7. Percival Willughby, *Observations in Midwifery*, quoted in Keith Wrightson, "Infanticide in Earlier Seventeenth-Century England," *Local Population Studies* 15 (1975): 11.

8. J. A. Sharpe, *Crime in Seventeenth-Century England: A County Study* (Cambridge: Cambridge University Press, 1983), 136.

9. J. A. Sharpe, "The History of Crime," 200.

10. Peter C. Hoffer and N. E. H. Hull, *Murdering Mothers: Infanticide in England and New England, 1558–1803* (New York: New York University Press, 1984), 8.

11. See Wrightson, "Infanticide in European History," 8.

12. 21 James I, cap. 27, *Statutes at Large from Magna Charta to the End of the Eleventh Parliament of Great Britain, Anno 1761*, ed. Danby Pickering (Cambridge: Joseph Bentham, 1763), vol. 7: 298. This act remained on the books until 1803. According to Hoffer and Hull, "Bastard neonaticides constituted over 70 percent of all murders of infants under nine years of age in the records. Concealment of pregnancy is mentioned in 55 percent of these cases." *Murdering Mothers*, 18.

13. *Proceedings at the Sessions-House in the Old-Bayly*, April 13–14 (London, 1681).

14. For further discussion of this statute, see Mark Jackson, "Suspicious Infant Deaths: the Statute of 1624 and Medical Evidence at Coroners' Inquests," in *Legal Medicine in History*, ed. Michael Clark and Catherine Crawford (Cambridge: Cambridge University Press, 1994), 65–69.

15. The 1576 law is 19 Eliz., cap. 3. See *Statutes at Large*, 6: 311. 7 James, cap. 4 provided that "every lewd woman . . . [which] shall have any bastard which may be chargeable to the parish, the justices of peace shall commit such lewd woman to the house of correction, there to be punished and set on work, during the term of one whole year" (*Statutes at Large*, 7:225). Earlier statutes also sought to control unmarried women.

The Statute of Artificers (1563), for example, allowed town authorities to order unmarried women between the ages of twelve and forty into service; those refusing could be sentenced to jail until they acquiesced (*Statutes at Large*, 6:168).

16. Mark Jackson, *New-Born Child Murder: Women, Illegitimacy and the Courts in Eighteenth-Century England* (New York: Manchester University Press, 1996), 30.

17. Wrightson, "Infanticide in Earlier Seventeenth-Century England," 10. Susan Amussen makes a similar argument in *An Ordered Society*, 113.

18. Jackson, *New-Born Child Murder*, 29.

19. Dolan, *Dangerous Familiars*, 132–33.

20. These are the plots of Thomas Brewer, *The Bloudy Mother* (London, 1609); Henry Goodcole, *Natures Cruell Step-Dames* (London, 1637); *Strange and Wonderful News from Durham, or the Virgins Caveat Against Infant Murder* (London, 1679); and Richard Watkins, *Newes from the Dead* (Oxford, 1651). I will discuss the first three of these pamphlets later in this section. For a discussion of *Newes from the Dead* and other pamphlets that deal with the case of Anne Greene, see below.

21. *News from Tyburn* (London, 1675), 7.

22. Keith Wrightson points out that such attitudes raise "the disturbing possibility that if Christian social morality had done much to overcome the practice of infanticide motivated by considerations of communal or familial interest, it may have exacerbated resort to it to avoid the stigma of illegitimacy." "Infanticide in European History," 5.

23. I borrow Peter Lake's term from "Deeds Against Nature," 264.

24. In fact, virtually all female faults were sexualized. Gossip was "a kind of incontinence of the mind"; curiosity was "a deflowering of the mind"; drunkenness was to be "a prostitute to wine." Mary Fissel, "Gender and Generation: Representing Reproduction in Early Modern England," *Gender and History* 7.3 (1995): 442. Linda Woodbridge explains that assigning the "label 'whore' to any unmarried non-virgin" was "a way of assimilating the puzzling maid/not maid into a recognizable category: to categorize was to understand. The unchaste never-married woman was a special sort of monster; her crime was heinous because it disrupted the schematic order of the world." *Women and the English Renaissance: Literature and the Nature of Womankind, 1540–1620* (Urbana: University of Illinois Press, 1984), 84.

25. *Deeds Against Nature, and Monsters by kinde* (London, 1614), sig. A4v. Page numbers cited hereafter in the text.

26. This quote derives from the 1610 statute cited above, note 15.

27. *A Warning to Sinners, Being a True Relation of a Poor Woman* (London, 1660), title page.

28. J. A. Sharpe, *Crime in Early Modern England, 1550–1750* (London: Longman, 1984), 177.

29. On the criminalization of poverty in the pamphlets, see Dolan, *Dangerous Familiars*, 128–29.

30. Amussen, *An Ordered Society*, 113.

31. Keith Wrightson, "The Nadir of English Illegitimacy in the Seventeenth Century," in *Bastardy and Its Comparative History*, ed. Peter Laslett, Karla Oosterveen and Richard Smith (Cambridge, Mass.: Harvard University Press, 1980), 187.

32. J. M. Beattie, *Crime and the Courts in England, 1660–1800* (Princeton: Princeton University Press, 1986), 114.

33. J. S. Cockburn, "Patterns of Violence in English Society: Homicide in Kent, 1560–1985," *Past and Present* 130 (1991): 95.

34. Thomas Brewer, *The Bloudy Mother* (London, 1609), sig. B3. Page numbers hereafter cited in the text.

35. Laura Gowing, "The Haunting of Susan Lay: Servants and Mistresses in Seventeenth-Century England," *Gender and History* 14.2 (2002): 187.

36. Gouge, *Of Domesticall Duties*, 663 and 652.

37. Paul Griffiths, *Youth and Authority: Formative Experiences in England 1560–1640* (New York: Oxford University Press, 1996), 274–75.

38. John Dod and Robert Cleaver, *A Godlie Forme of Householde Government: For the Ordering of Private Families, according to the direction of Gods word* (London, 1612).

39. Adrian Wilson, "The Ceremony of Childbirth and Its Interpretation," in *Women as Mothers in Pre-Industrial England: Essays in Memory of Dorothy McLaren*, ed. Valerie Fildes (New York: Routledge, 1990), 70–75. Other scholars disagree with Wilson about the churching ceremony, seeing it as a ritual purification of the polluted mother rather than a joyous reentry into the world. See, for example, William Coster, "Purity, Profanity, and Puritanism: the Churching of Women, 1500–1700," *Women in the Church: Papers Read at the 1989 Summer Meeting and 1990 Winter Meeting of the Ecclesiastical History Society*, ed. W. J. Sheils and Diana Wood (Oxford: Blackwell, 1990), 377–87, and David Cressy, "Purification, Thanksgiving and the Churching of Women in Post-Reformation England," *Past and Present* 141 (1993): 106–46.

40. As Peter Stallybrass explains, the "signs of the 'harlot' are her linguistic 'fullness' and her frequenting of public space." The signs of the chaste woman are "the enclosed body, the closed mouth, the locked house." "Patriarchal Territories: The Body Enclosed," in *Rewriting the Renaissance: The Discourses of Sexual Difference in Early Modern Europe*, ed. Margaret W. Ferguson, Maureen Quilligan, and Nancy J. Vickers (Chicago: University of Chicago Press, 1986), 127.

41. Gail Kern Paster argues that even for the married woman the enclosed and protected domain of the laboring woman is "hard to distinguish from one of concealment and shame, from the isolation ordinarily granted to acts of bodily evacuation." Further, she explains, "By ritually

sealing off the birthing chamber, even stopping up the keyholes, women at birth offer an ideologically weighted countersign to the bodily opening and emptying enacted in birth." *The Body Embarrassed: Drama and the Disciplines of Shame in Early Modern England* (Ithaca, N.Y.: Cornell University Press, 1993), 189.

42. On the role women played in criminal trials, see Jim Sharpe, "Women, Witchcraft, and the Legal Process," in *Women, Crime and the Courts in Early Modern England*, ed. Jennifer Kermode and Garthine Walker (Chapel Hill: University of North Carolina Press, 1994), 106–24. For a discussion of women's role in regulating illegitimate pregnancy, see Laura Gowing, "Ordering the Body: Illegitimacy and Female Authority in Seventeenth-Century England," in *Negotiating Power in Early Modern Society: Order, Hierarchy and Subordination in Britain and Ireland*, ed. Michael J. Braddick and John Walter (Cambridge: Cambridge University Press, 2001), 45–50.

43. Gowing, "The Haunting of Susan Lay," 192.

44. Michael Foucault, *Discipline and Punish: The Birth of the Prison*, trans. Alan Sheridan (New York: Vintage Books, 1995).

45. J. A. Sharpe, "'Last Dying Speeches': Religion, Ideology and Public Execution in Seventeenth-Century England," *Past and Present* 107 (1985): 156.

46. Henry Goodcole, *A True Declaration of the Happy Conversion, Contrition and Christian Preparation of Francis Robinson, Gentleman, who for Counterfeiting the Great Scale of England was Drawen, Hang'd and Quartered at Charing Cross, on Friday Last, being the Thirteenth Day of November 1618* (London, 1618), sig. A4.

47. See Belsey, *The Subject of Tragedy*, 190–91.

48. *Murther Will Out, Or, a True and Faithful Relation of an Horrible Murther committed Thirty Years Ago, by an Unnatural Mother* (London, 1675). For a discussion of the role of providence in the period, see Alexandra Walsham, *Providence in Early Modern England* (New York: Oxford University Press, 1999).

49. *Strange and Wonderful News from Durham, or the Virgins Caveat Against Infant Murther* (London, 1679), 4.

50. Erickson, *Women and Property*, 201.

51. As Lawrence Stone phrases the stereotypical view, "young widows, suddenly deprived of regular sexual satisfaction by a husband, were likely to be driven by lust in their search for a replacement." *The Family, Sex and Marriage*, 281. On the widow as stock character, see Charles Carlton, "The Widow's Tale: Male Myths and Female Reality in 16th and 17th Century England," *Albion* 10.2 (1978): 118–29.

52. *A True Narrative of the Proceedings at the Sessions-house in the Old-Bayly, At a Sessions there held On Wednesday the 17th of January 1676/7* (London, 1677), 6–7.

53. Henry Goodcole, *Natures Cruell Step-Dames: or, Matchlesse Monsters of the Female Sex* (London, 1637), 17. Page numbers cited hereafter in the text.

54. See Keith Wrightson, *English Society: 1580–1680* (London: Hutchinson, 1982), 102–3; and Steve Lee Rappaport, *Worlds Within Worlds: Structures of Life in Sixteenth-Century London* (New York: Cambridge University Press, 1989) 39–41.

55. Barbara J. Todd, "The Remarrying Widow: A Stereotype Reconsidered," in *Women in English Society, 1500–1800*, ed. Mary Prior (London: Methuen, 1985), 55.

56. Carlton, "The Widow's Tale," 128.

57. I borrow this term from Diane Purkiss, "Women's Stories of Witchcraft," 414.

58. Dolan, *Dangerous Familiars*, also comments upon the fairy tale aspect of the title page, 162.

59. Again, I borrow the term from Purkiss.

60. Quoted in Michael MacDonald, "The Inner Side of Wisdom: Suicide in Early Modern England," *Psychological Medicine* 7 (1977): 569.

61. Amussen, *An Ordered Society*, 115.

62. Quoted in Francus, "Monstrous Mothers," 150 n. 7.

63. Keith Wrightson, "Infanticide in European History," 3.

Notes to Chapter 5

1. Richard Watkins, *Newes from the Dead or a True and Exact Narration of the Miraculous Delivery of Anne Greene*, 2nd ed. (Oxford, 1651), 2. Page numbers cited hereafter in the text.

2. Sir William Blackstone, *Ehrlich's Blackstone*, vol. 2, ed. J. W. Ehrlich (New York: Capricorn Books, 1959), 524.

3. Michel Foucault, *Discipline and Punish*, 50. Several recent scholars have questioned this view of the public execution "as a theatre of punishment, in which the power of the centralising state was ritually inscribed in the flesh of the victim, a public demonstration of the power of the prince and the awful majesty of the law," seeing it instead as a subversion of that authority. Peter Lake, "Deeds Against Nature," 275. For a discussion of the public execution as a carnivalesque subversion of state authority, see Thomas W. Laqueur, "Crowds, Carnival and the State in English Executions, 1604–1868," in *The First Modern Society: Essays in English in Honour of Lawrence Stone*, ed. A. L. Beier, David Cannadine, and James M. Rosenheim (New York: Cambridge University Press, 1989), 305–55.

4. Sheila Delaney, *Writing Woman: Women Writers and Women in Literature, Medieval to Modern* (New York: Schocken Books, 1983), 188.

5. The earliest of these accounts is probably that told in two issues of

the *Mercurius Politicus*, no. 28, December 12–19, 1650, and no. 32, January 9–16, 1651. Joad Raymond includes these in *Making the News: An Anthology of the Newsbooks of Revolutionary England, 1641–1660* (New York: St. Martin's Press, 1993), 182–84. Petty's account appears in "History of the Magdalen (or The Raising of Anne Greene)," in *The Petty Papers, Some Unpublished Writings of Sir William Petty*, vol. 2, edited from the Bowood Papers by the Marquis of Lansdowne (New York: Augustus M. Kelley Publishers, 1967), 157–67. *A Declaration from Oxford, of Anne Greene, that was lately hanged but since Recovered* (London, 1651) is basically the same as Burdet's version but adds a brief description of a visitation from the angels that Anne experienced while she was dead. This version also includes the story of a woman who gave birth after she had been buried. Twenty-five years later, Greene's case was still notorious. John Evelyn mentions the event in his diary where he describes his friend Petty, "Doctor of Physick, . . . growne famous as for his Learning, so for his recovering a poore wench that had ben hanged for felonie, the body being beged (as costome is) for the Anatomie lecture, he let bloud, put to bed a warme woman, and with spirits and other meanes recovered her to life; The Young Scholars joyn'd and made a little portion, married her to a man who had severall children by her, living 15 yeares after, as I have ben assured." *The Diary of John Evelyn*, ed. John Bowle (New York: Oxford University Press, 1983), 252–53.

6. I first quote no. 28, December 12–19, 1650, then no. 32, January 9–16, 1651, in Raymond, *Making the News*, 182–84.

7. *A Declaration from Oxford, of Anne Greene* differs only slightly from *A Wonder of Wonders* and, although published anonymously, was apparently the first version of Burdet's pamphlet.

8. Burdet, *A Wonder of Wonders*, 2. Page numbers cited hereafter in the text.

9. Laqueur discusses the various subversions of the scaffold in "Crowds, Carnival and the State," cited above.

10. Willughby, *Observations in Midwifery*, 274, quoted in Mark Jackson, "Suspicious Infant Deaths: The Statute of 1624 and Medical Evidence at Coroners' Inquests," in *Legal Medicine in History*, ed. Michael Clark and Catherine Crawford (New York: Cambridge University Press, 1994), 70.

11. Amussen notes a conviction rate of 53 percent in Sussex from 1600 to 1640, *An Ordered Society*, 115. Other scholars posit different rates. J. A. Sharpe, for instance, found that conviction rates in Essex tended to fluctuate, from a maximum of 55 percent between 1630 and 1634 to a minimum of 10 percent from 1655 to 1659, *Crime in Seventeenth-Century England*, 134.

12. Thomas Percival, *Medical Ethics* (Manchester, 1803), 84, quoted in Jackson, "Suspicious Infant Deaths," 73.

13. Dolan, "'Gentlemen, I have one more thing to say, '" 166.

14. Jonathan Sawday describes anatomy as a kind of social/sexual control: the "science of *seeing*, and thus knowing and controlling the body, in order to harness its appetites and desires," in *The Body Emblazoned: Dissection and the Human Body in Renaissance Culture* (New York: Routledge, 1995), 219, but given the fascination with the female body revealed in cases such as this one, it seems just as likely that anatomy might also foster those appetites and desires.

15. Scholars have noted the remarkable change in attitudes toward the body that increased scientific knowledge brought about: "With the advance in understanding of anatomy and the corresponding development of private trade in corpses, we can find in the early eighteenth century a significant change in attitude towards the dead human body. The corpse becomes a commodity with all the attributes of a property. It could be owned privately. It could be bought and sold. A value not measured by the grace of heaven nor the fires of hell but quantifiably expressed in the magic of the price list was placed upon the corpse. As a factor in the production of scientific knowledge, the accumulated rituals and habits of centuries of religion and superstition were swept aside." Peter Linebaugh, "The Tyburn Riot Against the Surgeons," in *Albion's Fatal Tree: Crime and Society in Eighteenth Century England*, ed. Douglas Hay et al. (London: Allen Lane, 1975), 72.

16. Jane Todd, Old Bailey Session Papers, July 1727, 2. Quoted in Mark Jackson, "Suspicious Infant Deaths," 68.

17. Keith Thomas, "The Puritans and Adultery: The Act of 1650 Reconsidered," in *Puritans and Revolutionaries: Essays in Seventeenth-Century History presented to Christopher Hill*, ed. Donald Pennington and Keith Thomas (Oxford: Clarendon Press, 1978), 257.

18. "An Act for suppressing the detestable sins of Incest, Adultery and Fornication. 10 May, 1650," *Acts and Ordinances of the Interregnum, 1642–1660*, volume 2, collected and edited by C. H. Firth and R. S. Rait (Holmes Beach, Fla.: Wm. W. Gaunt and Sons, 1972), 388.

19. Thomas, "Puritans and Adultery," 267.

20. Foucault, *Discipline and Punish*, 68.

21. Dolan, *Dangerous Familiars*, 138.

22. Caroline Walker Bynum, *Fragmentation and Redemption: Essays on Gender and the Human Body in Medieval Religion* (New York: Zone, 1991), 186–94.

23. This reconstruction of the criminal as a saint occurs several times in this literature; see, for example, my examinations of Elizabeth Caldwell and various mothers, above. The connection between the women criminals in the popular literature and female saints does not seem strange at all if we agree with Stephen G. Nichols's argument that "hagiography is a mediated, scripted genre controlled by the institution of the church, designed to marginalize unauthorized prophetic voices such as those of

women. The only body that speaks in a hagiographical text is a dead body; it speaks, moreover, by having been turned into a text." Unpublished paper quoted in Maureen Quilligan, *The Allegory of Female Authority: Christine de Pizan's Cite des Dames* (Ithaca, N.Y.: Cornell University Press, 1991), 243. The crime literature also seeks to contain the subversive voices of women through the institutionalized authority of the state, though not always successfully.

24. Katharine Park, "The Criminal and the Saintly Body: Autopsy and Dissection in Renaissance Italy," *Renaissance Quarterly* 47.1 (1994): 23.

25. Raymond, *Making the News*, 172.

26. For an overview of the "Miracles of the Virgin," see John Edwin Wells, *A Manual of the Writings in Middle English, 1050–1400* (New Haven: Yale University Press, 1916), 165–70.

27. Alexandra Walsham, *Providence in Early Modern England*, 78.

28. Raymond notes the French versions (*Making the News*, 172–73). For the translated texts themselves and a fuller discussion of them, see Roger Chartier, "The Hanged Woman Miraculously Saved: An *occasionnel*" in *The Culture of Print: Power and the Uses of Print in Early Modern France*, ed. Roger Chartier, trans. Lydia G. Cochrane (Princeton: Princeton University Press, 1989), 59–91.

29. Chartier, "The Hanged Woman," 82.

Notes to *A True Discourse Of the practises of Elizabeth Caldwell*

1. A court session.

2. A form of punishment usually given to a person who stood mute or would not plead. The prisoner's body was pressed with heavy weights until he pleaded or died.

3. Very little is known about Gilbert Dugdale. In addition to this pamphlet, he also wrote an eyewitness account of the entry of James I into London in 1604 entitled *The time triumphant declaring in briefe, the arival of our soveraigne liedge Lord, King James into England* (London, 1604).

4. Robert Armin (c. 1568–1615), actor and writer in Lord Chandos's company and the Lord Chamberlain's Men, Shakespeare's company. He specialized in comic roles; it is likely that he played Dogberry, Touchstone, Feste, and Lear's Fool. Armin was the author of *Foole upon Foole* (1600); *Phantasma, the Italian Tail and His Boy (1609); Quips upon Questions; A Nest of Ninnies;* and a play, *The Two Maids of Moreclacke.* Mary Chandois, or Chandos, was the wife of William Brydges, Lord Chandos.

5. Composition.

6. A coarse, green wool cloth.

7. Falsehood.

8. One of Armin's nicknames.

9. Cheshire has played an important role in English history. The families descended from the original Saxons and Norman lords played an especially influential role and became known as Cheshire Knights.

10. Considered.

11. Foolishness.

12. Show, reveal.

13. A small coin; the reference is to Mark 12:42 and Luke 21:1–4, in which the widow offers all the coins she has to the poor.

14. To repay.

15. Used for emphasis, often expressing surprise or astonishment.

16. Propose.

17. Annuity.

18. Loose; astir.

19. Employed, paid by fees.

20. Promptings or instructions.

21. Gain, profit.

22. To put in irons or the stocks, to confine; also figuratively, to overthrow or disgrace.

23. Rat poison, especially arsenic.

24. A writ commanding the sheriff to take sureties for a prisoner's appearance.

25. Postponed.

26. A week.

27. The feast of St. Michael, September 29, one of the four quarterdays of the English business year.

28. Clergymen.

29. Deeply or sensibly felt, acute.

30. An official who pays troops or workmen; here, God.

31. Women who were pregnant and convicted of crimes could "plead the belly" and escape punishment, at least for the duration of their pregnancy.

32. Each of the distinct charges of an accusation or indictment.

33. Succeed or fare.

34. The area between Chester Castle and the city of Chester.

35. The text changes from black letter to roman type at this point to indicate the change to Elizabeth Caldwell herself as writer. The two letters preceding the pamphlet are also in roman type.

36. Genuinely.

37. A parable explaining the need to be prepared for Christ's coming. Matthew 25:1–13 tells the story of the ten virgins waiting for the bridegroom. Five of the virgins brought extra oil; the five foolish virgins had only what was in their lamps. The five without the extra oil soon realized

that they would run out of oil before the bridegroom came so they went to look for more. When they returned they were shut out of the wedding despite their repeated knocking.

38. Ecclesiastes 9:10.

39. Matthew 7:21.

40. Wish.

41. Jeremiah 31:18 and Matthew 18: 3.

42. John 6:44.

43. Psalms 51:10.

44. Way of life.

45. Ecclesiastes 11:9.

46. Reference to Noah and the flood in Genesis 7.

47. Daniel 5:5–28. The Balthazar Caldwell refers to is King Belshazzar.

48. Quickening, animating.

49. Hosea 4:6.

50. Luke 12:47.

51. Luke 10:16.

52. A sharp, pointed instrument, usually a wooden shaft with a spike on one end, used to command an ox. If the ox refused the command, the prick would be driven deeper into his flesh. To "kick against the prick" is to rebel, in this case against God. See Acts 9:5.

53. John 13:35.

54. A foreshadowing.

55. Strictly.

56. To act as defender.

57. City destroyed by God because of the wickedness of its inhabitants (Genesis 19:1–11).

58. Numbers 15:32–36.

59. Romans 6:16.

60. Exodus 31:13.

61. To incur debts.

62. Galatians 6:7.

63. Deuteronomy 29:19–20.

64. Ezekiel 18:27.

65. 1 Corinthians 10:12.

66. Luke 19:40.

67. 2 Kings 2: 23–24: "And he went up from thence unto Bethel. And as he was going up the way, little children came out of the city, and mocked him, and said unto him, Come up, thou bald head; come up, thou bald head. And he turned back, and looked on them, and cursed them in the name of the Lord. And two bears came out of the forest, and tore in pieces two and forty children of them."

68. A woman of advanced age; a grandmother.

Notes to *The Adultresses Funerall Day*

1. A brief statement or summary.

2. A person who makes an official visit of inspection or supervision, especially to an institution; specifically an ecclesiastic or lay commissioner appointed to visit churches, prisons, hospitals etc.

3. Henry Goodcole, 1586–1641, was a prolific pamphlet writer, apparently using his job as visitor at Newgate Prison for source material.

4. The fortieth day after Easter observed in commemoration of Christ's ascension into heaven.

5. The week beginning with Whit Sunday, (White Sunday), or Pentecost.

6. Biblical, seat of the affections.

7. To outdo or overcome in facing or confronting.

8. Disgusting beyond description.

9. To plot against.

10. Deadly, death producing.

11. One who mixes.

12. The practice of employing poison or magical potions in sorcery.

13. Obsolete for fascination, the casting of spells.

14. After Cornelius, emperor of Rome.

15. Empiric, an untrained practitioner in physic or surgery, a quack.

16. The keeping of boys for unnatural purposes.

17. The practice of sodomy.

18. The murder of a father, parent, near relative, ruler, etc.; also the crime of treason against one's country.

19. To run through from side to side with a sharp instrument.

20. Synonymous with the gallows; an upright post with a projecting arm from which the bodies of criminals were hung in chains or irons after execution.

21. Enoch ap Evans was executed in Staffordshire for killing his mother and brother for religious reasons. His story is told by Peter Studley in *The Looking Glasse of Schism: wherein by a narration of the murders, done by Enoch ap Evans, a downe-right Separatist, on his mother and brother, the disobedience of that sect, is set forth* (London, 1634); and Richard More, *A True Relation of the Murders Committed in the Parish of Clunne in the Country of Salop by Enoch ap Evans* (London, 1641).

22. To chase with malicious intent.

23. Tom and Canbery Bess were the aliases of Thomas Sherwood and Elizabeth Evans, who robbed and then killed their victims, and who were hanged for their crimes in 1635. The ballad "Murder Upon Murder" recounts their life of crime. Goodcole tells their story in *Heavens Speedie Hue and Cry Sent after Lust and Murther* (London, 1635).

24. In one of the more notorious crimes of the sixteenth century, Alice Arden had her husband murdered in Kent in 1551. Holinshed recounts

the crime in his *Chronicles of England, Scotland and Ireland*. The anonymous play *Arden of Feversham* is also based on this crime.

25. In February 1591, Mistress Ulalia Page of Plymouth and her lover, George Strangwich, murdered her husband. The story is told in *Sundrye Strange and inhumaine Murthers, lately committed* (London, 1591), usually attributed to Anthony Munday, and in several ballads, including several by Thomas Deloney.

26. At once, immediately (archaic use).

27. Kept company with.

28. All Saints' Day, November 1.

29. Duplicate manner.

30. Duplicate effect.

31. In the former mode.

32. Considering deliberately.

33. In the following mode; by secret intent.

34. The following effect; the act of abusing creatures.

35. As Jacob lay on his deathbed, he called his sons to his bedside in order to prophesy their futures. This reference is to his thoughts concerning Simeon and Levi (Genesis 49:5–7): "Simeon and Levi, brethren in evil, the instruments of cruelty are in their habitations. Into their secret let not my soul come: my glory, be not thou joined with their assembly: for in their wrath they slew a man, and in their self-will they dug down a wall. Cursed be their wrath, for it was fierce, and their rage, for it was cruel: I will divide them in Jacob, and scatter them in Israel."

36. Pertained or related to, concerned.

37. London prison.

38. A ruddy complexion was thought to be a sign of a sanguine humor, characterized by hopefulness and courage.

Notes to *Murther, Murther. Or, A bloody Relation*

1. Ephesians 5:25: "Husbands, love your wives, even as Christ also loved the church, and gave himself for it." Note the reversal in the pamphlet.

2. Merry, mirthful.

3. Luke 23:28: "But Jesus turned back unto them and said, 'Daughters of Jerusalem, weep not for me, but weep for yourselves, and for your children.'"

4. Genesis 2:24.

5. A stool consisting of jointed parts.

6. To be rid of. Also, euphemistically, "to put out of the way," murder.

7. Often used for familiar friend or chum.

8. A weight of 60 grains; one-eighth of an ounce.

9. A doctor or surgeon.

10. A very fine and delicate kind of glass, originally manufactured at Murano, near Venice.

Notes to *A Hellish Murder Committed by a French Midwife*

1. Although a new calendar dropping ten days from the year was introduced by Pope Gregory XIII in A.D. 1582, England continued to use the old style calendar until 1752. In England, the new year began on March 25. Thus dates for events occurring between January 1 and March 24 often indicate both years, as here, 1687/8.

2. Odd or whimsical ideas.

3. Common laborers.

4. Someone who fits together pieces of wood for doors and windows.

5. Written statement or accusation.

6. In English law two types of treasons exist: high treason and petit or petty treason. High treason is against the king or the safety of the commonwealth. Petty treason is an offense, usually murder, against a subject, specifically a servant against the master or a wife against her husband. The penalty for this crime was death.

7. Guarantee, bail.

8. A keeper of an eating house, inn, or tavern.

9. A memorandum as to the day and year and before whom an affidavit is sworn.

10. An apartment over the gate of a city or palace, often used as a prison.

11. Flare for lighting one's way.

12. A precinct of London, noted for the palace of the Savoy, which was converted by Henry VII into a hospital for the poor and renamed St. John's Hospital.

13. Mischievous behavior; a practical joke.

14. Delivered.

15. One who saws timber.

16. Dared.

17. Plotted together.

18. Good humored ridicule.

19. The guinea was a 20-shilling piece minted under Charles II in 1662.

20. Lawful dumping areas along the river.

21. A week.

22. A medallion.

23. Before us, in the court of King's Bench.

24. A warrant officer.

25. The duchy is the district between London and Westminster; a liberty

is a district within the county that is exempt from the jurisdiction of the sheriff.

26. A division of the county or shire having its own court.

27. Men employed to clean the cesspools and outdoor privies at night.

28. Privy.

29. A charnel house.

30. Perhaps an abbreviation for caption, the heading of a disposition, indictment, or other legal document indicating the names of the parties involved.

31. Invocations or oaths of vengeance.

32. Out of her house, in public view.

33. Heretics.

34. Heavy thread or twine used for tying up bundles.

35. Accomplices (archaic form).

Notes to *A pittilesse Mother*

1. The fortieth day after Easter, called Holy Thursday in England.

2. Incident.

3. Principal place in London where public executions were held.

4. The evening before Pentecost Sunday.

5. A monstrous sea creature of enormous size, used here to allude to Satan.

6. Cunning devices.

7. Fortune, lot.

8. Attacks.

9. Ecclesiastics or clergymen.

10. Roman Catholics.

11. Foolish.

12. Suspecting.

13. Traditionally, the pelican pecks herself until she bleeds and uses her blood to feed her babies. The pelican is used repeatedly during the period as the symbol of the good mother, an analogy filled with ambiguity and violence.

14. Against all maternal and natural instinct.

15. Enchantress in Greek mythology; when her husband, Jason, left her to marry Glauce, she killed the children she and Jason had produced and escaped to Athens. Medea is most often associated with vengefulness, jealousy, and sorcery.

16. Satiated.

17. At this time, many women had other women suckle their children rather than nursing themselves, though the practice was becoming controversial.

18. From behind the house, the back yard.

19. Common name for a child's nurse.

20. Several persons.

21. A writ instructing a jailer to hold a prisoner, a warrant.

22. A famous London prison.

23. The periodical sittings of the justices of the peace.

24. An object of religious veneration, especially an article (a part of the body or piece of clothing, for example) reputed to be associated with a saint or martyr.

25. Protestant Bible used by the Anglican Church and endorsed by the throne, as opposed to the Catholic Bible.

26. London prisons had different levels of accommodation for prisoners, based not on the severity of the crime they had committed but on the amount of money they had to bribe the keepers. The Master's side provided the most comfortable accommodations and usually housed the wealthiest prisoners.

Notes to *Blood for Blood*

1. The "Letter to the Reader" is in italics in the original text.

2. Used for conveying convicts to the gallows; also used to publicly shame and chastise offenders, especially lewd women.

3. To weigh or examine according to the standard of divine revelation.

4. At the right and proper time, opportunely.

5. One who makes an open profession of religion, a professed Christian.

6. Acts 28:3–6: "And when Paul had gathered a bundle of sticks, and laid them on the fire, there came a viper out of the heat, and fastened on his hand. And when the barbarians saw the venomous beast hang on his hand, they said among themselves, No doubt this man is a murderer, whom, though he hath escaped the sea, yet vengeance suffereth not to live. And he shook off the beast into the fire, and felt no harm. Howbeit they looked when he should have swollen, or fallen down dead suddenly: but after they had looked a great while, and saw no harm come to him, they changed their minds, and said that he was a god."

7. Two murder cases from the period. On August 6, 1657, Nathaniel Butler, an apprentice of a London silk maker, slit the throat of one of his fellow apprentices. His crime is the subject of several pamphlets: *Heaven's Cry Against Murder. A True Relation of the Bloody and Unparalleled Murder of John Knight; Blood Washed Away by Tears of Repentance*; and *A Full and the Truest Narrative of the Most Horrid, Barbarous and Unparalleled Murder Committed on the Person of John Knight* (London, 1657). Thomas Savage also murdered an apprentice in 1668; he survived the first attempt to hang him. See *A Murderer Punished and Pardoned, or*

A True Relation of the Wicked Life and Shameful-Happy Death of Thomas Savage; and *Gods Justice Against Murder, or the bloudy Apprentice Executed* (London, 1668).

8. Mark 9:48.

9. The second of the two divisions of the Decalogue, or Ten Commandments.

10. The verse quoted is Genesis 4:10. Revelation 6:10 cited by the authors is "And they cried with a loud voice, saying, How long, O Lord, holy and true, dost thou not judge and avenge our blood on them that dwell on earth?"

11. Evil personified; a name for the Devil or one of the fiends; in Milton, one of the fallen angels.

12. Proverbs 1:29: "For that they hated knowledge, and did not choose the fear of the Lord."

13. Titus 3:2: "To speak evil of no man, to be no brawlers, but gentle, shewing all meekness unto all men."

14. Benjamite who cursed David, see 2 Samuel 16:5–13.

15. Ecclesiastes 7:11: "Wisdom is good with an inheritance: and by it there is profit to it that see the sun."

16. Superiority.

17. The quote actually refers to 1 John 3:15.

18. Jacob cheats Esau out of Isaac's blessing. Isaac asks Esau to hunt game for a meal, promising Esau a deathbed blessing in return. Rebekah overhears the conversation and has Jacob slay two kids from the family's flock. She dresses him as Esau and tricks Isaac into bestowing the blessing on Jacob. Genesis 27:41: "And Esau hated Jacob because of the blessing wherewith his father blessed him: and Esau said in his heart, The days of mourning for my father are at hand; then will I slay my brother Jacob."

19. Romans 12:19: "Dearly beloved, avenge not yourselves, but rather give place to wrath: for it is written, Vengeance is mine; I will repay, saith the Lord."

20. Consanguinity, a relationship by blood, as opposed to affinity, a relationship by marriage.

21. Romans 1:28–31: "And even as they did not like to retain God in their knowledge, God gave them over to a reprobate mind, to do those things which are not convenient; Being filled with all unrighteousness, fornication, wickedness, covetousness, maliciousness; full of envy, murder, debate, deceit, malignity; whisperers, Backbiters, haters of God, despiteful, proud, boasters, inventors of evil things, disobedient to parents, Without understanding, covenant-breakers, without natural affection, implacable, unmerciful."

22. 1 Peter 3:8–9: "Finally, be ye all of one mind, having compassion one of another, love as brethren, be pitiful, be courteous: Not rendering evil for evil, or railing for railing: but contrariwise blessing; knowing that

ye are thereunto called, that ye should inherit a blessing." 1 Peter 3:11: "Let him eschew evil, and do good; let him seek peace, and ensue it."

23. Galatians 6:1–2: "Brethren, if a man be overtaken in a fault, ye which are spiritual, restore such an one in the spirit of meekness; considering thyself, lest thou also be tempted. Bear ye one another's burdens, and so fulfil the law of Christ."

24. Thread or yarn wound to a certain length upon a reel in a loose knot.

25. Deuteronomy 28 tells of the discontent and curses that come from sin and disobedience to God.

26. The seat of tender and sympathetic emotions; i.e., pity or compassion.

27. Surgeon, archaic.

28. Here, "in a state of stupor" or "having the senses dulled or deadened."

29. A cross or other sign made in lieu of a signature.

30. Matthew 18:17, a heathen; someone cut off from the church.

31. A petition.

32. A warrant for arrest.

33. Ezekiel 18:24: "But when the righteous turneth away from his righteousness, and committeth iniquity, and doeth according to all the abominations that the wicked man doeth, shall he live? All his righteousness that he hath done shall not be mentioned: in his trespass that he hath trespassed, and in his sin that he hath sinned, in them shall he die."

34. Nomadic tribes who lived in the remote regions in Asia Minor and North Africa. "To dwell in the tents of Kedar" is to be cut off from the worship of the true God. See Psalms 120:5.

35. The Central Criminal court in London.

36. Richard Baxter (1615–91), minister and writer of devotional literature, best known for *Saints' Everlasting Rest*, 1650.

37. Variant of "menstrual."

38. Mark 5:25–29 tells of a woman who bled for twelve years, but after she touched Christ's garment her blood dried up and she was healed.

39. In Matthew 4:1–11 Jesus is tempted by Satan; Matthew 4:12 to the end of the chapter tells of Jesus' ministry in Galilee and to Israelites.

40. The chaplain of the prison whose duty it was to prepare condemned prisoners for death.

41. The steps to the gallows.

42. Deuteronomy 17:13: "All the people will hear and be afraid, and will not be contemptuous again."

43. 1 Corinthians 10:12.

44. The gallows.

45. Psalms 31:5.

Notes to *Fair Warning to Murderers of Infants*

1. Although a new calendar dropping ten days from the year was introduced by Pope Gregory XIII in A.D. 1582, England continued to use the "old style" calendar until 1752. In England, the new year began on March 25. Thus dates for events occurring between January 1 and March 24 often indicate both years, as here, 1691/92.

2. The letter to the reader is in italics in the original text.

3. Proverbs 26:11: "As a dog returneth to his vomit, so a fool returneth to his folly."

4. The gallows from which executed criminals were hanged for public viewing, but here those actually hanged.

5. The place at which all the business of the court was transacted, synonymous with the court.

6. Reference to David and Bathsheba, 2 Samuel 11, 12.

7. To excel, to surpass.

8. The annual sessions of the High Court of Justice held in various counties of England and Wales, arranged in circuits.

9. Travail, that is, labor of childbirth.

10. Genesis 9:6.

11. The chaplain of the prison whose duty it was to prepare condemned prisoners for death.

12. A minister who does not conform to the Church of England.

13. A striking or remarkable display.

14. The month after childbirth.

15. Failure or weakness.

16. Joseph Alleine, *A Sure Guide to Heaven, or, An Earnest Invitation to sinners to turn to God in order to their eternal salvation* (London, 1691).

17. Matthew 26:41.

18. Easily, with little effort.

19. The seat of the tender and sympathetic emotions; pity, compassion, feeling.

Notes to *The Bloudy Mother*

1. Little is known about the author, Thomas Brewer (fl. 1624). The *Dictionary of National Biography* attributes "The Life and Death of the Merry Devill of Edmonton" and *A Knot of Fools* to him and notes his possible authorship of a broadside entitled "Mistress Turner's Repentance, who, about the poysoning of the Ho. Knight Sir Thomas Overbury, was executed the fourteenth day of November last."

2. Embryo, that is, the beginning.

3. Meaning unclear; abilities?

4. An allusion to the rope for hanging.

5. Loadstone or magnet.

6. Biblical, the seat of the affections.

7. The meaning of "Lena" is unclear. Perhaps it is a corruption of "leman," that is, sweetheart, illicit lover.

8. Dismissed, sent away.

9. Sometimes used as a vague title of dignity or a respectful form of address; the master or male head of a household; a husband.

10. The sense here is inexcogitable; that is, inconceivable.

11. To kill a baby accidentally by rolling on top of it while sleeping in bed with it.

12. Overdue payment.

13. Women typically served as witnesses in infanticide trials, searching the accused for signs of pregnancy or childbirth.

14. Someone who violates a law or convention.

15. Obstacles or impediments.

16. Supporter.

17. Dialect form of neckerchief, kerchief worn around the neck.

18. Pregnancy.

19. A bowl-shaped dish.

20. A fire-breathing she-monster usually represented as a composite of a lion, a goat, and a serpent.

21. Numbers 22–24: Balaam's ass sees an angel with a drawn sword standing before him, walks off the road, and collapses. Balaam, angered, strikes the ass three times with his staff. The ass, enabled to speak by God, asks, "Why have you hit me?" and "Have I ever led you astray?" Balaam is then allowed to see the angel, who reminds him to say only the words God puts in the prophet's mouth.

22. Bonds.

23. Annual sessions of the High Court of Justice held in various counties of England and Wales, arranged in circuits.

24. King's Bench Prison, a jail that imprisons criminals and debtors under the authority of the supreme court.

25. Turned off the ladder, hanged.

26. Smell, aroma.

27. Secret.

28. To live by fraud.

29. A wild ass, an unusually strong creature, yet also stupid; God still provides for them. See Psalms 104:10–15.

30. Early Christian theologian and bishop of Carthage who led the Christians of North Africa during a period of persecution from Rome. Upon his execution he became the bishop-martyr of Africa.

31. A late third to fourth century Christian apologist.

32. Biblical translator and monastic leader, traditionally regarded as one of the most learned of the Latin Fathers.

33. Trumpet.

34. Certainly, assuredly, archaic.

35. Twisted, contorted, in the sense of perverted.

Notes to *Deeds Against Nature*

1. The clearing of the jail of prisoners in order to bring them to trial.

2. Celebrated London prison.

3. The periodical sittings of justices of the peace, generally held quarterly.

4. The seat of the Central Criminal Court in London so called from the ancient bailey or ballium of the city wall between the Lud Gate and New Gate, within which it was situated.

5. Place of public execution.

6. Indulging to excess.

7. Figuratively, a rapacious person; one who preys upon society.

8. Was put to the touch, was put to the test.

9. A sitting or session of a legislative or judicial body.

10. Watchman who rang a bell at midnight outside a condemned prisoner's cell the night before execution, usually as a summons to prayer.

11. Wallet, purse, or bag for alms.

12. Great anger or resentment.

13. Enticed.

14. Outhouse or privy.

Notes to *Natures Cruell Step-Dames*

1. Place of public execution in London.

2. The *Short Title Catalogue* attributes this pamphlet to Henry Goodcole.

3. Stimulated, incited.

4. Psalms 140:11.

5. London prison for felons.

6. Surgeon.

7. James 4:7.

8. Matthew 26:41.

9. The devil doesn't sleep.

10. 1 Peter 5:9: "Whom resist steadfast in the faith, knowing that the same afflictions are accomplished in your brethren that are in the world."

11. Malignant, obsolete form.

12. Short prayer.

13. Verse 18.

14. Goodcole actually quotes Psalms 51 here.

15. Actually Goodcole quotes James 5:16.

16. John 20:23.

17. Paralytic, obsolete form.

18. Matthew 9:6.

19. The verse Goodcole refers to here is actually Isaiah 49:15.

20. A cask or vessel of varying capacity.

21. A spiced drink of hot sweetened milk curdled with wine or ale.

22. Drawn through the streets on an open cart as punishment; prostitutes were tied to the back of the cart and beaten along the way.

Notes to *Newes from the Dead*

1. The *Short Title Catalogue* attributes this pamphlet to Richard Watkins, 1623/4–1708.

2. Privy.

3. The periodic sittings of justices of the peace.

4. Hanged on the gallows.

5. Bodies of executed criminals were sometimes dissected for scientific purposes. See the discussion of this pamphlet, above.

6. William Petty (1623–1687), an anatomist in Oxford. Petty kept an extensive journal, upon which this account is apparently based. He is best known for his writings on political economics, particularly, *A Treatise of Taxes and Contributions* (1662) and *The Political Anatomy of Ireland* (1691).

7. Thomas Willis (1621–1675), another anatomist at Oxford, was author of *Cerebri anatome* (1664), the first monograph on the brain and spinal cord to be published in England.

8. Bindings, bandages.

9. Comforting, obsolete.

10. An enema.

11. A sweet, syrupy drink, especially one to which medicine may be added.

12. A poultice.

13. Had warm liquids applied to her skin.

14. Excess.

15. The distance from the tip of the thumb to the tip of the little finger.

16. Discharge, as of blood.

17. The sifting of barley or other grain prepared for brewing or distilling.

18. Menstrual discharge.

19. Labor of childbirth.

20. Orpheus — in Greek mythology, the Thracian poet and musician

whose music had the power to move inanimate objects and who attempted to rescue his wife, Eurydice, from Hades; Aeneas — the Trojan hero of Virgil's *Aeneid*. Both traveled to the underworld.

21. The god of the dead and ruler of the underworld. Orpheus failed to rescue his wife when he looked back at her and so violated the terms of his agreement with Pluto to return her from Hades.

22. The reference here seems to be to Virbius, a minor Roman deity who was a consort of Diana. Virbius is often identified with Hippolytus, whom Diana loved and who was dragged to his death by his horses. Diana persuaded the gods to bring him back to life.

23. Perhaps also punningly, to have an orgasm.

24. Greek Goddess of doom and destruction.

25. Persephone, the wife of Hades and daughter of Zeus and Demeter, who is the goddess of the underworld and of springtime. Persephone was taken to the underworld by her husband. Her mother, in grief at her daughter's absence, kept the world in perpetual winter. Eventually Persephone was allowed to return to her mother so the earth would flourish. However, because Persephone ate a pomegranate seed while in the underworld, she was required to spend one-third of the year in Hades with her husband.

26. Phoebe is the name of Artemis or Diana as goddess of the moon. Phoebe's orb is the moon.

27. Pyrrha and her husband Deucalion were the only humans who survived Zeus's flood. After the flood they prayed to Zeus, thanking him for their salvation and praying that he repopulate the world. Zeus instructed them to cover their faces and throw stones over their shoulders. Those thrown by Deucalion turned into men, those thrown by Pyrrha into women.

28. The wife and sister of Jupiter, patroness primarily of marriage and the well-being of women.

29. Having two different, especially contrasted qualities; half-and-half.

30. Both Democritus and Heraclitus were Greek philosophers; Democritus was known as the "Laughing Philosopher" in contrast to Heraclitus, the "Weeping Philosopher."

31. A mythical bird that lives five or six hundred years then burns itself to ashes on a funeral pyre, only to be reborn from its ashes.

32. Son of Theseus who spurned the advances of his stepmother, Phaedra, and was killed when Poseidon caused him to lose control of his horses. Artemis was so distraught that she convinced Asclepius to bring him back to life. Asclepius was successful but invoked the wrath of Zeus with so unnatural an act and was hurled into the underworld with a thunderbolt.

33. One of the women oracles in ancient Greece and Rome.

34. A disembodied spirit.

35. The wife of Orpheus, whom he failed to rescue when he looked back at her and so violated the terms of his agreement with Pluto to rescue her from Hades.

36. Asclepius, the god of medicine and healing. See also, note 32.

37. The fruit of the lotus tree was said to drug those who ate it.

38. The river of forgetfulness in Hades.

39. A thinker especially skillful in argumentation.

40. To give a wink to someone as a private signal or warning.

41. The hangman's rope.

42. Scholar skillful in argumentation.

43. A Latin verse printed in black letter (usually the beginning of the 51st Psalm: "Have mercy upon me, O God, according to Thy loving kindness: according unto the multitude of Thy tender mercies blot out my transgressions.") If a prisoner could read it, he could claim benefit of clergy and save his neck. This privilege became available to women in 1623, but since women were not ordained as clergy, it is unlikely they could use this defense.

44. The annual High Court sessions throughout England.

45. Punishment.

46. Proof or demonstration.

47. The ferryman who conveys the dead to Hades over the River Styx.

48. One of the three Fates: Clotho (the spinner), Lachesis (the alotter, who measures the length of thread spun by Clotho), and Atropos (inflexible or inevitable, she cuts the thread measured out by Lachesis); Clotho was the spinner of human fate.

49. Military attire, usually made of leather.

50. One of the three fates. See note 48.

51. New style, pertaining to the new calendar.

52. Begun.

53. Pare here is the obsolete form of pair, two associated things. Thus Greene is paired with the first Sun (Christ) because she too rose from the dead.

54. The end.

55. Umbilical cord.

56. To join by enclosing within a circle or a sphere.

57. Inclination, tendency.

58. Twin heroes in classical mythology. After Castor was killed, Pollux begged Jupiter to let him give his life in exchange for his brother's; Jupiter allowed the twins to divide their time evenly between Hades and heaven and created twin stars of the constellation Gemini in their honor.

59. The Greek king and tyrant Phalaris asked his chief inventor, Perillus, to come up with the cruelest system of torturing the king's enemies that he could. Perillus created a cast iron bull in which he would roast the king's enemies to death. Little did he realize that the king would use the 'torturing engine' on Perillus himself.

60. One of the three fates. See note 48.

61. See note 32.

62. Regeneration, rebirth.

63. Roger Bacon, an Oxford Franciscan, philosopher and alchemist, noted for his strange experiments. Robert Greene depicts him attempting to make a brass head speak in *Friar Bacon and Friar Bungay*. As the story goes, it spoke only three times while Bacon was asleep, saying first, "Time is," then later, "Time was," and finally, "Time is past."

64. River of forgetfulness.

65. A king of Crete, the son of Zeus and Europa. In Athenian drama and legend, Minos became the tyrannical exactor of tribute of children to feed the Minotaur (his son). He was eventually killed by the daughters of King Cocalus, who poured boiling water over him while he was bathing; he became a judge in Hades.

66. See note 21.

67. Asclepius. See note 36.

68. The Roman goddesses of fate; originally there was only one, Parca, the goddess of birth.

69. Italian counterpart of Hippolytus; first priest of Diana's cult at Aricia. See note 22.

70. Worn out horses, but also, punningly, a disreputable woman.

71. Roman for Hera, goddess of marriage and protectress of married women. Juno frequently thwarted the amorous designs of Zeus and took her revenge by punishing the women he loved or their offspring.

Bibliography

Abbreviations

STC: Pollard, Alfred W. and G. R. Redgrave. *A Short-Title Catalogue of Books Printed in England, Scotland, & Ireland and of English Books Printed Abroad, 1475–1640.* 2nd ed. London: Bibliographical Society, 1976.

Wing: Wing, Donald Goddard. *A Short-Title Catalogue of Books Printed in England, Scotland, Ireland, Wales, and British America, and of English Books Printed in Other Countries, 1641–1700.* 2nd ed. New York: Modern Language Association, 1994.

Primary Sources

An Account of the Manner, Behaviour and Execution of Mary Aubry, who was burnt . . . in Leicester Fields. London, 1687. Wing A319D.

Acts and Ordinances of the Interregnum, 1642–1660. Volume 2. Collected and edited by C. H. Firth and R. S. Rait. Holmes Beach, Fla.: Wm. W. Gaunt and Sons, 1972.

Bacon, Francis. "The Advancement of Learning." In *Critical Theory Since Plato,* edited by Hazard Adams. New York: Harcourt Brace Jovanovich, 1971.

Blackstone, Sir William. *Ehrlich's Blackstone.* Edited by J. W. Ehrlich. New York: Capricorn Books, 1959.

Blood Washed Away by Tears of Repentance. London, 1657. Wing B3224.

Bloody Newes from Dover. London, 1647. Wing B3267.

Brewer, Thomas. *The Bloudy Mother.* London, 1609. STC 3717.3.

Burdet, William. *A Wonder of Wonders.* London, 1651. Wing B5620.

A Cabinet of Grief: or, the French Midwife's Miserable Moan for the Barbarous Murther Committed upon the Body of her Husband. London, 1688. Wing C188.

Clinton, Elizabeth. *The Countesse of Lincolnes Nurserie.* Oxford, 1622. Reprinted in *The English Experience, Its Record in Early Printed Books Published in Facsimile,* no. 720. Norwood, N.J.: Walter J. Johnson, 1975.

Concealed Murther Reveil'd. London, 1699(?). British Library 515.1.2 (5).

"The Cruel Midwife." In *The Pepys Ballads,* vol. 7, edited by Hyder E. Rollins. Cambridge, Mass.: Harvard University Press, 1931.

The Cruel Mother, being A true Relation of the Bloody Murther Committed by M. Cook. London, 1670. Not in Wing.

Dalton, Michael. *The Countrey Justice.* London, 1618. Reprinted in *The English Experience: Its Record in Early Printed Books Published in Facsimile,* no. 725. Norwood, N.J.: Walter J. Johnson, 1975.

A Declaration from Oxford, of Anne Greene, that was lately hanged but since Recovered. London, 1651. Wing C586.

Deeds Against Nature, and Monsters by kinde. London, 1614. STC 809.

Deloney, Thomas. "The Lamentation of Master Pages Wife of Plimouth." In *The Roxburghe Ballads,* vol. 2, edited by Charles Hindley. London: Reeves and Turner, 1874.

The Distressed Mother, or a Sorrowful Wife in Tears. London, 1690(?). British Library 515.1.2 (2).

Dod, John and Robert Cleaver. *A Godlie Forme of Householde Government: For the Ordering of Private Families, according to the direction of Gods word.* London, 1612. STC 5386.

Dugdale, Gilbert. *A True Discourse Of the practises Of Elizabeth Caldwell. . . .* London, 1604. STC 7293.

Evelyn, John. *The Diary of John Evelyn.* Edited by John Bowle. New York: Oxford University Press, 1983.

Fair Warning to Murderers of Infants: Being an Account of the Tryal, Codemnation and Execution of Mary Goodenough. London, 1692. Wing F105.

A Full and the Truest Narrative of the Most Horrid, Barbarous and Unparalleled Murder Committed on the Person of John Knight. London, 1657. Wing F2292.

Gods Justice Against Murder, or the Bloudy Apprentice Executed. London, 1668. Wing G959A.

Goodcole, Henry. *The Adultresses Funerall Day: in flaming, scorching, and consuming fire.* London, 1635. STC 12009.

———. *Heavens Speedie Hue and Cry Sent after Lust and Murther.* London, 1635. STC 12010.5.

———. *Natures Cruell Step-Dames: or, Matchlesse Monsters of the Female Sex.* London, 1637. STC 12012.

———. *A True Declaration of the Happy Conversion, Contrition and Christian Preparation of Francis Robinson, who for Counterfeiting the Great Scale of England was Drawen, Hang'd and Quartered at*

Charing Cross, on Friday Last, being the Thirteenth Day of November 1618. London, 1618. STC 12013.

Gouge, William. *Of Domesticall Duties.* London, 1622. Reprinted in *The English Experience: Its Record in Early Printed Books Published in Facsimile,* no. 803. Norwood, N.J.: Walter J. Johnson, 1976.

Heale, William. *An Apologie for Women, or An Apposition to Mr. Dr. G. his assertion . . . that it was lawfull for husbands to beate their wives.* Oxford, 1609. Reprinted in *The English Experience, Its Record in Early Printed Books Published in Facsimile,* no. 665. Norwood, N.J.: Walter J. Johnson, 1974.

Heaven's Cry Against Murder. A True Relation of the Bloody and Unparalleled Murder of John Knight. London, 1657. Wing H1346.

A Hellish Murder Committed by a French Midwife, On the Body of her Husband. London, 1688. Wing H1384.

Holinshed, Raphael. *Holinshed's Chronicles of England, Scotland, and Ireland, in Six Volumes,* vol. 3. New York: AMS Press, 1965.

"Homily on the State of Matrimony." London, 1563. In *Daughters, Wives and Widows: Writings by Men about Women and Marriage in England, 1500–1640,* edited by Joan Larsen Klein. Chicago: University of Illinois Press, 1992.

Inquest after Blood, being a relation of the several Inquisition of all that have died by any violent death in the City of London. London, 1670. Wing I209B.

Jocelin, Elizabeth. *The Mothers Legacie to her Unborne Childe.* London, 1624. STC 14624.

Johnson, John, of Antwerp. *A True Relation of God's Wonderfull Mercies in preserving one alive, which hanged five days.* London, 1605? STC 14668.

Kyd, Thomas (?). *The Trueth of the most wicked and secret murthering of John Brewen, Goldsmith of London, committed by his owne wife through the provocation of one John Parker.* London, 1592. In *Illustrations of Early English Popular Literature,* vol. 1, edited by J. Payne Collier. New York: Benjamin Blom, 1966.

Leigh, Dorothy. *The Mothers Blessing.* London, 1616. STC 15402.

More, Richard. *A True Relation of the Murders Committed in the Parish of Clunne in the Country of Salop by Enoch ap Evans.* London, 1641. STC 23404.

A Murderer Punished and Pardoned, or A True Relation of the Wicked Life and Shameful-Happy Death of Thomas Savage and *God's Justice Against Murder or the Bloody Apprentice Executed.* London, 1668. Wing A996.

The Murderous Midwife, with her Roasted Punishment: being a True and Full Relation of a Midwife that was put into an Iron Cage with Sixteen wildcats, and so Roasted to death. London, 1673. Wing M3097.

Murther, Murther. Or, a bloody Relation how Anne Hamton, dweling in Westminster nigh London, by poyson murthered her deare husband. London, 1641. Wing M3084.

Murther Will Out, Or, a True and Faithful Relation of an Horrible Murther committed Thirty Years Ago, by an Unnatural Mother. London, 1675. Wing M3093.

News from Tyburn. London, 1675.

Parker, Martin. "A Warning for Wives, By the example of one Katherine Francis, alias Stoke, who for killing her husband, Robert Francis with a pair of Sizers, on 8 of Aprill at night, was burned on Clarkenwell-greene, on Tuesday, the 21 of the same moneth, 1629." In *A Pepysian Garland: Blackletter Broadside Ballads of the Years 1595–1639, Chiefly from the Collection of Samual Pepys,* edited by Hyder E. Rollins. Cambridge: Cambridge University Press, 1922.

Partridge, N., and J. Sharp. *Blood for Blood, or Justice Executed for Innocent Blood Shed.* London, 1670. Wing P630.

Petty, William. "History of the Magdalen (or The Raising of Anne Greene)." In *The Petty Papers, Some Unpublished Writings of Sir William Petty,* vol. 2, edited from the Bowood Papers by the Marquis of Lansdowne. New York: Augustus M. Kelley Publishers, 1967.

A Pittilesse Mother. That most unnaturally at one time, murthered two of her owne Children. London, 1616. STC 24757.

Proceedings at the Sessions-House in the Old-Bayly. London, 1681.

Rollins, Hyder E., ed. *A Pepysian Garland: Black-Letter Broadside Ballads of the Years 1595–1639, Chiefly from the Collection of Samuel Pepys.* Cambridge: Cambridge University Press, 1922.

Settle, Elkanah (?). *Epilogue to the French Midwifes Tragedy, who was burnt in Leicester-fields, March 2, 1687/8 for the barbarous murder of her husband Denis Hobry.* London, 1688. Wing S2680A.

Statutes at Large from Magna Charta to the End of the Eleventh Parliament of Great Britain, Anno 1761, vols. 6 and 7. Edited by Danby Pickering. Cambridge: Joseph Bentham, 1763.

Strange and Wonderful News from Durham, or the Virgins Caveat Against Infant Murder. London, 1679. Wing E6A.

Stubbes, Phillip. *A Christall Glasse for Christian Women: containing a most excellent discourse of the godlye life and Christian death of Mistresse Katherine Stubbes.* London, 1603. STC 23382.7.

Studley, Peter. *The Looking Glasse of Schism: wherein by a narration of the murders, done by Enoch ap Evans, a downe-right Separatist, on his mother and brother, the disobedience of that sect, is set forth.* London, 1634. STC 23403.

Sundrye Strange and inhumaine Murthers, lately committed. London, 1591. STC 18286.5.

Swetnam, Joseph. *The Arraignment of Lewd, Idle, Froward and*

Unconstant Women. In *Half Humankind: Contexts and Texts of the Controversy about Women in England, 1540–1640,* edited by Katherine Usher Henderson and Barbara F. McManus. Urbana: University of Illinois Press, 1985.

T. E. *The Lawes Resolution of Womens Rights; or, The Lawes Provision for Woemen. A Methodicall Colection of such Statutes and Customes, with the Cases, Opinions, Arguments and points of Learning in the Law, as do properly concerne Women.* London, 1632. Reprinted in *The English Experience, Its Record in Early Printed Books Published in Facsimile,* no. 922. Norwood, N.J.: Walter J. Johnson, 1979.

The Tragedy of Master Arden of Faversham. Edited by M. L. Wine. London: Metheun & Co., 1973.

A True and Perfect Relation of a most Horrid Murther Committed by One Philmore's Wife, Upon the Body of Her Own Child. London, 1686. Wing T2543A.

The True Discripcion of a Childe with Ruffes borne in the parish of Micheham in the Cou[n]tie of Surrey. London, 1566. STC 1033.

A True Narrative of the Proceedings at the Session-house in the Old Bayly, At a Session there held On Wednesday the 17th of January 1676/7. London, 1677. Wing T2820.

A True Relation of the Most Horrid and Barbarous Murders Committed by Abigail Hill of St. Olaves Southwark, on the persons of foure Infants. London, 1658. Wing T3008.

Vives, Juan Luis. *The Education of a Christian Woman: A Sixteenth-Century Manual.* Edited and translated by Charles Fantazzi. Chicago: University of Chicago Press, 2000.

A Warning-Piece to All Married Men and Women, Being the Full Confession of Mary Hobry, the French Midwife Who Murdered her Husband . . . for which she receiv'd Sentence to be Burnt alive. London, 1688. Wing W935.

A Warning to Sinners, Being a True Relation of a Poor Woman. London, 1660. Wing W940A.

Watkins, Richard. *Newes from the Dead, or a True and Exact Narration of the Miraculous Deliverance of Anne Greene.* 1st ed. Oxford, 1651. Wing W1072.

———. *Newes from the Dead, or a True and Exact Narration of the Miraculous Deliverance of Anne Greene.* 2nd ed. Oxford, 1651. Wing W1073.

Secondary Sources

Amussen, Susan Dwyer. "'Being Stirred to Much Unquietness': Violence and Domestic Violence in Early Modern England." *Journal of Women's History* 6.2 (1994): 70–89.

———. "Gender, Family, and the Social Order." In *Order and Disorder in Early Modern England*, edited by Anthony Fletcher and John Stevenson, 196–218. New York: Cambridge University Press, 1985.

———. *An Ordered Society: Gender and Class in Early Modern England*. Oxford: Basil Blackwell, 1988.

Aughterson, Kate, ed. *Renaissance Women: Constructions of Femininity in England*. New York: Routledge, 1995.

Baines, Barbara. "Effacing Rape in Early Modern Representation." *English Literary History* 65.1 (1998): 69–98.

Beattie, J. M. *Crime and the Courts in England, 1660–1800*. Princeton: Princeton University Press, 1986.

Beilin, Elaine V. *Redeeming Eve: Women Writers of the English Renaissance*. Princeton: Princeton University Press, 1987.

Belsey, Catherine. *The Subject of Tragedy: Identity and Difference in Renaissance Drama*. London: Routledge, 1985.

Burns, E. Jane. *Bodytalk: When Women Speak in Old French Literature*. Philadephia: University of Pennsylvania Press, 1993.

Bynum, Caroline Walker. *Fragmentation and Redemption: Essays on Gender and the Human Body in Medieval Religion*. New York: Zone, 1991.

Carlton, Charles. "The Widow's Tale: Male and Female Reality in 16th and 17th Century England." *Albion* 10.2 (1978): 118–29.

Chartier, Roger. "The Hanged Woman Saved: An *occasionnel*." In *The Culture of Print: Power and the Uses of Print in Early Modern France*, edited by Roger Chartier, translated by Lydia G. Cochrane, 59–91. Princeton: Princeton University Press, 1989.

Chaytor, Miranda. "Husband(ry): Narratives of Rape in the Seventeenth Century." *Gender and History* 7.3 (1995): 378–407.

Cockburn, J. S. "The Nature and Incidence of Crime in England 1559–1625: A Preliminary Survey." In *Crime in England 1550–1800*, edited by J. S. Cockburn, 49–71. Princeton: Princeton University Press, 1977.

———. "Patterns of Violence in English Society: Homicide in Kent, 1560–1985." *Past and Present* 130 (1991): 70–106.

Coster, William. "Purity, Profanity, and Puritanism: the Churching of Women, 1500–1700." In *Women in the Church: Papers Read at the 1989 Summer Meeting and 1990 Winter Meeting of the Ecclesiastical History Society*, edited by W. J. Sheils and Diana Wood, 377–87. Oxford: Blackwell, 1990.

Crawford, Patricia. "The Construction and Experience of Maternity in Seventeenth-Century England." In *Women as Mothers in Pre-Industrial England: Essays in Memory of Dorothy McLaren*, edited by Valerie Fildes, 3–38. New York: Routledge, 1990.

———. *Women and Religion in England, 1500–1720*. London: Routledge, 1993.

Cressy, David. *Birth, Marriage and Death: Ritual, Religion and the Life-Cycle in Tudor and Stuart England.* New York: Oxford University Press, 1997.

———. *Literacy and the Social Order: Reading and Writing in Tudor and Stuart England.* New York: Cambridge University Press, 1980.

———. "Purification, Thanksgiving and the Churching of Women in Post-Reformation England." *Past and Present* 141 (1993): 106–46.

Davies, Kathleen M. "Continuity and Change in Literary Advice on Marriage." In *Marriage and Society: Studies in the Social History of Marriage,* edited by R. B. Outhwaite, 58–80. New York: St. Martin's Press, 1981.

Davis, Natalie Zemon. *Fiction in the Archives: Pardon Tales and Their Tellers in Sixteenth-Century France.* Stanford: Stanford University Press, 1987.

Delany, Sheila. *Writing Woman: Women Writers and Women in Literature, Medieval to Modern.* New York: Schocken Books, 1983.

Dobb, C. "Henry Goodcole, Visitor of Newgate, 1620–1641." *Guildhall Miscellany* 4 (1955): 15–21.

Dolan, Frances E. *Dangerous Familiars: Representations of Domestic Crime in England, 1550–1700.* Ithaca, N.Y.: Cornell University Press, 1994.

———. "'Gentlemen, I have one more thing to say': Women on Scaffolds in England, 1563–1680." *Modern Philology* 92.2 (1994): 157–78.

———. "Home-Rebels and House-Traitors: Murderous Wives in Early Modern England." *Yale Journal of Law and the Humanities* 4.1 (1992): 1–31.

———. "The Subordinate('s) Plot: Petty Treason and the Forms of Domestic Rebellion." *Shakespeare Quarterly* 43.3 (1992): 317–40.

Doody, Margaret. "'Those Eyes Are Made So Killing': Eighteenth Century Murderesses and the Law." *Princeton University Library Chronicle* 46.1 (1984): 49–80.

Eccles, Audrey. *Obstetrics and Gynaecology in Tudor and Stuart England.* Kent, Ohio: Kent State University Press, 1982.

Erickson, Amy Louise. *Women and Property in Early Modern England.* New York: Routledge, 1993.

Ferguson, Margaret. "A Room Not Their Own: Renaissance Women as Readers and Writers." In *The Comparative Perspective on Literature: Approaches to Theory and Practice,* edited by Clayton Koelb and Susan Noakes, 93–116. Ithaca, N.Y.: Cornell University Press, 1988.

Fildes, Valerie. *Breasts, Bottles and Babies: A History of Infant Feeding.* Edinburgh: Edinburgh University Press, 1986.

Fissel, Mary. "Gender and Generation: Representing Reproduction in Early Modern England." *Gender and History* 7.3 (1995): 433–56.

Fitz, Linda. "'What Says the Married Woman?' Marriage Theory and Feminism in the English Renaissance." *Mosaic* 13.2 (1980): 1–22.

Foucault, Michel. *Discipline and Punish: The Birth of the Prison.* Translated by Alan Sheridan. New York: Vintage Books, 1995.

Fox, Adam. "Ballads, Libels and Popular Ridicule in Jacobean England." *Past and Present* 145 (1994): 47–83.

———. *Oral and Literate Culture in England, 1500–1700.* New York: Oxford University Press, 2000.

Foyster, Elizabeth. "'A Laughing Matter?' Marital Discord and Gender Control in Seventeenth-Century England." *Rural History* 4.1 (1993): 5–21.

Francus, Marilyn. "Monstrous Mothers, Monstrous Societies: Infanticide and the Rule of Law in Restoration and Eighteenth-Century England." *Eighteenth-Century Life* 21.2 (1997): 133–56.

Gaskill, Malcolm. *Crime and Mentalities in Early Modern England.* New York: Cambridge University Press, 2000.

Gowing, Laura. *Domestic Dangers: Women, Words, and Sex in Early Modern London.* New York: Oxford University Press, 1996.

———. "The Haunting of Susan Lay: Servants and Mistresses in Seventeenth-Century England." *Gender and History* 14.2 (2002): 183–201.

———. "Ordering the Body: Illegitimacy and Female Authority in Seventeenth-Century England." In *Negotiating Power in Early Modern Society: Order, Hierarchy and Subordination in Britain and Ireland,* edited by Michael J. Braddick and John Walter, 43–62. Cambridge: Cambridge University Press, 2001.

Griffiths, Paul. *Youth and Authority: Formative Experiences in England, 1560–1640.* New York: Oxford University Press, 1996.

Halasz, Alexandra. *The Marketplace of Print: Pamphlets and the Public Sphere in Early Modern England.* Cambridge: Cambridge University Press, 1997.

Harley, David. "Historians as Demonologists: The Myth of the Midwife-witch." *Social History of Medicine* 3.1 (1990): 1–26.

Haslem, Lori Schroeder. "'Troubled with the Mother': Longings, Purgings, and the Maternal Body in *Bartholomew Fair* and *The Duchess of Malfi.*" *Modern Philology* 92.4 (1995): 438–59.

Henderson, Katherine Usher, and Barbara F. McManus, *Half Humankind: Contexts and Texts of the Controversy about Women in England, 1540–1640.* Urbana: University of Illinois Press, 1985.

Hoffer, Peter C., and N. E. H. Hull. *Murdering Mothers: Infanticide in England and New England, 1558–1803.* New York: New York University Press, 1984.

Howard, Jean E. "Feminism and the Question of History: Resituating the Debate." *Women's Studies* 19.2 (1991): 149–57.

Hunt, Margaret. "Wife Beating, Domesticity, and Women's Independence in Eighteenth-Century London." *Gender and History* 4 (1992): 10–33.

Jackson, Mark. *New-Born Child Murder: Women, Illegitimacy and the Courts in Eighteenth-Century England*. New York: Manchester University Press, 1996.

———. "Suspicious Infant Deaths: The Statute of 1624 and Medical Evidence at Coroners' Inquests." In *Legal Medicine in History*, edited by Michael Clark and Catherine Crawford, 64–86. New York: Cambridge University Press, 1994.

Kahn, Coppélia. "The Absent Mother in *King Lear*." In *Rewriting the Renaissance: The Discourses of Sexual Difference in Early Modern Europe*, edited by Margaret W. Ferguson, Maureen Quilligan and Nancy J. Vickers, 33–49. Chicago: University of Chicago Press, 1986.

Kelly, Joan. "Did Women Have a Renaissance?" In *Women, History and Theory: The Essays of Joan Kelly*, 19–50. Chicago: University of Chicago Press, 1977.

Kermode, Jennifer, and Garthine Walker, eds. *Women, Crime and the Courts in Early Modern England*. Chapel Hill: University of North Carolina Press, 1994.

Klein, Joan Larsen, ed. *Daughters, Wives and Widows: Writings by Men about Women and Marriage in England, 1500–1640*. Chicago: University of Illinois Press, 1992.

———. "Women and Marriage in Renaissance England: Male Perspectives." *Topic* 36 (1982): 23–38.

Lake, Peter. "Deeds Against Nature: Cheap Print, Protestantism and Murder in Early Seventeenth-Century England." In *Culture and Politics in Early Stuart England*, edited by Kevin Sharpe and Peter Lake, 257–83. Stanford: Stanford University Press, 1993.

———. "Popular Form, Puritan Content? Two Puritan Appropriations of the Murder Pamphlet from Mid-Seventeenth-Century London." In *Religion, Culture and Society in Early Modern Britain: Essays in Honour of Patrick Collinson*, edited by Anthony Fletcher and Peter Roberts, 313–34. Cambridge: Cambridge University Press, 1994.

Laqueur, Thomas. "Crowds, Carnival and the State in English Executions, 1604–1868." In *The First Modern Society: Essays in Honour of Lawrence Stone*, edited by A. L. Beier, David Cannadine, and James M. Rosenheim, 305–55. Cambridge: Cambridge University Press, 1989.

Larner, Christine. "Crimen Exceptum? The Crime of Witchcraft in Europe." In *Crime and the Law: The Social History of Crime in Western Europe since 1500*, edited by V. A. C. Gatrell, Bruce Lenman, and Geoffrey Parker, 49–75. London: Europa, 1980.

———. *Witchcraft and Religion: The Politics of Popular Beliefs*. New York: Blackwell, 1984.

Linebaugh, Peter. "The Ordinary of Newgate and His Account." In *Crime in England, 1550–1800*, edited by J. S. Cockburn, 246–69. Princeton: Princeton University Press, 1977.

———. "The Tyburn Riot Against the Surgeons." In *Albion's Fatal Tree: Crime and Society in Eighteenth-Century England*, edited by Douglas Hay et al., 65–117. London: Allen Lane, 1975.

MacDonald, Michael. "The Inner Side of Wisdom: Suicide in Early Modern England." *Psychological Medicine* 7 (1977): 565–82.

———. *Mystical Bedlam: Madness, Anxiety, and Healing in Seventeenth-Century England.* Cambridge: Cambridge University Press, 1981.

MacFarlane, Alan. *The Origins of English Individualism.* New York: Cambridge University Press, 1985.

———. *Witchcraft in Tudor and Stuart England.* New York: Harper & Row, 1970.

Malcolmson, R. W. "Infanticide in the Eighteenth Century." In *Crime in England, 1550–1800*, edited by J. S. Cockburn, 187–209. Princeton: Princeton University Press, 1977.

Marshburn, Joseph H., and Alan R. Velie. *Blood and Knavery: A Collection of English Renaissance Pamphlets and Ballads of Crime and Sin.* Rutherford, N.J.: Fairleigh Dickinson University Press, 1973.

Miller, Jacqueline T. "Mother Tongues: Language and Lactation in Early Modern Literature." *English Literary Renaissance* 27.2 (1997): 177–96.

Newman, Karen. *Fashioning Femininity and English Renaissance Drama.* Chicago: University of Chicago Press, 1991.

Park, Katharine. "The Criminal and the Saintly Body: Autopsy and Dissection in Renaissance Italy." *Renaissance Quarterly* 47.1 (1994): 1–33.

Paster, Gail Kern. *The Body Embarrassed: Drama and the Disciplines of Shame in Early Modern England.* Ithaca, N.Y.: Cornell University Press, 1993.

Poole, Kristen. "'The fittest closet for all goodness': Authorial Strategies of Jacobean Mothers' Manuals." *Studies in English Literature* 35 (1995): 69–88.

Purkiss, Diane. "Women's Stories of Witchcraft in Early Modern England: The House, the Body, the Child." *Gender and History* 7.3 (1995): 408–32.

Quilligan, Maureen. *The Allegory of Female Authority: Christine de Pizan's Cite des dames.* Ithaca, N.Y.: Cornell University Press, 1991.

Radzinowicz, Leon. *A History of English Criminal Law.* London: Stevens & Sons, 1948.

Rappaport, Steve Lee. *World Within Worlds: Structures of Life in Sixteenth-Century London.* New York: Cambridge University Press, 1989.

Raymond, Joad. *Making the News: An Anthology of Newsbooks of Revolutionary England, 1641–1660.* New York: St. Martin's, 1993.

Rollins, Hyder E. "Analytical Index to the Ballad-Entries in the Registers of the Company of Stationers of London." *Studies in Philology* 21.1 (1924).

Rose, Mary Beth. "Where Are the Mothers in Shakespeare? Options for Gender Representation in the English Renaissance." *Shakespeare Quarterly* 42.3 (1991): 291–314.

Sawday, Jonathan. *The Body Emblazoned: Dissection and the Human Body in Renaissance Culture.* New York: Routledge, 1995.

Sharpe, J. A. *Crime in Early Modern England, 1550–1750.* London: Longman, 1984.

———. *Crime in Seventeenth-Century England: A County Study.* Cambridge: Cambridge University Press, 1983.

———. "The History of Crime in Late Medieval and Early Modern England: A Review of the Field." *Social History* 7.2 (1982): 187–203.

———. " 'Last Dying Speeches': Religion, Ideology and Public Execution in Seventeenth-Century England." *Past and Present* 107 (1985): 144–67.

———. "Women, Witchcraft and the Legal Process." In *Women, Crime and the Courts in Early Modern England*, edited by Jennifer Kermode and Garthine Walker, 106–24. Chapel Hill: University of North Carolina Press, 1994.

Stallybrass, Peter. "Patriarchal Territories: The Body Enclosed." In *Rewriting the Renaissance: The Discourses of Sexual Difference in Early Modern Europe*, edited by Margaret W. Ferguson, Maureen Quilligan, and Nancy J. Vickers, 123–42. Chicago: University of Chicago Press, 1986.

Stone, Lawrence. *The Family, Sex and Marriage in England, 1500–1800.* New York: Harper & Row, 1977.

Stretton, Tim. *Women Waging Law in Elizabethan England.* Cambridge: Cambridge University Press, 1998.

Tebeaux, Elizabeth, and Mary M. Lay. "The Emergence of the Feminine Voice, 1526–1640: The Earliest Published Books by English Renaissance Women." *JAC, a Journal of Composition Theory* 15.1 (1995); available at http://jac.gsu.edu/jac/15.1/Articles/4.htm, accessed 07/31/2002.

Thomas, Keith. "The Puritans and Adultery: The Act of 1650 Reconsidered." In *Puritans and Revolutionaries: Essays in Seventeenth-Century History presented to Christopher Hill*, edited by Donald Pennington and Keith Thomas, 257–82. Oxford: Clarendon Press, 1978.

———. *Religion and the Decline of Magic: Studies in Popular Beliefs in Seventeenth Century England.* New York: Scribner, 1971.

Todd, Barbara J. "The Remarrying Widow: A Stereotype Reconsidered." In *Women in English Society, 1500–1800*, edited by Mary Prior, 54–92. London: Methuen, 1985.

Travitsky, Betty S. "Child Murder in English Renaissance Life and Drama." *Medieval & Renaissance Drama in England: An Annual Gathering of Research, Criticism and Reviews* 6 (1993): 63–84.

———. "Husband-Murder and Petty Treason in English Renaissance Tragedy." *Renaissance Drama* 21 (1990): 171–98.

———. "The New Mother of the English Renaissance: Her Writings on Motherhood." In *The Lost Tradition: Mothers and Daughters in Literature*, edited by Cathy N. Davidson and E. M. Broner, 33–43. New York: Frederick Ungar Publishing, 1980.

———. "'A Pittilesse Mother'? Reports of a Seventeenth-Century English Filicide." *Mosaic* 27.4 (1994): 55–79.

Underdown, David. "The Taming of the Scold: The Enforcement of Patriarchal Authority in Early Modern England." In *Order and Disorder in Early Modern England*, edited by Anthony Fletcher and John Stevenson, 116–36. Cambridge: Cambridge University Press, 1985.

Walker, Garthine. "'Demons in Female Form': Representations of Women and Gender in Murder Pamphlets of the Late Sixteenth and Early Seventeenth Centuries." In *Writing and the English Renaissance*, edited by William Zunder and Suzanne Trull, 123–39. New York: Longman, 1996.

Walsham, Alexandra. *Providence in Early Modern England.* New York: Oxford University Press, 1999.

Warner, Marina. *Monuments and Maidens: The Allegory of the Female Form.* New York: Atheneum, 1985.

Watt, Tessa. *Cheap Print and Popular Piety, 1550–1640.* New York: Cambridge University Press, 1991.

Wells, John Edwin. *A Manual of the Writings in Middle English, 1050–1400.* New Haven, Conn.: Yale University Press, 1916.

Wiener, Carol Z. "Is a Spinster a Married Woman?" *American Journal of Legal History* 20.1 (1976): 27–31.

Willis, Deborah. *Malevolent Nurture: Witch-Hunting and Maternal Power in Early Modern England.* Ithaca, N.Y.: Cornell University Press, 1995.

———. "Shakespeare and the English Witch-Hunts." In *Enclosure Acts: Sexuality, Property, and Culture in Early Modern England*, edited by Richard Burt and John Michael Archer, 96–120. Ithaca, N.Y.: Cornell University Press, 1994.

Wilson, Adrian. "The Ceremony of Childbirth and Its Interpretation." In *Women as Mothers in Pre-Industrial England: Essays in Memory of Dorothy McLaren*, edited by Valerie Fildes, 68–107. New York: Routledge, 1990.

———. *The Making of Man-Midwifery: Childbirth in England, 1660–1770.* Cambridge, Mass.: Harvard University Press, 1995.

Wiltenburg, Joy. *Disorderly Women and Female Power in the Street Literature of Early Modern England and Germany.* Charlottesville: University Press of Virginia, 1992.

Woodbridge, Linda. *Women and the English Renaissance: Literature and the Nature of Womankind, 1540–1620.* Urbana: University of Illinois Press, 1984.

Wrightson, Keith. *English Society: 1580–1680.* London: Hutchinson, 1982.

———. "Infanticide in Earlier Seventeenth-Century England." *Local Population Studies* 15 (1975): 10–22.

———. "Infanticide in European History." *Criminal Justice History* 3 (1982): 1–20.

———. "The Nadir of English Illegitimacy in the Seventeenth Century." In *Bastardy and Its Comparative History*, edited by Peter Laslett, Karla Oosterveen, and Richard Smith, 176–91. Cambridge, Mass.: Harvard University Press, 1980.

Zunder, William, and Suzanne, Trull, eds. *Writing and the English Renaissance.* New York: Longman, 1996.

Index